Profile Books

Lloyds Bank Tax Guide 1998-99

Sara Williams is the publisher of *Small Company Investor* and *The AIM Guide*. She writes a weekly column in The Express and has contributed many articles on tax, finance and business for national newspapers, including The Daily Mail, Mail on Sunday and The Sunday Times. For a number of years she wrote for *Which?*, including the *Which? Tax Saving Guide* and the *Which? Book of Tax*. She is the author of the *Lloyds Bank Small Business Guide*. Sara Williams is a former investment analyst and lecturer in finance. She has been a public interest member for LAUTRO (Life Assurance and Unit Trust Regulatory Organisation), a council member of the Consumers' Association, and she is on the authorisation committee of the Institute of Actuaries.

John Willman is Consumer Industries Editor of the *Financial Times*. He has written extensively on personal finance and tax for *Which?*, including the *Which? Tax Saving Guide* and the *Which? Book of Tax*. Formerly publications editor at Peat Marwick McLintock (a firm of accountants), he was the editor of *Assessment and Taxes,* published by the Inland Revenue Staff Federation. He is the author of *Make Your Will, How to Sort Out Someone's Will* and the *Which? Guide to Planning and Conservation.*

Lloyds Bank

Tax Guide 1998-99

SARA WILLIAMS AND JOHN WILLMAN

PROFILE BOOKS

Published by Profile Books Limited
62 Queen Anne Street, London W1M 9LA

This edition published 1998

Copyright © Sara Williams and John Willman 1998
The moral right of the authors has been asserted

Consultants: Brian Clutterbuck, Jonquil Lowe and Jane Vass
Desk-top publishing and design: Paul Taylor
Editorial team: Penny Williams, Frances Worlock and Edwin Laing
Index: Moira Greenhalgh

Printed in Great Britain by The Bath Press

A CIP catalogue record for this book is available
from the British Library

ISBN 1 86197 060 9

CONTENTS

A MESSAGE FROM SIR BRIAN PITMAN LLOYDS TSB GROUP CHAIRMAN

This is the second year of self assessment and a year of further changes to the taxes we have to pay. Nearly nine million people are sent self assessment returns by the Inland Revenue to complete.

Everyone who completes a tax return needs to make sure they do it right and in time. So it is now more important than ever that people understand taxation and their own personal position.

The Lloyds Bank Tax Guide, now appearing in its 13th year, has achieved a reputation as one of the best and easiest ways to understand the complexities of personal taxation. It provides clear, simple and accurate information and this year has been comprehensively reorganised and updated to help with both self assessment and tax planning.

With our Tax Guide, our Personal Tax Management Service and the comprehensive range of financial services that we offer, our aim is to provide solutions to meet our customers' needs in a constantly changing financial world.

This guide will help readers to work out correctly the tax which they should be paying and to plan their financial affairs in an efficient manner.

I hope that you will find the Lloyds Bank Tax Guide useful.

© Lloyds TSB Group plc 1998

Brian Pitman

ACKNOWLEDGEMENTS

A tax guide of this type can not appear without the help and hard work of a multitude of people. Jane Vass helped tremendously by carrying out some of the updating and Brian Clutterbuck cast his eye over the final version spotting mistakes. At Lloyds Bank, we would particularly like to mention the support and enthusiasm of Sally Berry, along with Nicola Sears, Adrian Presland and Steve Wood.

In addition, Stephen Brough and Andrew Franklin at Profile Books and Stephen Page and his team at Fourth Estate have shown determination and commitment to bring the guide to as wide an audience possible.

Thank you.

Sara Williams and John Willman

NOTE
Both of us – along with everyone at Lloyds Bank and Profile Books Ltd – have made strenuous efforts to check the accuracy of the information. If by chance a mistake or omission has occurred, we are sorry that neither we, Lloyds Bank nor the Publisher can take responsibility if you suffer any loss or problem as a result of it. But please write to us c/o Profile Books Ltd if you have any suggestions about how we can improve the content of the guide.

Dear Reader

The Lloyds Bank Tax Guide went to press shortly after the 1998 Budget on March 17 – and much may change before the chancellor's proposals become law. If you want to keep abreast of developments, there are two ways to do it:

- send for our free update, which will be issued once the Finance Bill has become law (probably the end of July) – see below for instructions on what to do

- log on to the TaxGuide website – at www.taxguide.co.uk

You can also use either of these approaches to get two free guides offered to cover special circumstances:

- for filling in the special tax calculator for people with capital gains – p. 307

- for checking a Tax Calculation form for the tax year ending 5 April 1997 (the procedure for the tax year ending 5 April 1998 is on p. 351).

To get the paper versions of any of these, send an A4-sized self-addressed envelope with a 38p stamp on it to: Sara Williams and John Willman, Lloyds Bank Tax Guide, 62 Queen Anne Street, London W1M 9LA. Send one envelope for each guide requested, writing Update, Tax Calculator or Tax Calculation Form on the top left-hand corner as appropriate.

HOW INCOME TAX WORKS

Under self-assessment, the new tax regime introduced in the last tax year, you now operate the tax collection system in part or fully. You provide the records, fill in the tax return, and you may also work out the tax bill. You must pay what you owe by sending a cheque, along with your tax return, to the Inland Revenue by 31 January. If you prefer, you can send in your tax return to the Inland Revenue by 30 September. The tax you owe will be worked out by your tax inspector and you must pay it by 31 January.

However, it appears that not all taxpayers have got to grips with the new system as some 900,000 returns (out of the 9 million sent out) were not returned. It is expected that an extra £67 million will go into the Inland Revenue's coffers in penalties for late delivery of the return.

If any lessons are to be learned from last year, they should include the need to be organised from the start of the tax year. Remember that there are new:
- tax returns (pp. 13, 143)
- dates by which you have to fill in your tax return (p. 14)
- penalties you have to pay if you don't stick to all the rules (p. 19)
- rules about records which you must now keep (p. 12)
- dates to pay your tax bill (p. 15)
- rules about which income you will pay tax on (p. 148)
- dates for reporting income (p. 12)
- obligations which taxpayers must stick to (p. 12).

The taxes you might pay
There are a number of different ways in which the government raises money from taxpayers. Some of the taxes are as follows:
- income tax – some of your income is taxed at varying rates
- capital gains tax – some of the gains you make on investments or possessions may be taxed at varying rates
- inheritance tax – when you die, some of the money you leave to others could be taxed
- National Insurance – this is paid only by people who are earning,

employees, employers, the self-employed or partners.

Other taxes include council tax, corporation tax, value added tax, stamp duty and excise duties.

The tax returns for the tax year ending 5 April 1998 should land on your doorstep during April 1998. These will cover your income and gains, reliefs and allowances. The information you provide will be used to work out your income tax and capital gains tax bills.

How tax rules are changed

Parliament is responsible for changing the tax rules. The government of the day, advised by the Inland Revenue, produces a Budget, for this year held in March. Changes will apply from the start of the next tax year, which runs from 6 April to the following 5 April.

The Finance Bill with the changes suggested in the Budget will be published in May, debated in Parliament and the Finance Act passed before 5 July.

What is in this guide?

This tax guide explains the rules for income tax, capital gains tax, inheritance tax and national insurance. It covers most of the rules which the majority of taxpayers need to know, but it may not cover very specialised cases.

In Part I, the guide gives a broad outline of the rules and helps you to plan your affairs to minimise your tax bills. It covers what you need to know for the coming tax year (ending 5 April 1999) and beyond. It includes the changes made in the March 1998 Budget. By reading this section carefully and following its advice you should be able to save tax in the current and future tax years.

The guide went to the printers at the end of March 1998 and its advice is based on what was proposed in the Budget. Proposals are sometimes changed by debate in Parliament. You can receive notice of later changes in two different ways:

- contact our web site, www.taxguide.co.uk
- send an A4 stamped (38p), self-addressed envelope to Sara Williams and John Willman, 62 Queen Anne Street, London W1M 9LA

In Part II, the guide helps you to fill in your tax return and has the information and figures for the tax year ending 5 April 1998. It includes lots of tax-saving tips which help you to cut your tax bill for the last tax year.

A simple guide to income tax

There are many complexities and exceptions in the way that income is taxed. What follows is a broad brush approach to how income is taxed. It gives some important relationships:

Taxable income = (Income – Reliefs – Allowances)
Total income = (Income – Reliefs)
Income tax = Taxable income x the rate(s) of tax

Income is made up of what you earn from your job or self-employment and what you receive as income from other sources, such as investments. But not all the money you receive is income (see p. 5) and some income you receive is tax-free (see p. 370). Some income you receive has had tax deducted (called *net* – see pp. 6 and 66) and some income is paid without tax deducted (called *gross* – see pp. 6 and 373). Savings income (see p. 65) is a special case: much of it is paid with lower rate tax deducted and no further tax to pay unless you are a higher rate taxpayer.

Reliefs are amounts which you pay out and on which you get tax relief. They reduce your income before your tax bill is worked out. With some reliefs you get tax relief at your highest rate of tax, for example, pensions contributions. With other reliefs, the amount of tax relief is restricted to a certain figure, regardless of the rate of tax you pay; for example, mortgage interest to buy your home.

Allowances are amounts to which you are entitled because of your personal circumstances. They reduce your income before your tax bill is worked out.

EXAMPLE

Jessica Jones has income from self-employment of £10,000. She pays £1,000 into a personal pension scheme and she can claim a personal allowance for the tax year ending 5 April 1999 of £4,195. Her taxable income is:

	£
Income	10,000.00
Less Reliefs: pension contributions	1,000.00
	9,000.00
Less personal allowance	4,195.00
Taxable income	4,805.00
Less: tax at 20 per cent on first £4,300	860.00
tax at 23 per cent on next £505	116.15
Total tax bill	976.15

But some allowances, for example married couple's allowance, get a reduced rate of tax relief.

Taxable income is the figure on which you work out your tax bill. The amount of your income tax depends on how much taxable income you have and what rate of tax is paid on it (see below).

Total income is a figure that is not important for most taxpayers, but it is for the elderly (those in receipt of age-related allowances). The amount of total income determines whether you can receive these allowances in full or in a reduced amount (see p. 41). Total income can also affect some taxpayers paying life insurance premiums (see p. 71).

Total income is the amount you have after you have deducted some reliefs from income, but before deducting allowances. The reliefs you deduct to arrive at total income include pensions contributions, the gross amount of charitable covenants and charitable donations under Gift Aid and the pay-roll giving scheme, the gross amount of some maintenance payments and some loan interest (but not on a mortgage in MIRAS). Premiums for private medical insurance are not deducted.

The rates of tax
There are three different rates of tax:

- lower rate tax (20 per cent for tax years ending on 5 April 1998 and 1999)
- basic rate tax (23 per cent for tax years ending on 5 April 1998 and 1999)
- higher rate tax (40 per cent for tax years ending 5 April 1998 and 1999)

The levels at which these rates apply can vary from year to year. Here are the levels of income for each of these rates for the tax years ending 5 April 1998 and 5 April 1999:

Tax year ending 5 April 1998

Income band £	Size of band £	Tax rate %	Tax on band £
0 – 4,100	4,100	20	820
4,101 – 26,100	22,000	23	5,060
Over 26,100		40	

Tax year ending 5 April 1999

Income band £	Size of band £	Tax rate %	Tax on band £
0 – 4,300	4,300	20	860
4,301 – 27,100	22,800	23	5,244
Over 27,100		40	

INCOME, RELIEFS AND ALLOWANCES

Income, reliefs and allowances are the three elements in determining your income tax bill – and the three ways in which you can minimise the size of it. Look for opportunities to arrange your income to be tax-free (see p. 370 for a comprehensive list). In the case of a married couple, seek to distribute the income between the two of you to the greatest advantage. And don't forget to claim all your reliefs and allowances, including those from the past that you might have forgotten. You will find tax-saving tips throughout the guide; many of them are gathered together on pp. 30 – 39.

INCOME

Your income will be made of money or goods you receive or anything you get in return for a service – but not all money you receive counts as income (see below). The following will all normally be considered as income:

- what you earn from your work, including a job (see p. 203), a partnership (see p. 265) or self-employment (see p. 236). This includes salary, fringe benefits and business profits
- rent from letting out property (see p. 267)
- income from investments, such as interest, dividends and distributions (see pp. 65 and 148)
- pensions (from the state, your previous employer or your own plan)
- social security payments, such as jobseeker's allowance
- maintenance income, if the arrangement was made before 15 March 1988
- casual, occasional or miscellaneous income, such as freelance earnings, income received after you close a business, income from guaranteeing loans, dealing in futures, income from underwriting, certain capital payments from selling UK patent rights, accrued income including from gilt strips (see p. 154)
- income from a trust.

Payments that are not income
Some payments you receive are not income. For example:

- presents and gifts
- loans
- lottery prizes
- gambling winnings (unless it is your way of making a living)
- what you make from selling an asset (unless this is how you make a living)
- what you receive under a maintenance agreement made on or after 15 March 1988
- money you inherit.

Although these payments are not income, there may be other tax to pay on them – for example, capital gains tax or inheritance tax.

Tax-free income
There are many examples of income that is tax-free, including premium bond prizes or interest on National Savings Certificates. A comprehensive list is given on p. 370.

How is income paid to you
Income can be paid to you without any tax deducted *(gross)* or with tax deducted *(net)*. The tax can be deducted at the lower rate, the basic rate, the higher rate, or all three rates. The table on the right lists types of income, whether or not they are paid with tax deducted and if any further tax will be due. There are more details of income in Chapter 13.

If you need to give a figure for gross income when you have received net income, there are ready reckoners which help you to gross it up in Appendix B on p. 373.

RELIEFS

You make certain choices in your life. You might choose to buy a home using a mortgage. Or you might save now to give yourself a pension (over and above the state pension) when you retire. The government decides that it wants to encourage certain of your actions – for example, buying your own home, saving for a pension. So it allows you to deduct some or all of what you pay for these from your income before working out your income tax bill. These items are known as reliefs, outgoings or deductions.

A further advantage of reliefs is that they may lower the rate at which you pay tax. For example, if you pay pension contributions it might mean you pay tax at the basic rate of 23 per cent rather than the higher rate of 40 per cent. When this happens it means that the cost to you of some of these pay-

Types of income (for tax year ending 5 April 1999)

Type of income	Tax deducted?	At what rate?	More tax to pay? [1]
Earnings from a job	yes	LR, BR, HR	no
Taxable fringe benefits	yes, from earnings	LR, BR, HR	no
Pension from your former employer	yes	LR, BR, HR	no
Bank, building society interest	yes	LR [2]	yes – HR
British Government stocks [3]	you can choose	BR	yes – HR
Income from annuity	yes [4]	BR	yes – HR
Dividends from shares	yes	LR	yes – HR
Distributions from unit trusts	yes	LR	yes – HR
Income from an executor before a will is sorted out	yes	BR	yes – HR
Income from a trust	yes	generally 34 per cent	yes – HR
Income from self-employment	no		yes
Income from a partnership	no		yes
Social security benefits	no [5]		yes
Maintenance payments	no		sometimes
Rent from property	no		yes [6]

Key: LR = lower rate; BR = basic rate; HR = higher rate

(1) There could, of course, be more tax to pay if insufficient has been collected.

(2) Non-taxpayers can have interest paid without tax deducted – see p. 00.

(3) Tax is not deducted on stocks bought through the National Savings Stock Register (ask at the Post Office) or on War Loan (however it was purchased). From 6 April 1998, you will be able to receive interest without tax deducted on any stock.

(4) Tax is deducted from the part of the annuity which counts as income, not the part which counts as a return of the capital.

(5) But if you return to work, tax if due will be deducted from your earnings.

(6) But rent in the Rent a Room scheme is tax-free up to a limit. (For more details see p. 267.)

ments after tax can be low.

How you get tax relief

There are three ways in which you can get tax relief:

- you can make a lower payment by deducting the amount of the tax relief from the payment and keeping it yourself – for example, for your mortgage to buy your own home you pay interest on up to £30,000 of a loan in MIRAS after deducting tax relief of 10 per cent (15 per cent for tax year ending on 5 April 1998)
- you can get your tax relief through the PAYE system. It will be included in your Notice of Coding and thus you will pay less tax on your salary each month
- you can get your tax relief by claiming it in your tax return. If you are going to work out your own tax bill you would deduct the amount in your calculation and pay less tax. Or your tax inspector will work out the bill allowing for the deduction.

The table on the right lists types of reliefs and how you get them. There are more details about reliefs in Chapter 14.

ALLOWANCES

Everyone is entitled to an allowance to deduct from their income to ensure that some income is tax-free. This is called the personal allowance. But the amount of the allowance varies with age. There are other allowances that you may be able to claim – but these depend on your personal circumstances. There are details of allowances in the table on p. 10 and in Chapter 15.

Types of relief (for the tax year ending 5 April 1999)

Type of relief	Amount of relief	How do you get tax relief?
Charity: covenant	LR, BR or HR	LR, BR: make lower payments HR: either PAYE code or tax bill
Charity: single payments (Gift Aid)	LR, BR or HR	LR, BR: make lower payments HR: either PAYE code or tax bill
Enterprise Investment scheme (up to £150,000)	20%	through your PAYE code or tax bill
Home income scheme	BR	make lower payments or through your PAYE code or tax bill
Interest on a loan to pay inheritance tax	LR, BR or HR	through your PAYE code or tax bill
Interest on business loans	LR, BR or HR	through your PAYE code or tax bill
Job expenses	LR, BR or HR	through your PAYE code or tax bill
Maintenance payments[1]	15% of £1,900	through your PAYE code or tax bill
Mortgage interest[2] to buy your home	10% of the interest on a loan of £30,000	make lower payments if the loan is in MIRAS
Mortgage interest on a home you let	LR, BR or HR	a lower tax bill on rental income
Pension contributions	LR, BR or HR	through PAYE system
Personal pension payments	Employees BR or HR Self-employed LR, BR or HR	Employees BR: make lower payments HR: through PAYE code or tax bill Self-employed a lower tax bill
Private medical insurance for people aged 60 or over[3]	BR	make lower payments
Training for NVQ and SVQ – level 5	BR or HR	BR: make lower payments HR: through PAYE code or tax bill

Key: LR = lower rate; BR = basic rate; HR = higher rate

(1) This is the treatment under the new rules. From 6 April 1999, the relief will fall to 10%. For the tax treatment of maintenance paid under the old rules, see p. 48 (2) Rate of relief for tax year ending 5 April 1998 was 15 per cent (3) Tax relief on these policies abolished from 2 July 1997, but existing policies get it until they come up for renewal

Details of allowances

Allowance	Age	Tax year ending 5 April	Amount
Personal	up to 65	1998	£4,045
		1999	£4,195
	65-74	1998	£5,220[1]
		1999	£5,410[1]
	75 plus	1998	£5,400[1]
		1999	£5,600[1]
Married couple's	up to 65[2]	1998	15% of £1,830
		1999	15% of £1,900
	65-74	1998	15% of £3,185[1]
		1999	15% of £3,305[1]
	75 plus	1998	15% of £3,225[1]
		1999	15% of £3,345[1]
Blind person's	any	1998	£1,280
		1999	£1,330
Additional personal[2]	any	1998	15% of £1,830
		1999	15% of £1,900
Widow's bereavement[2]	any	1998	15% of £1,830
		1999	15% of £1,900

(1) The amount of these allowances is reduced if total income is above a certain amount. In the tax year ending 5 April 1998 the allowances were reduced if total income was £15,600 and over and in the tax year ending 5 April 1999 the income limit is £16,200. For more details see p. 41.
(2) From 6 April 1999, the relief will be restricted to 10% of the allowance

YOU AND YOUR TAX INSPECTOR

The popular image of the tax inspector is probably close to that of Hector, the character the Inland Revenue has used over the last year to publicise the change to self-assessment. In reality, your tax inspector is nothing like the pin-striped, bowler-hatted Hector. On the contrary, the whole of the Inland Revenue has been reshaped and updated over the last few years – a process which still continues and isn't due to be completed until 2002.

The Inland Revenue is in the middle of a fundamental change in organisation, helped along and precipitated by technological improvements and the switch to self-assessment. The process includes making the Revenue's working practices less cumbersome, reorganising the tax office structure and improving the service to customers. A major programme to rewrite tax laws without using jargon is also being implemented.

Under the old system, you might have needed to correspond with several different offices if you had different sources of income. And yet another office dealt with the collection of tax. Self-assessment has streamlined all this. You should have just one tax district, one tax reference and one calculation of income tax and capital gains tax due.

For most taxpayers, the plan is that your Taxpayer Service Office will send out your tax return, process it when you send it back and issue your PAYE code. In most cases, it will be the only tax office you need to deal with. Specialist Taxpayer District Offices will check that employers operate the PAYE system properly and chase up non-payers and tax evaders. A network of high-street Taxpayer Enquiry Centres will provide a face-to-face service, where

> **TAX-SAVING IDEA**
> Make sure you keep all your records, including the originals of certificates and your working papers. If you don't, you may end up paying more tax than you should because you can't provide the evidence to back up your tax return. And don't forget you can be fined for not keeping your records.

taxpayers can talk to tax staff who will be able to call up their records on computer screens and deal with queries.

YOUR OBLIGATIONS

New source of income or capital
If you don't receive a tax return, you must notify your tax inspector of any income or capital gains, which have not been previously declared, within six months of the end of the tax year in which you make the income or gain.

There are certain circumstances in which you don't have to notify your tax office. This applies, for example, if all the income comes under the PAYE system or if the income is dividends from shares which is paid with tax deducted at 20 per cent and you pay tax at no more than the basic rate.

You should also note that even if you do not know the amount of your new source of income or capital gain by the deadline by which you must tell your tax office you should not delay. You must tell your tax office of a new source as soon as you know of it.

Records
Since 6 April 1996 you have been required to keep records, for example, original copies of dividend vouchers, bank statements, certificates of interest received and any certificates showing foreign tax deductions, which you need to complete your tax return. If you don't have the original certificates, you can complete your tax return using information that can be verified by an external source. You don't have to send in your vouchers and other documents in order to get a tax refund. You must keep the originals in case of Inland Revenue enquiry, but if they are lost you will not be penalised

EXAMPLE
Roger Rose is an employee paying tax under the PAYE system. He buys some shares in a UK company in October 1997 and receives a dividend of £84 some two months later. He also decides to do some freelance consulting on the side, as well as his job. He doesn't know how much income that will bring in, since part of his payment will be in the form of commission.

Although he knows exactly how much income he will receive on his shares in the tax year ending 5 April 1998, he doesn't need to declare this income to the tax office until he fills in his tax return. This is because dividend income is paid with the equivalent of basic rate tax deducted. However, although he doesn't yet know what he will earn from his freelance business, he must tell his tax office about the business by 6 October 1998 (that is, six months from the end of the tax year in which the income is earned).

providing you can produce other evidence for the information. You also need to keep a copy of the working papers that you used to work out your calculations.

If you don't run your own business or have letting income, the period to keep records is one year from the date by which you must send back the tax return (31 January). However, this period is extended if there should be an enquiry into your affairs. Records must be kept until the enquiry is complete.

The period to keep records is also extended if you send in your return late or need to correct it after you have sent it in. The documents need to be kept until one year after the end of the quarter in which you amended the return or sent it in late. Quarters end on 31 January, 30 April, 31 July and 31 October.

> ### EXAMPLE
>
> Ashley Hickie is a self-employed journalist. He also has some savings, such as unit trusts and a building society account. He completes his tax return for the year ended 5 April 1998, including carrying out the calculation of his own tax bill, and returns it by 15 January 1999. Ashley must keep the dividend vouchers and certificate of interest, plus the working papers on this, until 31 January 2000. The records of his business and the working papers relating to it need to be kept much longer. He has to preserve them until 31 January 2004.

If you run your own business or receive any income from letting, you need to keep records for five years from the date by which you should send in your tax return (31 January). The records should include what you receive and spend in your business, for example, sales and purchase invoices.

The failure to keep records can result in a swingeing penalty (see p. 19).

THE TAX RETURN

Your tax return asks you for details of your income, deductions and allowances for the tax year just ended, ie the year ending on 5 April 1998. There is one basic tax return of eight pages sent to everyone who should receive a tax return. But there are also a lot of supplementary pages for particular types of income – self-employment, trusts, employment, share schemes, partnerships, land and property, foreign, capital gains and non-residence. You may not receive any of these or, in an extreme case, you might receive nine different supplements to the basic return. For more details about these supplements see p. 144.

In the past, it was acceptable to use such phrases as 'as returned' or 'as agreed' for income or the value of benefits. But you are now required to fill in the correct figure – otherwise you will not be able to work out how much income tax or capital gains tax you owe. This means you must get hold of the documents you need, including Forms P60 (your income from your job and the tax you have paid on it), P45 part 1A (your income and tax to date when you leave your job), P11D or P9D (your fringe benefits and expenses for the year), P2 (your notice of coding). Your employer has the responsibility to supply you with these forms (but not P2) by certain dates (see p. 22).

Deadlines for your tax return

There are two important dates to bear in mind. If you want to ask the Inland Revenue to work out your tax bill on your behalf, as your agent, rather than yourself or a tax adviser, your tax return must be sent in by 30 September. This is the date by which you must also submit your return even if you do your own tax calculation if you want any previous underpayment (£1,000 or less) to be deducted through the PAYE system, rather than you paying it with the rest of your tax bill.

There is a different date set for returning your tax return if you or your tax adviser choose to calculate what you owe in income tax. This is 31 January.

If you have missed the 30 September deadline and decide that after all you want the Revenue to calculate the tax due, you can still ask for this to happen. But your tax inspector won't guarantee to do this by the 31 January slot, so you may end up paying a penalty for late tax payment.

Where a tax return has been issued after 31 October, you are given three months to complete it and send it back to your tax office. But if the return is issued after 31 July and you want your tax inspector to calculate the tax due, it must be returned within two months.

If you don't send in your tax return

Failing to send back your completed tax return means you can be charged a penalty (see p. 19) and allows the

TAX-SAVING IDEA

If you are an employee paying tax under the PAYE system and you have some other income, for example from investments, on which you will need to pay tax, you should send in your tax return with your tax calculation by 30 September. If you do this, and the amount of tax due is £1,000 or less, you will not have to pay tax on this extra income by 31 January. Instead, it will be included into your PAYE code for the following tax year and you will pay tax on it with your monthly salary, thus spreading out and delaying the payment of your tax bill.

Inland Revenue to issue what's called a determination. Your tax inspector produces an estimate, to the best of his or her belief and using the best information available, of how much tax you should pay. The tax shown on this determination is payable; you cannot appeal against it or postpone it.

The only way you can overturn this estimate is to complete your tax return and self-assessment. You must do this within five years of the date by which you should have sent it in, or, if it is later, within a year of the determination by your tax inspector.

Your tax inspector cannot make a determination if five years have passed since the date by which you should have sent in your tax return. There will also be penalties and interest to pay (see p. 19).

TAX PAYMENTS

After completing your tax return, either you or your adviser or your tax office work out the amount of tax due on all types of income and capital gains. When you return your tax return, at least by the following 31 January, you send in the amount of tax that you have calculated as being due. This is the final bill for income tax for the year.

Interim payments

Self-assessment of income tax requires interim payments on account. These will be based on what you paid in income tax the previous year. The estimate will be what was due in the previous year, less amounts deducted at source, what is deducted through the PAYE system, tax credits and so on. There is no adjustment for changing levels of income, tax rates or allowances, but you can ask for it to be adjusted.

For any one tax year, apart from those paying through the PAYE system, the income tax due will be paid in three instalments. The first interim payment on account (normally half the amount of tax you paid in the previous year less any capital gains tax and tax deducted at source) will be on 31 January during the tax year. The second interim payment on account will be on 31 July following the end of the tax year. The final balancing income tax payment or repayment will be made after completion of the tax return on 31 January following the end of the tax year. Any capital gains tax due will also be paid with this third instalment.

However, there are rules which mean that these interim payments will not be required if they are small. Working on the basis of the tax due for the previous tax year, if the total tax payable, net of tax deducted at source (including PAYE), is less than £500 or if tax deducted at source (including PAYE) is more than 80 per cent of the total income tax plus Class 4 National Insurance due, then interim payments won't be required.

The effect of this new system will be that income tax will be paid either monthly through the PAYE system or half-yearly on 31 January and 31 July.

Employees can put off paying a final tax bill of £1,000 or less by asking for it to be included in next year's PAYE code. To achieve this, you have to send in your tax return by 30 September.

Statement of Account

During January 1998, you may have received a Statement of Account giving an estimate of what you should pay on 31 January 1998 and the same figure will be due on 31 July 1998. This estimate is based on the tax you paid for the tax year ending 5 April 1997. For how to check this statement see p. 367. And for how to appeal against it if you think that you won't be paying as much tax in the current tax year as is given in the Statement of Account, see p. 369. You will need to use form SA303 to claim to reduce your payments on account.

Interest and surcharges

Interest is payable on tax which is paid late or unpaid. On the other hand, any tax you have overpaid will also earn interest.

> ## TAX-SAVING IDEA
>
> Always check your Statement of Account to see if you can claim a reduction in interim payments. But if in doubt, it is better to pay slightly more rather too little on account – you will be charged interest if you pay too little, whereas tax you have overpaid will earn interest. The rate of interest charged on underpaid tax is roughly twice as much as that earned on overpaid tax.

The rate of interest due on unpaid tax is based on the average rate of borrowing, whereas that due on overpaid tax is based on average investment returns at the time less tax that would be paid. Any interest charged or received will be shown on your statement of account. Interest is automatically charged on any tax left unpaid by 31 January or 31 July following a statement of account. However, if the statement of account was issued late, although you sent in your tax return on time, the interest will only start 30 days after the date on the statement. Interest is also charged on any tax left unpaid by 31 January following the end of the tax year – that is by 31 January 1999 for the tax year ending 5 April 1998 – unless your tax return was issued late. If the tax is still not paid by 28 February 1999, there is a surcharge of 5 per cent of the unpaid tax. A further 5 per cent surcharge of the amount of tax still unpaid after 31 July 1999 is imposed. Interest will be added to any unpaid surcharge, starting 30 days after the notice of the surcharge.

CHANGES TO YOUR TAX RETURN

Mistakes and corrections

Sometimes you may not know a figure with 100 per cent accuracy by the time it comes to fill in your tax return. What you have to do is to put in your best estimate and work out the tax due on that. When you can supply the final figure, you should do so. If there is more tax to pay, you will have to pay interest (or will receive interest if a refund is due) but no surcharges or penalties unless you have been negligent or fraudulent.

It's also possible that you might make a mistake when you complete the return. You can correct an error at any time within 12 months after the date the return should be sent back – 31 January.

If you don't spot a mistake but the Inland Revenue picks up an obvious error, such as an arithmetical mistake or a misunderstanding of principle, your tax office will correct (or 'repair') the return within nine months of the date the return was sent in.

Either you or your tax office can amend your return to correct mistakes. Any tax due as a result of the revised self-assessment should be paid either by the normal payment date or 30 days after the making of the self-assessment (but this does not put off the date from which interest is charged).

Enquiries

Your tax inspector has the right to enquire into your tax return without giving any reason. A small proportion of all returns is selected at random for enquiry. A tax enquiry can be made into the return of an individual, a trustee, a partnership or a company. An enquiry can be made only once into the same tax return.

An enquiry is quite different from your right as a taxpayer or your tax inspector's right to correct or amend your tax return (see above).

Your tax inspector must give you written notice of an enquiry. If you sent in your tax return on time, the notice must be made by 31 January the following year. If you sent in your return late, the notice of an enquiry can be issued up to a year after the end of the quarter in which you sent in your return (quarter ends are 31 January, 30 April, 31 July and 31 October). With an amended tax return, the notice can be issued up to a year after the end of the quarter in which you amended it.

Once the Inland Revenue has said it is going to enquire into your tax return, you are not able to amend it until after the enquiry is complete.

Your tax inspector has the right to demand that you produce certain documents. When you receive a notice of an enquiry, you may also receive a notice to produce these within 30 days. You can produce copies, but your tax inspector may insist on seeing the originals. You can appeal within 30 days against this notice to produce documents.

You can also appeal to the general commissioners (see p. 21) if you consider that an enquiry should not have been undertaken or is being continued unnecessarily. The general commissioners can issue a notice to the Inland Revenue requiring it to close the enquiry.

If your tax return or its amendment is the subject of an enquiry your tax inspector will issue you with a formal notice telling you it is completed, how much tax you are considered to owe (if any) and requiring you to amend your self-assessment. You may also be required to amend your self-assessment before the completion of an enquiry if your tax inspector decides that it is too low. You will be given 30 days to amend your self-assessment in line with your tax inspector's conclusions. In certain conditions, you can also use this 30-day period to amend your self-assessment yourself with any changes which you had notified to your tax inspector. If you don't amend your self-assessment, your tax inspector has 30 days in which to do it for you. You can appeal against this Revenue amendment.

What your tax inspector can do if an enquiry has been completed

Although a second enquiry cannot take place, the law allows a discovery assessment if you have been acting fraudulently or negligently. A discovery assessment cannot be made if it is a mistake of arithmetic or principle on your part. Nor can it be made if the correct information was available to the Inland Revenue and it should have been possible to work out the correct tax.

A discovery means that your tax inspector has discovered that some income or gain on which you should have paid tax has not been included in your self-assessment, or the assessment is too low, or the amount of relief given is too much. A discovery assessment would be to collect the tax due. You can appeal against a discovery assessment (see p. 21).

PENALTIES, APPEALS AND COMPLAINTS

Penalties

A whole raft of penalties has been introduced to ensure the self-assessment system runs smoothly and taxpayers carry out their obligations:

- if you don't tell your tax office about a new source of income or capital gain within the required time limit, the maximum penalty imposed can be the amount of tax which would be assessed for that tax year. Interest can be charged on this penalty
- if you don't keep the records required under the self-assessment system, a penalty of up to £3,000 could be imposed. But there are certain exceptions to this, for example, if the documents which you have not kept are dividend vouchers or interest certificates – because there are other ways in which this income can be verified. Interest can be charged on this penalty
- failing to make the annual returns required from employers under the PAYE system and construction industry scheme by 19 May following the year of assessment would bring penalties starting at £100 for each month (or part of a month) by which they are overdue
- you are allowed to claim that you should not make interim payments of your tax bill (see p. 369), either because you will have no tax bill or because it will be covered by payments deducted at source (for example, earnings under the PAYE system or savings income paid with tax deducted). If you make an incorrect statement fraudulently or negligently, the maximum penalty is the amount or additional amount you would have paid on account if you had made a correct statement. Interest can be charged on this penalty
- if you fail to deliver your tax return, you can be fined £100 (or the amount of the tax due if less) and a further penalty of up to £60 a day may be set by the commissioners for each day it is late starting from the day you are notified by the commissioners – but this is likely to happen only if your tax office believes you may owe a substantial amount of tax. If your tax return is still not delivered six months after it was due you can be fined a further £100, and a delay of a year would mean that you could be charged a penalty of the amount of tax that would have been due. You can appeal against these penalties to the commissioners
- if you are in a partnership and you fail to deliver your partnership return, you can be charged the same penalties as above, but not the tax-geared penalty. There is no provision for reducing the £100 penalty
- if you fraudulently or negligently deliver an incorrect return, you can be charged a penalty equal to the amount of tax that would have been due
- if you don't produce the documents your tax inspector asks for during an enquiry, you can be charged a penalty of £50. If you still don't come up

with the documents, a daily penalty can be imposed. The amount will be £30, but it could rise to £150 if your tax inspector chooses to take it to the commissioners.

Penalties which are based upon an amount of tax that is due can be limited by certain factors which your tax inspector could take into account. These include disclosure, cooperation and gravity.

A claim for tax relief, allowance or tax repayment must be made in a tax return, unless it couldn't be included at that time or within the arrangements for correcting a return. If you make a claim independent of a return, you will need documentary proof and you must keep all the records relating to the claim. If you do not keep your records, you may be fined a penalty of up to £3,000, plus interest for each and every claim.

Appeals and complaints

You have the right to appeal against:

> **TAX-SAVING IDEA**
> You can appeal against the £100 penalty for missing the deadline for sending in your tax return. A reasonable excuse would be, for example, a prolonged postal strike, serious illness, the death of close relative, or loss of records due to fire, flood or theft. Pressure of work, a failure by your tax adviser or lack of information would not be regarded as a reasonable excuse.

- an assessment which is not a self-assessment
- an amendment to your self-assessment by the Inland Revenue after an enquiry into your tax return
- an amendment of a partnership statement where a loss of tax is discovered
- a disallowance, in whole or in part, of a claim or election included in a tax return.

You have to give written notice of appeal within 30 days after the issue of the notice of assessment, amendment or disallowance. But if you want to appeal against an amendment by the Revenue as a result of an enquiry, you cannot appeal until you have received notice that the enquiry is complete.

Even though you are appealing against the tax, it is due unless you also apply to postpone payment of the tax.

If you disagree about the amount of the tax bill, you should first of all exhaust the avenues within the Inland Revenue to try and reach an agreement. It is always worth appealing to your tax inspector – he or she may not have made the original decision. However, if it becomes clear that the two of you are not going to agree, there remains the option of appealing to the commissioners – and if that doesn't work you could appeal to the High Court, then to the Appeal Court and ultimately to the House of Lords.

There are two types of commissioners. The general commissioners are not tax experts, but often local people acting in the same way as magistrates. There will be a clerk with expert knowledge on hand to advise them. The second group are known as special commissioners. These are part of the Civil Service and tax experts in their own right.

If you are dissatisfied with the way the Inland Revenue handles your tax affairs, you should first complain to your tax inspector. If you get no satisfaction, you should direct your complaints to the regional controller responsible for your tax office (ask the tax office for the name and address). If this doesn't work, you should channel your next communication to the independent Revenue Adjudicator. The Adjudicator's remit covers matters such as excessive delay, errors, discourtesy or the way your tax inspector has exercised his or her discretion. Complaints about your tax bill must be dealt with through the normal appeals procedure.

THE PAYE SYSTEM

The government has used companies to collect tax from their employees for many a year. Your employer is an unpaid tax collector for the Inland Revenue using the PAYE system – Pay As You Earn. Every time employees are paid an amount of money, tax is deducted from the earnings and sent in a batch to the collector of taxes.

Your employer needs various bits of information to operate this system. The aim is that at the end of the tax year, each employee will have had the correct amount of tax deducted, although this does not always happen. Underpayments of tax might be collected in the following year through the PAYE system or in a tax bill at the end of the year.

Under the self-assessment system, an underpayment of tax which is calculated in a tax return, as long as it is £1,000 or less, and as long as you have returned your tax return by 30 September can be included in your PAYE code for the next tax year. This means that you will not have to pay the lump sum direct to the Inland Revenue, but it will be deducted in monthly instalments from your salary.

The Inland Revenue will tell your employer what your PAYE code is and will also supply tax tables so that your employer can deduct the right amount of tax. If the number in your code is 405, for example, you will be entitled to £4,059 free of tax for the tax year. If you are paid monthly, you will receive one-twelfth of £4,059 (that is £338) each month. If you are paid weekly, you will receive £4,059 divided by 52 each week free of tax. This would be £78.

The PAYE system is flexible and can be adjusted during the tax year. If you are entitled to more allowances, for example, because you get married, you should tell your tax inspector who should issue a new PAYE code. Your monthly after-tax earnings should rise once the new code has been received by your employer.

For how to check a Notice of Coding, see Chapter 28.

Your employer must give you certain forms by required dates so that you can use them to fill in your tax return. You should receive your P60 for the tax year ending 5 April 1998 by 31 May 1998. Form P9D or Form P11D should be received by 6 July 1998. Chase your employer if you don't receive them. You don't want to send in your tax return late because your employer is inefficient.

DEADLINES

Within 60 days

- Tell your tax office if you disagree with the statement of taxable social security benefits you receive from the benefit office

On or before 31 January 1998

- Make first interim payment on account of tax due for tax year ending 5 April 1998 according to the Statement of Account sent out early in January 1998

On or before 5 April 1998

- Claim for allowances and deductions for tax year ending 5 April 1992
- Apply to allocate the married couple's allowance to the wife or to split equally between the two of you for the tax year ending on 5 April 1999

April 1998

- Self-assessment tax returns sent to appropriate taxpayers

On or before 31 May 1998

- Form P60 should have been given to all employees by employer

On or before 4 June 1998

- Choose to pay tax in instalments on exercise of option in the tax year ending 5 April 1998 to acquire shares through an approved scheme

On or before 6 July 1998

- Form P9D (or Form P11D) should have been given to employees receiving fringe benefits by employer, plus details of other benefits provided by someone else

31 July 1998

- Second interim payment of tax due for tax year ending 5 April 1998

On or before 30 September 1998

- Send in tax return if you want Inland Revenue to work out tax due
- Employees who have underpaid tax by £1,000 or less should send in their tax return so that tax will be collected through the PAYE system

On or before 5 October 1998

- Tell your tax inspector about any new source of income or capital gain for year ending 5 April 1998

On or before 30 January 1999

- Claim to reduce payments on account for the tax year ending 5 April 1999 (see p. 369)
- Tell your tax inspector if you have reduced your payments on account by too little
- Send in your tax return, along with calculation of any income and capital gains tax due, plus payment for any unpaid tax for the year ending 5 April 1998
- Make first interim payment on account of tax due for tax year ending 5 April 1999 (statement received from Inland Revenue based on previous year's tax bill or your own self-assessment calculation)
- Choose to carry back personal pension payment made in the tax year ending on 5 April 1998 to the tax year ending on 5 April 1997

On or before 5 April 1999

- Claim for allowances and deductions for tax year ending 5 April 1993

On or before 31 January 2000

- Set losses made in a new business for the tax year ending 5 April 1998 against other income for the previous three tax years
- Set business losses made in the tax year ending 5 April 1998 against other income

On or before 31 January 2004

- Claim for allowances and deductions left out of tax return by mistake for the tax year ending 5 April 1998
- Set business losses made in the tax year ending 5 April 1998 against future profits of the same business

On or before 5 April 2004

- Claim unused relief for retirement annuities and personal pension schemes for tax year ending 5 April 1998.

TAX CHANGES FOR THE TAX YEAR STARTING 6 APRIL 1998

The Iron Chancellor didn't live up to his name in the Budget he announced on 17 March 1998. On the contrary, he took trouble to please a number of different sections of society by handing back quite a lot of the extra tax revenue which would have poured into the Exchequer coffers as a result of changes already announced in his first Budget in July 1997.

The other adjective used to describe him – reforming – appeared more accurate as the Budget did include some sweeping reforms, especially the Working Family Tax Credit. However, details of this are still sketchy as it will not be introduced until October 1999.

Income tax rates

Income tax rates are unchanged: the lower rate is 20 per cent, the basic rate 23 per cent and the higher rate 40 per cent. The rate applicable to trusts, which applies to income of discretionary and accumulation trusts, also remains at 34 per cent.

However, the bands of income to which these rates apply have been adjusted in line with inflation. The lower rate band is increased from £4,100 to £4,300. The basic rate limit is lifted by £1,000 to £27,100.

Allowances

Personal allowances are increased to compensate for inflation, putting the personal allowance up from £4,045 to £4,195, with corresponding changes for the allowances for those aged 65 or over during the tax year. The income limit for age-related allowances rose from £15,600 to £16,200.

Married couple's, additional personal and widow's bereavement allowances have been increased from £1,830 to £1,900. For the tax year starting 6 April 1999, the amount of relief will be restricted. Currently at 15 per cent, it will drop to 10 per cent.

The Chancellor also made one change to allowances which he backdated to

6 April 1997 (so this can be claimed on your 1998 tax return). The additional personal allowance can be claimed by husbands who have a child and whose wife is incapacitated. This now also applies to women whose husband is incapacitated.

Lastly, blind person's allowance will rise to £1,330.

Reliefs

The amount for relief on maintenance payments has been increased from £1,830 to £1,900. This will also be restricted to 10 per cent (currently 15 per cent) from 6 April 1999.

For maintenance payments made under the old rules (broadly those arrangements made before 15 March 1998 – see p. 46), relief in line with the married couple's allowance will be restricted to 10 per cent from 6 April 1999, but any extra paid up to the limit for the tax year ending 5 April 1989 will continue to get relief at the highest rate.

The amount of tax relief you will get on your mortgage falls from 6 April 1998 (this was a change announced in the July budget last year). The new figure is 10 per cent on the first £30,000 of loans to buy your home. This also applies if you can claim relief on a loan made before 6 April 1998 for home improvement and for a loan to buy or improve a home for a dependent relative or former or separated spouse. But the tax treatment of people aged over 65 who use their home to secure a loan to buy themselves an annuity is unaltered. They are still able to get interest relief on a loan of up to £30,000 at the basic rate (23 per cent).

Tax relief on private medical insurance was abolished in the last budget. Premiums due on policies taken out or renewed from 2 July 1997 will not qualify and premiums may have to rise to cover the amount of tax relief lost.

The Chancellor is proposing a special extension of Gift Aid from later in 1998 to the end of 2000. For donations to certain very poor countries, the minimum amount which qualifies for relief will be lowered from £250 to £100 during the year.

Savings and investment

The tax rate for income from savings, such as interest from bank or building societies, distributions from unit trusts or dividends on shares remains at 20 per cent for all but higher rate taxpayers, who will still pay 40 per cent.

However, from 6 April 1999, the rate of tax on dividends or distributions will become 10 per cent for lower and basic rate taxpayers to compensate for a cut in the tax credit from 20 per cent to 10 per cent. Non-taxpayers will no longer receive the tax credit. Higher rate taxpayers will pay tax at the rate of 32.5 per cent, thus leaving their after-tax income unchanged.

There has also been a change in the way British Government stocks are taxed from 6 April 1998. You can receive the interest gross rather than after the deduction of basic rate tax if you so choose.

The major changes in savings, which will occur on 6 April 1999, is the abolition of new PEPs and TESSAs and the introduction of Individual Savings Accounts (ISAs). However, the changes have been amended from those first mooted last year. All existing PEPs and TESSAs can continue to be held outside the new account but with the same tax advantages. The amount which can be saved in ISAs is £5,000 a year for ten years (£7,000 in 1999-2000 only). The new ISAs are described in more detail on p. 83.

The earnings cap which is placed on the maximum level of earnings for which you can make payments into a pension scheme, either occupational or personal, has been increased from £84,000 to £87,600 starting from 6 April 1998.

Inheritance tax
This is a tax which very few people pay (estimated around 17,500 in the tax year starting on 6 April 1998). The Chancellor has raised the inheritance tax threshold by £8,000 to £223,000 from 6 April 1998 onwards.

Capital gains tax
A number of fundamental changes have been proposed to the operation of capital gains tax, although not restructuring of the tax-free slice of net capital gains which an individual can make each year without paying tax. The amount has been lifted from £6,500 to £6,800. For trusts, the figure becomes £3,400.

The practice of bed and breakfasting, beloved of stockbrokers and shareholders, which has allowed investors to create gains each year to take advantage of the tax-free slice by selling one day and buying back the next, has been stopped for disposals of shares made on or after 17 March 1998 – see p. 120.

Indexation allowance, which removes the effects of inflation from the calculation of a capital gain, has been ended from 6 April 1998. To replace this, the Chancellor is introducing taper relief which depends on the length of time an asset has been held (see p. 123). For the first three years after 5 April 1998, all the gain will be taxable, falling after ten years to 60 per cent – making the effective rate of tax 24 per cent, where the current rate of capital gains tax is 40 per cent. The relief is more generous for business assets.

The capital gains tax rate structure will be rationalised for trusts and estates. From 6 April 1998, the unified rate will be 34 per cent.

Businesses
For the year to 1 July 1998, small and medium-sized businesses can claim 50 per cent first-year capital allowances on investment in plant and machinery (but not for expenditure on cars). From 2 July 1998 until 1 July 1999 it is proposed that first-year allowances will be 40 per cent.

It is proposed to rationalise the incentives to promote investment in new or unquoted companies. From 6 April 1998, capital gains tax reinvestment relief (which allows investors to defer capital gains tax indefinitely if the gain is reinvested in certain types of unquoted companies) will be merged with the Enterprise Investment Scheme. The amount an individual can invest in new shares under the new scheme and get income tax relief of 20 per cent will be increased to £150,000 a year. Other changes have been made, including restricting the scheme to investment in new shares, thus excluding existing shares, which are included under the existing capital gains tax reinvestment relief. The Chancellor has also tightened the company requirements to exclude certain property backed activities, such as farming and market gardening, nursing homes and so on and the relief will be available only for investments in companies with gross assets of £10 million or less before the investment or £11 million including the investment.

The new taper relief for working out capital gains (see above) will be more generous for business assets, which includes those used for carrying on a trade or shares held in qualifying companies. The maximum effective rate of tax for business assets held for ten years will be 10 per cent.

As this treatment of business assets is so generous, retirement relief for capital gains will be phased out, beginning with the tax year starting on 6 April 1999. The relief will cease to be available from 6 April 2003.

Professionals who used a cash basis for working out their tax bill, rather than the more widely used earnings basis, will find that it is no longer acceptable to the Inland Revenue from the tax year starting on 6 April 1999. This will primarily affect barristers.

To cut red tape and help businesses, the Inland Revenue and the Contributions Agency will be merged. The two organisations will also offer a service to new employers to help them deal with tax and national insurance for their first employee.

Employees
There are three changes affecting employees.

The rules for taxing redundancy settlements (excluding the £30,000 redundancy exemption) will be made fairer. Ex-employees will now be taxed only on the value of the benefits which they actually enjoy and only at the time they are enjoyed (rather than straight away on termination).

The taxable value of petrol provided for private motoring in company cars has been increased by 20 per cent over and above the usual increases. This extra increase will be made each year until the tax year ending 5 April 2003. This is to discourage the use of company cars for private motoring.

The foreign earnings deduction has been abolished for employees going abroad for short periods from 17 March 1998.

Stamp duty
Property transfers (excluding shares) may attract higher rates of stamp duty from 24 March 1998, except for transfers as a result of contracts exchanged before 17 March 1998. Where the price is £250,000 but less than £500,000 the rate will be 2 per cent; for property where the price is more than £500,000 the rate will be 3 per cent.

National Insurance
From April 1999, employees and employers will pay National Insurance only on the portion of earnings above the NIC starting point. The starting point for employers' contributions will be lifted to the level of the personal allowance under the income tax system. Above that level contributions will be at a single rate of 12.2 per cent.

Working Family Tax Credit
The government is proposing that this will be introduced in October 1999 and replace Family Credit (paid through the Benefits Agency). The Working Family Tax Credit will be paid through the tax system from April 2000 and will increase the take-home pay of those who qualify.

SEVENTY-FIVE WAYS
TO SAVE TAX

CHAPTER 5

Here are 75 tips to cut your tax bill. None of them requires you to turn your life upside down in search of tax savings.

All taxpayers

- Make sure you keep all your records, including the originals of certificates and your working papers. You can be fined for not keeping your records (p. 12).

- Keep careful records – apart from the legal requirement, it could help you pay less tax. Note down all the expenses you could claim: if you are an employee (see p. 221); if you are self-employed (see p. 248); if you let out property (see p. 270).

- Don't be late sending in your tax return. The 1998 tax return must be sent back by 31 January 1999 if you want to avoid an automatic £100 penalty (see p. 19).

- Always check your tax forms. As soon as you receive a Tax Calculation or PAYE Coding Notice make sure your tax inspector has got the sums right (see Chapter 28).

- If you are asked to make payments on account, check that you're not paying more than you need to. The figures will be based on last year's tax bill. If you expect your income to be lower this year or your allowances and reliefs to be higher, you can make reduced payments (see p. 369).

- Investigate the past. It may not be too late to claim an allowance or deduction you have forgotten about. Some of the more important deadlines for claims are given on pp. 22-4.

- If you want to give money to charity, think about covenants, payroll-giving schemes and Gift Aid – you'll get tax relief on the gifts. There are more details on pp. 186-8 and p. 207.

- Look closely at any gifts you make to charity by covenant or through Gift Aid. If you are a non-taxpayer or pay tax at the lower rate, you will not be able to keep all the tax relief you deduct at the basic rate from the gifts (p. 188). If your husband or wife pays tax, it may be better if he or she makes the gifts.

Married

- If you are married, consider reorganising your investments so your investment income is paid to the partner who pays least tax on it.

- Married couples where one partner has a low income and can't use up all their allowances can transfer the married couple's allowance and blind person's allowance to their partner (see p. 198).

- If you are single and there is a child under 18 living with you at the start of the tax year, you may be able to claim the additional personal allowance, the same amount as the married couple's allowance (£1,830 for the tax year ending 5 April 1998, £1,900 for the tax year beginning 6 April 1998). You may also be entitled to claim this allowance if you are married but separated, or married to someone who is totally unable to look after himself or herself (see p. 195).

- If you are separated or divorced and paying maintenance under arrangements made before March 1988, it could pay you to change the way you get tax relief on the payments (see p. 50).

- If you separate from your husband or wife, don't agree to make their mortgage payments as part of any maintenance arrangements – you won't get tax relief on mortgage interest. Give the money to your ex-spouse and he or she can claim the tax relief (see p. 51).

Employees

- If you pay tax under the PAYE system and have some other income, for example from investments, on which you will need to pay tax, make sure you send your tax return back by 30 September – even if you are working out your own tax bill. If the amount of tax due is £1,000 or less, the tax on this extra income will be deducted from your earnings under PAYE in the tax year which begins on 6 April 1999 – not as a lump sum by 31 January.

- If you are an employee, see if you can negotiate the introduction of share option schemes (p. 228). These can be free of income tax.

- There is a long list of fringe benefits which are tax-free whatever your level of earnings – try to take advantage of them in your negotiations with your boss. These perks are still free of tax: entertainment by your suppliers or customers at cultural or sporting events (within certain rules); air miles (which enable you to make cheap flights); and non-cash gifts costing up to £100 from a third party (see p. 86).

- Fringe benefits which are not tax-free can still be a tax-efficient way of being paid. The taxable value put on them may be much lower than the value to you. There is a rundown of how they are taxed in Chapter 9 (p. 86).

- If you have a company car, keep an eye on your business mileage as the end of the tax year approaches or if you are about to change your car. If your business mileage is approaching a rate of 2,500 or 18,000 miles a year, try to use the car for work enough to qualify for the reduction in the tax bill if you travel more than either of these amounts on business (see p. 95). Keep good records of your business mileage so you can substantiate your claims.

- If you plan to keep a company car for some years, you will pay less tax if it is registered just before the end of the tax year (April 5). The taxable value of a car which is more than four years old at the end of the tax year is reduced by one-third (see p. 95). If you buy a car just after the start of a tax year, it will be almost five years old before you get the reduction.

- Be aware that if you want a large, luxurious company car, you will be taxed fairly heavily for the privilege (see p. 95). Do your sums carefully before accepting a company car if you are just below the limit for paying higher rate tax (£27,100 in the tax year beginning 6 April 1998). If you have the option, consider taking a cheap, lightly taxed company car and taking the rest of the car allowance in cash which you can invest in a tax-free investment, such as additional contributions to your pension plan.

- Working parents should try to persuade their employers to provide child-care facilities, as this fringe benefit is tax-free. Your private childcare arrangements are not eligible for tax relief (see p. 87).

- If you often work away from home and think you may be affected by changes in what expenses you can claim (see p. 222), start keeping a note now of your costs of normal commuting. It may help you to establish what costs of travel you can claim.

- If you can arrange your work so you count as self-employed rather than an employee, you will be able to claim a wider range of expenses (see p. 248). But remember there may be disadvantages in not having the protection of employment law. For more about the distinction between employees and the self-employed, see pp. 203 and 236.

- If you borrow to buy shares in a company where you work, you may be able to get tax relief on the loan (see p. 182). The company must be largely owned by its employees or you must have a large stake in it.

- If you become unemployed and are not claiming social security benefits, ask your tax inspector for a rebate of tax paid when you were working.

Self-employed

- If you leave a job in the middle of a tax year to become self-employed, ask your tax inspector for a rebate. It will help your finances, although not cut your actual tax bill.

- If you are self-employed or in partnership and your turnover is less than £15,000 a year, take advantage of the ability to send in three-line accounts (see p. 245). This won't save you any tax, but it may cut your book-keeping and accountancy fees.

- You can still claim as an expense for your business something you use partly for business and partly in your private life, for example, using your home for work, sharing the car (p. 248).

- You can get a higher-than-normal first-year capital allowance on plant and machinery bought between 2 July 1997 and 1 July 1999 inclusive – 50 per cent in the first of these years, 40 per cent in the second (see p. 256). This concession, for small and medium-sized businesses, gives you the tax relief faster than with the normal annual capital allowance of 25 per cent.

- When you first start your business, claim capital allowances on any equipment you already own but take into the business, for example, a car, desk and so on (see p. 257).

- You do not have to claim all the capital allowances you are entitled to. It may save you more tax to claim less and carry forward a higher value to the next year when your profits may be higher or your personal allowances lower (p. 257).

- If you are married and run your own business, consider employing your spouse if he or she does not work. It could save money if your spouse's tax rate (including National Insurance contributions – see p. 262) would be lower than yours.

- If you are in business and buying assets, see if they can be treated as short-life assets. The cost can be reclaimed over five years, whereas the writing-down allowances available on other sorts of assets mean the cost is reclaimed much more slowly (see p. 256).

- If you make a tax loss in your business, there are several ways this can be used to reduce tax on other income. Choose the one that will save you the most tax (see p. 260).

Investments

- The government offers lots of tax incentives to persuade you to save for a pension. Take advantage of them. Chapter 8 (p. 72) tells you how to take them up.

- If you're approaching retirement, consider making extra contributions towards a pension. If you work for an employer, you can get tax relief on additional voluntary contributions (AVCs) to your employer's scheme (p. 74). With contributions to a personal pension scheme, you can get tax relief on a higher proportion of your earnings as you get older (p. 77).

- Take advantage of the rules that allow you to backdate contributions to personal pensions (see p. 78). You may be able to get a higher rate of tax relief – for example, if you paid tax at the higher rate in a previous tax year. If you haven't made the maximum contributions allowed in previous tax years, you can claim the unused relief up to six years later to make a bigger contribution.

- If you pay tax at the top rate of 40 per cent, tax-free investments can be attractive. Even if you could get a higher rate of return on a taxable investment, the after-tax return could be considerably lower.

- Non-taxpayers investing in banks, building societies and other investments where tax is deducted from the income should claim it back from the Inland Revenue. With interest from banks and building societies, you can arrange for it to be paid without deduction of tax if you are a non-taxpayer (see p. 68).

- If you want to give some capital to your children, any income it produces over £100 a year will be counted as yours (see p. 290). Choose investments that produce a tax-free income or gain (see pp. 151 and 103).

- If you are elderly, watch out for the income trap – the level of income where the extra allowances paid to people aged 65 or over are withdrawn. The withdrawal is phased, but it means you are effectively taxed at a higher-than-normal rate on each extra £1 of income (see p. 42). Consider tax-free investments if this is the case.

- If you invest in shares, investment trusts or unit trusts, make sure you invest the maximum in a personal equity plan before PEPs are replaced by Individual Savings Accounts on 6 April 1999 – there's no tax to pay on the income or gains. You can invest up to £9,000 a year in PEPs – and a couple can invest double that amount. If you buy shares in a privatisation issue, transfer these into your PEP (see p. 80).

- Investing in a tax exempt special savings account (TESSA) means tax-free interest on up to £9,000 of savings – as long as you can leave the money for the full five years (p. 81). If you haven't already got one, open a TESSA before the closing date for new accounts of 5 April 1999.

- Open an individual savings account (ISA) as soon as they are introduced on 6 April 1999 (see p. 83). There will be no tax to pay on income or gains on the investments in ISAs and you won't lose the tax relief if you withdraw your money. So you can use an ISA even for temporary savings and boost the returns.

- If you receive shares through an employee profit-sharing scheme or a savings-related share option scheme in the tax year ending 5 April 1999, transfer the £3,000 maximum for a tax year into a single-company PEP (see p. 80). This will mean no income tax on the dividends and no capital gains tax when you eventually sell the shares.

- Investors should consider having some investments which give a capital gain rather than income. There is a tax-free allowance of net capital gains (£6,800 in the tax year beginning 6 April 1998) which you can make each tax year (see p. 71).

- If you took out a life insurance policy before midnight on 13 March 1984, the chances are that you get tax relief on the premiums (currently at 12.5 per cent). However, altering the policy (for example, increasing the benefits unless this is done automatically under the policy) could mean losing the tax relief (see p. 71). Consider carefully before altering – perhaps you can achieve your objective in another way.

- If you get income from trusts, it comes with a tax credit – you can reclaim some or all of this if it is more than you should have paid (see p. 289). Unless you pay tax at the higher rates, you are almost certainly entitled to a tax rebate on income from discretionary trusts.

- People investing in growing businesses can claim tax relief on up to £150,000 in a tax year through the Enterprise Investment Scheme. There is also generous tax relief for investing in venture capital trusts (see p. 81).

- If you get income from investments abroad on which you have paid foreign tax, tax credit relief can reduce the amount of UK tax you pay (see p. 280).

Homeowners

- The cost of borrowing money to buy a home can be reduced by the tax relief on mortgage interest paid on up to £30,000 of loans. You can get the tax relief on a range of loans – it doesn't have to be a mortgage. You can use the loan to buy a home anywhere in the UK or Ireland – even if it is a caravan or houseboat. Chapter 7 (p. 54) tells you the rules so you get the maximum relief.

- A married couple can choose to share the tax relief on mortgage interest however they like. If some split other than an equal one would save you tax, make an allocation of interest election (see p. 56 for when it would pay to do this).

- If you have a home improvement loan taken out before 6 April 1988, consider carefully before you replace it with another loan with a lower rate of interest. You would not be able to claim tax relief on the interest paid on the replacement loan (see p. 58).

- You can be away from your home for quite long periods and still get mortgage interest tax relief (the various concessions you can claim are on p. 58). You'll also need to keep an eye on the capital gains tax position – don't lose private residence relief which means you pay no capital gains tax on your only or main home (see p. 62).

- Do you have more than one home? You may have to pay capital gains tax when you sell your second home (p. 61). But you can choose which of your homes counts as your main one, make sure you nominate the home that is likely to incur the biggest capital gains tax bill.

- Do you want an income of over £80 a week tax-free? If you let out a room in your home under the rent a room scheme, you can take £4,250 of gross rent a year tax-free. This relief can reduce your tax bill even if the income is higher (see p. 267).

- If you let out your home, you might do better to switch from mortgage interest tax relief to claiming the interest as an expense against letting income. You get the tax relief at your highest rate of tax and there's no £30,000 limit on the loan (see p. 59).

- If you let out your second home, try to make sure you meet the conditions for the rent to be taxed as income from furnished holiday lettings (p. 269). You can claim a wider variety of deductions against tax, and you may be able to avoid capital gains tax when you sell the home.

- You can claim a tax allowance for the wear and tear incurred in letting out furnished property (see p. 277).

- If you have made a loss letting out property, you may be able to use this to reduce other parts of your tax bill (see p. 273).

- If you've let out part or all of your home, lettings relief could mean no capital gains tax to pay when you dispose of it (see p. 63).

Capital gains tax

- Try to use the tax-free allowance for capital gains tax every year – you can't carry over unused allowances to other years. Think about selling some shares showing a profit and buying them back a month later to make a gain that uses up the allowance (see p. 120).

- Husband and wife are each entitled to the tax-free allowance of net capital gains – £6,800 for the tax year beginning 6 April 1998 (see p. 125). Consider reorganising your possessions so each of you can use up the limit before either starts paying capital gains tax.

- If you are going to dispose of assets, split the disposals over several years. You can then claim the tax-free allowance for capital gains to reduce the bill each year.

- If you are facing a capital gains tax bill on the disposal of one large asset, you could sell assets that are showing losses to set against the gain. If you don't really want to get rid of these other assets, you can buy them back some time later (see p. 126).

- If you own valuables such as antiques, a second home or collectables, keep careful records of what they cost you to buy and maintain. You could face a capital gains tax bill when you dispose of them – allowable expenses can reduce the tax bill (p. 108).

- If you are thinking of making a gift to charity of an asset which is showing a loss, think again. It would be better to sell the asset and give the money to the charity (see p. 103).

- Do not forget to claim losses if you dispose of something like shares or valuables at a loss. Losses can be set off against taxable gains, and carried over to later years. But you must claim them within time limits (see p. 115). Keep careful records so you don't forget them later!

- If you face a big capital gains tax bill, think about investing the gain in growing companies. Reinvestment relief can defer the bill (see p. 127).

Inheritance tax

- Draw up a will. There are simple steps you can take to minimise the tax payable on your estate when you die and to reduce the complications for those you leave behind (see p. 134). Making a will helps you to start thinking about inheritance tax.

- Make as full use as possible of the gifts you can make which do not fall into the inheritance tax net. Gifts on marriage and those made out of normal income are tax-free (p. 134).

- Share your wealth with your husband or wife so you can each make tax-free gifts. There is no capital gains tax to pay on gifts between a married couple (p. 135).

- Use life insurance to blunt the impact of inheritance tax. Policies written in trust go straight to the beneficiary and don't form part of your estate (see p. 136). If you pay the premiums out of your normal spending, they are tax-free gifts (see p. 133).

- If you own a small business or farm, take professional tax advice. There are extensive tax reliefs which can mean you pay little or no capital gains tax (p. 128) or inheritance tax (p. 137), but they are complicated and need careful planning.

- There are steps you can take to reduce an inheritance tax bill after a death (see p. 141). In particular, you can rearrange inheritances in ways that reduce the amount of tax.

MARRIAGE AND DIVORCE

Married couples are treated as two independent taxpayers by the Inland Revenue. They are taxed on their own income and gains and have their own allowances. Each is responsible for filling in their own tax return and paying their own tax bills.

However, there are some aspects of the tax system which recognise that husband and wife are more than just two individuals living together. One is that the Chancellor still blesses marriage with the wedding gift of an extra income tax allowance – the married couple's. Another is they can transfer some allowances between them in certain circumstances. Gifts between husband and wife don't normally fall into the net for capital gains tax or inheritance tax. And by sharing their wealth, a couple can each use their tax-free allowances to reduce the amounts paid in tax.

This chapter explains the opportunities to save tax in marriage. It sets out the rules for what happens when marriages come to an end, and the taxation of maintenance payments. And it gives some brief guidance on what happens if you are widowed. For how marriage affects mortgage interest tax relief, see p. 56, and information about capital gains tax is on p. 105, and on inheritance tax on p. 135.

MARRIAGE

Married couple's allowance
A husband and wife are each entitled to a personal tax allowance in the same way as single people. And if they are 65 or over during the tax

> **TAX-SAVING IDEA**
> If one of you pays tax at a higher rate than the other, you should consider giving investments which produce a taxable income to the partner who would pay least tax on the income.
> Gifts between married couples must be genuine – you can't hand them over with strings attached. If you are reluctant to give away the investments completely, consider putting them into joint names with your spouse so the income is shared equally (see p. 44).

year, they can claim the higher amounts of personal allowance for older people (see below). This personal allowance is deducted from total income (see right) in arriving at the taxable income on which the individual's tax bill is calculated

But they can also claim married couple's allowance which can be allocated to either the husband or the wife, or split equally between them. Unlike the personal allowance, the married couple's allowance reduces their tax bill by a fixed amount – it is not used to reduce their income for tax purposes. For the tax year beginning 6 April 1998, for example, the allowance is £1,900 for people under the age of 65. Tax relief is given at 15 per cent against this amount – giving a maximum tax-saving of £285 for the tax year. For the tax year beginning 6 April 1999, the rate of tax relief will be cut to 10 per cent.

EXAMPLE

Janet Lardon is a high flier on a salary of £60,000 a year and income from shares and savings accounts of £5,000 a year before tax. She pays tax at the higher rate of 40 per cent on her earnings – and that will be the rate for any additional income from investments.

She decides to share the investments with her husband Ted, who pays tax at the basic rate only. She puts them in their joint names, so £2,500 of the investment income is taxed as his. He has to pay tax on dividends and interest only at the lower rate of 20 per cent (see p. 66), so they save higher rate tax of 20 per cent of £2,500, that is £500 a year.

The married couple's allowance goes automatically to the husband. However, the husband and wife can ask their tax inspectors to set it against the wife's income – they should both sign Inland Revenue Form 18 before the start of the tax year it is to apply to. The same procedure would be required if they subsequently wanted the allowance switched back to the husband.

TAX-SAVING IDEA

If one of you does not pay tax, allocate the married couple's allowance to the partner who does. If this means changing the current allocation, do it before 6 April 1999 if you want it to come into force for the tax year which begins on that date.

Either partner can ask for half the allowance to be allocated to their income – again this must be done before the start of the tax year.

For those aged 65 or over
As with the personal allowance, there are higher rates of married

couple's allowance for people who are 65 or over at any time during the tax year. The figures for this tax year and the last tax year – and the maximum tax-savings – are given in the table below.

Age of older partner during tax year	Tax year ending 5 April 1998		Tax year ending 5 April 1999	
	maximum allowance £	maximum tax-saving £	maximum allowance £	maximum tax-saving £
Under 65	1,830	274.50	1,900	285.00
65-74	3,185	477.75	3,305	495.75
75 and over	3,225	483.75	3,345	501.75

As with the married couple's allowance for under-65s, it will normally be given to the husband. It can be switched to the wife or split equally between the pair – but only the amount under-65s get can be allocated in this way. The extra allowance for those aged 65 and over always goes to the husband.

This additional amount is gradually reduced if the husband's 'total income' is above a certain level – even if the couple are getting the allowance because of the wife's age. Total income is broadly all your income less deductions such as pension contributions (see p. 4).

If the husband's total income in the tax year ending 5 April 1999 is £16,200 or more, his personal allowance is first reduced by £1 for each extra £2 over the limit until he is getting the same allowance as the under-65s. This would be when his 'total income' had reached £18,630 (£19,010 if 75 or over). Then the married couple's allowance is similarly reduced until it is the same as for the under-65s. This would be when his total income reached £21,440 (£21,900 if he is 75 or over, or £21,520 if he isn't but his wife is).

If the husband is under 65, he won't get the higher personal allowance, so if his total income is over £16,200 it will immediately start to reduce the married couple's allowance. He will end up with the same allowance as under-65s if total

> **TAX-SAVING IDEA**
>
> If one of you is 65 or over and the husband's 'total income' is £16,200 or more in the tax year which began on 6 April 1998, see if you would save tax by giving investments that produce a taxable income to the wife. Even if the husband is under 65, his total income could be reducing the amount of married couple's allowance you get.

income is £19,010 (£19,090 if his wife is 75 or over).

The total income limit for the tax year ending on 5 April 1998 was £15,600.

Transfer of allowances because of low income

If either husband or wife has a tax bill which is too low to use up all their married couple's allowance, they can ask to have the unused part deducted from the tax bill of their spouse. You can do this after the end of the tax year in which you got the allowance – and it can cover the extra allowance paid to a husband where one of you is 65 or over. (See p. 190 for how to claim this.) The same is true if you get blind person's allowance and can't fully use it because your income is too low. It can be transferred to your partner even if not blind.

You have up to five years and ten months after the end of the tax year to transfer the unused allowances. So for the tax year ending 5 April 1998, you can make a claim any time up to 31 January 2004. But if you know in advance that your income will not be big enough to benefit from these allowances, you can ask your tax inspector to transfer the part you estimate will be unused to your spouse's PAYE code.

EXAMPLE

Jasper Duffy, 68, has a total income of £19,750 – of which £9,300 a year is from savings and investments. Because his total income is over the £16,200 limit, it reduces the amount of personal allowance he gets to the amount for under-65s. But it is also high enough to reduce the married couple's allowance the Duffys get by £1 for each £2 over £18,630.

He decides to share his savings and investments equally with his wife Ellen, whose total income is well below the £16,200 limit. He puts them all into their joint names, which means only half the income they produce is his. This reduces his total income by half of £9,300 = £4,650 to £15,100.

The Duffys will thus get the full amount of married couple's allowance for people aged 65 and over. And Jasper will get the full higher personal allowance for those aged 65 and over.

Allowances in the year of marriage

In the tax year of your marriage, you get a proportion of the married couple's allowance. The proportion depends on the date of the wedding (see table overleaf).

If you have a child living with you when you marry, you can carry on claiming the full additional personal allowance for single parents (which is the same as the married couple's allowance) instead of a fraction of the married couple's allowance. You can't claim additional personal allowance after the tax year of your marriage unless your spouse is totally unable to look after himself or herself throughout the tax year (see p. 195). (Note that until the tax year beginning 6 April 1997, only men could claim the additional personal allowance in such circumstances.)

Date of marriage before	Tax year ending 5 April 1998		Tax year ending 5 April 1999	
	maximum allowance £	maximum tax-saving £	maximum allowance £	maximum tax-saving £
6 May	1,830	274.50	1,900	285.00
6 June	1,678	251.70	1,742	261.30
6 July	1,525	228.75	1,583	237.45
6 August	1,373	205.95	1,425	213.75
6 September	1,220	183.00	1,267	190.05
6 October	1,068	160.20	1,108	166.20
6 November	915	137.25	950	142.50
6 December	763	114.45	792	118.80
6 January	610	91.50	633	94.95
6 February	458	68.70	475	71.25
6 March	305	45.75	317	47.55
6 April	153	22.95	158	23.70

Jointly owned assets

If you have investments which are jointly owned, your tax inspector will assume the income from them is split equally between you. If the investments are not owned in equal proportions, you can have the income divided between you to reflect your actual shares of it. You do this by both signing a declaration of beneficial interests on Form 17 (available from tax offices) and sending it to your tax inspector.

The new split of joint income applies from when the declaration is signed – it can't be backdated. If you acquire new assets on which the 50:50 split is not to apply, you must make a further declaration. Note the split for income will also be used to allocate any gain on selling an asset between you when you dispose of it (see p. 105).

SEPARATION AND DIVORCE

You should tell your tax inspector when you separate – even if you have yet to make a deed of separation or seek a court order. The Inland Revenue will treat you as no longer living with your husband or wife if you have parted in circumstances that make it look as if the separation is permanent.

You should tell the Inland Revenue even if you weren't paying tax before – contact your local tax office (under Inland Revenue in the telephone book). You will be asked to fill in a form about the separation and provide documentation about it. You must also tell your tax inspector if you get back together again or remarry.

Tax allowances
Each of you retains your personal allowances. And each of you will also retain any married couple's allowance you were getting before the separation – but only for the rest of the tax year.

If either of you has a child under 18 living with you at the start of the tax year, you can claim additional personal allowance – worth the same as married couple's (see p. 195).

EXAMPLE
Joe and Jenny Barrett separate on 15 April 1998. They have three children under 18, one of whom is to live with Joe while the other two will live with Jenny. Before separation they split the £1,900 married couple's allowance between them.

For the tax year beginning 6 April 1998, each will get the personal allowance of £4,195, an additional personal allowance for having a child living with them of £1,900 and half the married couple's allowance – £950. That makes total allowances of £7,045. Of this total tax relief is at 15 per cent only on the £2,850 of additional personal and married couple's allowances.

In the tax year which begins on 6 April 1999, each will get the personal allowance and additional personal allowance. Neither will then be entitled to married couple's allowance.

Where a couple separated on or before 5 April 1990, the husband could go on getting married couple's allowance as long as he wholly maintained his wife by making voluntary payments. This can continue until the couple divorce.

Maintenance payments
Maintenance can take several forms, including direct payments of cash or the provision of support such as a home. Where this is provided voluntarily – that is, payment cannot be enforced – the person paying it gets no tax relief and the person getting it does not have to pay tax on what they receive.

But most maintenance payments are made under enforceable agreements, such as a deed of separation, court order or assessment by the Child Support Agency. There is some tax relief for most enforceable maintenance payments, provided they are enforceable in the UK or another country in the European

Economic Area (the EU plus Iceland, Liechtenstein and Norway).

But the amount of tax relief the giver gets on maintenance payments – and how the recipient is taxed on them – depends on when the arrangements were made. What follows below is an explanation of the rules that have applied to new arrangements made in the last ten years or so.

The old rules (pre-1988 or so) are set out on p. 48 – and apply to the following:

- court orders made on or before 30 June 1988, provided they had been applied for on or before 15 March 1988
- maintenance agreements made on or before 14 March 1988 – if you wrote to your tax inspector on or before 30 June 1988
- any agreement made on or after 15 March 1988 which replaces such court orders or agreements – provided the person who receives the payments is unchanged.

Rules for new maintenance arrangements

Under the new rules for arrangements since 1988, any maintenance payments you receive are tax-free. This applies even if you remarry and payments continue for a child, for example.

Thus the person receiving the maintenance can have other income up to the amount of the personal allowance (£4,195 for the tax year beginning 6 April 1998) before paying income tax.

If you make enforceable maintenance payments to an ex-husband or ex-wife, you can get tax relief equivalent to the married couple's allowance. So for the tax year beginning 6 April 1998, you get tax relief of 15 per cent on payments you make up to the level of the married couple's allowance of £1,900. If you are already getting tax relief under the old rules below, it is deducted from the amount you can get under the new rules.

You don't get any tax relief on payments made direct to a child, or to someone you weren't married to. Lump sum payments are excluded – as are any payments which already qualify for tax relief (such as mortgage interest payments). The tax relief ends if the ex-spouse remarries.

The maximum you can get under the new rules is the same however many former spouses you are making maintenance payments to. But it is in addition to any other tax allowances, such as part or all of the married couple's allowance you are allowed to keep during the year of separation.

EXAMPLE

Lewis and Monica Lomax separated on 6 October 1992. Their three children live with Monica, and Lewis makes enforceable maintenance payments of £90 a week (£4,680 a year) from his salary of £25,000 a year. Monica has a job which pays £12,500 a year.

Monica will pay no income tax on the maintenance payments. In the tax year beginning 6 April 1998, Monica's tax bill will be calculated as follows:

Earnings		£12,500.00
Less personal allowance		£4,195.00
Taxable income		£8,305.00
Tax due:	20 per cent of £4,300	£860.00
	23 per cent of £4,005	£921.15
		£1,781.15
Less additional personal allowance: 15 per cent of £1,900		£285.00
Total tax		£1,496.15

So Monica's after-tax income is £12,500 less £1,496 tax plus maintenance of £4,680 – a total of £15,684 for the tax year beginning 6 April 1998.

Lewis's tax bill for the same tax year is calculated as follows:

Earnings		£25,000.00
Less personal allowance		£4,195.00
Taxable income		£20,805.00
Tax due:	20 per cent of £4,300	£860.00
	23 per cent of £16,505	£3,796.15
		£4,656.15
Less tax relief on maintenance payments: maximum is 15 per cent of the £1,900 married couple's allowance		£285.00
Total tax		£4,371.15

Thus Lewis has an after-tax income of £25,000 less £4,371 tax, less maintenance payments of £4,680 – a total of £15,949 for the tax year beginning 6 April 1998.

You get the tax relief on these maintenance payments through your PAYE code (see p. 362) or through an adjustment to your tax bill. You do not deduct any tax from the maintenance payments you make.

EXAMPLE

Conrad Murdoch pays £3,000 a year maintenance to his former wife Theresa and £2,000 direct to each of his two children under a court order which falls under the old rules. In the tax year ending 5 April 1989, he paid £2,500 to Theresa and £1,250 to each of the two children – a total of £5,000. He earns £40,000 a year, while Theresa earns £9,500.

In calculating her tax bill for the tax year beginning 6 April 1998, Theresa first calculates how much of her £3,000 maintenance payment is taxable. She can deduct two sums from it:

- the £1,900 married couple's allowance for the tax year
- the £500 increase she received over what she was given in the tax year which ended on 5 April 1989.

Thus she can deduct £1,900 + £500 = £2,400 from the £3,000 of maintenance she received – leaving just £600 which is taxable. Theresa's tax bill is calculated as follows:

Earnings	£9,500.00	
Taxable maintenance payments	£600.00	
Total income		£10,100.00
Less personal allowance		£4,195.00
Taxable income		£5,905.00
Tax due: 20 per cent of £4,300	£860.00	
23 per cent of £1,605	£369.15	
		£1,229.15
Less additional personal allowance: 15 per cent of £1,900		£285.00
Total tax		£944.15

So Theresa's after-tax income is her £9,500 earnings, plus £3,000 maintenance payments, less £944 tax – £11,555 for the tax year which began on 6 April 1998.

Rules for old maintenance payments

If the maintenance arrangements were made before the 1988 deadlines listed above, the old rules for the taxation of enforceable maintenance payments apply. They also cover any agreements made since those deadlines which replace, vary or add to such arrangements.

Taxation of payments received

Under the old rules, payments received by an ex-wife or ex-husband are tax-free only within limits. The limit is the married couple's allowance, which is £1,900 for the tax year beginning 6 April 1998, plus any increase in maintenance payments made since the tax year ending 5 April 1989. If you get

The two children can each deduct the personal allowance of £4,195 from the maintenance they receive in the tax year beginning 6 April 1998. As this is more than the £2,000 they each get, they pay no tax on their maintenance payments. Each of them could have another £4,195 – £2,000 = £2,195 of income before paying tax.

In calculating his tax bill for the tax year beginning 6 April 1998, Conrad first calculates how much of his maintenance payments qualify for tax relief. He can get tax relief on no more than he paid in the tax year ending 5 April 1989 – £5,000. He will get tax relief at 15 per cent on the first £1,900 of this, and at his top rate of tax on the remaining £5,000 – £1,900 = £3,100. His tax bill will be as follows:

Earnings		£40,000.00
less allowances:		
maintenance allowable at top rate	£3,100.00	
personal allowance	£4,195.00	
Total allowances		£7,295.00
Taxable income		£32,705.00
Tax due:	20 per cent of £4,300	£860.00
	23 per cent of £22,800	£5,244.00
	40 per cent of £5,605	£2,242.00
		£8,346.00
Less tax relief on first £1,900 of		
maintenance payments at 15 per cent		£285.00
Total tax		£8,061.00

Thus Conrad has an after-tax income of £40,000, less £8,061 tax, less maintenance payments of £7,000 – a total of £24,939 for the tax year which began on 6 April 1998.

more than this, the excess is added to your taxable income and you pay tax on it at your top rate. If you remarry and continue receiving the maintenance, you no longer get the £1,900 tax-free.

Anything paid direct to a child under a court order is fully taxable – though again, not any increase on the court order paid since the tax year ending 5 April 1989. The child will be entitled to a personal allowance to set against the income. Once the child is 21, the payments become tax-free.

Payments to a child under a legally binding agreement are tax-free. If these are paid after deduction of basic rate tax, the child may be able to claim a refund if it is more than he or she should have paid.

Tax relief on payments made

Under the old rules, you can get tax relief on maintenance you pay to an ex-wife or ex-husband, and on some payments to your children. You cannot get tax relief on payments to an unmarried partner.

The maximum amount you get tax relief on is the amount you got tax relief on in the tax year ending 5 April 1989. For the tax year beginning 6 April 1998, you get tax relief at 15 per cent on what you pay, up to £1,900 – the amount of the married couple's allowance. If the amount qualifying for tax relief is more than the married couple's allowance, you get tax relief on the excess at your top rate of tax.

If you pay more maintenance now than in the tax year ending 5 April 1989, you won't get any tax relief on the increase. So if you got tax relief on payments of £3,000 in the tax year ending 5 April 1989, that is the maximum on which you will get tax relief in the tax years ending 5 April 1998 and 1999. With payments to a child, you get tax relief only if they are paid under a court order to a child under the age of 21.

Switching from the old rules to the new

It could pay you to switch to the new rules if you would get more tax relief on the maintenance payments you make.

This could happen if you made maintenance payments of less than £1,900 in the tax year ending 5 April 1989 and you are now paying more than this. Under the old rules, you are restricted to tax relief on what you paid then; under the new rules, you would get tax relief on the equivalent of the married couple's allowance – £1,900 for the tax year beginning 6 April 1998.

But if you switch to the new rules, you would lose any tax relief on payments you make to your children under a court order.

You can switch from the old rules for taxing maintenance payments to the new rules, simply by filling in Inland Revenue Form 142. To have the payments taxed under the new

> ### Example
>
> Conrad and Theresa Murdoch look at whether it would pay them to switch to the new rules. They quickly see they are better off sticking to the old rules where Conrad gets tax relief on £5,000 of payments; under the new rules, his tax relief would be limited to £1,900 of payments in the tax year which began on 6 April 1998.

rules, you must tell your tax inspector within a year of the end of the tax year in which you made the payments. So for payments you make in the tax year beginning 6 April 1998, you must make the change on or before 5 April 2000. Once you have made the change to the new rules, you cannot go back to the old ones.

What happens to your home?
Once you are separated, you are likely to need two homes. You can each get tax relief on interest you pay on loans to buy your only or main home (see p. 53).

However, if you pay the interest direct to the lender on behalf of your ex-spouse, you won't get tax relief (unless you bought the home for the ex-spouse on or before 5 April 1988 – see p. 58). The best financial arrangement is for you each to pay the mortgage for the home you live in.

Capital gains tax and inheritance tax on separation

> ### EXAMPLE
> Damian Boland makes enforceable maintenance payments of £2,100 a year to his ex-wife Debbie under an agreement originally drawn up in 1986 to support her and their child. But he has been steadily raising the amount over the years – he paid £1,300 in the tax year ending 5 April 1989. So the amount he gets tax relief on under the old rules is pegged at £1,300. He gets tax relief of 15 per cent of £1,300 – £195 a year.
>
> Under the new rules, Damian would get tax relief on maintenance payments up to the level of the married couple's allowance – £1,900 for the tax year ending 5 April 1998. He would be better off switching, when he would get tax relief of 15 per cent on £1,900 = £285.00. And since the married couple's allowance has risen each year in line with other tax allowances, the value of the tax relief should rise.

You can carry on making gifts to your ex-husband or ex-wife in the year of separation without falling into the net for capital gains tax. After this, gifts may lead to a capital gains tax bill in the same way as for any other gifts (see p. 102).

However, if one of you moves out of the family home and gives or sells it to the other within three years of the separation, there will be no capital gains tax to pay. Even after that, there may be no capital gains tax if your ex-spouse is still living there and you have not claimed any other property as your only or main home.

If you bought a home for your ex-spouse on or before 5 April 1988, there will be no capital gains tax to pay when you dispose of it, as long as the ex-spouse has lived in it rent-free ever since.

Gifts between a separated husband and wife are free of inheritance tax (see p. 133). Once you are divorced, gifts may fall into the inheritance tax net unless they are for the maintenance of the ex-spouse or any children.

WIDOWED

When your husband or wife dies, you keep the married couple's allowance for the rest of the tax year in which the death happens. And if you have living with you a child or children under 18 at the start of the tax year, you can get additional personal allowance.

Widows can also get widow's bereavement allowance – £1,900 for the tax year beginning 6 April 1998. The amount of tax relief is restricted in the same way as for married couple's allowance – the rate is 15 per cent for the tax year beginning 6 April 1998. This allowance can also be claimed in the tax year after the one in which you are widowed.

You can go on getting additional personal allowance for as long as a child who is under 18 at the start of the tax year is living with you.

HOME AND TAX

Buying a home is probably the biggest purchase you will make. Your mortgage payments are almost certainly the largest outgoing in your household budget. And your home is also likely to be your most valuable asset.

This chapter tells you how to keep the cost of the mortgage as low as possible by claiming all the tax relief you are entitled to on the interest. It also explains how to make sure you don't pay a hefty capital gains tax bill if you sell your home for a lot more than you paid for it.

MORTGAGE INTEREST TAX RELIEF

You can get tax relief on interest you pay on loans of £30,000 or less to buy your only or main home. Your only or main home is normally the one you live in for most of the time, although you may be able to get tax relief on loans for homes you are not currently living in (see p. 58).

The rate of tax relief from 6 April 1998 is 10 per cent. So every £1 of interest you pay within the £30,000 limit will be reduced by 10p tax relief to 90p. A gross interest rate of 8 per cent will then be 7.2 per cent after the tax relief.

For the tax year ending 5 April 1998, the rate of tax relief was 15 per cent. The lender will have increased your mortgage payments to reflect the lower tax relief from 6 April 1998 onwards.

How you get the tax relief
In most cases, you get the tax relief in the form of lower monthly payments to the lender. For example, if £100 interest is due on your mortgage, you pay £100 minus tax relief of 10 per cent: £100 – £10 = £90. You get the tax relief even if you don't pay tax, or you pay less than the tax relief you get.

This system is known as mortgage interest relief at source (MIRAS) and the scheme is operated by most lenders such as building societies, banks and insurance companies. They reclaim the tax relief direct from the Inland Revenue.

MIRAS does not include loans which are only partly for buying a home. If this applies to your loan – or your lender is not in MIRAS – you will have to claim the tax relief direct from the Inland Revenue (see p. 181). In this case, you will get tax relief only if you have enough income to pay tax.

Which loans qualify for relief?
The relief is available on loans to buy a house or flat, leasehold or freehold, in the UK or the Republic of Ireland. You can also claim it for a houseboat designed to be used as a home. And loans for a caravan (or mobile home) used as your only or main home are also eligible.

You can get tax relief on the interest paid on most sorts of loans used to buy your only or main home, including personal loans from banks and other lenders. The loan doesn't have to be a mortgage secured on your home to qualify. But you won't get tax relief on interest paid on a bank overdraft or credit card debts – even if these are incurred on your home. And there's no tax relief on interest for loans which have to be repaid within a year of being taken out, unless the lender is a bank, stockbroker or discount house.

You can still get the tax relief if part of the loan is used to pay the costs of buying the home such as stamp duty, valuers' fees, legal bills and insurance premiums (for example, for a mortgage indemnity policy). And if the loan is increased because you fall behind on the payments or to cover insurance premiums, the amount of loan on which you can get mortgage interest tax relief can be increased by up to £1,000 (or 12 months' payments arrears, if greater).

If you remortgage your home to change lenders or borrow more, you will get mortgage interest tax relief on the new loan provided you got it on the old loan it replaces.

Bigger mortgages
If your loan to buy your only or main home is more than £30,000, you get the tax relief on only a proportion of the interest. For example, if your loan is £40,000, the proportion of interest on which you get tax relief is:

$$\frac{£30,000}{£40,000} = \frac{3}{4}$$

If your loan is in MIRAS, it will automatically give you the right amount of tax relief.

If you are buying your home with two or more loans which add up to over £30,000, you get the tax relief on the earliest loans first, up to the £30,000 limit. For example, if you had a loan of £25,000 topped up with another £10,000 loan, you would get tax relief on all the interest on the first loan. That would leave unused mortgage interest tax relief of £30,000 − £25,000 = £5,000. So you would get tax relief on the following share of the interest on the second loan:

$$\frac{£5,000}{£10,000} = \frac{1}{2}$$

Your loan could creep up above £30,000 if you miss some interest payments (or don't increase your payments when the mortgage rate goes up). You can get tax relief on all the interest you pay as long as no more than £1,000 of interest is added to the loan.

Bridging loans

If you take out a bridging loan to buy a new home before you have sold your old one, you can get tax relief on the interest for up to £30,000 of the bridging loan, as well as on £30,000 of loans on your old home. This second lot of tax relief is available for up to 12 months (longer if you can persuade your tax inspector that there is good reason for the delay in selling your old home).

It doesn't matter which of the homes you live in during the transitional period. But you will have to pay back the second lot of relief if you do not move into the new home at the end of the bridging period.

Home income schemes

People aged 65 or over can get tax relief on a mortgage loan taken out as part of a home income scheme. Under such a scheme, an insurance company lends up to £30,000 against the security of the home. The loan is used to buy an annuity which pays a regular income that leaves the home-owner with money to spend after making the mortgage payments.

Provided 90 per cent or more of the loan is used to buy the annuity, tax relief is given on the interest payments at the basic rate of tax − 23 per cent for the tax year ending 5 April 1998 and the tax year beginning 6 April 1998.

In practice, these schemes make financial sense only for people in their seventies, when the rate of income paid by the insurance company in return for the lump sum is high enough to more than cover the mortgage costs. Some types of home income schemes have led to losses for investors in recent years. Avoid schemes where the income can vary up or down, or where interest on the mortgage can be added to the loan.

Rolling the mortgage over to a new home
Normally, when buying a new home you pay off the old loan and take out a new one. However, if you carry a loan over from one home to another, you can go on getting tax relief on the loan.

This concession was introduced in 1993 to help people who wanted to move but could not repay their mortgages because their homes were worth less than the loan outstanding (this is known as negative equity). Provided the lender agreed, they could sell the home and carry the loan over to the new one.

This provision can also be useful if you have taken out a fixed-rate mortgage for a set term and want to move before the end of the term. Repaying such a loan early usually involves paying several months' interest as a penalty, so you can instead roll the loan over to your new home.

Married couples
A married couple get tax relief on interest they pay for loans of £30,000 or less in total. If the loan is in one of their names only, that person gets all the tax relief. With a mortgage in their joint names, the mortgage interest tax relief will be divided 50:50 between them. But you can allocate the tax relief between husband and wife in any way you choose, simply by signing a form.

For loans covered by MIRAS it makes no practical difference how the relief is allocated. However, if the loan is outside MIRAS and one partner pays little or no tax, the couple should allocate all the interest to the other partner to get the tax relief in full.

To change the way relief is allocated, both husband and wife must sign Form 15. You have up to a year after the end of the tax year to make the choice. So for the tax year ending 5 April 1998, you have until 5 April 1999 to send in Form 15.

The allocation can be varied from year to year, simply by filling in a new Form 15. To revert to a 50:50 split, you should withdraw the allocation on Form 15-1.

Newlyweds
If a newly married couple each owned homes before marriage and move into one of them after the wedding, they can go on getting tax relief on the interest on the other for up to a year. Alternatively, they may decide to buy a new matrimonial home. In this case, they can go on getting tax relief on the mortgage interest for the two other homes for up to a year after the wedding –

effectively getting three lots of tax relief.

Sharers

If two or more single people buy a home together, or a married couple buy with another couple or single person, the tax relief is restricted to interest on £30,000 of loans per home – irrespective of the number of people sharing it.

For example, two single people would share between them the tax relief on the interest paid for £30,000 or less of loans (that is on £15,000 of loans each). Where a married couple shares with a single person, the couple would get tax relief on interest they pay on two-thirds of the £30,000 limit (£20,000) with one-third (£10,000) for the single person.

If a sharer has a loan smaller than his or her entitlement, the unused part can be transferred to the other sharers – the example shows how this works.

Sharers who took out loans before 1 August 1988 to buy a home in which they still live are each entitled to tax relief on £30,000 of mortgage interest. So two single people who have shared a home since before that date can get tax relief on the interest paid on up to £60,000 of such loans. These rules continue to apply until the loans are paid off, replaced with a new loan or switched to a new home. If two such sharers marry, the maximum

EXAMPLE

Len Mallory, Norma Openshaw and Peter Quince decide to buy a house, with a one-third share each. Each of them has some savings, so they end up with different loans: Len of £12,000, Norma of £7,000 and Peter of £14,000.

The three are jointly entitled to tax relief on interest of up to £30,000 of loans. This is divided equally between them, so each is entitled to tax relief on interest on up to £10,000 of loans.

Norma's £7,000 loan is less than her £10,000 entitlement – so she gets tax relief on all the interest she pays. That leaves £10,000 – £7,000 = £3,000 of her entitlement unused. This can be divided between Len and Peter so they can get tax relief on more than £10,000 of loans.

Norma's unused £3,000 entitlement is divided between Len and Peter in proportion to the amount by which their mortgages exceed £10,000:

Len's mortgage is £2,000 over the £10,000 limit; Peter's excess is £4,000.

The total of their excesses is £2,000 + £4,000 = £6,000. So Len will get £2,000 ÷ £6,000 = $^1/_3$ of Norma's unused £3,000 allowance, that is £1,000. Peter gets £4,000 ÷ £6,000 = $^2/_3$, that is £2,000.

This means Len will get tax relief on £11,000 ÷ £12,000 = $^{11}/_{12}$ of the interest he pays. Peter will get tax relief on £12,000 ÷ £14,000 = $^6/_7$ of his mortgage interest.

amount of loans on which they can get tax relief immediately falls from £60,000 to £30,000.

Home-improvement loans

If you took out a loan before 6 April 1988 to improve your only or main home, the interest paid on it could be added to the interest paid on loans to buy it when calculating your mortgage interest tax relief. You can go on getting the tax relief for such home improvement loans for as long as they last. But if you pay off the loan and replace it with a new one – at a lower rate of interest, say – you won't get tax relief on the interest on the new loan.

A home for an ex-spouse or dependent relative

You could get tax relief on a loan taken out on or before 5 April 1988 to buy or improve a home for a separated or former spouse or dependent relative. You can go on getting the tax relief on such loans as long as the ex-spouse or dependent relative continues to live in the home as their only or main residence. If you pay off such a loan and replace it with a new loan – at a lower rate of interest, say – you won't get tax relief on the interest on the new loan.

Dependent relatives are:

- your mother or mother-in-law if widowed, separated or divorced
- any relative of yours or your spouse who is unable to look after themselves because of permanent illness, disablement or old age (over 64 at the start of the tax year).

The tax relief is given only if the dependent relative lives in the home rent-free.

Absence from home

Mortgage interest tax relief is meant for your only or main home. But you can be away from the home for up to a year without losing tax relief on the mortgage interest payments. And if you have moved out but not yet sold the home, you can go on getting the tax relief for up to a year (longer if you can persuade your tax inspector that selling the home is proving difficult).

You may also be able to go on getting tax relief if work takes you away from home. If you work for an employer who requires you to live away from home, you can go on getting mortgage interest tax relief for up to four years provided you're expected to return within that period. If you're still away after four years, the tax relief ends. But if you move back in for at least three months, further such absence of up to four years is allowed.

Servants of the Crown who move abroad because of their jobs can be away indefinitely without losing the tax relief. So can those who have to live in job-related accommodation, provided they intend to live in the house they own eventually. Job-related accommodation is living accommodation provided for one of the following reasons:

- it is necessary to live in it to do the job properly – for example, a residential housekeeper
- it is customary to live in it for that sort of work and living there helps do the job better – a hotel manager
- it is essential for security reasons.

There is a similar exemption for the self-employed who have to live in work-related accommodation (for example, over the shop or at the club). They can go on getting mortgage interest tax relief on their own homes provided they intend to live in them eventually.

Working from home
If you use part of your home for business, you may still be able to go on getting mortgage interest tax relief through MIRAS – provided the business use is incidental. For example, if you occasionally work from home or use part of it on occasions as an office or place to store work tools.

If you start to use your home for more substantial work or business purposes, tell the lender. The loan may have to leave MIRAS, although you should still be able to get mortgage interest tax relief on it (and perhaps also set off some of the interest against business income – see p. 248).

If you let your home
If you let out no more than one-third of your home, you can go on getting mortgage interest tax relief through MIRAS. But if you let out more than one-third, you should tell the lender and your tax inspector. You will no longer get mortgage interest tax relief through MIRAS – although you can claim it directly from the Inland Revenue if you are still entitled to it.

Whether or not you are in MIRAS, you may be better off not claiming mortgage interest tax relief but deducting the interest from rental income when working out the profit or loss of your letting business (see p. 276). There are several possible advantages:

- all the interest qualifies for tax relief – mortgage interest tax relief covers interest on £30,000 of loans only
- the tax relief is at your highest rate of tax – not just the 10 per cent given for mortgage interest tax relief
- if the interest is more than your property income in one tax year, you can carry forward the loss to set against property income in the future.

If your loan is not in MIRAS, you can choose each year whether to claim mortgage interest tax relief or set the interest against letting income (see p. 276).

If your loan is in MIRAS, you have to opt out of it if you want the interest to be set against letting income. Write and tell your tax inspector within 22 months of the end of the tax year in which you first want this to happen. So if you want the interest paid in the tax year ending 5 April 1998 to be set against letting income for that year, tell the tax inspector by 5 February 2000. Once you have opted out of MIRAS, you will not be able to return to it unless the letting business ends.

CAPITAL GAINS TAX ON HOMES

If you sell most types of investments (including property) for more than you paid for them, there may be capital gains tax to pay (see Chapter 10). But if you sell your only or main home, there is normally no capital gains tax to pay unless the garden is excessively large (see below) or you are making a business out of buying and selling homes. This exemption from capital gains tax is known as private residence relief.

However, if you own more than one home, only one of them qualifies for private residence relief. And you might lose the relief if you use the home for business, leave it for prolonged periods or let it out. If you do have to pay capital gains tax on selling a home, it can mean a hefty tax bill – the gain, adjusted for inflation, is taxed at your top rate of income tax.

Which homes?
Private residence relief is given for your only or main home, whether it is a house or flat, freehold or leasehold, and wherever in the world it is situated.

You must occupy the home exclusively as your residence if it is to be free of capital gains tax. If part of the home is used for work or business, you may have to pay tax on part of the gain (see p. 62). And letting out some or all of your home can also mean a capital gains tax bill (see p. 63).

If you live in a caravan or houseboat, there's normally no capital gains tax to pay on it, even if it is not your only or main home. Caravans and boats count as wasting assets with a useful life of 50 years or less – and are thus outside the net for capital gains tax (see p. 103). But if you own the land on which a caravan stands, you might have to pay capital gains tax if you sell it, unless the caravan was your only or main home.

A home which an ex-spouse or dependent relative lives in rent-free is also free of capital gains tax provided it fell into this category on or before 5 April 1988 (see p. 58 for who qualifies). This exemption lasts only as long as the ex-spouse or dependent relative continues to live in the home.

Gardens

Private residence relief applies to both your home and garden. But there are rules to stop people taking advantage of it to avoid capital gains tax on dealing in land.

If the area of your home and garden exceeds half a hectare, there may be tax to pay on the gain you make on the excess. The gain on any excess will be free of tax only if you can convince your tax inspector that a garden of that size is appropriate for the home (for example, it is a Capability Brown garden designed for the house).

If the area of the home and garden is less than half a hectare, you can sell part of the garden without having to pay capital gains tax. But if you divide the garden to build a second home which you sell off, there could be tax to pay on the gain. And if you sell the home and keep some of the land, there may be capital gains tax to pay when you eventually sell the land.

If you own more than one home

If you own more than one home, you can choose which of your homes is your main one and thus free of capital gains tax. It doesn't have to be the one you live in most of the time, or the one on which you get mortgage interest tax relief.

So you should think about which home is likely to make the largest gain and nominate it for private residence relief. You must make your choice and tell your tax inspector in writing within two years of buying the second home. Newlyweds who have kept the two homes they owned while single should tell their tax inspector which is to get private residence relief within two years of the marriage.

You can alter your choice at any time, but you cannot backdate the change by more than two years. Again, write and tell your tax inspector that you wish to change your choice and when you want the change to run from.

If you don't nominate one of your homes for private residence relief, your tax inspector will decide – probably on the basis of which home you spend the most time at. You can appeal against this decision in the normal way (see p. 20), but you will have to produce proof that the other home really is your main one.

Working from home

If any part of your home is used exclusively for work, there may be a capital gains tax bill when you sell the home. This applies to work for your own business (if you are self-employed) and work for an employer.

So if you use one or more rooms entirely for work (as an office or workshop, for example), there will be tax to pay on a proportion of the gain when you come to sell the home. You will have to agree the proportion with the tax inspector, who may calculate it by reference to the number of rooms you use or their floor area. If you claim a proportion of the rent and council tax as business expenses (see p. 249) or as expenses of employment (see p. 221), the same proportion of the gain is likely to be taxable. But in modest cases you may be able to persuade your tax inspector to allow you the expenses without a capital gains tax bill.

For details of how the taxable gain will be worked out – and ways to reduce the tax bill – see Chapter 10.

Away from home

If you don't live in your home for all the time you own it, you might lose some of the private residence relief – even though it is the only home you own or you have nominated it as your main home. Normally you will have to pay capital gains tax on the following proportion of the taxable gain:

$$\frac{\text{Number of complete months of absence}}{\text{Number of complete months of ownership}}$$

Only months of ownership or absence since 31 March 1982 count in working out the proportion – gains before that date are outside the scope of the tax (see p. 111).

In practice, you can be away from the home for considerable spells of absence without losing any private residence relief. You can retain it during absence for the following periods:

- the first year of ownership while you are building, rebuilding or modernising the home, or because you can't sell your old home. This can be extended for another year if you can convince the tax inspector it is necessary. To retain the exemption, you must move in within the one-year (or two-year) period
- the last three years of ownership – even if you have already moved out
- any other absences totalling up to three years, provided you live in the home both before the first absence and after the last.

You may also be able to retain private residence relief if work takes you or your spouse away from home. If you work for an employer who requires you to live away from home in the UK, you can go on getting private residence relief for up to four years of absence, provided you return to the home afterwards (unless you are prevented by the job). If your employer requires you to work abroad, you can get private residence relief on your home indefinitely.

Provided you intend to live in your home in the future, private residence relief continues if you or your spouse are required to live in job-related accommodation (see p. 59). Self-employed people who have to live in work-related accommodation (for example, over the shop or at the club) can go on getting private residence relief on their own homes as long as they intend to live in them eventually.

You can add together some or all of these reasons to continue getting private residence relief for longer periods of absence – as the example shows.

Capital gains tax on lettings

There is no capital gains tax to pay if you take in a lodger who is treated as a member of the family – sharing your living rooms and eating with you. But in other circumstances, there may be capital gains tax to pay when you sell a home that has been let out wholly or in part.

If you let out the whole house for a period, the gain attributable to that period is taxable.

If you let part of your home, you may have to pay capital gains tax on

E X A M P L E

Linda March bought a house on 24 June 1987. On 6 July 1990 her employer sent her on an overseas posting lasting until 10 November 1992. On Linda's return to the UK, her employer sent her to work away from home until 15 August 1996. She lived in the home until 22 October 1996, when she bought a new home, eventually selling her old home on 27 February 1998.

During the ten years and nine months Linda owned the home, she was absent for three periods totalling seven years and three months. But she will get private residence relief for the entire time she owned the house:

- the two years and four months from July 1990 to November 1992 count for private residence relief because they are a period of employment spent entirely abroad
- the three years and nine months from November 1992 to August 1996 are less than the four years of employment elsewhere in the UK possible without losing private residence relief
- the year and four months from October 1996 to February 1998 are part of the last three years of ownership.

the part that is not occupied by you. If you let two of your six rooms, for example, one-third of the gain on selling the home is taxable (less if you haven't let the two rooms for all the time that you've owned the home).

However, there may still be no capital gains tax to pay if you can claim lettings relief, for homes which have been wholly or partly eligible for private residence relief. Lettings relief reduces the taxable gain by £40,000, or the amount of private residence relief if this is lower – the example shows how it works.

Property dealings
If you regularly buy and sell houses for profit, there might be a capital gains tax bill when you sell one – even if you have been living in it as your only or main home. This is meant to catch people who are making a business out of doing up unmodernised homes for sale.

If your property dealings are on a substantial scale, you could find yourself classified as a dealer in land. You would then have to pay income tax on the profits like any other self-employed person (see p. 236).

EXAMPLE

Jane Mortimer lived in a home for four years and then let it out for six. She sold it making a taxable gain of £50,000.

Jane qualifies for private residence relief for the four years she lived in it, plus the following three years – seven years in all. The gain attributable to the remaining three years is $^3/_{10}$ of the £50,000. This £15,000 is taxable.

Jane next works out how much lettings relief she is entitled to. The amount is the lower of £40,000 or the value of private residence relief on the house, which is £50,000 – £15,000 = £35,000. She can reduce the gain by £35,000; that means no taxable gain on the letting.

SAVING AND INVESTING

The ordinary saver faces a wider choice of investments than ever before. Banks, building societies and National Savings are vying to look after your spare cash. Many more people have become shareholders through employee share-ownership schemes, privatisations and the conversion of building societies into companies. And millions are saving for their retirement through personal pensions.

To encourage savings, the government has introduced a series of tax incentives for investors, including a lower rate of income tax for interest and dividends and tax relief on pension contributions. There are also special tax rules to tempt savers into long-term life insurance policies, personal equity plans (PEPs), tax-exempt special savings accounts (TESSAs), the Enterprise Investment Scheme (EIS) and venture capital trusts (VCTs). And from 6 April 1999 onwards, there will be new individual savings accounts (ISAs) which will offer tax concessions for an even wider range of savings and investments.

This chapter guides you through the various types of savings and investments and how they are taxed. It tells you the rules to follow if you want to cash in on the tax breaks offered by the government. And it explains the rules for the new individual savings accounts – and what will happen to PEPs and TESSAs after ISAs are introduced.

INCOME TAX ON INVESTMENTS

Income from some investments is tax-free (that is, there is no income tax to pay). For a list of these, see p. 151.

All other investment income is taxable. With more and more investments, tax is deducted from the income before it is paid to you. There is no further tax to pay on such income unless you pay tax at the higher rate. If you should have paid less tax than was deducted, you will normally be able to get a refund.

Interest paid after deduction of tax

Interest on most kinds of savings is now normally paid after tax has been deducted from it. This applies to building society accounts, bank accounts, local authority loans and bonds and National Savings First Option Bonds.

On these types of interest, tax is deducted at 20 per cent from the gross income before handing it over to you. There is no further tax bill if you pay tax at the lower or basic rate only on your income – which is the case for the vast majority of taxpayers. If you pay tax at the higher rate, there will be extra tax to pay on this income (see opposite). If your income is too low to pay tax, you should be able to reclaim some or all

EXAMPLE

Sonny Dasgupta pays tax at 40 per cent on his income. National Savings certificates offer him an average return of 5.35 per cent a year tax-free over five years. He could get 7.5 per cent a year over the same period in a bank high interest account.

Sonny invests in the National Savings certificates, since that will give him 5.35 per cent a year whatever his tax rate. The interest rate he would get on the bank account after paying tax at 40 per cent would be 60 per cent of 7.5 per cent, that is 4.5 per cent a year.

GROSSING-UP

If you receive investment income after some tax has been deducted from it, what you receive is known as the net income. But you may need to work out how much the income was before tax was deducted from it (the gross income).

You can find the gross income by grossing-up the net income (that is the income after deduction of tax) using the ready reckoners in Appendix B (p. 373), or by using the following formula:

$$\text{Amount paid to you} \times \left(\frac{100}{100 - \text{rate of tax}} \right)$$

For example, if you receive £50 of income after tax has been deducted at 20 per cent, the grossed-up amount of the income is:

$$£50 \times \left(\frac{100}{100 - 20} \right)$$

$$= £50 \times \frac{100}{80}$$

$$= £62.50$$

of the tax which has been deducted (see overleaf).

The savings income is treated as your top slice of your income. This means it does not reduce the amount of earnings or other income that can be taxed at the lower rate of 20 per cent – £4,300 for the tax year which began on 6 April 1998.

Higher rate tax on income paid after deduction of tax

If you get interest after tax has been deducted and pay tax at the higher rate of 40 per cent, there will be a further tax bill to pay – as the example below shows. The higher rate tax will be collected by the Inland Revenue in one of two ways:

- by increasing the amount of tax you pay on your earnings through PAYE (see p. 366)
- through the payments you have to make in January and July under the self-assessment system (see p. 15).

EXAMPLE

Niamh Fagan gets £640 interest on her building society account in the tax year beginning 6 April 1998. Tax has already been deducted from the interest at 20 per cent before it is credited to her account, so this £640 is the net (that is, after deduction of tax) amount.

To work out the gross (before deduction of tax) amount of interest, Niamh must add the tax back to the net amount. The grossed-up amount of interest is:

$$£640 \times \left(\frac{100}{100 - 20} \right)$$
$$= £640 \times \frac{100}{80}$$
$$= £800$$

In other words, Niamh has paid £800 – £640 = £160 in tax and this covers her basic rate tax on the interest.

If Niamh should pay tax at 40 per cent on this interest, her overall tax liability is 40 per cent of £800 = £320. Since she has already paid £160 in tax, she has to pay only £320 – £160 = £160 in higher rate tax. This leaves her with £640 – £160 = £480 of interest after higher rate tax has been paid.

Too much tax deducted?

If too much tax has been deducted from your interest, the excess can be claimed back. This would happen if the rest of your income is below the level at which you pay tax – as the next example shows.

EXAMPLE

Niall O'Halloran is 12 years old and has no income apart from the interest he gets on £3,000 given to him by his grandparents. During the tax year beginning 6 April 1998, he gets interest of £150 which is paid after deduction of tax at 20 per cent.

Like all taxpayers, he is entitled to a personal allowance of £4,195 for the year. Since his taxable income is much less than the personal allowance, he can claim back the tax deducted from it.

To work out the size of his rebate, Niall grosses up the net amount of interest he received:

$$£150 \times \left(\frac{100}{100 - 20} \right)$$
$$= £150 \times \frac{100}{80}$$
$$= £187.50$$

So the gross amount of interest Niall received was £187.50. Since he can claim back all the tax deducted, he will get a rebate of £187.50 – £150 = £37.50.

To claim back the tax, ask your tax inspector for Tax Claim Form R40. Fill this in and send it back with the certificates showing the amount of tax deducted (the bank or building society can supply these). You can send in the completed form before the end of the tax year to get the repayment as soon as possible so long as the amount of tax involved is more than £50 and you've had all the savings income for the tax year paid to you after tax has been deducted (including share dividends – see opposite).

If your income is too low to pay tax at all, you can arrange with the bank or building society to be paid interest without deduction of tax. Fill in Form R85 which is available from banks, building societies and post offices, as well as from tax offices. A copy is in Inland Revenue leaflet *IR110 A guide for people with savings*, which also contains useful hints on checking whether you will pay tax or not.

Arranging for interest to be paid without deduction of tax not only saves you the trouble of claiming back the tax which has been deducted, it means you get the money much earlier. However, interest on joint accounts can be paid without deduction of tax to just one of the two account-holders only if the bank or building society can arrange it. There are hefty penalties for making a false declaration.

Gilt-edged stock
Interest paid on government stock (gilts) you buy through the National Savings Stock Register is paid gross – without deduction of tax. With gilts you buy directly, interest was usually paid net, after deduction of tax. But with gilts bought on or after 6 April 1998, interest will be paid gross unless you ask the Bank of England to pay it net. Interest on gilts you owned before 6 April 1998 will continue to be paid net unless you ask the Bank of England to pay it gross.

Shares and unit trusts
Dividends from UK companies and distributions from authorised unit trusts are paid with a tax credit – the amount is given on the tax voucher which comes with the dividend or distribution. There is no further tax bill if you pay tax at the lower or basic rate only on your income – which is the case for the vast majority of taxpayers. What happens for higher rate taxpayers and those with so little income they pay no tax will change from 6 April 1999 onwards.

Up to and including 5 April 1999
For dividends and distributions paid up to and including 5 April 1999, the tax credit is 20 per cent of the gross dividend or distribution. So if you receive a dividend of £80, the grossed-up amount of this dividend is:

$$£80 \times \left(\frac{100}{100 - 20} \right)$$
$$= £80 \times \frac{100}{80}$$
$$= £100$$

The tax credit will be £100 – £80 = £20.

The tax on the grossed-up amount of dividends and distributions is 20 per cent for lower rate and basic rate taxpayers. Since this is the same amount as the tax credit, they need pay nothing extra. People whose income is too low to pay tax can claim back the £20 tax credit, as with the tax deducted from interest (see opposite).

If you pay tax at the higher rate, there will be extra tax to pay – in the same way as for interest on savings (p. 67). Higher rate taxpayers pay tax on the grossed-up amount of dividends and distributions at 40 per cent. So on a net dividend of £80, your total tax bill should be 40 per cent of the grossed-up amount of £100 = £40. Since you have a tax credit for £20, the higher rate tax due would be £40 – £20 = £20. This would leave you with £80 – £20 = £60 after paying the higher rate tax.

From 6 April 1999 onwards
For dividends and distributions paid on or after 6 April 1999, the tax credit falls to 10 per cent of the gross dividend or distribution. So if you receive a dividend of £80, the grossed-up amount of this dividend will be:

$$£80 \times \left(\frac{100}{100-10}\right)$$
$$= £80 \times \frac{100}{90}$$
$$= £88.89$$

The tax credit will be £88.89 – £80 = £8.89.

The tax on the grossed-up amount of dividends and distributions will fall to 10 per cent for lower rate and basic rate taxpayers. Since this is the same amount as the tax credit, they will still need to pay nothing extra.

But people whose income is too low to pay tax will no longer be able to claim back the tax credit. They would therefore be better off by investing in shares through an individual savings account (ISA) which can reclaim the tax credit – see p. 83.

If you pay tax at the higher rate, there will be extra tax to pay in the same way as previously. Higher rate taxpayers will pay tax on the grossed-up amount of dividends and distributions at 32.5 per cent – a figure which ensures they are no worse off as a result of the fall in the tax credit. So on a net dividend of £80, your total tax bill should be 32.5 per cent of the grossed-up amount of £88.89 = £28.89. Since you have a tax credit for £8.89, the higher rate tax due would be £28.89 – £8.89 = £20. This would leave you with £80 – £20 = £60 after paying the higher rate tax – the same as before the change.

INVESTING FOR CAPITAL GAINS

One way of reducing your income tax bill is to invest for capital gains rather than income. Capital gains tax is paid on increases in the value of investments – for example if the value of shares rises. The chargeable gain is added to your income and taxed at the same rate as interest or dividends.

But there's no tax to pay if your total net capital gains in the tax year beginning 6 April 1998 are below £6,800. A husband and wife can each make total net capital gains of this amount before paying capital gains tax. And you can make paper gains of more than the £6,800 limit, because of the deductions you can make in calculating your total net capital gains. These include expenses incurred in acquiring, owning or disposing of the investment and losses on other investments. And taper relief means the tax bill is reduced if you have owned the investment for more than three years from 6 April 1998.

For more about capital gains tax and how to minimise it, see Chapter 10, p. 102.

LIFE INSURANCE POLICIES

Life insurance can be used as a form of investment, since some types pay out a tax-free lump sum when the policy matures. There are various conditions to be met if the proceeds of a life insurance policy which pays out in your lifetime are to be tax-free – in particular, that the policy involves paying regular premiums for at least ten years. With most endowment, unit-linked and whole life policies, these conditions are normally met so you don't have to pay tax on the proceeds. There may be some tax to pay if you cash in a savings-type life insurance policy after less than ten years or three-quarters of the term, if this is shorter (see p. 168).

Some insurance companies make a deduction from the proceeds of unit-linked policies to cover their capital gains tax. This deduction is your share of the company's tax bill, not a tax charge on you personally – so you cannot claim it back if you don't pay capital gains tax.

Tax relief on life insurance premiums
With certain types of life insurance policies taken out before 14 March 1984, you were able to get tax relief on the premiums (within limits). Provided you haven't substantially changed the policy, you can go on getting the tax relief which is now $12^{1}/_{2}$ per cent of the premiums. In most cases you get it by paying reduced premiums to the insurance company – you pay $87^{1}/_{2}$ per cent of

the gross premium and the insurance company reclaims the 12$^1/_2$ per cent tax relief from the Inland Revenue.

You can get tax relief on no more than £1,500 of gross premiums (£1,312.50 of net premiums) in any tax year – or one-sixth of your total income if this is greater. If you pay more than the limit, the taxman will reclaim the excess tax relief you have been given by paying reduced premiums. If you change the policy, you may lose the tax relief. For example, you will lose the tax relief if you extend the term of the policy, increase the cover or convert it to a different type of policy. But you won't lose the tax relief if the value of the policy increases automatically as part of the policy (for example, if it increases by 5 per cent every year). Check with the insurance company.

PENSIONS

The government offers handsome tax incentives to encourage you to provide for your retirement by saving with an employer's pension scheme or through your own personal pension. These mean that saving for the future through a pension often provides a better return than any other type of investment:

- there is tax relief on your contributions to the scheme (within limits)
- any employer's contributions made for you are not taxable as your income or as a fringe benefit
- the fund the money goes into pays no further income tax or any capital gains tax
- you can trade in some pension to get a tax-free lump sum when you retire.

Employers' pension schemes

The tax incentives for saving through an employer's pension scheme are available only if it is approved by the Inland Revenue. Approved schemes must offer benefits within set limits:

- the maximum pension is two-thirds of your final salary
- the maximum tax-free lump sum is 1$^1/_2$ times your final salary
- the maximum lump sum payment which can be made on death in service (the life insurance cover) is four times your final salary.

> ### TAX-SAVING IDEA
> Everyone should try to make sure that they are saving for retirement through a pension – and the earlier you start, the better the pension you should get at the end. Don't delay. You can get tax relief at your highest rate of tax. This means a contribution of £1,000 costs you just £600 if you are a higher rate taxpayer, and just £770 if you are a basic rate taxpayer for the year beginning 6 April 1998. The fund into which you pay your contributions pays no income or capital gains tax.

There are also limits on the benefits that can be paid out to widows and widowers. For example, the maximum widow's or widower's pension is two-thirds the pension the deceased would have got.

There is a further restriction on the pension benefits from an approved scheme set up on or after 14 March 1989, or if you joined an older scheme on or after 1 June 1989. The amount of final salary which can be taken into account is limited by the pension scheme earnings cap which is £87,600 for the tax year beginning 6 April 1998 (£84,000 for the tax year ending 5 April 1998). If the cap applies to you, the maximum you can draw in the tax year which began on 6 April 1998 are:

- a maximum pension of £58,400 (two-thirds of £87,600)
- a maximum lump sum of £131,400 (1$^{1}/_{2}$ times £87,600)
- a maximum payment for death in service of £350,400 (four times £87,600).

Other benefits such as widow's and widower's pensions are also subject to the pension scheme earnings cap.

> ### EXAMPLES
>
> Marion Mould is an employee. Her monthly contributions of £50 to an employer's pension scheme are deducted from her salary before tax is worked out under the PAYE scheme.
>
> Margaret May is an employee. She doesn't contribute to her employer's pension scheme, but saves in a personal pension scheme instead. She saves £50 a month, but only hands over £38.50 to the pension provider, because she has deducted £11.50 (basic rate tax at 23 per cent for the year beginning 6 April 1998). The pension provider claims back the £11.50 from the Inland Revenue.
>
> Marcia Mumps is self-employed, saving £50 a month in a personal pension scheme. She hands over £50 each month to the pension provider. She claims her basic rate tax relief in her tax return, deducting it from her income before working out how much tax she should pay on 31 January.

Contributions to an employer's scheme

The amount you are required to contribute to an employer's pension scheme is decided by your employer, but cannot exceed 15 per cent of your earnings (this can include the value of fringe benefits). Provided the pension scheme is approved by the Inland Revenue, you get tax relief at your highest rate of tax on these contributions. Your contributions will be deducted from your income before working out how much tax has to be paid under PAYE (although your National Insurance contributions are worked out on your full pay, that is, before deduction of pension contributions).

However, if the scheme was set up on or after 14 March 1989, or you joined it on or after 1 June 1989, contributions are restricted to 15 per cent of earnings up to the pension scheme earnings cap mentioned above. For the tax year beginning 6 April 1998, that means you can get tax relief on maximum contributions of 15 per cent of £87,600, that is £13,140.

If you leave an approved pension scheme within two years of joining, your pension contributions can be repaid only after tax has been deducted at a flat rate of 20 per cent, to recover the tax relief you have had.

Additional voluntary contributions

Very few people qualify for the maximum permitted amount of an employer's pension – if only because job changes usually mean losing some pension entitlement. If you are in this position and want to save for your retirement, you should consider additional voluntary contributions (AVCs). These enjoy the same tax benefits as an approved pension scheme, so should grow faster than if you invested the money yourself.

You can choose between two different ways of investing your AVCs:
- through your employer's pension scheme (in-scheme AVCs)
- by making your own arrangements with an insurance company, bank, building society or unit trust manager (free-standing AVCs).

You get full tax relief on AVCs, provided the total amount you contribute in pension contributions does not exceed the 15 per cent limit. So if your employer's pension scheme contributions are 6 per cent, you can pay up to 15 – 6 = 9 per cent in AVCs.

EXAMPLE

Brenda Robertson earns £28,000 a year from a job and does not belong to her employer's pension scheme. She is 44 and is therefore entitled to tax relief at her top rate of tax on personal pension contributions of up to 20 per cent of her net relevant earnings.

To work out her net relevant earnings, Brenda adds the £28,000 salary to the £1,890 value of her fringe benefits and deducts the £180 of allowable expenses she can claim. Thus her net relevant earnings are £28,000 + £1,890 – £180 = £29,710.

So Brenda can get tax relief on personal pension contributions of 20 per cent of £29,710 = £5,942. If her top rate of tax is 23 per cent in the tax year which began on 6 April 1998 her tax bill will be reduced by 23 per cent of £5,942 = £1,367. The £5,942 of contributions will cost Brenda only £4,575 after allowing for the tax relief.

AVCs can be used to increase the pension you will get, the widow's or widower's pension and your life cover. But you can increase the tax-free lump sum only if the AVCs began on or before 7 April 1987. You cannot use AVCs to buy pension benefits greater than the maximum limits set by the Inland Revenue for approved schemes. If you inadvertently contribute so much that the benefits would exceed the limits, some of the AVCs will be paid back when you retire, with a deduction to cover the tax relief you have had on the contributions.

Personal pensions

If you save through a personal pension plan, you can build up a fund with an insurance company, bank, building society or other pension provider that provides you with an income for retirement. Your employer can also contribute to your personal pension plan, as will the government if you contract out of the state earnings-related pension scheme (SERPS) into an appropriate personal pension plan. You can begin to draw this pension any time after the age of 50 (younger for certain professions such as sports-playing).

The amount of pension you draw depends on the size of the fund – which in turn depends on the amount contributed and the investment performance of the fund. However, there are limits on the size of the tax-free lump sum you can take: the maximum is a quarter of the fund accumulated from your contributions and your employer's, with a cash limit of £150,000 if you took out the personal pension on or before 26 July 1989.

Personal pension plans taken out before 1 July 1988 are known as retirement annuity contracts and are subject to slightly different rules. The maximum tax-free lump sum is three times the pension the remainder of the fund will buy – which is usually more than you can take with a new-style personal pension. On the down side, your employer can't get tax relief on contributions to a retirement annuity contract, and you can't start drawing the pension until you are 60. If you have a retirement annuity contract, you can convert it into a personal pension plan at any time simply by telling the insurance company.

How much tax relief?

The amount of contributions you can get tax relief on depends on three factors:

- your net relevant earnings (see p. 77)
- your age
- whether you are saving in a personal pension plan or a retirement annuity contract.

Net relevant earnings for employees are earnings from non-pensionable jobs, including the taxable value of fringe benefits but after deduction of allowable expenses. For self-employed people, it is taxable profits after deducting certain payments made to your business after deduction of tax (for example, patent royalties or covenant payments). In the case of a partnership, it is your share of the partnership profits. With furnished holiday lettings, net relevant earnings are your profits from the lettings.

EXAMPLE

Philip Brampton is aged 55 and has a personal pension plan. His net relevant earnings for the year beginning 6 April 1998 are expected to be £100,000, and a man of his age could contribute 30 per cent of net relevant earnings to a personal pension. But the pension scheme earnings cap for the year is £87,600, so the maximum he can save is 30 per cent of £87,600, which is £26,280.

TAX-SAVING IDEA

If you are saving through a retirement annuity contract and your earnings are below the pension scheme earnings cap, consider taking out a personal pension plan as well. You can contribute a higher percentage of your net relevant earnings with a personal pension, allowing you to save more.

EXAMPLE

Mark Fisher is aged 55 and has a retirement annuity contract. His net relevant earnings for the year beginning 6 April 1998 are £100,000. Because it is a retirement annuity contract, there is no earnings cap. The limit on investment for his age is 20 per cent of net relevant earnings. Mark can invest up to £20,000 in his pension for the year.

EXAMPLE

Shelagh Fitzherbert is contributing to both a retirement annuity contract and a personal pension plan – this gives her more flexibility about when she starts drawing benefits and spreads the risk in case either turns out to be a poor investment. Her earnings for the tax year beginning 6 April 1998 are £40,000 and she is 52.

This means she can invest 20 per cent of £40,000 = £8,000 in her retirement annuity contract, or 30 per cent of £40,000 = £12,000 in her personal pension plan. Tax relief is always given for the retirement annuity first, and she chooses to put £8,000 into it. That leaves her with £12,000 – £8,000 = £4,000 that she can invest in her personal pension plan.

The amount of your net relevant earnings on which you can get tax relief depends on your age at the start of the tax year and the type of personal pension:

Age at 6 April	Personal pension %	Retirement annuity %
35 or less	$17^{1}/_{2}$	$17^{1}/_{2}$
36-45	20	$17^{1}/_{2}$
46-50	25	$17^{1}/_{2}$
51-55	30	20
56-60	35	$22^{1}/_{2}$
61-74	40	$27^{1}/_{2}$

Any contributions made by your employer to your personal pension plan count towards the limits above. And the maximum net relevant earnings that can be used to calculate the amount you can get tax relief on with a personal pension plan is the pension scheme earnings cap which applies to employers' pensions (see p. 73). For the tax year beginning 6 April 1998, the pension scheme earnings cap is £87,600 – so the maximum for someone aged 35 or less is $17^{1}/_{2}$ per cent of £87,600 – that is, £15,330.

As noted above, your employer can't get tax relief on contributions to a retirement annuity contract. But there is no earnings cap with a retirement annuity, so highly paid people can save more. If you are saving with both, the tax relief goes first to the retirement annuity contributions, and the amount reduces the maximum you can put into a personal pension plan.

Life insurance cover
If you die before drawing a personal pension or retirement annuity, the contributions are normally paid into your estate – usually with interest. But many personal pension providers also offer some sort of optional life insurance cover, and you can get tax relief on the premiums for this up to a maximum of 5 per cent of your net relevant earnings. Whatever is spent on this life insurance cover is deducted from the maximum amount you can contribute to your personal pension.

Backdating contributions and unused tax relief
You can claim extra tax relief on payments to personal pension plans or retirement annuity contracts by backdating contributions to a previ-

---

TAX-SAVING IDEA
If you're a high earner and have both a retirement annuity contract and a personal pension plan, you might be able to save more without falling foul of the pension scheme earnings cap with the retirement annuity.

ous tax year or claiming unused tax relief for up to six previous tax years. The rules are known as 'carry-back', 'bring back' and 'carry-forward' – and they allow you to make maximum use of the tax relief even if you do not have enough cash to save in a particular year.

You can choose to carry back payments made in one tax year to the previous tax year. For example, you could carry back payments made in the tax year beginning 6 April 1998 to the tax year ending 5 April 1998. And if you had no net relevant earnings in the year ending 5 April 1998, you could carry the payments back to the year ending 5 April 1997 – but no further. You might choose to carry back payments if your rate of tax in the previous year was higher than your current rate of tax, thus saving money – see the example right.

Alternatively, you can carry forward unused tax relief from the previous six tax years. You can do this only if you have already made your maximum contribution for the current year, and the tax relief will be at the tax rates for the year in which you use it up. Unused relief from the earliest years is used first, as the example opposite shows.

How do you get the tax relief?
If you are self-employed, you get tax relief on contributions to either a personal pension plan or a retirement annuity contract by claiming it in your tax return. This means you make the payments gross to the pension provider – that is, without deducting any tax relief.

EXAMPLE

Alan Perry is 37 and has a retirement annuity contract into which he pays £5,000 a year – normally well within his limits for tax relief. But the year beginning 6 April 1998 is a bad one and he earns only £20,000 – so his maximum contribution is $17^1/_2$ per cent of that, or £3,500. He gets tax relief for that year at 23 per cent, his top rate of tax – 23 per cent of £3,500 saves him £805.

But the previous year he had earnings of £45,000, and could have made contributions to his retirement annuity of $17^1/_2$ per cent of that figure, or £7,875. Since he had paid in his usual £5,000, he had £7,875 – £5,000 = £2,875 of unused allowance.

He can backdate £1,500 of the contribution made in the tax year beginning 6 April 1998 to the previous year. But he decides to backdate £2,875, since he paid tax at 40 per cent in that tax year and will get more tax relief. This leaves him the opportunity to put away another £2,875 – £1,500 = £1,375 at a later date.

EXAMPLE

James Loch's net relevant earnings for the last six complete tax years are set out below. He has his 36th birthday in February 1998, which means the maximum personal pension contributions on which he can get tax relief rises from $17^1/_2$ per cent of net relevant earnings to 20 per cent from 6 April 1998.

Tax year ending 5 April	Net relevant earnings £	Maximum premiums £	Premiums paid £	Unused relief £
1994	20,000	3,500	2,000	1,500
1995	15,000	2,625	2,000	625
1996	20,000	3,500	2,000	1,500
1997	22,000	3,850	2,000	1,850
1998	24,000	4,200	2,000	2,200
1999	22,000	4,400	2,000	2,400

James contributed £2,000 a year to his personal pension, which means that by the end of the tax year ending 5 April 1999, he has unused relief for the previous six years of £10,075. He could make a lump sum payment of £10,075 in the tax year beginning 6 April 1999 in addition to whatever contribution he could make based on his earnings for that year. If he wanted to pay in an extra £5,000, he would use the unused tax relief starting with the tax year ending 5 April 1994 (£1,500), then the following two years (£625 + £1,500 = £2,125) and £1,375 from the tax year ending 5 April 1997. The tax relief is at his highest rate of tax in the year he makes the payments – the one beginning 6 April 1999.

If you are an employee, you will get tax relief on contributions to a personal pension plan by paying them net of basic rate tax. So if the basic rate of tax is 23 per cent and you contribute £1,000 to a personal pension plan, you would hand over £770 (that is, £1,000 less 23 per cent of £1,000). If you are a higher rate taxpayer, you will have to claim the extra tax relief on your tax return – see p. 177.

With a retirement annuity contract, you make your payments without deducting any tax relief. You must claim the tax relief in your tax return (see p. 175). Your PAYE code may be adjusted to give you the tax relief through lower tax deductions from your earnings (see p. 362).

PERSONAL EQUITY PLANS

A personal equity plan (PEP) is a way of investing in various stockmarket investments without paying income tax or capital gains tax on the proceeds. The tax year ending 5 April 1999 is the last year that you can invest in PEPs – from 6 April 1999 onwards, they will be replaced by individual savings accounts (ISAs). Below are details of the rules for PEPS in the run-up to 6 April 1999. For what happens when ISAs are introduced, see p. 83.

To invest in a PEP, you have to be 18 or over. You can put up to £6,000 in a PEP in the tax year ending 5 April 1999, either by single lump sum, regular monthly instalments or several payments. Your money is invested in shares, unit trusts, investment trusts and certain types of corporate bonds, convertible shares and preference shares. The shares must be listed on the Stock Exchange, traded on the Alternative Investment Market (AIM) or quoted on broadly equivalent exchanges in another European Union countries. Unit trusts and investment trusts must invest at least 50 per cent of their funds in such shares or bonds. Where less than 50 per cent is invested thus, the maximum you can invest in such unit and investment trusts is £1,500.

You can also invest £3,000 in the tax year ending 5 April 1999 in a single-company PEP which holds shares in only one company (they are sometimes known as corporate PEPs). These are normally set up by the company which issued the shares, often for employees in share-ownership schemes – such as savings-related share option schemes (see p. 229) and employee profit-sharing schemes (see p. 227). Such employees can transfer their shares into a single-company PEP up to the £3,000 limit. There will be no capital gains tax to pay on the transfer, no income tax on the dividends and no capital gains tax on the profits on selling the shares – provided the transfer takes place within six weeks of the shares being issued.

In the tax year ending 5 April 1999, a husband and wife can each invest up to £6,000 in general PEPs and £3,000 in single-company PEPs – up to £18,000 altogether. The only time you would pay tax on PEP proceeds would be if some of your money were held as cash on deposit and earned interest which was paid out to you. If more than £180 of interest was paid out to you in a year, the plan manager would have to deduct tax at 20 per cent and hand this over to the Inland Revenue. The net interest is treated in the same way as any other interest you receive after deduction of tax – higher rate taxpayers would face an additional tax bill (see p. 67).

If you buy newly-issued shares (in a privatisation, say), you can put them into your PEP, so long as your total investment in the PEP remains within the limit for the tax year. You wouldn't then have to pay income tax on the dividends or capital gains tax when you sell them. You must do this within six weeks of the share allocation being announced.

TAX EXEMPT SPECIAL SAVINGS ACCOUNTS (TESSAS)

A tax exempt special savings account (TESSA) allows you to save with a bank or building society without paying income tax on the interest, provided you save for five years. If you haven't already opened a TESSA, you have until 5 April 1999 to open one – after that, the new individual savings account (ISA) will take over. But while no new TESSAs can be opened after that date, existing ones will be allowed to run their course. Below are details of the rules for TESSAs – for what happens when ISAs are introduced, see p. 83.

To open a TESSA, you must be 18 or over. The maximum you can save is £9,000 over five years which you can build up by regular savings (up to £150 a month), by lump sum deposits or a combination of both. No more than £3,000 can be invested in the first year of your first TESSA, and the maximum in each of the remaining years is £1,800. But if you open a second TESSA within six months of the first one completing its five years, you can put in all the capital saved in the first one – though not the interest. A husband and wife can each invest up to £9,000 in a TESSA, a total of £18,000.

If you need income from your TESSA, you can draw out up to 80 per cent of the interest. But you must leave at least 20 per cent – the equivalent of the tax which would have been deducted from the interest with a normal savings account. If you draw out more than this – or withdraw any of the capital – the TESSA comes to an end and tax will be deducted from all the interest added to your TESSA at the 20 per cent rate for savings income. If you are a higher rate taxpayer, there could be extra tax to pay (see p. 67). If your income for the tax year is too low to pay tax, you might be able to claim back some or all of the tax deducted (see p. 68).

INVESTING IN GROWING BUSINESSES

Enterprise Investment Scheme (EIS)
If you invest £500 or more in new shares issued by certain unquoted trading companies on or after 6 April 1998, you can get tax relief on the investment – provided you hold the shares for five years or more. Investments in EIS approved investment funds which invest in such companies also qualify – even if less than £500. If you dispose of the investments after the five years is up, there will be no capital gains tax to pay when you sell your investment.

You get income tax relief at 20 per cent on up to £150,000 of such investments in the tax year beginning 6 April 1998. But if you make the investment on or after 6 April 1998 and on or before 5 October 1998, half the investment up to a maximum of £25,000 can be set off against your income for the tax year ending 5 April 1998. With a married couple, husband and wife can each invest up to these limits.

The rules for the EIS were changed in the 1998 Budget. Under the previous set-up, which ended on 5 April 1998, tax relief of 20 per cent was given on investments of up to £100,000 in any tax year. Up to £15,000 invested in the first six months of the tax year could qualify for tax relief in the previous tax year. Investments could be in existing shares provided they had been issued on or after 1 January 1994.

Making EIS investments can also allow you to put off paying capital gains tax on disposing of other assets if you are able to claim reinvestment relief (see p. 127). To get the relief, you must reinvest the proceeds within a period starting one year before and ending three years after making them.

The companies you can invest in must be unquoted; this includes those with shares traded on the Alternative Investment Market (AIM). They have to be trading companies, which excludes those engaged in banking, insurance, share-dealing, dealing in land or property, leasing and legal or accountancy services. The company must be trading in the UK, but it does not have to be registered or resident in the UK. Investments in schemes where a substantial part of the return is guaranteed or backed by property made on or after 2 July 1997 are also excluded because they do not carry the degree of risk envisaged when the EIS was introduced.

You won't get tax relief on investments if you are connected with the companies – broadly this means being an employee or director or owning over 30 per cent of the shares. In deciding how much of a company you own, you must include the holdings of connected persons – your spouse and you and your spouse's children, parents and grandparents (but not brothers or sisters) – and associates such as business partners. Once you have made your EIS investment, however, you can take part in the active management of the company as a paid director (or 'business angel') provided you had not been connected with the company before you made the EIS investment.

You can't claim the tax relief until the company has carried out its qualifying trade for at least four months, and you lose it if it ceases to do so within three years. If you sell the shares within five years, you lose tax relief on the amount you sell them for (that is, if you sell them for more than they cost you, you have to pay back all the relief). If you sell the shares after five years and the company still qualifies under the scheme there will be no capital gains tax to pay on any gain you make. If you make a loss, this can be set off against other income or capital gains – reducing your overall tax bill for the year.

Business Expansion Scheme
The Business Expansion Scheme (BES), which used to offer tax relief on a wider range of investments than the Enterprise Investment Scheme, came to an end on 31 December 1993. But although no new investments have been possible under the BES since, there is still no capital gains tax to pay when you sell BES investments which you made after 18 March 1986.

Venture capital trusts
If you buy new ordinary shares in a venture capital trust (VCT) which invests in or lends money to certain unquoted trading companies, you can get tax relief on an investment of up to £100,000 in any tax year. A venture capital trust is similar to an investment trust and must be quoted on the Stock Exchange. Unquoted trading companies are defined in broadly the same way as for the Enterprise Investment Scheme.

You get income tax relief at 20 per cent on your investment, provided you hold the shares for five years or more. Any dividends paid out by the venture capital trust and gains you make when you sell the shares are tax-free. In addition, you can claim reinvestment relief (see previous page).

INDIVIDUAL SAVINGS ACCOUNTS
The new individual savings account (ISA) will be introduced from 6 April 1999 onwards for anyone who is 18 and over. The idea is that it will give you the same sort of tax incentives to save as PEPs and TESSAs – no tax on any income or gain made – but cover a wider range of investments.

ISAs will be provided by a range of financial institutions, and will allow you to save in several ways:

* cash savings accounts (as with TESSAs)
* shares and unit trusts (as with PEPs, but with fewer restrictions)
* life insurance policies
* National Savings.

You will be able to invest up to an annual limit of £5,000 in ISAs each year. Of this £5,000, no more than £1,000 can be in cash savings accounts and no more than £1,000 in life insurance policies. But in the first year of ISAs – the tax year beginning 6 April 1999 – you can invest up to £7,000, with the maximum in cash savings accounts being £3,000.

A husband and wife can each have their own ISAs and invest up to the limits. So a married couple can put £14,000 into ISAs in the tax year beginning 6 April 1999, and £10,000 a year thereafter.

Any interest, dividends or distributions paid out will be free of income tax. You can withdraw your money any time without losing the tax relief, and there will be no capital gains tax to pay when you cash in part or all of an ISA. And for the first five years, there will be a 10 per cent tax credit paid into your ISA with share dividends and unit trust distributions (see p. 70).

If you own PEPs when ISAs are introduced on 6 April 1999, you can keep them – they do not have to be transferred to an ISA as originally planned. Any share dividends and unit trust distributions paid into your PEPs will come with a 10 per cent tax credit for the five years after 6 April 1999, as with an ISA.

If you have a TESSA when ISAs start up, it can continue until it has finished its five-year term. Keep saving in it if you can afford to – it won't be deducted from the amount you can put into ISAs. When the five years is up you can transfer the capital into an ISA in addition to the maximum investment you can make in an ISA for the year. Anything which is not transferred into an ISA is taxed in the same way as any other savings – so you will pay tax on the interest on it.

Shares you get from an approved employee profit-sharing scheme (p. 227) or savings-related share option scheme (p. 229) can be transferred into an ISA at their market value. The value of the shares will

TAX-SAVING IDEA
If you haven't got a TESSA and can afford to start one before individual savings accounts start on 6 April 1999, do so. You can continue to save in the TESSA, paying no tax on the interest, in addition to saving the maximum allowed with ISAs.

TAX-SAVING IDEA
Here's a three-step process for getting the best out of individual savings accounts:
1. Save as much as you can in ISAs – there are no tax penalties for withdrawing your money if you need it.
2. Keep your PEPs when ISAs are introduced – this will further increase the amount you can invest free of tax on income and gains.
3. If you have a TESSA, switch as much as you can into an ISA when it ends.

count towards the annual investment limit for an ISA, but there will be no capital gains tax on the transfer. Newly issued shares or those you get when a mutual insurance company or building society converts to a public limited company cannot be transferred to an ISA.

FRINGE BENEFITS

CHAPTER 9

Many employers give their employees non-cash fringe benefits as part of their pay package. Typical examples are employer's contributions to a pension scheme, company cars, luncheon vouchers or interest-free loans to buy your season ticket for the railway.

Many fringe-benefits are tax-free, and even those which are not can remain good value for employees because the taxable value put on them may be less than it would cost you to pay for the benefit yourself.

TAX-FREE FOR ALL

There are many fringe benefits which are tax-free for all employees regardless of what you are paid – see the list below. There are also a number of other benefits which are tax-free for some employees, but not all. There are more details of these on p. 93.

Your employer's own products or services provided to you at less than the price to the general public are tax-free as long as providing them does not cost your employer anything; for example, goods sold to you at the wholesale price, cheap conveyancing for solicitors which does not require the firm to take on extra staff, or free bus travel for bus company employees which does not displace fare-paying customers.

The following are also tax-free:

- free or subsidised meals at work, provided they are available to all employees and are not provided in a public restaurant
- luncheon vouchers (or equivalent) up to a maximum of 15p a day
- your employer's contributions to a pension, life insurance or sick pay insurance policy for you (but premi-

> **TAX-SAVING IDEA**
> There is a long list of fringe benefits which are tax-free whatever your level of earnings – try to take advantage of them in your negotiations with your boss.

ums to a private medical insurance policy for you do count as a taxable fringe benefit)
- routine medical check-ups or medical screening for you or your family
- the costs of medical treatment while you are working abroad (or insurance to cover it)

TAX-SAVING IDEA
Working parents should try to persuade their employers to provide childcare facilities, as this fringe benefit is tax-free. Your private childcare arrangements are not eligible for tax relief.

- nurseries and playschemes run by your employer (if the childcare is not on your employer's premises, then the employer must participate in financing and arranging the care)
- living accommodation provided it is either necessary for you to do your job, or beneficial and customary for someone in your line of work (for example, a caretaker). This benefit is not tax-free if you are a director, unless you have no material interest in the company, and you are either a full-time working director, or a director of a non-profit-making company or charity
- living accommodation provided as part of special security arrangements, and other security precautions, if there is a threat to your security because of your job
- if you live in accommodation which is tax-free for one of the two reasons above, any council tax paid by your employer is also a tax-free benefit
- the provision of a car-parking space at or near your work
- travelling expenses paid for your spouse if he or she has to accompany you on a business trip abroad because your health does not allow you to travel abroad alone
- reasonable extra travel or overnight subsistence expenses paid to you because of disruption to public transport by industrial action
- the cost of transport home if you are occasionally required to work late after public transport has shut down or cannot reasonably be used
- financial help with the cost of travelling between home and work if you are severely and permanently disabled and cannot use public transport
- some retraining and counselling costs paid for by your employer when you leave your job, providing you have worked for your employer for at least two years
- the cost of fees and books for further education or training courses paid for by your employer if the course is either necessary or directly beneficial for your work, or if you are under 21 when starting a general educational course. If you have to be away from your normal workplace for not more than 12 months, and will return to it after training, some travel and subsistence costs may be tax-free
- truly personal gifts from your employer of an appropriate size and nature

(excluding cash), including gifts on marriage, and long-service awards of things or shares in the company. However, long-service awards are tax-free only if they are to mark service of 20 years or more, they do not cost more than £20 for each year of service, and you have received no similar award in the previous ten years

TAX-SAVING IDEA

These perks are also still free of tax: entertainment by your suppliers or customers at cultural or sporting events (within certain rules); air miles (which enable you to make cheap flights); and non-cash gifts costing up to £150 from a third party.

- suggestion scheme awards (see Incentive awards on p. 208)
- entertainment for you or your family provided by someone other than your employer purely as a gesture of goodwill – but not if there are any strings attached, or if it counts as payment for your services
- small non-cash gifts from someone other than your employer. To qualify, the total cost of all gifts you received from the same donor must not be more than £150 in any tax year, and they must not be provided on any sort of condition, for example, that you will provide some particular service
- annual parties or similar functions, such as a Christmas dinner or summer party, which are open to staff generally and cost no more than £75 a head per year to provide
- sports facilities generally available to all staff and their families (and not available to the general public)
- incidental overnight expenses paid or reimbursed by your employer if you are away overnight on business, such as newspapers and phone calls home. The maximum payment is £5 a night (£10 outside the UK); if more is paid, the whole of the payment becomes taxable, not just the excess
- relocation expenses if you move house for your job, such as the costs of buying and selling homes, some travel and subsistence expenses, and bridging loan expenses. There is a maximum of £8,000 per move; you will be taxed on anything over this figure.

TAXABLE FOR ALL

There are four types of benefits which are always taxable. These are:

- assets transferred to you or payments made for you
- vouchers and any goods or services paid for by credit card
- living accommodation provided by your employer (apart from the few exceptions listed on p. 87)
- mileage allowances if you use your own car for work.

Assets transferred to you or payments made for you

Your employer may give you as a present, or allow you to buy it cheap, an item such as a television set, furniture, groceries or your employer's own product. These payments in kind may be taxed in a number of ways depending on how you earn and whether you have the alternative of cash instead.

If you earn less than £8,500 (see p. 93)

The taxable value is the second-hand value of the payment in kind (whether or not you actually sell it). Since many assets have a much lower second-hand value than the cost of buying them new this can be advantageous to you.

If you earn at the rate of £8,500 or more (see p. 93)

The tax rules are tougher for those who earn at a rate of £8,500 or more, or directors. They pay tax on the larger of:

- the second-hand value, or
- the cost to the employer of providing the asset, including ancillary costs such as installation or servicing. Remember, though, that if it is the employer's own product, you pay only the extra cost to the employer. So if it does not cost the employer anything (after taking into account anything you have paid for it) it should be tax-free, unless it has a second-hand value.

If you are being given something you have already had the use of (apart from a car, telephone or mobile phone), the taxable value is the larger of the following, less any amount you have paid:

- the market value when you are given it, or
- the market value of the asset when it was first loaned out (either to you or to anyone else), less the total amount on which tax has already been charged. This is because assets which have been on loan will already have had some tax paid on them.

If you are given a car, telephone or mobile phone, for example on leaving a job, you are taxed on its second-hand value when you are given it, less anything you pay for it. If you buy your company car for a low price, you may have to pay tax on the difference between the price you paid and what your tax office reckons it would fetch on the open market.

> **TAX-SAVING IDEA**
> Fringe benefits which are not tax-free can still be a tax-efficient way of being paid. The taxable value put on them may be much lower than the value to you.

Cash or perks?

You may be given the alternative of either a particular payment in kind, such as free board and lodging, or cash. If you have a perk you can convert into money either immediately or at short notice, you have to pay tax on the value of the cash alternative, even if you opt for the perk. However, note that there is a concession for some workers, including farm workers, and for cash alternatives to cars (see p. 97).

Payments made for you
However much you earn, you pay tax on the full amount of any bill paid directly by your employer on your behalf, such as:

- your phone bill
- your personal credit card bill
- your council tax (unless it is tax-free because you live in tax-free accommodation, see p. 87)
- rent paid direct to your landlord
- a tax bill.

Note, though, that this normally applies only to payments settled directly by your employer, for example to the telephone company, the credit card company or your landlord. If you were given cash to settle the bill yourself, it should already have been added to your other pay on your payslip and taxed through PAYE.

Vouchers and credit cards
You may be given a voucher for a particular service (for example, a season ticket), a credit token or a company credit or charge card. If so, you are taxed on their cash equivalent unless they appear in the list of tax-free fringe benefits on p. 87 (for example, luncheon vouchers, gift vouchers which count as a small gift). Cash vouchers worth a specified amount of cash will usually be taxed under PAYE.

For vouchers and cards which do count as a taxable fringe benefit, broadly speaking you pay tax on the expense incurred by the person who provided them, less any amount that you have paid yourself. You will not have to pay tax on any annual card fee or interest paid by your employer.

Company credit cards and charge cards are often provided as a convenient way of paying business expenses. But you will have to pay tax on anything which is not an allowable business expense.

Living accommodation
In some cases living accommodation may count as a tax-free fringe benefit – see the list on p. 87. But if it does not, it counts as a taxable perk however much you earn. It includes houses, flats, houseboats and holiday homes but

not board and lodging or hotel-type accommodation where typically you get food and other services.

The taxable value of the accommodation is based on the higher of:
- the rateable value of the property, or
- if the property is let, the rent paid for it.

From the taxable value, you can deduct anything you pay for the accommodation, and also, if part of the property is used exclusively for your work, a proportion for that.

Rateable values are still used, although rates are no longer payable. However, for properties in Scotland, where rateable values were revalued more recently than elsewhere, only a percentage of the rateable value is used (found by multiplying the rateable value by 100 and dividing by 270). If there is no rateable value your employer will have to agree a value with your tax office.

If the tax is based on the rateable value, there may be an extra charge if the property cost more than £75,000, including the cost of any improvements made before the current tax year, but deducting anything you paid towards the cost. Broadly, you pay interest at the Inland Revenue's official rate at the start of the tax year (6.75 per cent at 6 April 1997) on the excess over £75,000, reduced in line with the number of days you do not have the property if it is provided for only part of the year. You can deduct any rent you pay not already deducted when working out the basic taxable value, and an amount for business use.

Mileage allowances

If you use your own car for work most employers pay you a mileage allowance which can be quite generous. Any profit you make on your mileage allowance will be taxable.

There are three different methods of working out your profit. You can choose which suits you best. Inland Revenue leaflet *IR125 Using your car for work* is helpful. Note that:
- business mileage excludes travel between home and work – see p. 222 for how 'grey areas' are treated
- motoring expenses are fuel, insurance, servicing, repairs, road tax and tax relief on loan interest to buy the car (or capital allowances if you buy it outright).

Method 1: Exact

You keep records of your business mileage, your overall mileage and your overall motoring expenses. At the end of the tax year, you divide your business mileage by your overall mileage to find what percentage of your mileage is down to your work. Then multiply your overall expenses by the same percentage to find out how much of these you can claim as business expenses. If your mileage allowances come to more than this, the excess is your profit (unless your employer has a dispensation, see p. 210).

Method 2: Quick

You need only keep records of your business mileage. The Inland Revenue has a scale of pence per mile (the Fixed Profit Car Scheme scales) which it estimates to be the average cost of running a car of various engine sizes, including fuel, insurance, depreciation, servicing and road tax. You pay tax only on any mileage allowance you receive above this scale. At the end of the tax year you multiply your business mileage by the appropriate pence per mile. If your mileage allowances come to more than this, the excess is your profit.

Scale charges under the Fixed Profit Car Scheme

	Tax-free rate per mile	
	on the first 4,000 miles in the tax year	*on each mile over 4,000 miles in the tax year*
Size of car engine	1998-99	1998-99
up to 1,000 cc	28p	17p
1,001-1,500 cc	35p	20p
1,501-2,000 cc	45p	25p
over 2,000 cc	63p	36p

Rates for 1997-98 are the same

Method 3: Fixed Profit Car Scheme

Your employer has agreed with your tax office that method 2 should apply when working out employees' profit. If so, the figures will not appear on your P11D, but your employer should give you the taxable figure, or the information you need to work it out. If your employer's mileage allowances are not worked out using the same engine sizes as those shown in the table, the scale charges are matched as closely as possible. If the same allowance is paid whatever the size of car, the average of the two middle bands is used.

Which method?

You do not have to stick with the Fixed Profit Car Scheme, even if your employer operates it, but using the scheme's scales is much simpler than keeping full records. Keep records for a few months to see how similar your actual cost per mile is to the Fixed Profit Car Scheme scale. Then:

- if your car happens to be more expensive to run than average, choose the exact method (but you must keep records of all your expenses)
- if its running costs are average, or cheaper than average, choose the Fixed Profit Car Scheme if your employer runs one, or the Quick method

> **T AX - SAVING IDEA**
> Check out which method of calculation (see opposite) will give you the lowest profit on your mileage allowance.

- if you find that your mileage allowances come to less than the amount of your actual business expenses, you will be able to claim a loss.

TAXABLE FOR SOME, TAX-FREE FOR OTHERS

The following benefits are tax-free if you earn at a rate of less than £8,500 and are not a director:

- a company car or van
- a mobile phone
- private medical or dental insurance
- services without a second-hand value, such as hairdressing at work
- loans of things or money.

However, these benefits are taxable for employees who earn at the rate of £8,500 or more. You cannot get around this by asking to be paid under £8,500 and getting substantial perks instead. To work out whether you earn at a rate of £8,500 a year, you need to take into account two rules:

Rule 1
Your earnings for this purpose are any kind of pay you receive for the job – that is, including your expenses and the taxable value of any perks worked out as if you earned £8,500 or more. However, you can exclude any tax-free profit-related pay, your contributions to an employer's pension scheme, and payroll giving donations.

Rule 2
The earnings are worked out assuming you work full-time for a whole year. So if you leave a job half-way through the year, having earned £5,000, you will still count as earning more than £8,500 – because in the second part of the year you would have earned another £5,000, that is, £10,000 in total.

If you are a director you are automatically counted as earning £8,500 or more unless all of the following three conditions apply:

- you are either a full-time working director or a director of a charity or non-profit-making concern
- you do not own or control more than 5 per cent of the share capital
- you earn under £8,500.

Your employer should take account of your rate of earnings when filling in your taxable benefits and their cash equivalent: you can tell what category you fall into depending on whether you get a form P11D (which is the form for people who earn at a rate of £8,500 or more) or P9D (the alternative form if you earn under £8,500).

Company cars

The rules for taxing company cars have become less favourable over the years and many employers now give their staff the choice of whether to take a car or cash. If you only need a car for work occasionally, note that a 'pool car' is tax-free. To qualify it must not normally be kept overnight near your home, it must be used by more than one employee, and any private use must be a consequence of business use. But before you can work out which option is better for you, you need to be able to work out the taxable value of a company car and any free fuel you get.

The baseline for a car's taxable value is 35 per cent of its price. So a £15,000 new car has a basic taxable value of £5,250. The price is defined as the list price of the car at registration (not the dealer's price), including delivery

---

Example

Sanjay O'Hanlon got a new company car in March 1994 with a price of £15,000. From the tax year ending 5 April 1995 (when this system of taxing company cars was introduced) the basic taxable value for each tax year was 35 per cent of this, £5,250. But he does at least 2,500 miles on business in it each year, so he can claim a one-third deduction. One-third of £5,250 is £1,750, so the taxable value is £5,250 – £1,750 = £3,500. £3,500 is added to his pay for tax purposes each year, when working out his PAYE code.

However, in March 1998 the car had its fourth birthday. This means that he can claim a further one-third deduction for the whole of the tax year ending 5 April 1998. The deduction is one-third of £3,500, that is £1,167, so the car's taxable value for the tax year ending 5 April 1998 was £2,333. Had the car been registered just a month later, after 5 April 1994, he would have had to wait until the tax year ending 5 April 1999 for the further reduction.

charges, VAT and car tax (but not road tax). Any contribution you make towards the cost of the car is deducted from its price, up to a limit of £5,000, and the maximum price for tax purposes is capped at £80,000. For cars without a list price, your employer will have to reach agreement with the Revenue, usually on the basis of published car price guides. The market value is used for classic cars worth at least £15,000 and aged 15 years or more at the end of the tax year.

You cannot create an artificially low price by getting a basic model and adding accessories. The price includes any accessories fitted before the car was made available to you, and any accessories or set of accessories worth more than £100 which are fitted after that. Accessories needed because you are disabled are excluded.

This system of taxing company cars means that you are taxed on roughly the whole price of the car over three years. You are also taxed on free fuel you get (see p. 97), although other running costs borne by your employer, such tax, servicing and insurance, are tax-free. However, you can make various deductions from the basic taxable value if:

- you do at least 2,500 miles on business in the car each year – deduct one-third of the taxable value for 2,500 to 17,999 business miles each tax year, two-thirds of the taxable value for 18,000 or more business miles
- the car is more than four years old at the end of the tax year in question – deduct one-third of the taxable value you ended up with after any business mileage deduction

- you have to pay towards your private use of the car – deduct the amount you pay. Note that you cannot deduct a contribution you make voluntarily, in order to get a better car, say.

If you qualify for more than one deduction, the taxable value is worked out on a cumulative basis – first you deduct one-third of the basic taxable value, then you deduct a further third (or two-thirds) from the result. The cash contribution towards your private use is deducted last.

Changing, getting or losing a company car

At some point your company car is almost certain to be unavailable for part of a tax year, because you changed it, or you started or stopped getting one. The tax system recognises this by reducing the taxable value of the car in line with the number of days in the tax year for which the car was unavailable. The same applies if you didn't have the car (or a replacement) for at least 30 days at a stretch during the tax year. The number of miles you need to do to qualify for the business mileage reductions is also reduced proportionately.

However, you may want to work out your own figures during the tax year in order to decide whether a company car will be beneficial for you. If so, beware of confusion if you have to adjust the figures to account for time when the car was unavailable. The method shown in the example below is the simplest but the Revenue tends to talk in terms of days unavailable, and then deducts a figure for those days from the full-year figure. So in the example, Sanjay's tax office would probably work out the days for which the first car was unavailable (254) and then deduct $^{254}/_{365}$ths from the full-year figures.

EXAMPLE

Sanjay changes his company car on 1 August 1998. He has had his old company car for only 111 days in the tax year, so the taxable value is $^{111}/_{365}$ of the full year's value. But first he needs to check that he is still entitled to the business mileage deduction he usually gets. He multiplies the normal business mileage limit that applies (2,500 miles) by $^{111}/_{365}$ to get 760 but his actual mileage is comfortably above this. The taxable value for a full tax year would be £2,333; the taxable value for the 111 days is £2,333 x $^{111}/_{365}$ = £709.

Sanjay has to do a similar calculation for his brand new company car, using its price, but this time he cannot claim the reduction for a car aged four years or more. This time he adjusts all the figures by the number of days he had the new car: 365 – 111 = 254.

Two company cars?

If your employer provides you and your household with two company cars, you do not get a full business mileage reduction on the second (least-used) car. You have to do at least 18,000 business miles in the second car order to qualify for a reduction, and then it is only a one-third reduction.

Giving up cars for cash

If you do decide that you would rather have cash than a company car, you will of course be taxed on the cash. Employees have to pay National Insurance contributions on extra cash but not on company cars. However, there is no employees' National Insurance to pay on earnings over £25,220 (in the tax year ending 5 April 1999) so if you are over this limit there would be no extra National Insurance to pay anyway.

Fuel for company cars

If you get a company car, you may get free fuel for private use as well. This is taxed according to a fixed scale of charges added to your taxable income. The only reduction you get is if you have the car for only part of the year, in which case the scale charge is worked out in line with the number of days, in the same way as for cars. The only way in which you can avoid the scale charge is by being required by your employer to reimburse all the cost of fuel used for private purposes, and actually doing so. However, fuel provided for the travel between home and work for disabled employees is tax-free.

In the budget, the Chancellor proposed that the car fuel scale charges will rise by 20 per cent a year or more each year until the tax year ending 5 April 2003. This is to discourage employers from offering and employees from accepting free fuel.

Car fuel scale charges

	Engine size, cc		
	0-1,400	1,401-2,000	2,001+
Petrol			
1997-98	£800	£1,010	£1,490[1]
1998-99	£1,010	£1,280	£1,890[1]
Diesel			
1997-98	£740	£740	£940
1998-99	£1,280	£1,280	£1,890

[1]These figures also apply for cars without a cylinder capacity

Vans

A van provided by your employer for your private use is lightly taxed, compared with a company car. The basic taxable value of a van is £500, and there is no tax charge for free fuel. You may also qualify for the following reductions:

- the taxable value is reduced to £350 if the van is aged four years or more at the end of the tax year
- if the van is shared with other employees and is not exclusively yours for any period of more than 30 days at a stretch, the taxable value is split between all the employees concerned
- the taxable value is reduced in line with the number of days within the tax year for which it is unavailable (in the same way as for company cars, above)
- any amount you have to pay for the use of the van is deducted from the taxable value.

Cheap or free loans

The basic rule is that if your employer provides a cheap or interest-free loan, you have to pay tax on the difference between the interest you pay and the interest worked out at an official rate set from time to time by the Inland Revenue. You do not need to worry about any of this, however, if:

- your employer lends money as part of its normal business, comparable loans were available to members of the general public (a substantial proportion actually being sold to them), and the loan was made to you on the same terms as those comparable loans. Such loans are tax-free from 6 April 1994, even if they were first taken out before then
- the total loans you have outstanding are no more than £5,000 throughout the tax year. If you have several loans, one of which qualifies for tax relief, then the qualifying loan is ignored when deciding whether the other loans fall within the limit. If, for example, you have a £1,000 personal loan and a £50,000 mortgage (on which you get tax relief), only the mortgage will be treated as a taxable loan.

To work out the tax on a loan, you take the average amount owing during the year (the whole amount, not just the amount above £5,000), adjusted if the loan was only outstanding for part of the year. You then multiply the average loan by the average official rate of interest for the period in the year during which the loan was outstanding (your tax office should be able to tell you this). Lastly, you deduct the interest you were actually liable to pay during the tax year, to find the amount on which you will be taxed.

EXAMPLE

Lene Mikkelsen has a £10,000 loan from her employer to help buy her flat, at a special low interest rate of 5 per cent (compared with an average official interest rate of 7.08 per cent). She paid off £1,000 of the loan halfway through the year. The taxable value of the perk is £197.60, worked out as follows:

Amount outstanding:
At start of tax year	£10,000
At end of tax year	£9,000
Average:	£19,000 ÷ 2 = £9,500.

Interest payable at official rate	£9,500 x 7.08% =	£672.60
Actual interest payable		£475.00
Difference (taxable value)		£197.60

As the loan qualifies for tax relief, Lene can claim tax relief on both the actual interest payable (£475) and the difference between that and the interest payable at the official rate (£197.60), a total of £672.60. As the loan is to buy a home, the tax relief for the year ending 5 April 1998 is 15 per cent of the total – a £100 saving.

If you think that you will lose out under this averaging method, you can choose to calculate the figures using the daily amounts of the loan and official rates of interest. However, you have to use the same method for all your taxable loans, and the calculations can get quite complex. If you want to make this choice, you have to tell your tax office within roughly 21 months of the end of the tax year in question.

Note that under either method, if the loan qualifies for tax relief, you get tax relief on both the interest you actually paid and the difference between that and the official rate of interest. Effectively, the tax relief is worked out assuming you paid the official rate of interest. Note that if it is a home loan, you may already have had relief on the interest you actually paid, under MIRAS (see Chapter 7).

Mobile phones

The taxable value of a mobile phone provided for you (or a member of your household) is a flat £200. The taxable value is reduced if the phone is unavailable for part of the year, in the same way as company cars above. You are not taxed, however, if you pay the full cost of any outgoing private calls.

In practice, many employers have arranged either a dispensation or a PAYE Settlement Agreement (see p. 210) for mobile phones, which is why you may not see them on your P11D (and of course they are not taxable at all unless you earn at a rate of £8,500).

Private medical or dental insurance
If your employer pays premiums for a private medical expenses policy for you (for example, through a group scheme for all employees), the amount is a taxable benefit. The same applies to dental insurance schemes. You pay tax on the cost to your employer, less any amount you pay for the benefit.

Other benefits
There is a variety of other perks taxable only if you earn at the rate of £8,500 a year or more. These include:

- relocation expenses which would normally be tax-free but which are above the £8,000 tax-free limit for each move
- childcare provided by your employer – workplace nurseries and playschemes should be tax-free, but if your employer just pays for you to arrange your own childcare, this will count as a taxable benefit
- services supplied, such as free hairdressing, holidays, gardening or a free chauffeur – but remember that you pay tax only on the extra cost to your employer, so services that your employer provides as part of their normal business may be tax-free
- share schemes or share options which are not tax-free. See Chapter 18 for more on these
- subscriptions and fees paid for by your employer for you to join professional bodies, societies, leisure or sports clubs etc. Note that if you pay for these yourself, you may be able to claim them against your tax if they are necessary for your work (see p. 224)
- any income tax paid for you by your employer, other than through PAYE – but only if you are a director. This may sometimes apply if PAYE was not deducted from your pay at the proper time, and the tax was later paid for you
- the value of anything provided for your use, except for cars, vans, mobile phones and living accommodation (for example, a television, furniture, a yacht or aircraft). The value is 20 per cent of the market value when it was first provided (to you or to anyone else), plus any expense of providing it met by your employer. If you are later given whatever it is, you will be taxed as explained on p. 89
- help with educating your children (unless this is nothing to do with your

job, for example it is pure coincidence that your child gets one of the generally available scholarships your employer's firm provides).

MINIMISING CAPITAL GAINS TAX

If you own items which increase in value, you may find yourself paying capital gains tax. For example, shares, unit trusts, land, property and antiques can increase in price, giving you a capital gain. If you sell them – or even give them away – you may be faced with a tax bill at up to 40 per cent of the chargeable gain

The average taxpayer is unlikely to pay capital gains tax, however. There is a long list of assets on which gains are tax-free, including your only or main home, private cars and other personal belongings (see opposite). If you do part with an asset which falls into the capital gains tax net, you can deduct from the gain any money you've spent acquiring and owning it. You can also deduct any losses you've made on other assets.

Then there is indexation allowance to reduce the part of the gain caused by inflation between 1982 and 1998 (replaced by tapering relief from 6 April 1998 onwards). There are special reliefs which can reduce or eliminate the gain made on selling business assets, farms or growing businesses. And if there is still any chargeable gain left after all these deductions, there is an annual tax-free allowance that can swallow up another £6,800 of chargeable gains in the tax year beginning 6 April 1998.

This chapter explains how capital gains tax works and the details of the various reliefs and allowances. It tells you how to keep your capital gains tax to a minimum. And it sets out the complicated rules for calculating the tax when you buy and sell in shares. But it begins with a guide to when you might face this tax.

When do you have to pay capital gains tax?
You may have to pay this tax whenever you dispose of an asset. What is meant by dispose is not defined by law. But if you sell an asset, swap one asset for another or give something away, this will normally count as a disposal. So will the loss or destruction of an asset (although not if you replace or restore it by claiming on an insurance policy, or by using some types of

compensation from an overseas government).

There are some occasions when there is no capital gains tax to pay, regardless of what is being disposed of or how much it is worth:

- assets passed on when someone dies
- gifts to a husband or wife, unless separated (p. 51)
- gifts to charity.

Although there are no taxable gains in these circumstances, there are also no losses if the asset is worth less than when you acquired it.

TAX-SAVING IDEA

If you are thinking of making a gift to charity of an asset which is showing a loss, think again. You won't be able to claim the loss to reduce other taxable gains.

Ideally, find something which is showing a taxable gain to give – there will be no tax to pay on the disposal. Alternatively, sell the asset which is showing a loss and give the proceeds to the charity. That would create an allowable loss which could reduce your tax bill on other disposals.

EXAMPLE

Leonie Dale wants to give a house she used to let out to students to a charity for the homeless. It has become badly run-down and would produce a capital loss of £40,000 if sold on the open market.

However, she also owns shares which are showing a chargeable gain of much more than £40,000. She decides to sell the house to produce an allowable loss and at the same time sells some shares to produce a similar gain – saving around £10,000 in capital gains tax. She gives the proceeds of the house sale to the charity together with a donation of £5,000 towards the expense of buying another house for their purposes.

Tax-free gains

There is no capital gains tax to pay on any gain you make on the following assets:

- your home (though not a second home in most cases – see p. 60)
- private cars
- personal belongings – known as chattels – sold for less than £6,000 (see p. 113)
- wasting assets with a useful life of 50 years or less (for example, a boat or caravan), so long as you could not have claimed a capital allowance on it
- British money, including sovereigns dated after 1837
- foreign currency for your personal spending abroad (including what you spend on maintaining a home abroad), but not foreign currency accounts

- gains on insurance policies, unless you bought them and were not the original holder (though you may have to pay part of the insurance company's capital gains tax bill – see p. 71)
- betting, pools or lottery winnings
- National Savings investments such as National Savings Certificates and Capital Bonds
- Personal equity plans (PEPs) – see p. 80
- Individual savings accounts (ISAs) – see p. 83
- Business Expansion Scheme (BES) shares bought after 18 March 1986, provided you have owned them for at least five years and they carried on their qualifying activity for at least three years (see p. 83)
- Enterprise Investment Scheme (EIS) shares, provided you have owned them for at least five years and they carried on their qualifying activity for at least three years – see p. 82
- shares in venture capital trusts (VCTs) – see p. 83
- terminal bonuses on Save-As-You-Earn (SAYE) contracts
- British Government stock and any options to buy and sell such stock
- certain corporate bonds such as company loan stock and debentures issued after 13 March 1984 and options to buy and sell such bonds
- interests in trusts or settlements, unless you bought them
- decorations for bravery, unless you bought them
- certain gifts for the public benefit (p. 133)
- damages or compensation for a personal injury or wrong to yourself or in your personal capacity (for example, libel)
- compensation for being given bad investment advice that left you worse off after being persuaded to buy a personal pension between 29 April 1988 and 30 June 1994.

Disposals of land to housing associations may also be free of capital gains tax.

If an asset is one where there is no capital gains tax to pay on disposal, any loss you make on it cannot normally be used to reduce your overall tax bill. But if you dispose of a chattel worth £6,000 or less at a loss, you may be able to use this to reduce your tax bill (see p. 113).

Who has to pay?
Capital gains tax applies to you as an individual in your private life or in your business whether self-employed or in partnership. Trustees may also have to pay capital gains tax on the assets that are held in trust (see opposite).

Any capital gains tax for the tax year ending 5 April 1998 will have to be paid by 31 January 1999, along with the final payment for any income tax still unpaid from the same tax year. Capital gains tax for the tax year beginning 6 April 1998 will have to be paid by 31 January 2000.

Married couples

A husband and wife are treated as two single people for capital gains tax purposes, and each is responsible for paying their own capital gains tax bills. With assets jointly owned by husband and wife – second homes, shares, valuables and so on – the gain or loss should be split 50:50 between you unless you have told your tax inspector that they are not owned equally.

If assets are held in your joint names unequally, you need to complete a declaration of beneficial interests using Form 17. If the asset produces income, you may already have filled in Form 17 to allocate the income other than 50:50 (see p. 44). There is no need to fill in another for capital gains tax purposes.

Trusts

Where assets are held in trust, the trustees are liable for capital gains tax on disposals of the assets in the trust, in much the same way as individuals. However, the slice of net taxable gains which is free of capital gains tax in any tax year is half the figure that applies to individuals. So for the tax year ending 5 April 1998, the first £3,250 of net chargeable gains is free of tax for a trust; for the tax year which began on 6 April 1998, the tax-free allowance for trusts is £3,400.

The rate of capital gains tax paid by trustees for the tax year ending 5 April 1998 is 23 per cent, unless it is a discretionary trust (including an accumulation trust) when the rate is 34 per cent. For disposals on or after 6 April 1998, the rate of capital gains tax is 34 per cent for all types of trust.

WORKING OUT THE GAIN FOR THE TAX YEAR ENDING 5 APRIL 1998

The way capital gains tax works changes from 6 April 1998 onwards and details are given on p. 123. Below are the rules for disposals before that date – these apply in filling in your 1998 tax return which covers capital gains for the tax year ending 5 April 1998.

For disposals on or before 5 April 1998, the gain or loss is worked out broadly as follows:

Step 1: Find the final value of the asset – what you get for selling it or its market value if given away.

Step 2: Find its initial value – normally what you paid for it or its market value (see below).

Step 3: Deduct the initial value from the final value to find the gross capital gain or gross capital loss.

Step 4: If you incurred any allowable expenses in acquiring, owning or disposing of the asset, these can be deducted from the gross capital gain or loss to give the net capital gain or net capital loss. (See p. 108 for more about expenses.)

Step 5: If you have made a net capital gain, you can reduce this by claiming indexation allowance which reflects the impact of inflation on the figures (p. 110). You may also be able to claim special reliefs to reduce the gain further or increase a net capital loss – for example, when disposing of your only or main home (p. 60) or retiring from your business (p. 128).

Step 6: The figure you end up with after all these deductions is the chargeable gain or allowable loss on the asset. Add together all your chargeable gains for the tax year and subtract any allowable losses to get your total chargeable gain. If your allowable losses outweigh the chargeable gains, there will be no capital gains tax to pay for this tax year – and the net allowable loss can be used to reduce your tax bill elsewhere in various ways (see p. 114).

Step 7: If you have made a total chargeable gain, subtract the tax-free capital gains allowance for the tax year from it – this was £6,500 for the tax year ending 5 April 1998.

Step 8: You can now subtract any losses carried over from previous tax years (see p. 114 for details).

Step 9: If there is anything left after all these deductions, it is added to your taxable income for the year and income tax is charged on it at the lower rate, basic rate or higher rate as appropriate.

There are special rules for calculating the gains on assets owned on or before 31 March 1982 (see p. 111). And the detailed rules for working out the gains on shares and unit trusts – including what happens when you buy and sell batches of the same shares or unit trusts – are on p. 116.

Initial and final value
In most cases, the value of an asset when you acquire or sell it is what it cost

EXAMPLE

Ben Barber bought a painting for £2,000 in April 1985, paying a buyer's fee to the auction house of £200. In the same week, he spent £500 having the painting cleaned. The painting was sold in May 1997 for £20,000, with a seller's fee of £3,000 for the auction house. Ben calculates the tax due as follows:

Step 1: The final value of the painting is what he sold it for – £20,000.

Step 2: The initial value is what he paid for it – £2,000.

Step 3: He deducts the initial value from the final value to find the gross capital gain of £18,000.

Step 4: He incurred allowable expenses of £3,700: the £200 fee paid when buying the painting, the £500 spent on cleaning it and the £3,000 fee paid when selling it. He deducts this from the £18,000 gross capital gain to get the net capital gain of £14,300.

Step 5: He can claim indexation allowance for the £2,000 cost of buying the painting, the £200 buyer's fee and the £500 cleaning charge. The allowance is £1,769 (for how he calculated this, see p. 111). Ben subtracts this indexation allowance from the net capital gain of £14,300 to get a chargeable gain of £12,531.

Step 6: This is his only chargeable gain for the tax year ending 5 April 1998, and he has no allowable losses for that tax year. So Ben has a total chargeable gain of £12,531 for the tax year.

Step 7: The tax-free allowance for the tax year ending 5 April 1998 is £6,500. He subtracts this from the total chargeable gain to get £6,031.

Step 8: He has no losses carried over from previous tax years to reduce this figure further.

Step 9: The £6,031 is added to Ben's taxable income for the tax year ending 5 April 1998 and income tax is charged on it. His income is already high enough for him to be paying tax at the higher rate of 40 per cent, so that is the rate he pays on the gain.

So Ben must pay 40 per cent of £6,031 – a capital gains tax bill of £2,412.40.

you to acquire it or what you get on selling it. If you acquired something by inheritance, its initial value is its probate value.

With a gift, the value is its market value: what anyone selling it at the time of the gift would get for it on the open market. However, in certain circumstances, the initial value of a gift may be what the giver acquired it for if you agreed at the time of the gift to take over the giver's capital gain (see below).

The market value is also the final value if you dispose of an asset to a connected person, however much you sell it for. For capital gains tax, a connected person includes your husband or wife, your business partner and their spouse, a relative of yours or these others (brother, sister, parents, child, grandchild) and the spouse of one of these relatives.

There are special rules for valuing assets owned before April 1982 (see p. 111).

Gifts

With some things you are given, you may have agreed to take over the giver's capital gains tax bill by agreeing to a claim for hold-over relief (see p. 126). Since 14 March 1989, this can be done for only a limited range of gifts, but before that date it could be done with almost anything.

When you come to dispose of an asset on which hold-over relief has been claimed when you got it, its initial value is what the giver acquired it for, not its market value when you were given it.

E X A M P L E

In December 1988 Suzy Richmond gave an antique diamond ring valued at £8,500 to her daughter Emma. Suzy had bought the brooch herself four years previously at a cost of £4,000. They claimed hold-over relief.

In December 1997 Emma sold the ring for £12,000. Because hold-over relief had been claimed on the gift, her net gain was not £12,000 – £8,500 = £3,500. Instead, Suzy's original purchase price of £4,000 is taken as the initial value. And Emma can claim as an allowable expense the £200 bill for restoring the ring paid by Suzy in June 1986.

So Emma's net gain (ignoring indexation allowance) was £12,000 – £4,000 – £200 = £7,800.

Allowable expenses

Deducting the initial value of an asset from its final value gives you the gross capital gain or gross capital loss. However, you can then deduct certain

EXAMPLE

When Melanie Hill sold her holiday cottage in September 1997 for £108,000, she feared an enormous capital gains tax bill – she had bought it in August 1988 for £52,000. But she soon realised there were a lot of expenses she could claim to reduce the capital gain:

- acquisition costs of £1,735 – the £790 legal bill incurred in buying it, the £520 stamp duty and the £425 surveyor's fee for inspecting and valuing it
- improvement costs of £18,750 – the cost of installing modern plumbing and central heating, rewiring and building an extension which were all paid for in May 1989
- disposal costs of £3,575 – legal bills for the sale of £1,725 and £1,850 commission paid to the estate agent.

The net capital gain is worked out as follows:

Final value		£108,000
minus allowable expenses:		
original cost	£52,000	
acquisition costs	£1,735	
improvement costs	£18,750	
disposal costs	£3,575	
Total allowable expenses		£76,060
Net capital gain		**£31,940**

However, Melanie won't pay capital gains tax even on this net capital gain of £31,940 – she can claim indexation allowance (see p. 110).

allowable expenses in computing the gain on an asset for capital gains tax. These include:

- acquisition costs, such as payments to a professional adviser (for example, surveyor, accountant, solicitor), conveyancing costs and stamp duty, and advertising to find a seller
- what you spend improving the asset (though not your own time)
- what you spend establishing or defending your rights or title to the asset
- disposal costs, similar to acquisition costs, but including the cost of valuing it for capital gains tax.

Deducting these expenses gives you the net capital gain or net allowable loss. If the asset was a gift to you and the giver got hold-over relief (see opposite), you can also claim any allowable expenses incurred while the giver owned it.

EXAMPLE

Martin Thompson buys a house which he converts into a pair of flats. He spends £5,000 converting one into a weekend retreat for himself and £3,000 on doing up the other one to sell off.

Each of the flats is given identical valuations at the time of the sale. So any money spent on the whole house can be divided equally between the two flats. He can therefore claim the following expenses to reduce the gain on flat he sells off:

- the £3,000 spent improving the flat he sells off
- the expenses of selling the flat
- half the expenses of buying the house including the purchase price.

Part disposals

If you dispose of part of an asset, you will need to allocate expenses between the part you are getting rid of and the part you have kept.

Any expense connected only with the part being disposed of can be fully deducted from the proceeds in working out the gain. Anything connected only with the part you are keeping cannot be deducted. But some of the expenditure will be impossible to allocate in this way, and will thus have to be divided between the two parts, in proportion to their value. The proportion of such a cost that you can deduct from the gain is as follows:

$$\frac{\text{Disposal proceeds}}{\text{Disposal proceeds} + \text{Value of the part retained}}$$

There are special rules for allocating costs to shares and unit trusts where holdings are divided or added to (see p. 116).

Indexation allowance

If you end up with a net capital gain after deducting allowable expenses from the gross capital gain, you can claim indexation allowance to remove some or all of the gain created by inflation since March 1982. If there is a net capital loss, you can't claim indexation allowance, however – indexation allowance cannot be used to create or increase a loss.

To calculate indexation allowance, multiply the initial value and each allowable expense by the following:

$$\frac{\text{RPI in disposal month} - \text{RPI in expenditure month}}{\text{RPI in expenditure month}}$$

EXAMPLE

Ben Barber works out the indexation allowance he can claim on the painting he disposed of in May 1997 (see p. 107). He can claim the allowance for the original cost of £2,000, the buyer's fee of £200 and the cleaning costs of £500 – all of this £2,700 was spent in April 1985.

The RPI in April 1985 was 94.78
The RPI in May 1997 was 156.9

The indexation allowance is as follows:

$$£2,700 \times \frac{\text{RPI May 1997} - \text{RPI April 1985}}{\text{RPI April 1985}}$$

$$= £2,700 \times \frac{156.9 - 94.78}{94.78}$$

$$= £2,700 \times 0.655$$
$$= £1,769$$

Ben's chargeable gain on the painting is therefore £14,300 – £1,769 = £12,531

RPI stands for Retail Prices Index (figures for the RPI since March 1982 are given in the Tax Return Guide sent to you by the Inland Revenue). The expenditure month is the month in which the payment of the initial value or the allowable expense became due.

Work out this sum for the initial value and each allowable expense to three decimal places, and add together the answers. Subtract this from the net capital gain to produce the chargeable gain. If the indexation allowance is bigger than the net capital gain, it reduces the gain to zero – it cannot be used to create a loss.

Assets owned on or before 31 March 1982

If you owned an asset on or before 31 March 1982, only the gain since that date is liable to capital gains tax. Any gain made before 1 April 1982 is effectively tax-free. With such assets, the initial value is normally its market value on 31 March 1982. You cannot deduct expenses incurred on or before that date. Indexation allowance runs from March 1982.

In some circumstances, using the 31 March 1982 value could artificially inflate your gain or loss. Suppose, for example, you bought something in

1978 which fell in value before 31 March 1982 and has risen in value since. Basing the gain on the 31 March 1982 value would make the gain larger than the amount you've actually made since that date. Similarly, if you dispose of something which rose in value while you owned it before 31 March 1982 and fell in value afterwards, this could produce a bigger loss than you actually made.

Thus when calculating the gain or loss on assets owned before 1 April 1982, you need to work out the sums using two different methods:

- the rebased chargeable gain – using the value on 31 March 1982 and ignoring costs incurred on or before that date
- the actual gain – using the original cost you paid for it and allowing for allowable expenses incurred on or before 31 March 1982 (with indexation allowance on them running from that date).

The two answers are then compared in what the Inland Revenue calls the kink test:

- if both methods produce a gain, the smaller gain is used to calculate your tax bill
- if both methods produce a loss, the smaller loss is allowable
- if one produces a gain and the other a loss, the disposal is assumed to produce no gain or loss.

To avoid all this palaver, you can make a rebasing election, which means all your gains and losses on assets owned on or before 31 March 1982 will be based on their market value on that date. This will avoid having to keep

---

Example

Jim Brooke carries out the kink test on the home he rents out which he sold for £120,000 in December 1997.

He had bought it in June 1979 when he had paid £20,000 for it, with acquisition costs and other allowable expenses before 1 April 1982 of £2,000. Its value at 31 March 1982 was £16,300.

The net capital gain using the 31 March 1982 value as the initial value would be £120,000 – £16,300 = £103,700. The net capital gain based on what he paid for it in June 1979 and expenses before 1 April 1982 would be £120,000 – £20,000 – £2,000 = £98,000.

Both methods produce a gain, so the capital gains tax bill will be based on what Jim paid for it in June 1979 since that produces the smaller gain. If Jim had already opted for all his pre-1 April 1982 assets to be treated as if they were acquired on that date, his tax bill would be based on the larger figure produced by using the market value on 31 March 1982.

complicated records (although it could mean paying more tax if you have assets which fell in value before 31 March 1982 and have risen in value since).

If you want to make a rebasing election, tell your tax inspector in writing within two years of the first disposal of such an asset on or after 6 April 1988. This is likely to be the first disposal to which the rebasing rules apply. The election is irrevocable – so make sure it will pay for you. For more details, see Help Sheet IR280 *Rebasing – assets held at 31 March 1982*.

Special rules for personal belongings – chattels

If personal belongings, known as chattels by the Inland Revenue, are sold for less than £6,000, the gain is tax-free. Chattels are defined as tangible, movable property and include furniture, silver, paintings and so on. A set (for example, a silver tea-set) counts as one chattel for this exemption.

If a chattel is sold for more than the tax-free limit, the taxable gain is restricted to $5/_3$ of the amount of the disposal over the limit. So the maximum gain on a chattel sold for £7,200 would be $5/_3$ of £7,200 – £6,000 = $5/_3$ of £1,200 = £2,000.

E X A M P L E

William Baxter bought a piece of furniture for £4,000 and sold it for £7,500 in the tax year ending 5 April 1998. This produces a gain of £7,500 – £4,000 = £3,500. The sale price is over the £6,000 chattels limit so the gain is not tax-free. But for capital gains tax purposes, the gain cannot be more than $5/_3$ of £7,500 – £6,000. This is $5/_3$ of £1,500 = £2,500, thus reducing William's taxable gain by £1,000.

In most cases, disposing of an asset that would produce a tax-free gain means that you cannot claim any allowable loss made on such an asset. With a chattel, you can claim a loss even if it is sold for less than £6,000 – but the loss is calculated as if it had fetched £6,000.

E X A M P L E

William Baxter sold another piece of furniture for £4,500 which he had bought for £9,500. His gross loss is calculated as if he had sold it for £6,000: it is therefore £9,500 – £6,000 = £3,500 – rather than the £5,000 loss William actually made.

For more about chattels, ask for Help Sheet *IR295 Chattels and capital gains tax*.

Capital losses

If the initial cost of an asset and its expenses add up to more than its final value, you have made a net capital loss on that asset. Net capital losses are deducted from your chargeable gains to find the total chargeable gain on which your capital gains tax bill is based. If your net capital losses are bigger than your total chargeable gains, the difference – your net allowable loss – can be carried over to reduce your total chargeable gain in a later tax year.

Note that a loss made when you dispose of an asset to a connected person (p. 108) can be set off only against a gain made to a connected person. This applies even if the loss was made when you disposed of the asset for a genuine commercial value.

The tax-free allowance

The first slice of total chargeable gain in any tax year is free of capital gains tax. For the tax year ending 5 April 1998, the tax-free allowance is £6,500.

If you don't use all your tax-free allowance in one year, you can't carry the unused part over to another year. So try not to reduce your total chargeable gain below the level of the tax-free allowance by claiming too much by way of losses. You have to deduct losses from gains made in the same tax year, even if this reduces your net gains below the tax-free level.

E X A M P L E

Gus Henry made chargeable gains of £7,500 in the tax year ending 5 April 1998 and allowable losses of £3,250 in the same year. All the losses have to be set off against the gains for this tax year, even though this brings the net chargeable gain below the tax-free allowance of £6,500 for the tax year.

So his net chargeable gain is £7,500 – £3,250 = £4,250 – on which no tax is payable.

Losses from previous years

If your total chargeable gain is bigger than the tax-free allowance, you can use any losses from previous tax years to reduce your tax bill. If you have enough such losses, you can reduce your total chargeable gain to the level of the tax-free allowance and pay no capital gains tax at all.

You must use losses from the last tax year before those from earlier years.

But note that – unlike with losses from the same tax year – you don't have to deduct more than is necessary to get down to the tax-free amount.

Losses can never be carried back to an earlier tax year, except in the year when you die. Your executors will be able to carry back these losses to set against gains you made in the three previous tax years – starting with the gains in the most recent year. There is further information in Help Sheet *IR282 Death, personal representatives and legatees*.

E X A M P L E

Elizabeth Ong has a total chargeable gain for the tax year ending 5 April 1998 of £8,000. The tax-free amount for that tax year is £6,500, which would mean paying capital gains tax on £8,000 – £ 6,500 = £1,500. But she has losses of £3,500 carried over from previous years and she can use £1,500 of this amount to reduce her total chargeable gain to nil – with no capital gains tax to pay.

That still leaves her with £3,500 – £1,500 = £2,000 of unused losses to be carried forward to the tax year beginning 6 April 1998 and beyond.

Claiming losses
You have to claim losses within five years and ten months of the end of the tax year in which they were made. So losses made in the tax year ending 5 April 1998 must be claimed by 31 January 2004.

You can claim the losses by giving details on the Capital gains pages of the tax return – enter the amount in box 8.2 and give details in column 8 on page CG2 when entering the asset that made the loss. Alternatively, write and tell your tax inspector.

Calculating your capital gains tax bill
If there is anything left after deducting expenses, indexation allowance, the tax-free allowance and losses, it is added to your taxable income for the year and income tax is charged on it.

So if your income is already high enough for you to be a higher rate taxpayer, you will pay tax on your chargeable gains at the higher rate of 40 per cent. If you are a basic rate taxpayer – even after your chargeable gains are added to your income – you'll pay tax on the gains at the basic rate of 23 per cent. And if your income is so low that you pay tax only at the lower rate of 20 per cent, you will pay tax on your gains at the lower rate also – until the combined total is high enough to mean you pay tax at the basic rate on some of it.

For example, in the tax year ending 5 April 1998, your gains were taxed at the higher rate of 40 per cent if your taxable income was more than £26,100. If your taxable income and gains came to less than £4,100, you paid tax on your chargeable gains at the lower rate of 20 per cent. Anything between those two limits was taxed at the basic rate of 23 per cent.

SHARES AND UNIT TRUSTS

Shares and unit trusts are treated in the same way as other assets for capital gains tax purposes. But if you buy and sell shares in a particular company or units in a particular unit trust, how do you decide which you have bought or sold when working out the gain? And there are further complications when companies merge, are taken over or otherwise reorganise their capital. This section explains the special rules for working out the gains and losses on share transactions. There are also two Help Sheets: *IR284 Shares and capital gains tax*, and *IR285 Share reorganisations, company takeovers and capital gains tax*.

Valuing shares
The market value of shares bought and sold on one of the Stock Exchange markets is normally the amount you paid for them or got for selling them.

But you should use the market value when valuing gifts or disposals to a connected person (see p. 108) – use the prices recorded in the Stock Exchange Daily Official List (which can be supplied by a stockbroker or bank). The market value is the lower of the following two figures, calculated using prices on the date of the gift or disposal:

- the selling price, plus a quarter of the difference between the selling price and the (higher) buying price – the quarter-up rule
- the half-way point between the highest and lowest prices of recorded bargains for the day.

With any disposal of unquoted shares, the market value must be agreed with the Share Valuation Division of the Inland Revenue. This cannot be negotiated in advance and reaching agreement can be a lengthy business. For more about the Share Valuation Division, see Inland Revenue leaflet SVD1.

Unit trusts and investment trusts
The gain on disposing of unit trusts and investment trusts is worked out in the same way as for shares. If you receive an equalisation payment with your first distribution from a unit trust, this is a return of part of your original investment and should be deducted from the acquisition price in working out your gain or loss.

Which shares or unit trusts have you sold?

If you buy one batch of shares in a company and later sell it without any other dealings in the shares, it is quite simple to calculate the gain or loss. But if you buy shares in the same company on different occasions and then sell them – together or in parcels – it is not so easy to identify which you have sold and what they cost you.

For this reason, shares of the same class in the same company acquired on or before 5 April 1998 are normally pooled. This means they are treated as a single asset, even if they were acquired at different times. If one share from a pool of ten is disposed of, the gain is taken to be one-tenth of the gain on the whole pool. A similar procedure applies to unit trusts.

The gain made on the whole pool is worked out by comparing its value at the time of the sale with the indexed cost of buying the shares or units that went into it. The following example shows how pooling works.

Shares bought on or before 5 April 1982

Shares owned on or before 5 April 1982 and on or after 6 April 1965 are kept in a separate pool, and treated like other assets owned before 1 April 1982:

- the gain is based on their value on 31 March 1982, unless it is to your advantage to base it on their cost when you bought them (see p. 111)
- indexation allowance runs only from March 1982.

If you have shares in a company bought after 5 April 1982 and some bought on or before that date, any shares you sell are assumed to come from the pool of those acquired after 5 April 1982 first. Only when all those have been sold do you start to sell shares in the pool acquired on or before 5 April 1982.

Shares bought before 6 April 1965

Shares acquired before 6 April 1965 are kept completely separate. They are the last to be sold if you have bought batches since that date – all shares bought after that date are sold first. When you come to sell pre-April 1965 quoted shares, it is assumed the last to be bought are the first to be sold.

However, you can elect for your shares acquired before 6 April 1965 to be added to your pre-April 1982 pool. This is usually to your advantage, as their value on 31 March 1982 is likely to be higher than what you paid for them more than 17 years before.

Example

Diana Nichols bought 2,000 ordinary shares in United Enterprises PLC in June 1983 at a cost of £7,000. In December 1988, she added another 2,000 United Enterprises shares for £10,000. That gave her a pool of 4,000 such shares. She sold 1,000 of them in July 1997 for £7,500.

Since she has sold a quarter of her pool of United Enterprises shares, Diana's taxable gain on the sale will be a quarter of the taxable gain she would have made if she had sold the lot in July 1997. She works out the taxable gain on the whole pool in July 1997 using the following figures for the Retail Price Index (RPI) on the dates of transactions:

- June 1983 – 84.84
- December 1988 – 110.3
- July 1997 – 157.5

First Diana calculates the indexed cost of the pool at each stage in buying and selling the shares. This involves adding indexation allowance to the value of the pool at each transaction.

The first purchase in June 1983 started off the pool with a value of £7,000. The next transaction was the purchase of a second batch of shares in December 1988. By this date, the value of the first batch had increased by the amount of indexation allowance due since June 1983. This is worked out as follows:

$$£7,000 \times \frac{\text{RPI December 1988} - \text{RPI June 1983}}{\text{RPI June 1983}}$$

$$£7,000 \times \frac{110.3 - 84.84}{84.84}$$

$$= £7,000 \times 0.300$$

$$= £2,100$$

Shares sold within ten days of buying them

If you sold shares before 17 March 1998 within ten days of buying shares in the same company, the shares you sold are assumed to be the most recently acquired ones, in the following order:

- any bought on the same day as the sale were sold first
- any others bought in the ten days before the sale went next
- only if you sold more than you bought in the previous ten days did the shares come from the pool.

After 17 March 1998, the new rules on bed and breakfasting (see p. 120) mean any bought within 30 days after the sale of the same shares are treated as having been bought after shares bought on the same day. There is no indexation allowance if you sold shares within ten days of buying them.

By December 1988, the indexed cost of the June 1983 shares was £7,000 + £2,100 = £9,100. The second purchase of shares at £10,000 took the indexed value of the pool to £9,100 + £10,000 = £19,100.

No more United Enterprises shares had been bought by the time of the first sale in July 1997. So the indexation allowance due on the pool since December 1988 was as follows:

$$£19,100 \times \frac{\text{RPI July 1997} - \text{RPI December 1988}}{\text{RPI December 1988}}$$

$$= £19,100 \times \frac{157.5 - 110.3}{110.3}$$

$$= £19,100 \times 0.428$$
$$= £8,175$$

The indexed cost of the pool was therefore £19,100 + £8,175 = £27,275 in July 1997. However, Diana sold only 1,000 of the 4,000 shares in July 1997 – a quarter of the pool. So the indexed cost of the shares she sold was one-quarter of £27,275 = £6,819.

Since she sold the shares for £7,500, her taxable gain is:

$$£7,500 - £6,819 = £681$$

The indexed cost of the remaining 3,000 shares in Diana's pool in July 1997 is:

$$£27,275 - £6,819 = £20,456$$

EXAMPLE

Suppose in the example above that Diana Nichols also had 1,000 United Enterprises shares bought in November 1980. These would be held in a separate pool from the 4,000 shares bought after 5 April 1982 (the two batches dealt with above). The 1,000 shares sold in July 1997 would come from the post-April 1982 pool – so the gain would be as worked out above.

If Diana sold another 3,000 of her United Enterprises shares, those would also come from her post-April 1982 pool. Any further sales would then come from her pre-April 1982 pool. The initial value of the shares from that pool would be their value on 31 March 1982, and indexation would run from that date.

Bed and breakfasting

Until 17 March 1998, many investors used to sell some shares towards the end of the tax year and buy them back the next day to realise a gain which could help them use up the tax-free allowance. This could also be done to realise a loss for offsetting gains made on other assets. This was known as 'bed and breakfasting', since the sale was at the end of one day and the repurchase at the beginning of the next so the shareholder didn't miss out on any rises in the share price.

For disposals of shares on or after 17 March 1998, this can no longer be done. If you sell shares and buy them back within 30 days of the sale, the shares you sell are matched to those you buy back, not shares bought earlier. So if you sell some shares for £5 each which you originally bought for £3 and then buy them back for £5 the next day, the initial value of the shares you sold will be £5 each, not £3 – and there would be no gain realised.

> ## TAX-SAVING IDEA
>
> It could still pay you to sell some shares towards the end of the tax year to use up the tax-free allowance. In the tax year beginning 6 April 1998, you can have chargeable gains of £6,800 tax-free – saving up to £2,720 in capital gains tax. You could buy the same shares back after the 30 days – taking the risk that the shares shoot up in price during the 30 day-period. Or you could buy different shares – perhaps in a similar company. Remember to take the costs of buying and selling shares into account in deciding whether to do this.

Employee share schemes

Employee share schemes allow employees to acquire shares in their companies free or cheaply – and if they are certain types approved by the Inland Revenue, without an income tax bill. However, there could be a capital gains tax bill when the shares are disposed of. The initial cost of the shares and when you are deemed to have received them depends on the type of scheme:

- approved savings-related share option schemes – you acquire the shares at the market value on the day you opted to buy them
- approved profit-sharing schemes – you acquire the shares at the market value on the day they are allocated to you, even though you can't sell them for three years
- approved discretionary share option schemes – you acquire the shares at the price you pay for them on the day you exercise the option. If you paid anything for the option, this an allowable expense.

You can transfer up to £3,000 of shares into a single company personal equity plan (PEP) direct from approved profit-sharing and savings-related share option schemes (see p. 227). The shares transferred in this way will be free of capital gains tax on the transfer or when they are eventually sold. There will be a similar provision with the new individual savings account (see p. 83).

Help Sheet *IR287 Employee share schemes and capital gains tax has more details.*

Rights issues
If you get extra shares through a rights issue or a bonus issue, they are allocated to the relevant pool. So if half your shares are in the post-April 1982 pool and half in a pre-April 1982 pool, the rights issue is split 50:50 between the two pools. Whatever you pay for the rights issue is added to the initial costs of the two pools, with any indexation allowance running from the time the payment is made.

Stock dividends and accumulation unit trusts
If you get extra shares instead of dividends, this is known as a stock dividend (or scrip dividend). The value of the new shares is the amount of dividend forgone excluding the value of the tax credit – the cash equivalent. Indexation allowance runs from the date of the dividend.

Accumulation unit trusts work in a similar way, with extra units allocated to the appropriate pool.

Takeovers and mergers
If you own shares in a company which is taken over, you may get shares in the new parent company in exchange for your old shares. This exchange does not count as a disposal. The new shares are assumed to have been acquired at the cost of the old ones and on the same dates.

If part of the price for the old shares is cash, this is a disposal. For example, if you get half cash, half shares, you have disposed of half the old shares.

When mutuals become PLCs
Some building societies and mutual insurance companies are converting to public limited companies or are involved in other organisational changes that may produce benefits for members. If you receive shares or cash – or both – in such circumstances, there may be a bill for income tax or capital gains tax. Ask the building society or insurance company for guidance.

Payment by instalments
If you have bought newly issued shares, you may have paid for them in instalments. Indexation allowance on the full purchase price runs from when

the shares were acquired only if all the instalments were paid within 12 months of acquisition. If instalments are paid more than 12 months after the shares were acquired, indexation allowance on those instalments runs from when the payments were made.

However, if you paid in instalments when buying newly issued shares in a privatised state enterprise, indexation allowance runs from the date you acquired the shares (even though you hand over some of the money months or even years later).

Monthly savings schemes

If you have invested in unit trusts or investment trusts through a monthly savings scheme, working out your gains and losses could be very complicated. You would have to work out the gain and indexation allowance for each instalment you invested when making a disposal. You can opt for a simplified way of working out the initial costs and indexation allowances which assumes that all 12 monthly instalments for a year are made in the seventh month of the year (the year is the accounting year of the fund).

So if you invested £100 a month in a fund with an accounting year that runs from 1 January to 31 December, you could assume that you invested 12 x £100 = £1,200 in July, the seventh month.

You may have to add in or deduct extra amounts:

- any distribution or dividend reinvested during the year is added to your investment. So a £50 dividend added to your fund in the above example would take the amount you had invested in July to £1,200 + £50 = £1,250
- extra savings over and above the regular instalments are included, provided you don't add more than twice the monthly instalment in any month – a bigger payment is treated as a separate investment
- if you increase the monthly instalments, the extra is added to the year's investment so long as the increase is in or before the seventh month (if later, it is added to next year's fund)
- small withdrawals are deducted if they are less than a quarter of the amount invested in the year by regular instalments (if withdrawals exceed this amount, the simplified calculation cannot be used).

To opt for this simplified method, you must write to your tax inspector within two years of the end of the first tax year after 6 April 1988 in which you dispose of the units or shares and any of the following applies:

- you face a capital gains tax bill
- the disposal proceeds are more than twice the amount of the tax-free

band for the year (£6,500 for the tax year ending 5 April 1998, £6,800 for the tax year beginning 6 April 1998)
* your other disposals in the year create net losses.

WORKING OUT THE GAIN FROM 6 APRIL 1998 ONWARDS

From 6 April 1998 onwards, the way capital gains tax works changes. The following is a brief summary of the new rules, based on the skimpy information released after the 1998 Budget on 17 March. Much of this may change as the full details are worked out and debated. A full explanation of the new rules will be in next year's edition of the Lloyds Bank Tax Guide – in time for you to do the calculations for the 1999 tax return which covers capital gains for the tax year beginning 6 April 1998.

For disposals on or after 6 April 1998, the gain or loss will be worked out broadly as follows:

* the net capital gain or net capital loss on each asset will be worked out as before, by finding the final value and deducting the initial value and any allowable expenses in acquiring, owning or disposing of it
* if the asset was owned before 6 April 1998, you will still be able to deduct indexation allowance – but only up to April 1998
* losses from the same tax year and previous tax years will then be deducted from the net gains – if you have disposed of more than one asset, they will be deducted first from the gains made on the assets acquired most recently after 5 April 1998
* the resulting net gains will then be reduced by taper relief (see below)
* the tax-free allowance (£6,800 for the tax year beginning 6 April 1998) will be deducted from the total of tapered gains and capital gains tax charged on the result.

Taper relief
Taper relief replaces indexation allowance for periods after 5 April 1998. It reduces the amount of the gain which is chargeable to tax according to how long the asset has been owned after that date. The reduction is bigger for business assets, as the table overleaf shows.

This means that with assets acquired on or after 1 April 1998, there will be no indexation allowance. If it is a non-business asset, the percentage of the gain which is chargeable will drop to 95 per cent once you have owned it for two full years after 5 April 1998, 90 per cent after three full years and so on.

Number of complete years asset owned after 5 April 1998	Percentage of gain chargeable	
	Non-business assets	Business assets
0	100	100
1	100	92.5
2	100	85
3	95	77.5
4	90	70
5	85	62.5
6	80	55
7	75	47.5
8	70	40
9	65	32.5
10	60	25

With assets owned before 1 April 1998, you will get indexation allowance up to April 1998 and taper relief for the period of ownership after 5 April 1998. If you owned the asset before 17 March 1998, you will be given one extra year after 5 April 1998. So if you bought the asset on 1 January 1998 and sold it on 1 July 2000, you would be treated as having owned it for three years after 5 April 1998 – the two complete years after that date plus the one extra year.

If you transfer an asset to your husband or wife after 5 April 1998, the taper relief will be based on the number of years you both owned the asset. If you dispose of something you were given on which hold-over relief was claimed (see p. 126), only the period you owned it counts for taper relief.

Shares and unit trusts

Taper relief means that shares and unit trusts acquired on or after 6 April 1998 will no longer be pooled, as before (see p. 116). Each batch bought on or after that date will be treated separately, so that the right amount of taper relief can be given when a disposal is made.

Disposals after 5 April 1998 will be matched with acquisitions in the following order:

- first, shares acquired the same day
- second, shares acquired at any time in the next 30 days – part of the new measure to stop 'bed and breakfasting' (see p. 120)
- third, shares acquired before the day of sale and after 5 April 1998 – with the most recent acquisitions first (last in, first out, or LIFO)
- fourth, shares in the pool acquired between 6 April 1982 and 5 April 1998

- fifth, shares acquired between 6 April 1965 and 5 April 1982
- finally, shares acquired on or before 5 April 1965.

HOW TO REDUCE OR DELAY YOUR CAPITAL GAINS TAX BILL

There are a number of ways to reduce or delay a CGT bill. For a start, it is important to claim all the allowable expenses you can (p. 108), indexation allowance (p. 110) and taper relief (p. 123). Also, take advantage of the special rules for disposing of assets owned before 31 March 1982 (p. 111). Then use the tax-free capital gains allowance you can make each year (see p. 114) and don't overlook losses which you can set off against gains (see p. 114).

These are all ways to minimise your tax bill once you have made a disposal. But there are several steps you can take before reaching a disposal to keep your tax bill down:

- take advantage of the allowances of your husband or wife (below)
- make the best use of losses (see p. 126)
- pass the tax bill for gifts of business assets and certain other gifts on to the recipient if possible, or pay it in instalments if not (p. 126)
- invest the gains from any disposals in growing businesses if you don't need the proceeds immediately – you may be able to defer the tax bill by claiming reinvestment relief on buying shares in certain types of small companies (p. 127)
- claim the special reliefs which can reduce your tax bill if you are disposing of a business or farm (see p. 128).

It will help in minimising your capital gains tax bill if you keep a record of the assets you have acquired which may fall into the tax net, together with relevant receipts (for example, for allowable expenses).

Husbands and wives

Husbands and wives are treated as separate individuals for capital gains tax (see p. 105). They pay tax on their own gains and can deduct their losses only from their own gains. They have their own tax-free allowances to deduct from their own net chargeable gains.

But if a married couple living together dispose of assets to each other, this

> **TAX-SAVING IDEA**
> Since there is no capital gains tax on gifts between husband and wife, you can effectively double your tax-free band if you are married by giving assets to your spouse to dispose of. So in the tax year which began on 6 April 1998, a married couple can effectively make £13,600 of disposals.

is ignored for the purposes of capital gains tax. For example, if a husband buys shares worth £10,000 in June 1998 and gives them to his wife at a later date, her gain or loss when she sells them will be calculated as if she had bought them for £10,000 in June 1998. Anything they pay each other on such transfers is ignored.

A married couple is treated as living together unless legally separated or where the separation appears to be permanent. Gifts between husband and wife in the year of separation are free of capital gains tax, but after this, tax may be payable. For more about marriage and capital gains tax, see Help Sheet *IR281 Husband and wife, divorce and separation*.

Making the best use of losses

If your allowable losses in a tax year look likely to mean you will not be able to use the whole tax-free allowance for the year, there are two options:

- make more disposals to increase your chargeable gains – by selling some shares that have done well, for example
- hold back on loss-making disposals to a later year when there are no gains or they can be used to reduce future gains.

Gifts

If you give away certain assets or sell them for less than their market value, you can avoid paying capital gains tax by claiming hold-over relief. This means the recipient is treated as having acquired the assets when you did and having paid the costs you paid (less anything paid to you). The recipient's agreement is necessary, since he or she is taking over the tax bill for your period of ownership.

Hold-over relief is available only for the following gifts, however:

- business assets (see p 129)
- heritage property
- gifts to political parties
- gifts which result in an immediate inheritance tax bill (mainly gifts to certain trusts and companies).

If the person you have made the gift to becomes non-resident without having sold or given it away, you might have to pay a capital gains tax bill.

There is no point in claiming hold-over relief if your net taxable gains for the year, including the gift, will be within the tax-free band (£6,500 for the tax year ending 5 April 1998, £6,800 for the tax year beginning 6 April 1998). There would be no capital gains tax for you to pay, but you might add to the tax the person you are making the gift to has to pay eventually.

If you make a gift of land or certain types of shareholdings which doesn't qualify for hold-over relief, you may be able to pay the capital gains tax in ten annual instalments. The shareholdings which qualify are a controlling shareholding in a company or minority holdings in unquoted companies. Interest is charged on the unpaid tax, except with agricultural property. For more about hold-over relief, see Help Sheet *IR295 Relief for gifts and similar transactions.*

Reinvestment relief

If you're facing a capital gains tax bill that you can't reduce by claiming losses or other reliefs, consider the gain in the shares of certain types of small companies. You can claim reinvestment relief which allows you to defer the tax bill.

To get the relief you have to invest in the ordinary shares of unquoted companies – companies which are not listed on the UK Stock Exchange or any other recognised stock exchange. Investments in companies quoted on the Alternative Investment Market (AIM) are eligible, provided they meet the other requirements for reinvestment relief. The main one is that the company must be trading in certain qualifying sectors or be a holding company for such trading companies.

For investments to qualify for reinvestment relief from 6 April 1998 onwards, they must be in shares that are eligible for tax relief under the Enterprise Investment Scheme (see p. 81). The most important change is that the shares must be newly issued.

To get reinvestment relief, you must make the investment any time between one year before and three years after the disposal that produces the gain. The amount of the gain that you reinvest will be taxed only when you eventually sell the shares – although you could then defer the tax bill again by reinvesting any gain in more qualifying shares and claiming further reinvestment relief. Otherwise, the deferred gain will be taxed only if you emigrate or the company ceases to be a qualifying one during the three years after you acquired the shares.

To claim reinvestment relief, you must tell your tax inspector within five years after the 31 January in the year following the tax year in which you make the disposal or acquire the shares. So if you made the disposal and bought the shares in the tax year ending 5 April 1998, you have until 31 January 2004 to make the claim. Use the form at the end of Help Sheet *IR291 Reinvestment relief.*

Businesses and farms

If you are disposing of a business or farm, you could face an enormous tax bill on the gain. There are two important reliefs to reduce the impact on entrepreneurs and others who create small businesses:

- retirement relief when you retire from your business (below)
- roll-over relief if you replace business assets (opposite).

What follows is a brief introduction to indicate their scope. But with large sums at stake, it would pay to seek professional advice on these reliefs to ensure you meet the complex requirements.

Retirement relief

Retirement relief reduces the tax bill if you dispose of a business when aged 50 or more, or less if you are retiring because of ill-health. It is to be phased out over four years from 6 April 1999, since the new taper relief will allow up to 75 per cent of the gain on selling business assets to be free of capital gains tax (see p. 123). But until retirement relief disappears, it is a valuable concession for businesses.

The maximum relief is for people disposing of a business owned for at least ten years. Until the tax year beginning 6 April 1999, up to £250,000 of the capital gain can be tax-free and only half the gain between £250,000 and £1,000,000 is taxable. If you have owned the business for less than ten years, the amount on which you can get relief is reduced by 10 per cent for each year less than ten – the example opposite shows how this works.

In the tax year beginning 6 April 1999, the £250,000 exemption limit will be reduced by £50,000 to £200,000 and the £1,000,000 half-exemption limit reduced by £200,000 to £800,000. Similar reductions will follow each tax year thereafter, so the relief will end by the tax year beginning 6 April 2003. Over this period, the amount of gain free of tax under taper relief – which is subject to no maximum – will begin to build up.

With retirement relief, a husband and wife can each make claims if they are eligible – effectively doubling the limits for a married couple who share ownership of the business. And you do not have to retire to claim it unless you are making your claim when aged under 50.

If you are selling or disposing of your business before 50, you must be retiring because of your ill-health (which is strictly defined) to claim the relief. If you wish to claim this relief because of ill-health, you must do so on or before the second 31 January after the end of the tax year in which you dispose of the business. So if you disposed of the business in the tax year end-

E X A M P L E

Harry Singh, aged 65, started a business 30 years ago and sold it in May 1997. The gain after indexation allowance was £500,000. He is entitled to the maximum retirement relief as he had the business for more than ten years.

Harry can claim full relief on the first £250,000 plus relief on half the gain between £250,000 and £1,000,000:

$$£250,000 + 50 \text{ per cent of } (£500,000 - £250,000)$$
$$= £250,000 + 50 \text{ per cent of } £250,000$$
$$= £250,000 + £125,000$$
$$= £375,000$$

Harry's taxable gain is:
$$£500,000 - £375,000 = £125,000$$

The first £6,500 of taxable gains in the tax year ending 5 April 1998 is free of capital gains tax, so tax is charged on:
$$£125,000 - £6,500 = £118,500$$

Harry's taxable income is £45,000 on which he pays tax at the higher rate of 40 per cent. His tax bill is therefore:
$$40 \text{ per cent of } £118,500 = £47,400$$

ing 5 April 1998, you can claim retirement relief on ill-health grounds up to 31 January 2000.

Retirement relief applies to business assets, and to shares in a company in which you have at least 5 per cent of the voting rights, providing you have been a full-time director or an employee of the company for the past ten years.

You can still get retirement relief if you have owned several different businesses in the last ten years. Providing that each business qualifies for the relief, and the gap between each is not more than two years, you can add together the separate periods of business activity over the past ten years to calculate the total period that counts for the relief.

Roll-over relief

Roll-over relief allows you to defer the capital gains tax bill when you sell or otherwise dispose of assets from your business, providing you replace them in the three years after the sale or the one year before it. You can claim this roll-over relief even if you do not buy an identical replacement as long as you use the proceeds to buy another qualifying business asset. Assets which qualify include land or buildings used by the business, goodwill, fixed plant and machinery.

You usually get the relief by deducting the gain for the old asset from the acquisition cost of the new one. So when you come to sell the new asset, the gain on it has been increased by the gain on the old asset. However, if you replace again, you can claim further roll-over relief, and currently capital gains tax will not have to be paid until you fail to replace the business asset.

You can make a claim for roll-over relief up to six years after the end of the tax year in which you dispose of the asset or the year in which you replace it if this is later.

INHERITANCE TAX

There is no space on the 1998 tax return for inheritance tax. This is because it is largely a tax on what you leave when you die (including gifts made in the seven years before). And few people are affected by inheritance tax – just one in 45 estates currently falls in its net.

Do not ignore it, however. The tax rate is a hefty 40 per cent of anything over £223,000. There is plenty that can be done to reduce the amount paid – as long as you plan carefully. As one former chancellor said a few years ago: 'It is largely paid by people of modest means who either cannot or simply do not make careful plans to avoid it.'

This chapter tells you how inheritance tax works and how to reduce the amount that goes to the Inland Revenue. It also has some guidance on what can be done to reduce an inheritance tax bill after the event; there is some scope to ease the burden even then.

HOW INHERITANCE TAX WORKS

When you die, everything you own – your home, possessions, investments and savings – goes into your estate. So does money paid out by life insurance policies unless they are written in trust (see p. 136), and the value of things you have given away but reserved the right to use for yourself (gifts with reservation – see p. 138). Debts such as outstanding mortgages and funeral expenses are deducted from the total to find the value of your estate.

Some or all of your estate may be free of inheritance tax: anything left to your husband or wife, or to a UK charity, for example (for a full list of what is tax-free, see p. 133). These tax-free bequests and legacies are deducted from the value of your estate before the tax bill is worked out.

Then any gifts to other people in the seven years before your death which are not tax-free are added. So are gifts made to a trust for a disabled person, or to an accumulation and maintenance trust for children and grandchildren under 25.

If the resulting total exceeds a certain limit – £223,000 for deaths on or after 6 April 1998 – inheritance tax is payable on the amount over the limit at 40 per cent. (For deaths in the tax year ending 5 April 1998, the limit was £215,000.)

So if the total is £250,000, tax is payable on £250,000 – £223,000 = £27,000. This gives a tax bill of 40 per cent of £27,000, that is £10,800.

Inheritance tax due on what you leave on death is paid out of your estate. But if inheritance tax is due on a gift made before your death, it must be paid by the person you made the gift to. They may be able to reduce the amount payable if the gift was made more than three years before death by claiming tapering relief:

Years between gift and death	*% of inheritance tax payable*
Up to 3	100%
More than 3 and up to 4	80%
More than 4 and up to 5	60%
More than 5 and up to 6	40%
More than 6 and up to 7	20%

Inheritance tax may also have to be paid on gifts to certain types of trust made more than seven years before death. The tax, which must be paid at

---

EXAMPLE

Angela Framing died in April 1998, leaving an estate worth £287,000 (largely the value of her home counties house). In December 1993, she had made a taxable gift of £10,000 to help a grandchild with the cost of studying for an MBA at a leading business school. Subsequently, in August 1994, she gave another grandchild a taxable gift of £5,000 to start a business.

The calculation of the inheritance tax due starts with the earliest taxable gift – the £10,000 made just over four years before her death. There is no tax to pay on this gift, since it is well below the £223,000 threshold for inheritance tax applying in April 1998 when she died. Nor is there any inheritance tax to pay on the 1994 gift of £5,000. It brought her total of taxable gifts to £15,000 – still well below the £223,000 tax threshold.

In calculating the tax due on Angela's estate, the £15,000 of taxable lifetime gifts is added to the £287,000 left on death to produce a total of £302,000. The first £215,000 of that is free of tax, leaving £302,000 – £223,000 = £79,000 on which tax is due.

Tax at 40 per cent on £79,000 is £31,600 – tax that will be entirely paid out of Angela's estate.

the time of the gift, can also affect the tax payable on death. If you are involved with such trusts, you should seek professional advice from an accountant or solicitor – this chapter does not deal with their complexities.

Gifts free of inheritance tax

Gifts that are always tax-free:

- gifts between husband and wife – even if the two are legally separated. But only the first £55,000 is tax-free if the gifts are to someone who is not domiciled in the UK (domicile reflects the individual's natural home, see p. 306)
- gifts to UK charities
- gifts to certain national institutions such as the National Trust, National Gallery, British Museum (and their Scottish, Welsh and Northern Irish equivalents)
- gifts of certain types of heritage property such as paintings, archives, land or historic buildings to non-profit-making concerns like local museums
- gifts of land in the UK to registered housing associations
- gifts of shares in a company into a trust for the benefit of most or all of the employees which will control the company.
- gifts to established political parties.

Gifts that are tax-free on death only:

- lump sums paid out on your death by a pension scheme provided the trustees of the scheme have discretion about who gets the money
- refunds of personal pension contributions (and interest) paid directly to someone else or a trust – in other words, not paid into your estate
- the estate of anyone killed on active military service in war or whose death was hastened by such service.

Gifts that are tax-free in lifetime only:

- anything given to an individual more than seven years before your death – unless there are strings attached (see p. 138)
- small gifts worth up to £250 to any number of people in any tax year. But you can't give anyone more than this limit and claim exemption on the first £250 – if you give someone £500, the whole £500 will be taxable unless it is tax-free for one of the other reasons below
- regular gifts made out of normal income. The gifts must come out of your usual after-tax income and not from your capital. After paying for the gifts, you should have enough income to maintain your normal standard of living
- gifts on marriage to a bride or groom: each parent of the bride or groom can give £5,000, grandparents or remoter relatives £2,500 and anyone else £1,000. The gifts must be made before the great day – and if the mar-

riage is called off, the gift becomes taxable
- gifts for the maintenance of your family – an ex-husband or wife, certain dependent relatives and children under 18 or still in full-time education. The children can be yours, stepchildren, adopted children or any other children in your care
- up to £3,000 in total a year of other gifts. If you don't use the whole £3,000 annual exemption in one year, you can carry forward the unused part to the next tax year only. You can't use the annual exemption to top up the small gifts exemption. If you give someone more than £250 in a year, all of it must come off the annual exemption if it is to be free of inheritance tax.

PLANNING FOR INHERITANCE TAX

If your estate is likely to be well below the threshold for paying inheritance tax, there is no need to worry about it. But if it looks as if you are above it, there is much you can do to reduce the tax bill. An important first step is to draw up a will which will make you think about what you own and how you want it to be disposed of after you die.

> ### TAX-SAVING IDEA
> Draw up a will. There are simple steps you can take to minimise the tax payable on your estate when you die and to reduce the complications for those you leave behind.

Most of the ways of minimising inheritance tax involve making gifts which are free of tax or making taxable gifts more than seven years before your death. But remember your heirs will still be better off even if tax is due on your estate. Don't give away so much that you or your spouse are left impoverished in old age, merely to cheat the Inland Revenue of every last penny of tax.

Tax-free gifts
If you do have some resources to spare, make as full use as possible of the tax-free small gifts, gifts on marriage and such like. And make sure your spouse has enough to make similar gifts free of inheritance tax.

If you want to make larger gifts, the earlier you make them the better – because inheritance tax may have to be paid on a gift if you die within seven years of making it. (For this

> ### TAX-SAVING IDEA
> Make as full use as possible of the gifts you can make which do not fall into the inheritance tax net. Gifts on marriage and those made out of normal income are tax-free.

reason, lifetime gifts are often described as potentially exempt transfers (PETs). They are potentially free of inheritance tax but you must survive for seven years after they are made for the tax to be avoided.)

Even if you die within seven years of making a gift, the inheritance tax paid by the person you made the gift to will be reduced by tapering relief (see p. 132) if the gift is made more than three years before your death. Note that gifts in your lifetime, other than cash, may mean a capital gains tax bill.

Share your wealth
A married couple can share their wealth – what they give to each other is free of inheritance tax. Each can then make tax-free gifts and leave a taxable estate of up to £223,000 without paying inheritance tax.

In practice, it may not be easy to split your worldly goods and give them away during your lifetime. It may make more sense to pass all or most of them on to the survivor so he or she has enough to live on. But this principle of estate-splitting is a basic strategy to be followed where possible.

> # EXAMPLE
> Veronica McGrath wants to give away as much as possible free of inheritance tax before she dies.
>
> First, she gives £1,000 a year to each of her three children – taking advantage of the £3,000 a year annual exemption. Then she makes £250 gifts every year to each of her ten grandchildren – a total of £2,500 a year free of inheritance tax as small gifts. She also gives the maximum £2,500 to any of her grandchildren who get married.
>
> She can afford to pay the premiums on insurance policies on her own life out of her normal income. So she takes out policies written in trust (see p. 136) for each of her three children. The premiums come to £60 a month each and will be tax-free as regular gifts made out of normal income (when she dies, the money from the insurance policies will be paid straight to the children without being taxable).
>
> Overall, Veronica manages to give away almost £7,000 a year free of inheritance tax. This is nearly £50,000 in a seven-year period, and even if she dies within seven years of starting this programme of gifts there will be no inheritance tax to pay on them.

Your home
Your home is almost certainly your most valuable possession – and may be the main reason why your estate ends up over the threshold for paying inheritance tax. But it is one of the hardest assets to remove from the tax net – assuming you intend to go on living in it until you die.

For example, you can't make a life-time gift of it to your children on condition you can continue to live in it. That would count as a gift with reservation (see p. 138), and the home would be treated as yours.

You might be able to reduce the size of your estate somewhat by sharing the ownership of the house. If your home is jointly owned with someone under a joint tenancy, your share automatically goes to the survivor when one of you dies. But if you jointly own your home with some-one else as a tenancy in common, you can bequeath your half-share to anyone you please.

For example, if you had a tenancy in common with your spouse, you could bequeath half of your half-share to your spouse and the other half to the next generation. This would reduce the size of your spouse's estate but leave him or her in control of the home.

There is no inheritance tax to pay if you leave part or all of a home to your spouse, since gifts between hus-band and wife are always tax-free. But a gift to anyone who is not your husband or wife is taxable.

Life insurance

If you want to make sure there is enough money to pay an inheritance tax bill on a home or business, you can take out a term life insurance policy which pays out if you die within seven years of giving it away. And if you plan to leave a large asset on death, whole life insurance policies pay out whenever you die, again providing cash to pay the inheritance tax.

> ## EXAMPLE
> Alan and Meg Riordan realise they are going to face a hefty inheritance tax bill when they die, since most of their assets are in Alan's name. They decide to start an active pro-gramme of making tax-free gifts and estate-splitting.
>
> They adopt a similar approach to Veronica McGrath in making gifts. Since each of them can make these tax-free gifts, they are soon passing on around £100,000 to their children and grandchildren every seven years.
>
> They also divide their assets between them, and bequeath a fur-ther £200,000 each to their chil-dren in their wills, with the rest to each other. When the first dies, the £200,000 bequest to the children will be below the threshold for inheritance tax.
>
> The second to die will thus leave £200,000 less to fall into the tax net. And the Riordans will have saved £100,000 from inheritance tax for each seven years of the life-time gifts programme.
>
> By starting 15 years before their deaths, the Riordans manage to pass on £400,000 more without tax than if they had left it all in Alan's name. This saves their heirs £160,000 in inheritance tax.

Make sure you have any such policies written in trust to the person you want to have the money. The proceeds will then be paid directly to that person on your death and be free of inheritance tax. If the policy is not written in trust, the money will be added to your estate and inheritance tax charged on it (there will also be a delay before your heirs can get their hands on it until probate is granted).

The premiums for a policy written in trust count as gifts, but will be free of inheritance tax if the policy is for your spouse. And if you pay the premiums out of your normal spending, they will be tax-free whoever benefits.

Shares

The market value of any shares left on death (or given away in the previous seven years) must normally be included in your estate in working out the inheritance tax bill. But some sorts of shares qualify for business relief, which reduces the value for inheritance tax purposes – or even removes them from the calculation altogether:

- shares in a listed company which form a controlling interest – for gifts made on or after 10 March 1992 and inheritance tax bills which arise out of deaths on or after that date, the value of the shares is halved
- shares quoted on the Unlisted Securities Market (USM) or Alternative Investment Market (AIM) – no inheritance tax provided they have been held for at least two years
- unquoted shares and those traded on the Over the Counter (OTC) markets are also eligible for business relief on the same basis as AIM shares.

Your own business or farm

If you own or have an interest in a small business or a farm, seek professional advice on inheritance tax, since there are substantial concessions which can reduce or eliminate the tax:

- business relief means there will be no inheritance tax to pay on business assets such as goodwill, land, buildings, plant, stock, patents and so on (reduced by debts incurred in the business)
- agricultural relief can mean no inheritance tax on the agricultural value of owner-occupied farmlands and farm tenancies (including cottages, farm buildings and farm houses). There are also reliefs for landowners who let farmland.

Estate freezing

Estate freezing is a way of freezing some of the value of your wealth now so the increase in value in future years benefits someone else.

A simple way of doing this is by investing in an endowment or unit-linked life insurance policy written in trust for your children or grandchildren (see Life insurance, above). Any growth in its value accumulates in the policy free of inheritance tax. Some unit trust managers can do something similar with investments in unit trusts.

A more ambitious approach is to set up an accumulation and maintenance trust for your children or grandchildren. You put some capital in and any income from it is either reinvested or used for the maintenance, education or benefit of the beneficiaries at the discretion of the trustees. When the beneficiaries reach the age of 25, either the capital is shared out or they become entitled to the income from it. If you live for more than seven years after making gifts to such trusts, there is no inheritance tax to pay.

If you are thinking of setting up a family trust, consult a professional tax adviser such as a solicitor or accountant.

INHERITANCE TAX PLANNING PITFALLS

You might think that there are some rather obvious wheezes that will help you avoid inheritance tax. It is unlikely that the Inland Revenue will not have thought of them and blocked their use.

Gifts with strings attached

If you give something away but reserve the right to use it, it counts as a gift with reservation – and is treated as remaining your property. The gift would not be recognised for inheritance tax purposes and its value would be added to your estate when you died.

For example, if you give your home to a child on condition that you can go on living in it until your death, this would count as a gift with reservation. This could apply even if there was no formal agreement that you go on living in the home. If the gift was made after 17 March 1986, it counts as subject to a reservation if you go on using it.

Associated operations

If you try to get round the inheritance tax rules by making a series of gifts, the Inland Revenue is allowed to treat them as associated operations which form a single direct gift.

For example, you might think you could give an extra £5,000 to an adult child by making ten tax-free gifts of £250 to friends which they pass on. The taxman will treat this as a single £5,000 gift, however – and one subject to inheritance tax.

Related property
In working out the value of a bequest or gift, the Inland Revenue treats as yours property which it reckons is related to yours – in particular, anything owned by your husband or wife. This means you can't reduce its value by splitting it up with your spouse.

Suppose, for example, you own 30 per cent of the shares in a company and your spouse owns another 30 per cent. The Inland Revenue will value your 30 per cent as worth half the value of a 60 per cent controlling interest, which is generally higher than the value of a 30 per cent minority interest. Property will also be treated as related if it has been owned at any time in the previous five years by a charity, political party or national institution to which you or your spouse gave it.

EASING THE PAYMENT OF INHERITANCE TAX

Inheritance tax is due six months after the end of the month in which the death happened. In practice, it can often take longer for the executors or personal representatives to sort out the will and tidy up the dead person's affairs. As part of the process of seeking probate, they must submit an Inland Revenue account, listing the value of the dead person's property (including property owned jointly with anybody else) and the amounts of any debts. Probate will not be granted until the tax has been paid.

Interest is charged if the tax is paid after the six-month deadline, running from the time the tax was due. Likewise, if you pay too much inheritance tax, you will get interest on the over-payment from the Inland Revenue.

If you take out a loan to pay inheritance tax before probate is granted, you can get tax relief on the interest on it for up to 12 months.

Payment by instalments
You can spread the pain of paying inheritance tax over ten equal yearly instalments with two sorts of assets:
- land and property
- a business, including certain holdings of unquoted shares.

This option is allowed only with bequests on death and lifetime gifts where the recipient still owns the property when the death occurs. Interest has to be paid on the delayed tax with land and property, unless it is business property or agricultural land.

If you want to pay in instalments, tell the Inland Revenue before the normal payment date for the tax. The first instalment is due on the date the whole tax would have been payable.

Reducing the tax on bequests that have fallen in value

If you inherit investments or land and buildings which fall in value after the death of the person who bequeathed them, you might be able to reduce your inheritance tax bill.

For investments, this applies to quoted shares (including those quoted on the AIM) and authorised unit trusts which fall in value or become worthless in the year after death:

- if sold during this period for less than they were worth on death, the sale price can be used to value them for inheritance tax purposes instead of their value on death
- if cancelled without replacement, they are treated as having been sold immediately before the date of cancellation for the nominal sum of £1
- if suspended and remaining suspended a year after the death, their value at the first anniversary can be used for inheritance tax purposes instead of their value on death.

When this relief is claimed, however, all such investments sold in the year after death are revalued in this way. So if some shares or unit trusts have been sold for more than they were worth on death, this would offset any loss made on other shares or unit trusts.

For land or buildings, you can ask for the inheritance tax bill to be recalculated if you sell them within four years of the death for less than their probate value. The inheritance tax bill will be worked out on the actual sale proceeds instead. Again, if this relief is claimed, all land or property sold during the four-year period is revalued for inheritance tax purposes at what it was sold for, rather than what it was worth on death.

Facing a second inheritance tax bill within five years?

If you inherit something that has only recently been subject to inheritance tax, the tax due on this second change of ownership is reduced by what is known as quick succession relief. Provided the death which led to the first payment was within five years of the death that has led to a second tax bill, the second bill can be reduced by a fraction of the first bill.

If the first death was within one year of the second death, the second bill is reduced by the following fraction of the first bill:

$$\frac{\text{Value of inheritance at the time of first transfer}}{\text{Value of inheritance at transfer + tax paid on first transfer}}$$

If the first death was more than one year before the second death, the fraction is reduced by 20 per cent for each complete year between the two. The example, right, shows how quick succession relief works.

Changing inheritances after a death

If you are facing an inheritance tax bill, one option to reduce it is to vary the inheritances covered. Whether or not there is a will, those who are entitled to a share of a dead person's estate can agree to vary the way the estate is divided up.

For example, the variation could direct some of the estate towards tax-free bequests – from the children to the dead person's husband or wife, for example. Or it might be used to jump a generation, so it goes straight to the grandchildren rather than adding further to the wealth of the children and the amount of tax that would have to be paid on their deaths.

The procedure is to draw up a deed of variation in writing, which must be signed within two years of the death by all those who will lose out. If it increases the amount of tax, the personal representatives of the dead person

EXAMPLE

Maurice Thornton inherits a half-share of his mother's estate, worth £150,000. Inheritance tax of £16,000 is due on this share.

However, Maurice's mother had inherited £80,000 from her father only two and a half years earlier – an inheritance on which tax of £20,000 had been paid. Because Maurice's legacy is within five years of his mother's own legacy, he is entitled to reduce the inheritance tax on his legacy by a fraction of what was paid on hers.

The fraction of the tax bill on his mother's legacy which can be taken into account is worked out as follows:

$$\frac{£80,000}{£80,000 + £20,000}$$
$$= \frac{£80,000}{£100,000}$$
$$= \frac{4}{5}$$

This, expressed as a decimal, is 0.8, which is reduced by 20 per cent for each complete year between Maurice's mother's legacy and her death. Since this period was two and a half years, the 0.8 is reduced by 2 x 20 per cent = 40 per cent. Forty per cent of 0.8 is 0.32.

Thus the tax on Maurice's estate is reduced by 0.8 – 0.32 = 0.48 of the tax due on the legacy when he got it (£20,000), that is, £9,600. This results in a tax bill of £16,000 – £9,600 = £6,400.

must also sign it. It should clearly state which inheritances are being changed and how.

A variation can be carried out only once, so it is important to get it right. A solicitor can advise on drawing up the document – if children under 18 and unmarried are involved, it will be necessary to obtain a court order.

HOW TO FILL IN YOUR TAX RETURN

When you receive your tax return for the tax year ending 5 April 1998, this is what you should have:

- an eight-page booklet entitled Tax Return. We show you how to complete these pages in Chapters 13 to 16
- a Tax Calculation Guide. There are three versions of the tax calculation guide. We show you how to complete this tax calculator in Chapter 27 and give you some examples in Chapter 28
- supplementary pages for the tax return to cater for your individual circumstances – there are nine sets of supplementary pages (see below). We explain how to complete these pages in Chapters 17 to 25
- a Tax Return Guide. This consists of 30 pages which explain how to complete the eight pages of the tax return (see above) plus how to fill in the Employment supplementary pages.

What you should do next
Step 1
Make sure you have the correct supplementary pages.

Step 2
If one or more of the supplementary pages you need are missing, contact the Inland Revenue. The Orderline is open every day from 8 am to 10 pm, except on Christmas Day. The phone number is 0645 000 404.

Step 3
Gather together all your records and supporting documentation, which you need to fill in the tax return.

Step 4
Fill in your supplementary pages FIRST, using the advice in Chapters 17 to 25 of this Guide.

Step 5
After filling in the supplementary pages, complete the tax return.

Step 6
If you are not going to work out your tax bill yourself, send in your tax return and supplementary pages by 30 September 1998.

Step 7
If you want to calculate your own tax, use Chapter 27 and the tax calculation working sheet in your Tax Calculation Guide.

Step 8
If you are an employee and the tax you owe is £1,000 or less, choose to send in your tax return, supplementary pages and tax calculation by 30 September. Then you can ask to pay your tax bill through the PAYE system on a monthly basis starting in April 1999.

Step 9
Otherwise send in your tax return, supplementary pages and tax calculation by 31 January, and send your final tax payment for the tax year ending 5 April 1998 at the same time.

THE SUPPLEMENTARY PAGES

On page 2 of the basic tax return you are asked nine questions. You have to answer yes or no to each of these questions. If you answer YES to a question you will need to fill in the corresponding supplementary page. If you have not been sent that page or pages automatically you will need to ask for it from the Orderline (see p. 00).

Employment

Q 1   Were you an employee, or office holder, or director, or agency worker in the year ended 5 April 1998?   NO   YES   EMPLOYMENT YES

You are required to fill in the Employment supplementary page if you come into any of the above categories. The Inland Revenue will regard you as an employee even if you work on a part-time or casual basis. There are more guidelines on who counts as an employee in Chapter 17 (p. 203).

Share schemes
If you receive your shares or options under one of the special approved schemes which is tax-free and you kept to the rules of scheme, you aren't

required to complete this supplementary page. You will have to fill it in if in the tax year ending 5 April 1998 you have received shares or options in any other way or you have broken the rules of an approved scheme. Chapter 18 on p. 226 gives a lot of background information on share schemes and guides you through the completion of this supplementary page.

Self-employment

If you carried on a trade, profession or vocation as a self-employed person during the tax year ending on 5 April 1998 you need to complete this supplementary section. Chapter 19 on p. 236 has guidelines on who counts as self-employed.

If you are in partnership you need to complete a different set of supplementary pages (see below).

Partnership

If you are in business with one or more partners, you should answer YES to this question and complete a set of supplementary pages. There is a short version and a long version. You will find guidance on which version you should complete in Chapter 20 (p. 265).

Land and Property

You need to complete this supplementary page if you receive income from land and property, furnished holiday accommodation, or providing furnished accommodation in your home during the tax year ending 5 April 1998. However, if you provide additional services, such as meals, you will need to complete the Self-employment supplementary pages, as you are considered to be carrying on a trade. You can get more guidance by turning to Chapter 21 (p. 267).

Foreign

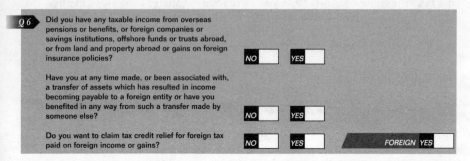

There are four supplementary pages which have space to give details about your foreign savings, pensions and benefits, property income and other investment income from abroad. Ask for it if you received any such income in the tax year ending 5 April 1998. You will need to fill it in even if you got no income, but you first got income from this source before 6 April 1994. If you turn to Chapter 22 (p. 280) you will find more information on what is foreign income and how it is taxed.

Trusts etc

You need to complete this supplementary page if you were a beneficiary, a settlor or had income from the estates of someone who had died. You can find more information and guidance on filling in the supplementary page in Chapter 23 (p. 288).

Capital gains

You must complete this supplementary page if you have made a capital gain (with some exceptions – see below) or you wish to claim an allowable capital loss for the tax year ending 5 April 1998.

You won't need to return the supplementary page if your gains were less than £6,500 (which is the tax-free slice for the year) and if the gain was from selling your home and it is free of tax and the other assets which you disposed of (leaving out assets which on which gains are tax-free) were less than

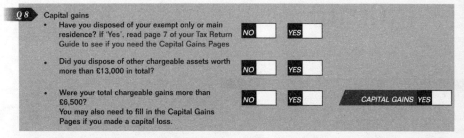

£13,000 altogether for the year. For more information on which gains are tax-free and guidance on whether the gain on selling your home will be taxable or not, see Chapter 24 (p. 294).

Non-residence etc

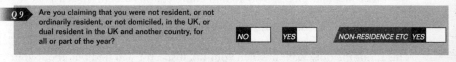

For the tax year ending 5 April 1998, if you consider yourself to be not resident in the UK, or not ordinarily resident (or not for part of the year), or not domiciled or resident but resident in a country with which the UK has a double taxation agreement, then you will need to complete this supplementary page. Chapter 25 (p. 303) will give you guidance.

INCOME

CHAPTER 13

The first stage in working out your income tax bill for the tax year ending 5 April 1998 is to find your taxable income. The basic tax return on pages 3 and 4 sets out various different types of income, such as income from savings and investments, pensions and benefits, maintenance income received and other bits and pieces. You should complete this section to tell your tax inspector what types of income and how much of each type you received. You may find it helpful to read Chapter 8.

This is not the only way in which your tax inspector will find out about your income. It is your obligation to notify any new source of income within six months of the end of the tax year in which you first get it. There are also supplementary pages, including Employment, Self-employment and Land and property, where you must give details of other sorts of income.

You don't need to enter in the tax return any income which is tax-free. A comprehensive list is given in Appendix A (see p. 370).

INCOME *for the year ended 5 April 1998*

When entering your income in the tax return, you should enter the amount you received in the year ending on 5 April 1998 (although in a few cases there are special rules for what counts as received). If you receive income of the same type from more than one source – for example, you have several savings accounts – enter totals for each type, but keep records for each separate account in case your tax office asks to see them.

SAVINGS AND INVESTMENT INCOME

Q 10 Did you receive any income from UK savings and investments? NO ☐ YES ☐ If yes, fill in boxes 10.1 to 10.32 as appropriate. Include only your share from any joint savings and investments

You can get an income from your investments or savings in the form of interest or dividends; for example, interest on a building society account or dividends from shares. Although the income from both these sources can be paid out to you, this is not always the case. For example, interest can be added to your account rather than paid out, and with distributions from unit trusts (a form of dividends) it can be reinvested if you choose. It counts as income whether it is paid out to you or not. If you have any investment income (unless it is tax-free, see p. 151), you should tick the YES box at Q10 and fill in boxes 10.1 to 10.32.

Only enter details of investments you own. If you own an investment jointly, you need to enter only the amount in the tax return which is your share. If you are married, the income from a jointly-owned investment will be split equally. But if you own an investment in a different proportion, the income can be split to reflect ownership (see p. 44).

There are many opportunities for tax saving and tax planning with investments. Turn to Chapter 5 and Chapter 8 which should help you maximise your tax-efficient investing.

If you are the beneficiary of a bare trust, that is one in which you have an immediate absolute title to (a share of) the capital and income, you should enter the amount of your share of the income on page 3. Your trustee will be able to give you the details of your share.

Your income from investments includes income from investments which you have given to your children (aged 17 or less on 6 April 1997). You need to enter details if the amount of the income is £100 or more before tax in a tax year.

> ### TAX-SAVING IDEA
> Take advantage of the many ways you can save which are free of tax: pensions, TESSAs, PEPs, many National Savings products. These are especially helpful if you are a higher rate taxpayer. But watch out for possible changes in the tax rules – see Chapter 8 for changes to TESSAs and PEPs. If you are a basic rate taxpayer, check to see that any expenses, for example on managing a PEP, are not more than the tax you save.

Which investment income should not be included on page 3 of your tax return?

You shouldn't include in your tax return any investment income which is tax-free (see box on p. 151). If all your investment income is tax-free, tick the NO box at Q10.

These other types of income may be taxable but should go elsewhere in the tax return. They include:

- income from an annuity under a personal pension plan or retirement annuity contract or trust scheme. These should be included on page 4 under Q11
- gains on UK life insurance policies or life annuities or capital redemption policies. These should be included on page 4 under Q12
- a share of any partnership investment income should be entered in the Partnership pages
- accrued income charges on British Government stocks should be included on page 4 of the tax return under Q13
- annual payments from UK unauthorised unit trusts should go on page 4 under Q13.

The documents you need
Get together all your dividends vouchers, interest statements or tax deduction certificates and trust vouchers.

EXAMPLE

Sidney Barrow has the following investments and accounts: National Savings Certificates, a personal equity plan, a TESSA account and a bank current account which pays interest on credit balances. If he didn't have the bank current account he could tick the NO box. But the interest payable on his bank current account means that he has to tick the YES box.

TAX-SAVING IDEA

Married couples who have different tax rates should adjust their investments between the two of them so the investments are in the name of the person paying the lower rate of tax.

INTEREST

■ *Interest*

If you closed an account in the tax year ending 5 April 1998
You may be affected by special rules if you closed an account which you had opened before 6 April 1994 and which paid out interest gross. The main

TAX-FREE INVESTMENT INCOME

Some investment income is free of income tax. This income does not have to be entered in the tax return at all. Income from the following investments is tax-free:

- premium bonds
- a TESSA account (tax exempt special savings account), but not if you closed your account before the five years was up
- a PEP (personal equity plan), but not if you withdraw more than £180 in interest
- SAYE schemes
- National Savings Ordinary account (but only up to the first £70 of interest)
- National Savings Certificates, including the index-linked ones
- National Savings Children's Bonus Bonds
- Ulster Savings Certificates, if you normally live in Northern Ireland and you bought the certificates or they were repaid while you were living there
- dividends on shares in venture capital trusts.

There are other less obvious forms of investment income which are also tax-free and don't need to be entered in the tax return:

- interest awarded by a UK court as part of a claim for damages for personal injury or death. There is an extra-statutory concession which means that this can also apply to awards from a foreign court
- if you are a trustee, before-tax interest which is paid out direct to beneficiaries from the payer, but through your authority.

investments covered by these rules are taxable National Savings accounts (listed on p. 154), British Government stocks not bought through a stockbroker and some bank accounts.

Before self-assessment, such income was taxable on the basis of income received in the preceding year. In the year of closing an account you were taxed on the actual amount paid, and your tax office would revise your tax bill for the year before that to tax you on the actual amount paid if this would result in a higher tax bill. These closing-year rules might still affect you if:

- you closed your account in the tax year ending 5 April 1998. In this case, your tax bill for the tax year ending 5 April 1997 may need to be revised upwards. Enter in the Additional information box on page 8 of the return the source of the income, the date it ended and the amount of interest received in the tax year ending 5 April 1997. Also include the 1997-98 income in the appropriate box on page 3 of the tax return

- you closed your account in the tax year ending 5 April 1997. You should have been taxed on the actual amount received in that year, but, in order to move to the new system of taxing you on the basis of the current income received, the tax return instructed you to enter half the total amount received between 6 April 1995 and 5 April 1997. If you did so, you might have paid too much tax. Enter in the Additional information box the source of the income, the date it ended and the amount of interest received in the final year.

Banks and building societies

Interest from UK banks, building societies and deposit takers

Most saving income is now paid with tax deducted and the current rate of tax is 20 per cent. Income from most accounts in UK banks, building societies, finance houses, organisations offering high-interest cheque accounts and other licensed deposit takers is paid after deduction of tax. There is no further tax bill to pay if you pay tax at the lower or basic rate only on your income, which applies to most taxpayers. If you pay tax at the higher rate, there will be extra tax to pay, at the rate of 20 per cent (see p. 67).

	Taxable amount
– where **no tax** has been deducted	10.1 £

You may have received interest from your bank or building society paid gross, that is without tax deducted. The most common circumstance where this might apply is if you have registered to receive interest gross because you are a non-taxpayer (see p. 68).

Add up all the interest you have received without tax deducted from your bank, building society or deposit taker in the tax year ending 5 April 1998 and enter it in box 10.1.

If you are a beneficiary of a trust and you are entitled to income as it arises, you should include in box 10.1 any untaxed interest paid direct to you because the trustee has authorised the payer to do so.

Don't include National Savings interest here.

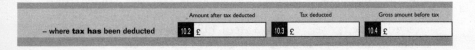

	Amount after tax deducted	Tax deducted	Gross amount before tax
– where **tax has** been deducted	10.2 £	10.3 £	10.4 £

You can get the information for these boxes from your statements or pass books or ask your bank, building society or deposit taker direct to give you a tax deduction certificate. Enter the totals for all three figures in the boxes.

You may have received cash or shares when two or more building societies have merged or a building society has converted to a company or been taken over by a company. You may have to pay either income or capital gains tax and your building society should be able to tell you this. If you have received a cash payment on which you should pay income tax, put the details in boxes 10.2 to 10.4. If you don't know whether you have to pay income tax, put the details under Q13 on page 4, but also tick box 22.3 on page 8 and explain the situation in the Additional information box. Any capital gain should be entered in the Capital gains supplementary pages. If you have received shares, you may need to supply details only when you dispose of the shares.

Unit trusts

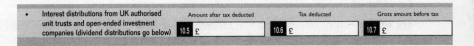

Some types of unit trusts and open-ended investment companies pay interest rather than dividends. These include unit trusts which invest in British Government stocks and other fixed-interest distributions. In these cases, 20 per cent tax has been deducted from the income before you get it in the same way as for bank or building society interest (see left) and you will get a tax voucher telling you the amount paid. You may be able to claim some or all of it back, or you may have to pay more tax in the same way as for bank or building society interest.

The interest may not be paid out to you but automatically reinvested in accumulation or other units. However, you still have to enter the interest in your tax return.

Add up all the interest you receive after tax has been deducted and enter the total in box 10.5. Put the tax deducted in box 10.6. Then add together boxes 10.5 and 10.6 and enter the sum in box 10.7 (gross amount before tax). If you received interest without any tax deducted, enter nil in boxes 10.5 and 10.6 and enter the before-tax amount in box 10.7.

When you buy units in a unit trust, part of the purchase price includes an amount of income which the trust has received but not yet paid out. The first payment you receive will include an equalisation payment, which is not income, but is a refund of the original purchase price you paid. It is not taxable, so do not enter it here. (But it is deducted for CGT purposes).

National Savings

National Savings (other than FIRST Option Bonds and the first £70 of interest from a National Savings Ordinary Account)

Taxable amount

10.8 £

You will receive interest paid before deduction of tax from the following National Savings investments:

- Ordinary Account
- Investment Account
- Deposit Bonds
- Income Bonds
- Capital Bonds
- Pensioners' Guaranteed Income Bonds

Tot up the before-tax interest you received (or added to your account) in the tax year ending 5 April 1998. See p. 150 if you closed an account. You don't include the first £70 of interest on a National Savings Ordinary Account, as this is tax-free (as are many other National Savings investments – see box on p. 151).

Enter the total amount you received in box 10.8.

National Savings FIRST Option Bonds

Amount after tax deducted	Tax deducted	Gross amount before tax
10.9 £	10.10 £	10.11 £

This investment is an exception among the range of National Savings investments. Interest is paid with tax deducted. Enter in box 10.9 the amount you received, in box 10.10 the amount of tax deducted and in box 10.11 the amount of interest before tax.

British Government stock and other interest-paying investments

Other income from UK savings and investments (except dividends)

Amount after tax deducted	Tax deducted	Gross amount before tax
10.12 £	10.13 £	10.14 £

There is a hotch-potch of interest from other investments which should be entered here. Depending on the nature of the interest, it may be paid without tax being deducted or after tax is deducted. Tot up the relevant amounts and enter in boxes 10.12 to 10.14. If no tax has been deducted, put the interest in box 10.14 only and put nil in boxes 10.12 and 10.13. Remember the special rules on p. 150 if you closed an account. If tax has been deducted fill in all the boxes.

Here is a list of the investments to include:

- certificates of tax deposit when the certificate is applied to payment of a tax bill
- British Government stock (see below)
- other loan stocks (see p. 156)
- loans to an individual or organisation
- income from credit unions or friendly societies
- interest from Enterprise Zone trusts
- discount on relevant discounted securities (enter in box 10.14)
- discount from gilt strips (enter in box 10.14)
- income from securities to which you have sold or transferred the right to the income, but not the security – even if you have not received the income (enter in box 10.14)
- purchased life annuities (see p. 156).

British Government stock

Tax at the rate of 20 per cent for the tax year ending 5 April 1998 has already been deducted from the interest on most British Government stocks (or gilts) before you receive it. Your interest payment should be accompanied by a tax voucher which lets you know how much tax has been deducted. If you are a non-taxpayer, you should be able to claim back the amount deducted. If you are a basic rate taxpayer, there is no more tax to pay. Enter the appropriate amounts in the three boxes 10.12, 10.13 and 10.14.

There are a few examples where the interest is paid without any tax deducted. If you buy your British Government stocks through the Post Office (the National Savings Stock Register), the interest will be paid before tax. With $3^1/_2$ per cent War Loan (as well as, since 7 June 1997, a few other stocks), however purchased, the interest is before tax. And with small amounts of interest (£2.50 gross each half year) there is no tax deducted. From 6 April 1998 all interest from British Government stocks will be paid before tax, unless you have asked to have it after tax. If you are already receiving interest after tax, you will carry on receiving it this way unless you ask to have it paid before tax.

If you own fixed-interest securities with a nominal value in excess of £5,000, and you buy or sell them, there are special tax rules designed to stop tax avoidance by turning income into capital gains. Ask your tax inspector to send you Inland Revenue leaflet *IR68 Accrued Income scheme*.

Other loan stocks

There are other loan stocks, such as local authority loans and stocks, which you can buy as well as British Government stocks. These pay interest with tax deducted. If you are a non-taxpayer, you can reclaim the tax deducted and you can arrange for the interest to be paid before it is deducted.

Annuities

An annuity is an investment made with a life insurance company. You invest a lump sum and in return the insurance company will pay you an income. Sometimes this could be for a particular period, say ten years, or it could be until you die. The income which you receive is considered to be in two parts: some of it is your original investment being returned to you. There is tax to pay on only the interest.

The annuity payment is made to you with tax at the rate of 20 per cent of the interest part already deducted. The tax voucher which accompanies the payment will tell you how much tax has been deducted. If you are a non-tax-payer you can claim back the tax deducted.

With an annuity which you buy as part of your pension, the tax treatment is different. Tax will be deducted from the whole payment through the PAYE system. Details of annuities bought under personal pension schemes or retirement annuity contracts should be entered on page 4 of the tax return under Q11.

DIVIDENDS

■ *Dividends*

You will receive share dividends from UK companies and distributions from authorised unit trusts with no more basic rate tax to pay because you also receive a tax credit. The payments are accompanied by a tax voucher which sets out the amount of the tax credit (and for the year ending 5 April 1998 the amount is 20 per cent, the same as on other forms of savings). You work out the gross amount of dividend by adding together the net dividend and the tax credit (see p. 69).

If you are a beneficiary of a trust and you are entitled to income as it arises, include in these boxes any dividends or distributions shown on your trust voucher.

Shares in UK companies

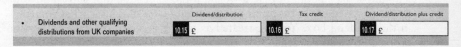

	Dividend/distribution	Tax credit	Dividend/distribution plus credit
• Dividends and other qualifying distributions from UK companies	10.15 £	10.16 £	10.17 £

Your dividend voucher should show the amount of the dividend and the tax credit. Put these in boxes 10.15 and 10.16 and add them together to enter the sum in box 10.17. Note that foreign income dividends or scrip dividends are included below in boxes 10.21 to 10.26.

Companies can make other kinds of distributions as well as dividends, for example, payment in kind. A distinction is drawn between qualifying and non-qualifying distributions. A non-qualifying distribution is broadly one which gives a future rather than a current claim on the company's assets, such as a bonus issue of redeemable shares. Qualifying distributions should be entered in boxes 10.15 to 10.17 (non-qualifying distributions are entered below in boxes 10.30 to 10.32).

Unit trusts

	Dividend/distribution	Tax credit	Dividend/distribution plus credit
• Dividend distributions from UK authorised unit trusts and open-ended investment companies	10.18 £	10.19 £	10.20 £

Distributions from most authorised unit trusts are treated in the same way as dividends (see p. 69). If you have invested in an accumulation unit trust, you don't receive the income but the unit trust managers reinvest it for you in more units. However, for tax purposes this is treated in exactly the same way as if you received the cash. You will receive a tax voucher with a tax credit.

Your dividend vouchers show the amount of the dividend and the tax credit. If you own units in more than one unit trust, add up the distributions and tax credits and enter the totals for each in boxes 10.18 and 10.19. Add them together to get the entry for box 10.20. Don't enter any equalisation payments (see p. 154).

Scrip dividends

If you receive new shares instead of cash as a dividend, this is known as a

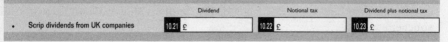

	Dividend	Notional tax	Dividend plus notional tax
• Scrip dividends from UK companies	10.21 £	10.22 £	10.23 £

scrip dividend. The value of the scrip dividend is known as the cash equivalent and is the amount of cash dividend forgone. It should be shown on your dividend statement as the appropriate amount of cash. This is what you enter in the dividend box. You are treated as having received the cash equivalent grossed up at 20 per cent.

If you pay tax at the basic rate only, there is no further tax to pay. If you pay tax at the higher rate of 40 per cent, there will be 20 per cent extra tax to pay. But unlike a cash dividend you cannot claim back any tax credit if you are a non-taxpayer.

Enter in box 10.21 the appropriate amount of cash. In box 10.22 enter the notional tax. For the tax year ending 5 April 1998, this is found as follows:

$$\left(\text{cash equivalent} \times \frac{100}{80} \right) - \text{cash equivalent}$$

Or you can take 25 per cent of the cash equivalent.

Enter this figure in box 10.22. Add together boxes 10.21 and box 10.22, and enter the sum in box 10.23.

EXAMPLE

Barry Badger is a non-taxpayer. He has a few shares in Wonderland plc, a company listed on the stockmarket. The company offers a choice of a cash dividend of £80, paid with a tax credit of £20, or a scrip dividend which would give a cash equivalent of £80 and notional tax paid of £20. Barry chooses the cash dividend, because as a non-taxpayer he can claim back the tax credit of £20, giving him an income of £100. He could not claim back the notional tax paid on the scrip dividend.

Foreign income dividends

	Dividend	Notional tax	Dividend plus notional tax
• Foreign income dividends from UK companies	10.24 £	10.25 £	10.26 £

If a company pays share dividends out of profits from a foreign source, the company can pay dividends under the foreign income scheme. From the shareholder's point of view, these are the same as ordinary dividends, except that non-taxpayers cannot claim back the tax credit.

Your dividend voucher should show the dividend (put in box 10.24) and the notional tax (put in box 10.25). Add these together and put the sum in box 10.26.

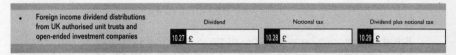

Your dividend voucher should show the amount of the foreign income distribution (put in box 10.27) and the tax treated as paid or notional tax (put in box 10.28). Add boxes 10.27 and 10.28 together to get the figure to enter in box 10.29. Note that the notional tax cannot be reclaimed by a non-taxpayer.

If you have invested in an accumulation unit trust and don't actually receive the distribution because it is automatically reinvested, you should still show the distribution in your tax return.

Don't enter the amount of any equalisation payment (see p. 154).

Non-qualifying distributions

A non-qualifying distribution is broadly one which gives a future rather than a current claim on the company's assets, such as a bonus issue of redeemable shares. The amount of the distribution is the nominal value of the securities you received less any consideration (for example, cash) you paid. If you pay tax at the lower or basic rate, there is no more tax to pay. If you pay tax at the higher rate, an amount of lower rate tax is treated as already paid by you and set against your tax bill.

Enter the amount of the distribution in box 10.32. Multiply box 10.32 by 20 per cent to get the amount of notional tax to enter in box 10.31. Leave box 10.30 blank.

For loans written off, contact your tax adviser or tax office.

PENSIONS AND SOCIAL SECURITY BENEFITS

INCOME *for the year ended 5 April 1998, continued*

Q 11 Did you receive a UK pension, retirement annuity or Social Security benefit? NO ☐ YES ☐ If yes, fill in boxes 11.1 to 11.13 as appropriate.

If you received none of these, tick the NO box and go to Q12.

But if you received one or more of these, you will need to find out whether what you received should be entered here in your tax return. Some pensions and benefits are not taxable.

What pensions and benefits should not be included in your tax return

If you received any of the following, you do not need to give details here in the tax return because they are tax-free:

- additions to your state pension or social security benefits which you get because you have a dependent child
- Christmas bonus for pensioners
- family credit and childcare allowance
- maternity allowance
- social fund maternity payments
- student grants
- school uniform grants
- child benefit
- child's special allowance (only payable to those already claiming before 6 April 1987)
- one-parent benefit
- war orphan's benefit
- guardian's allowance
- war widow's pension and some pensions paid to other dependants of deceased Forces and Merchant Navy personnel. Ask the Orderline for Help Sheet *IR310 War Widow's and Dependant's pensions*
- widow's payment
- severe disablement allowance
- pensions and benefits for wounds or disability in military service or for other war injuries
- industrial disablement benefit
- incapacity benefit for the first 28 weeks (but not taxable after that time if you were receiving invalidity benefit before 13 April 1995 unless there is a break in your claim; incapacity benefit replaced invalidity benefit)
- disability living allowance
- disability working allowance

- attendance allowance
- housing benefit (rent rebates and allowances)
- council tax benefit
- most income support
- payments from the social fund
- jobfinder's grant, most YT training scheme allowances, employment rehabilitation and training allowances
- similar benefits paid by foreign governments.

Refunds of surplus additional voluntary contributions are not entered here. Details should be put in boxes 12.10 to 12.12. Overseas pensions and taxable benefits paid under the rules of another country should be entered in the Foreign supplementary pages (covered in Chapter 22).

What pensions and benefits should be entered in your tax return
Details of the following should be entered here:

- state retirement pension, the basic pension and state earnings related pension
- old person's pension for people aged 80 or over
- widow's pension
- widowed mother's allowance
- industrial death benefit
- jobseeker's allowance (this has replaced unemployment benefit and income support if you are out of work)
- invalid care allowance
- statutory sick pay and statutory maternity pay paid by the DSS
- taxable incapacity benefit
- pension from a former employer or a pension from your late husband or wife's employer
- pension from a personal pension scheme or retirement annuity contract or trust scheme
- pension from a free-standing additional voluntary contribution
- pension for injuries at work or for work-related illnesses
- pension from service in the armed forces
- income withdrawals from a personal pension plan where the purchase of an annuity has been delayed.

If you receive any of the above pensions or benefits, tick the YES box in answer to Q11.

The documents you need
You will need to gather together certain information such as the details of your state pension and your P60, which your pension payer may have given

you, or any other certificate of pension paid and tax deducted. Details of any taxable amounts of social security benefits, such as jobseeker's allowance, incapacity benefit or any other taxable state benefits will also be required – ask your benefit office.

State pensions and benefits

Enter the amount of pension or benefit you were entitled to for the tax year ending 5 April 1998, whether or not you actually received that amount in the year. You should enter the total of all the weekly amounts which you were entitled to in the year, even if you chose to receive your pension or benefit monthly or quarterly.

State retirement pension

		Taxable amount for 1997-98
• State Retirement Pension	11.1	£

The state retirement pension is taxable but paid without tax deducted. So if you have other income you will find that tax on your state retirement pension might be collected from your other income.

In box 11.1, you should enter the amount you were entitled to receive in the tax year ending 5 April 1998, but excluding any amount paid for a dependent child and the Christmas bonus.

A married woman might receive a pension which is based on her husband's contributions and not her own (but not any dependency allowance which he receives for her before her 60th birthday). She can claim a personal allowance to deduct from her pension and the pension should be entered in her tax return, not her husband's.

Widow's pension

• Widow's Pension	11.2	£

Enter the full amount you were entitled to receive in the tax year ending 5 April 1998, including any earnings-related additional pension, in box 11.2.

For more information on the benefits available to widows, ask for leaflet *NP45 A guide to widow's benefits* from your local Benefits Agency office.

Widowed mother's allowance

- Widowed Mother's Allowance   11.3 £

You should include in box 11.3 the flat rate basic allowance which you were entitled to and any earnings-related increase. But don't include any child dependency increase.

Industrial death benefit

- Industrial Death Benefit Pension   11.4 £

In box 11.4 you should enter the yearly pension you are entitled to receive under the industrial death benefit scheme. But do not include industrial death benefit child allowance which is tax-free.

Jobseeker's allowance

- Jobseeker's Allowance   11.5 £

Jobseeker's allowance is taxable but paid without any tax deducted. There are two kinds of allowance, one based on your National Insurance contribution record and one means-tested. There is a limit on the overall amount that is treated as taxable.

Income support is not taxable if you are 60 or over, a single parent living with a child under 16 or staying at home to look after a severely disabled person. Any amount you receive over the standard weekly amount of jobseeker's allowance for a couple or single person is not taxable.

The benefit office will usually have given you a statement of the total jobseeker's allowance paid and the taxable portion. You should enter the taxable amount in box 11.5. If you haven't received a statement, tell your tax office. You have 60 days to check your statement to see if it is correct.

Invalid care allowance
Enter the amount you were entitled to receive in the tax year ending 5 April

• Invalid Care Allowance	11.6 £

1998. Include any addition for a dependent adult, but exclude any additional amount for a dependent child, because this is tax-free.

Statutory sick pay and statutory maternity pay

• Statutory Sick Pay and Statutory Maternity Pay paid by the Department of Social Security	11.7 £

Generally, these are paid by your employer and taxed under the PAYE system (see p. 21). They will be included in your P60 or P45. Details should be entered in the Employment supplementary pages.

But if your employer didn't pay you, and the Department of Social Security did so instead, enter the total received here in box 11.7.

Taxable incapacity benefit

	Tax deducted	Gross amount before tax
• Taxable Incapacity Benefit	11.8 £	11.9 £

Some incapacity benefit is tax-free. You will not pay tax on it when you receive it during your first 28 weeks of incapacity or you are receiving it for a period of incapacity which began before 13 April 1995, and for which invalidity benefit used to be payable.

The Department of Social Security will give you a form showing you whether your incapacity benefit is taxable or not. If it is taxable, enter the amount of the benefit in box 11.9 and any tax that has been deducted in box 11.8.

Other pensions

■ *Other pensions and retirement annuities*

Apart from the state pension, you can get a pension from your employer, from what you have paid into a personal pension scheme or a retirement annuity contract.

You should enter here details of pensions paid to you by someone in the UK who is not paying on behalf of someone outside the UK. Pensions received

	Amount after tax deducted	Tax deducted	Gross amount before tax
• Pensions (other than State pensions) and retirement annuities	11.10 £	11.11 £	11.12 £

from abroad will be entered in the Foreign pages (see p. 283).

You should total the amount you receive from all your pensions (excluding state pension) and put it in box 11.10. You should include in the total:

- annuity payments from a personal pension scheme
- if you have taken advantage of the ability to defer buying the annuity, perhaps because annuity rates were low, the income withdrawals which you receive during the deferred period
- any annual payments from a retirement contract or trusts scheme.

Put the amount of tax deducted in box 11.11. The information about an employer's pension should be on Form P60 and for other pensions from a certificate given to you by the pension payer. Adding up boxes 11.10 and 11.11 should give you the total for box 11.12, unless you have received some non-cash benefit. If you have, you'll need to ask your tax office what to do.

There are some special pensions which can be partially free of UK tax.

Tax-free pensions
Part of your pension may be tax-free if you receive it as a former employee who was awarded a pension on retirement because you were disabled by injury on duty or a work-related illness. If that pension is more than the amount you would receive if you had retired at the same time on the grounds of ordinary ill-health, the extra amount is free of tax. You should not enter any tax-free amounts in the tax return, unless you also qualify for the 10 per cent deduction below. In this case, enter the full pension received in box 11.12 and the tax-free part in box 11.13.

	Amount of deduction
• Deduction – see the note for box 11.3 on page 14 of your Tax Return Guide	11.13 £

10 per cent deduction
This applies to some UK pensions for service for certain overseas governments. Only 90 per cent of the pension is taxed.

Enter the full pension received in box 11.12 and the 10 per cent deduction in box 11.13.

OTHER INCOME TO BE ENTERED HERE

Q 12 Did you receive any of the following kinds of income?   NO   YES   If yes, fill in boxes 12.1 to 12.12 as appropriate.

The income includes taxable maintenance or alimony, gains on UK life insurance policies, life annuities or capital redemption policies or refunds of surplus additional voluntary contributions.

If you tick the NO box you should go to Q13.

Maintenance income

	Income receivable	Exempt amount	Income less exempt amount
• Taxable maintenance or alimony	12.1 £	12.2 £	12.3 £

Maintenance you receive could be taxable. It depends on whether your maintenance agreement was made under the old rules or the new rules.

If you receive maintenance under the new rules you do not pay tax and you do not need to enter the amount in your tax return. Even if you remarry and carry on receiving maintenance from your former husband or wife, for example, for your child, the maintenance received will be tax-free.

A maintenance agreement is made under the new rules if:
- it was made on or after 15 March 1988 (unless it merely alters or replaces an arrangement to which the old rules apply)
- it was made before 15 March 1988, but you didn't tell your tax inspector about it in writing by 30 June 1988
- it is a court order which was applied for after 15 March 1988
- it was a court order made after 30 June 1988 (unless it is merely altering or replacing an arrangement to which the old rules apply)
- it is assessed by the Child Support Agency
- the person paying the maintenance has opted for it to be taxed under the new rules.

If the maintenance you receive is made under a legally-binding agreement not in the list above, it will be taxed under the old rules. This means that you may have to pay income tax on it and will need to enter the details in boxes 12.1 to 12.3.

Under the old rules, the first £1,830 in the tax year ending 5 April 1998 is tax-free. Anything else you receive above this is taxed at your top rate of tax, except that, if what you receive in maintenance has increased since the tax year ending 5 April 1989, you pay no tax on this extra bit. If you remarry and you carry on receiving maintenance, the first £1,830 will no longer be tax-free.

If your child receives maintenance under the old rules paid direct to him or her, rather than to you for his or her benefit, there is no tax-free band. What he or she receives, up to the amount received in the tax year ending 5 April 1989, counts as taxable income, but the child can set his or her personal allowance against it (giving a tax-free band of £4,045 in the tax year ending 5 April 1998.

If you are receiving maintenance from your parents and are over 21, you do not have to pay tax on it.

If your maintenance is taxable, you have to pay tax on the lower of:
- the amount you were due to receive and did receive between 6 April 1988 and 5 April 1989, or
- the amount you were due to receive and did receive between 6 April 1997 and 5 April 1998.

In box 12.1 put in the lower of these two amounts. If you receive maintenance from more than one source under the old rules, treat each maintenance payment separately when working out the taxable amounts. Add together the taxable amounts and put the total in box 12.1.

The first £1,830 for the tax year ending 5 April 1998 is tax-free if:
- you received it from your separated or former husband or wife; and
- it is for yourself or for the support of a child aged under 21 of whom you are both the parents, or whom you have treated as part of the family; and
- you have not remarried; and
- you did not, during the tax year ending 5 April 1998, live again with your separated husband or wife who pays the maintenance.

If all these apply to you, you can claim your tax-free bit of maintenance. In box 12.2 put the lower of the taxable maintenance you received (the figure in box 12.1) or £1,830.

Deduct box 12.2 from box 12.1 and enter the difference in box 12.3.

There is an example on p. 168 and more information in Chapter 6.

Life insurance policies

Gains on life insurance policies, contracts for life annuities or capital redemption policies are treated as investment income and may be taxable.

The tax treatment of life insurance policies depends on whether they are qualifying or non-qualifying. Most types of life insurance which involve you paying regular premiums are qualifying; if you pay just a single premium, it will almost certainly be a non-qualifying policy, which has less favourable tax treatment.

Taxation of qualifying policies

The life insurance company will have paid tax on the income and gains which its life fund makes as they arise. And so, with qualifying policies, there is not usually any income or capital gains tax to pay when the policy matures – that is, it comes to the end of its agreed period or the person insured by the policy dies.

The exception to this is if you cash in or make a policy paid up before the end of the agreed period. A policy might be treated as non-qualifying if this happens before ten years or, if this is less, three-quarters of its term.

Taxation of non-qualifying policies

The tax treatment of non-qualifying policies is less favourable than for the qualifying ones and it is possible that income tax might be due when you receive the proceeds. Most insurance policies are treated as having already paid basic rate tax, but the basic rate tax is notional only and cannot be reclaimed by a non-taxpayer or lower rate taxpayer.

But if you are a higher rate taxpayer, or become one when you add the proceeds of your policy to your other taxable income, there will be higher rate tax due on it. There may also be a loss of age allowance (see p. 42).

The proceeds are treated as a chargeable gain and the amount of the gain is usually what you receive less what you have paid during the life of the policy. If the person insured has died and the policy pays out, the gain is taken as the cash-in value of the policy, if this is less than you receive.

You may be able to draw an income from your non-qualifying policy by cashing part of it. Under the current rules, these withdrawals won't be taxed at the time as long as you have not cashed in 5 per cent or more of what you paid for each year of the policy. But at the end of the policy, the amount you have withdrawn will be added to the gain to work out the tax due. If you don't cash the full 5 per cent each year, you can carry forward the unused amount, meaning that you might be able to cash more than 5 per cent in a later year without paying tax at the time. However, you will eventually be taxed on what you have received during the life of the policy, unless you are no longer a higher rate taxpayer when it comes to an end (see below). Selling a non-qualifying policy is treated the same as a policy maturing or being cashed in.

The gain on a non-qualifying policy is added to your taxable income for the year. But there is no basic rate tax due. For the tax year ending 5 April 1998, there will be higher rate tax to pay if your taxable income and the gain come to £26,100 or more.

If the policy is treated as having had basic rate tax deducted, the rate of tax to pay is 40 − 23 = 17 per cent for the tax year ending 5 April 1998. This could still mean a large tax bill in the year of the gain. But you may be able to benefit from top-slicing relief which spreads the gain you make over the years of the policy. Broadly, you work out the average gain for each year you have held the policy, calculate the amount of tax that would be due if the average gain was added to your income and multiply this by the number of whole years the policy was held. The tax return asks you to enter the number of years so that top-slicing relief can be worked out.

Although most gains from UK insurances are treated as having had basic rate tax deducted, gains from certain life annuities and friendly societies' tax exempt policies are not treated in this way, that is, there is no notional tax paid. Your insurance company should be able to tell you how your gain is treated. And you may have received a chargeable event certificate showing your gains and the other information you need to fill in your tax return.

If you have made a gain and it is not treated as having had basic rate tax deducted, put the amount of the gain in box 12.5 and the number of complete years since the insurance was made in box 12.4.

If you have made a gain and it is treated as having had basic rate tax deducted, put the amount of the gain in box 12.8 and the notional tax in box 12.7 (23 per cent of the amount in box 12.8). Enter the number of complete years in box 12.6.

Where you have made more than one sort of gain, or you hold a cluster of policies, things become complex. You will probably need to put additional information in the section on page 8 of the tax return. Ask the Orderline (see p. 143) for a copy of Help Sheet *IR320 Gains on UK life insurance policies*. Consult your tax office or tax adviser for more guidance.

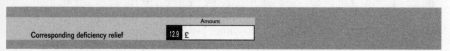

	Amount
Corresponding deficiency relief	12.9 £

If you had a life insurance policy on which you made a loss on final surrender, you may be able to claim a relief to ensure that the amount treated as income is not more than the total gain made under the policy. Ask for Help Sheet *IR320 Gains on UK life insurance policies*.

Repayment of additional voluntary contributions

	Amount received	Notional tax	Amount plus notional tax
• Refunds of surplus additional voluntary contributions	12.10 £	12.11 £	12.12 £

Additional voluntary contributions are extra payments you can make to your employer's or your own free-standing additional voluntary contribution scheme (see p. 179). A condition of the contributions is that they cannot buy you pension benefits greater than the maximum limits set by the Inland Revenue for approved schemes. If you inadvertently contribute so much in additional voluntary contributions that the benefits would exceed the limits, the excess will be paid back to you at retirement, with a deduction to cover the tax relief the contributions have enjoyed.

Your certificate from your pension scheme provider should show you the amount of surplus contributions and the tax refunded to you. Enter the total amount in box 12.12, the amount actually repaid to you in box 12.10 and the tax deducted in box 12.11.

Any other income

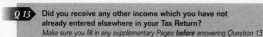

Q 13 Did you receive any other income which you have not already entered elsewhere in your Tax Return?
Make sure you fill in any supplementary Pages before answering Question 13.

NO □ YES □

If yes, fill in boxes 13.1 to 13.6 as appropriate.

You should have already filled in the appropriate supplementary pages for income from employment, self-employment, trusts, abroad and so on. You may have other odd bits of income not yet entered. For example:

- freelance or casual income
- profits from the odd literary or artistic activity
- income received after you close a business (post-cessation receipts). This could include money which you have recovered from a bad debt or royalties arising after the business ceased from contracts made before it ceased. You can claim to have this treated as income for the year in which the business ceased (tick box 22.5 on page 8 of the tax return). Or you can enter the total here
- any recovery of expenses or debts for which you claimed relief as post-cessation expenses
- sale of patent rights if you received a capital sum
- receipts from covenants entered into for genuine commercial reasons which are in connection with the payer's trade, profession or vocation. Losses cannot be set against this income
- rental from leasing equipment you own
- income from guaranteeing loans, dealing in futures and some income from underwriting
- accrued income on the transfer of securities (but not if the nominal value of securites in the tax year ending 5 April 1998 was £5,000 or less)
- annual payments received in the year including annual payments received from UK unauthorised unit trusts, and annual payments paid by former employers which do not count as a pension. Expenses and losses cannot be deducted from this income.

You should also enter in this section any cashbacks or other incentives which you received to take out a mortgage if there is tax to pay. Ask the person who gave you the incentive or check with your tax office to find out if it is taxable. Include it in box 13.3.

Some part of income received under a permanent health insurance policy may be taxable and should be entered here. This does not include income from a policy which you paid for yourself, as that is tax-free. Income from your employer for sickness and disability should go on the Employment pages. But if you have left your employer and you are still receiving benefits because you are covered by your former employer's scheme, you should enter that amount here (part might be tax-free if you contributed to the cost of the scheme). Check with your tax office if you are not sure how much is taxable, and ask for leaflet *IR153 Tax exemption for sickness or unemployment insurance payments*.

If you received any other income which should be taxed but which you have not put anywhere else, you should tick the YES box at Q13.

You need to keep careful records of the income and the expenses.

If you are self-employed and make losses in your business, one option available to you is to deduct the loss from any other income which you have in that year or the next year. See p. 260 for your other options. You can deduct the losses from all the income listed above except from the covenant income received, the annual payments and benefits from a permanent health insurance policy.

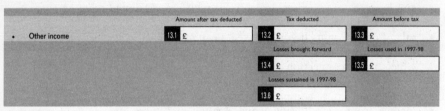

Enter the amount of income after any tax deducted and after any allowable expenses or capital allowances in box 13.1. If you made a loss put nil. In box 13.2, put the amount of tax deducted from the payments you received. Add together boxes 13.1 and 13.2, to find the figure for box 13.3.

If you made a loss in box 13.3, you can deduct it from some other income in a future year. Put it in box 13.6.

If you have made losses in earlier years, either from your business or other income, enter the amount of unused allowable losses brought forward in box 13.4. If you have any income in box 13.3, and unused losses brought forward in box 13.4, you can deduct the losses from box 13.3, reducing it to nil (and thus cutting your tax bill). Put in box 13.5 the amount of losses you are using this year. Note that you only use these pages for losses from your business if you haven't used the supplementary pages.

If you have several types of other income, the calculation can become complex. Help Sheet *IR325 Other income* has a worksheet to help you.

RELIEFS

You can pay less tax by spending more money on things the government wants to encourage – and thus gives tax relief on – such as pensions and training. In some instances you can get tax relief at your highest rate of tax, which could be 40 per cent. Assuming that you want to spend the money, buying any of these things could be highly advantageous. You claim for them on page 5 of the basic tax return.

You get your tax relief in different ways. Frequently you get basic rate tax relief by deducting it from what you spend. Any higher rate tax relief that is due you will claim here in the tax return and give yourself the relief when you are working out your tax bill. Or you could get higher rate relief through your PAYE code. Non-taxpayers will not have to repay the tax deducted, except in the case of covenants and Gift Aid.

If you don't get basic rate relief by deducting it from what you pay, you will claim the relief here in the tax return and get it by deducting the amount from the tax you owe on 31 January or through your PAYE code.

> **TAX-SAVING IDEA**
> You can go back six years to claim deductions which you forgot to claim at the time or didn't know you were able to. You will get tax relief at the rate you should have got it if you had claimed the deduction at the right time.

The documents you need
You must gather together all the supporting documents you need to be able to prove to your tax inspector that you are entitled to the relief you are claiming. These could include:

- certificates of premiums paid from your pension provider
- receipts of payments paid for vocational training
- certificates of interest paid on loans
- maintenance agreements, court order, Child Support Agency assessments
- share certificate in a venture capital trust
- Forms EIS3 or EIS5 (for Enterprise Investment Scheme)
- details of covenants paid or lump sums to charity under Gift Aid.

What deductions can you claim

You can claim here for:

- pension contributions
- additional voluntary contributions to a pension scheme
- vocational training payments
- interest paid on qualifying loans
- maintenance payments
- investments in growing business (venture capital trusts or Enterprise Investment scheme)
- payments to charities (through covenants or Gift Aid)
- post-cessation expenses for a business and losses on relevant discounted securities
- certain payments to a trade union or friendly society.

You may wonder why there is nowhere in the tax return to put payments for private medical insurance for people aged 60 and over. Although tax relief on these policies was abolished from 2 July 1997, existing policies continued to get it until they came up for renewal. No entry is needed because the basic rate tax relief was given by reducing your payments to the insurer, and higher rate tax relief was not available.

PENSIONS

For the tax year ending 5 April 1998, you can get tax relief at your highest rate of tax on contributions to a pension scheme. If you are an employee, your employer can also make contributions to an approved pension scheme for you, and these would also get tax relief (and not count as a

> ### EXAMPLE
> Tony Jabot is wondering which is the best way to save for his retirement. He considers tax-free investments such as PEPs or TESSAs or taking out a personal pension plan. The tax treatment of PEPs, TESSAs or the pension fund is similar in that no tax is payable on any income or capital gains generated while your money is invested. But with a pension scheme, the government helps Tony to invest with tax relief on his contributions. He is a basic rate taxpayer. If he invested £1,000 in a personal pension plan, it would cost him just £770 in the year ending 5 April 1998.

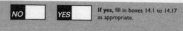
fringe benefit for you). There are more details about saving for your pension in Chapter 8.

You can save for a pension through an employer's pension scheme or a personal pension scheme if you are an employee, and through a personal pension scheme if you are self-employed or a partner.

With an employer's pension scheme, you are likely to get tax relief on your contributions deducted at source (they will be deducted from your salary before your employer works out your income tax through the PAYE system). If this is the only way you are saving for a pension, you can tick the NO box and go on to Q15. Obviously, if you are not saving at all for a pension, you should also tick the NO box.

What you should claim for

In the tax return you can claim tax relief for payments into two different types of pension scheme:

- retirement annuity contracts (new contracts not available from 1 July 1988)
- personal pension plans (not available before 1 July 1988)

If you started saving for a pension before 1 July 1988, unless you converted it into a personal pension, your scheme will be a retirement annuity contract. If you started saving for a pension on or after 1 July 1988, you will be saving in a personal pension plan. You could have started a personal pension plan in addition to a retirement annuity contract.

Although it is possible for you to have both a retirement annuity contract and a personal pension scheme, you cannot get double the tax relief. The tax relief for the retirement annuity contract is always given before the relief for the personal pension scheme. Relief for retirement annuity contract reduces the relief for the personal pension. The Inland Revenue has produced Help Sheet *IR330 Pension payments* which has an explanation and working sheets.

Retirement annuity contracts

Under the heading of Retirement annuity contracts you need to give information about your payments in the tax year ending 5 April 1998, about any you wish to carry back to an earlier year, and about any payments you have

Qualifying payments made in 1997-98	14.1 £		1997-98 payments used in an earlier year	14.2 £		Relief claimed
						box 14.1 *minus* (boxes 14.2 and 14.3, but not 14.4)
1997-98 payments now to be carried back	14.3 £		Payments brought back from 1998-99	14.4 £		14.5 £

made since 5 April 1998 which you want to bring back to get tax relief in this tax return.

In Box 14.1, enter the amount of payments which you have made to a retirement annuity (started before 1 July 1988) in the year before 5 April 1998. You will be entering gross figures (before deduction of tax).

You are allowed to carry back pension payments (see p. 78). You may have already claimed tax relief on some of the amount in box 14.1, for example, for the year ending 5 April 1997. If you have done so, enter the amount used in an earlier year in box 14.2.

If you now want to carry back some of what you paid in the year ending 5 April 1998 to the previous tax year (or possibly the one before that, see p. 78), put this amount in box 14.3. On this amount you will get tax relief at the rate of tax you paid in the previous year.

EXAMPLE

Paul Taylor has a retirement annuity contract. For the year ended 5 April 1998, he earned £20,000 and is aged 37. He can save £3,500 within the limits of 17.5 per cent of his net relevant earnings. He made payments of £3,000 and enters this figure in box 14.1. However, £1,000 of his pension contributions were made before he returned his tax return for the last tax year and he had asked for them to be carried back to the year ending 5 April 1997. He enters that amount in box 14.2. He chooses now to carry back a further £1,000 to the last tax year as he was a higher rate taxpayer and this would mean he would get more tax relief. The figure of £1,000 is entered in box 14.3.

The amount of tax relief he is now claiming on his contributions in the year ended 5 April 1998 is box 14.1 minus box 14.2 minus box 14.3, that is £3,000 minus £1,000 minus £1,000. He is claiming relief on pension contributions of £1,000 for the year ended 5 April 1998.

Between 5 April 1998 and the date you are filling in your tax return, you may have made some pension payments. If you want these to be included in your tax return for the year ending 5 April 1998 (see p. 78), enter the amount in box 14.4.

The amount of relief you are claiming for your retirement annuity contract payment for the tax year ending 5 April 1998 will be worked out in box 14.5 (box 14.1 minus box 14.2 minus box 14.3). If the amount you are claiming for this year is greater than the percentage limit (see p. 78), you may have unused relief from the previous six years which could be set against the excess.

There is no place on the tax return to claim unused relief carried forward from earlier years. Simply enter the pension contributions actually made, but keep your workings in case the Inland Revenue queries your payments. Use the working sheets which come with Help Sheet *IR330 Pension payments*.

For more information on retirement annuity contracts, see p. 75.

Personal pension plans

■ *Self-employed contributions to personal pension plans*

Qualifying payments made in 1997-98	14.6 £	1997-98 payments used in an earlier year 14.7 £	Relief claimed
1997-98 payments now to be carried back 14.8 £		Payments brought back from 1998-99 14.9 £	box 14.6 *minus* (boxes 14.7 and 14.8, but not 14.9) 14.10 £

If you are self-employed and contributing to a personal pension plan (started after 1 July 1988), you claim your tax relief in boxes 14.6 to 14.10.

Under the heading of Personal pension plans, you need to give information about your payments in the tax year ending 5 April 1998, about any you wish to carry back to an earlier year, and about any payments you have made since 5 April 1998 which you want to bring back to get tax relief in this tax return.

In Box 14.6, enter the amount of payments which you have made to a personal pension scheme (started on or after 1 July 1988) in the year before 5 April 1998. The self-employed pay before-tax amounts to the pension provider, so you will be entering gross figures (before deduction of tax).

You are allowed to carry back pension payments (see p. 78). You may have already claimed tax relief on some of the amount in box 14.6, for example, for the year ending 5 April 1997. If you have done so, enter that amount used in an earlier year in box 14.7.

If you now want to carry back some of what you paid in the year ending 5 April 1998 to the previous tax year (or possibly the one before that, see p. 78), put this amount in box 14.8. On this amount you will get tax relief at the rate of tax you paid in the previous year.

Between 5 April 1998 and the date you are filling in your tax return, you may have made some pension payments. If you want these to be included in your tax return for the tax year ending 5 April 1998, enter the amount in box 14.9.

The amount of relief you are claiming for your personal pension scheme will be worked out in box 14.10 (box 14.6 minus box 14.7 minus box 14.8). If the amount of relief you are claiming for this year is greater than the percentage limit (see p. 77), you may have unused relief from the previous six years which could be set against the excess. There is no place for this on the tax return. You claim it and the Inland Revenue has to ask you for your workings. Use Help Sheet *IR330 Pension Payments*.

For more information on self-employed contributions to personal pension plans, see p. 75.

■ **Employee contributions to personal pension plans** (include your gross contribution - see the note on box 14.11 in your Tax Return Guide)

Qualifying payments made in 1997-98	14.11 £		1997-98 payments used in an earlier year	14.12 £		Relief claimed
						box 14.11 minus (boxes 14.12 and 14.13, but not 14.14)
1997-98 payments now to be carried back	14.13 £		Payments brought back from 1998-99	14.14 £		14.15 £

Employees pay their contributions into a personal pension plan after deducting basic rate tax. So you will need to adjust the figures you paid to enter the gross amount here. For the year ending 5 April 1998, divide the amount you paid by 0.77.

In Box 14.11, enter the gross amount of payments which you have made to a personal pension scheme (started on or after 1 July 1988) in the year before 5 April 1998.

You are allowed to carry back pension payments (see p. 78). You may have already claimed tax relief on some of the amount in box 14.11, for example, for the year ending 5 April 1997. If you have done so, enter that amount used in an earlier year in box 14.12.

If you now want to carry back some of what you paid in the year ending 5 April 1998 to the previous tax year (or possibly the one before that, see p. 78), put this amount in box 14.13. On this amount you will get tax relief at the rate of tax you paid in the previous year.

TAX-SAVING IDEA

Make the most of the amount you are allowed to save in a pension scheme if you are an employee. You can save up to 15 per cent of your earnings including fringe benefits. Top up contributions to an employer's scheme if you can by making additional voluntary contributions either to your employer's scheme or to one of your own (known as a free-standing additional voluntary contributions scheme).

Between 5 April 1998 and the date you are filling in your tax return, you may have made some pension payments. If you want these to be included in your tax return for the tax year ending 5 April 1998, enter the amount in box 14.14.

The amount of relief you are claiming for your personal pension scheme for the tax year ending 5 April 1998 will be worked out in box 14.15 (box 14.11 minus box 14.12 minus box 14.13). If the amount of relief you are claiming for this year is greater than the percentage limit (see p. 77), you may have unused relief from the previous six years which could be set against the excess. There is no place for this on the tax return. You claim it and the Inland Revenue has to ask you for your workings. Use Help Sheet *IR330 Pension Payments*. If you do not get a tax return, you need to claim using Form PP42 (from your pension scheme administrator).

For more information on employee contributions to personal pension plans, see p. 75.

Additional voluntary contributions

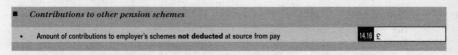

- ■ *Contributions to other pension schemes*

- • Amount of contributions to employer's schemes **not deducted** at source from pay   14.16 £

If you are going to qualify for less than the maximum permitted amount of an employer's pension and want to improve the benefits you will get, you can get tax relief on additional voluntary contributions (see p. 74).

If you paid your contributions in a lump sum, it is possible that you did not get tax relief at the time. If that is the case, enter the amount you paid to your employer's scheme at box 14.16. Don't enter the amount of additional voluntary contributions on which you have already received tax relief through the PAYE system.

• Gross amount of free-standing additional voluntary contributions paid in 1997-98	14.17 £

Instead of paying additional voluntary contributions into your employer's scheme, you can choose to invest in the fund of a pension provider, such as a life insurance company or unit trust manager. These are known as free-standing additional voluntary contributions.

When you made your payment to the pension provider, you would have made it after basic rate tax was deducted. But in box 14.17, you have to enter the gross amount. Take the amount you paid and divide it by 0.77 to give the gross figure. Using the tax return you will be able to claim higher rate tax relief if you are entitled to it.

OTHER RELIEFS YOU CAN CLAIM

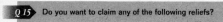

Q 15 Do you want to claim any of the following reliefs?   NO   YES   If yes, fill in boxes 15.1 to 15.12, as appropriate.

Your tax return on page 5 lists out the possible reliefs you might be able to claim. If you are entitled to any of these deductions from your income, put a tick in the YES box. Otherwise tick the NO box and go to Q16.

Vocational training

	Amount of payment
• Payments you made for vocational training	15.1 £

You can get tax relief at your highest rate of tax for fees you paid for training which would count towards the National Vocational Qualifications and Scottish Vocational Qualifications. From 6 May 1996, if you are aged 30 or over you can also get tax relief on fees for full-time vocational courses lasting between four weeks and a year, whether or not they lead to the qualifications.

Relief at the basic rate is normally deducted from the payments you make so you can benefit even if unemployed. You can get higher rate tax relief on vocational training if applicable, so you need to claim for it in your tax return.

Enter at box 15.1, the amount of the payment you have made for the tax year ending 5 April 1998, that is after the deduction of basic rate tax.

You are entitled to relief only if you are not receiving or entitled to receive financial assistance for a course under a government scheme. Nor can you claim if you are doing the course mainly for your own recreation.

Loan interest

You can get tax relief on interest you pay on loans of £30,000 or less to buy your only or main home (or to improve it but only if the loans were taken out on or before 5 April 1988 – see p. 58).

The rate of tax relief is 15 per cent, dropping to 10 per cent from 6 April 1998. So every £1 of interest you pay within the £30,000 limit will be reduced by tax relief to 85p (90p from 6 April 1998).

Most taxpayers get their tax relief through MIRAS (mortgage interest relief at source). Under this system, you make reduced payments to your lender. Your lender receives the amount of tax relief direct from the Inland Revenue. And you get the relief whether you pay tax or not. If your mortgage is in MIRAS, put nothing in box 15.2.

If your mortgage is **NOT** in MIRAS, claim here for tax relief. You will need a certificate of interest from your lender (but do not send this with your tax return unless your tax office asks to see it). If your mortgage is for more than £30,000 or if your home is used partly for business, you will have to work out what proportion of the interest you can claim (see pp. 54 and 59).

You also qualify for tax relief on mortgage interest if you took out a loan on your only or main home in order to buy an annuity and you are aged 65 or more. This is commonly known as a home income scheme (see p. 55). The tax relief on such loans is usually given through the MIRAS system. If it is not, it also needs to be claimed here. These loans qualify for tax relief at the basic rate of tax, so you need to adjust the amount you enter here in order to produce the right result when taken into the calculations together with other (less favourably treated) mortgages. Help Sheet *IR340 Relief on loans not in MIRAS* will guide you through the calculations.

Interest on other qualifying loans

Claim here for tax relief on the interest for a variety of loans, including loans to buy:

- a share in or putting capital into a co-operative partnership (but not if you are a limited partner)
- plant or machinery for use in your job if you are an employee or partner (if you are self-employed you claim in the Self-employment supplementary pages)
- shares in a close company (see below). To be eligible you should own more than 5 per cent of the company or be a shareholder and work for most of your time in the business.

A close company is one which is controlled by a small number of people. Broadly, it should have five or fewer 'participators', such as shareholders, or it should be controlled by shareholder directors.

You may also be able to claim relief here if you are an employee and get a low-interest or interest-free loan from your employer which counts as a taxable benefit (see p. 98).

Don't enter here to claim tax relief on the interest on a loan for a self-employed business (use box 3.47) or to buy a property you let (use box 5.4). Nor should you enter overdraft or credit card interest, which does not qualify for tax relief here.

Maintenance payments

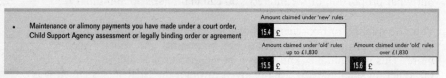

You are entitled to tax relief on payments you make to your former or separated spouse and your children, but not if these are voluntary payments (that is you can't be forced to make them). And you can't get tax relief on payments made to or for your children if they are 21 plus.

Payments on which you can get tax relief include those made under:

- a Court Order
- a Child Support Agency assessment
- a written agreement
- a verbal agreement made before 15 March 1988, if written details were received by your tax inspector by 30 June 1988.

There are different rules about tax relief on maintenance payments depending on when the agreement was made. Chapter 6 on p. 40 explains the distinctions between the old and new rules and gives tax-saving ideas.

TAX-SAVING IDEA

Be careful that you don't alter an arrangement to pay maintenance under the old rules which means that the tax treatment changes and it comes under the new rules. Treatment under the new rules could be much less generous.

What to enter if your maintenance comes under the new rules

If your payments come under the new rules what you should enter in box 15.4 is the lower of £1,830, which is the maximum payments each year on which you can get tax relief under the new rules, and the amount you paid in the year ending 5 April 1998. If your former husband or wife has remarried during the tax year ending 5 April 1998, you are not entitled to tax relief on any payments made after he or she remarried. If what you paid before the date of marriage is less than £1,830, enter that amount.

EXAMPLE

Peter Smith pays maintenance to his ex-wife and child. The agreement was made in 1992, so it comes under the new rules. In the year ending 5 April 1998 he paid £5,000. He is entitled to tax relief of the lower of what he paid (£5,000) or £1,830. He puts £1,830 in box 15.4.

He is entitled to tax relief on his maintenance payments at the rate of 15 per cent. On the £1,830 which he can claim under the new rules he will get tax relief of 15 per cent of £1,830, which is £274.50.

You can get tax relief on maintenance payments only up to a total of £1,830, no matter how many ex- or separated husbands or wives you have.

You will need to give the dates of the court order, agreements and so on in the section headed Additional information on page 8 of the tax return.

You do not get tax relief at the rate of tax you pay. This is a fixed-rate relief and is 15 per cent for the year ending 5 April 1998 (and for the year ending 5 April 1999).

What to enter if your maintenance comes under the old rules
You can get tax relief on the amount of maintenance payments which you paid and got tax relief on in the tax year ending 5 April 1989, unless you were due to pay less and did pay less in the tax year ending 5 April 1998. If the lower of these two amounts is less than or equal to £1,830, enter it in box 15.5. If it is more than £1,830, put £1,830 in box 15.5 and the excess in box 15.6. You have to split up the payments like this because tax relief on the first £1,830 is only 15 per cent, but on the excess you get relief at your top rate of tax.

You can get tax relief on maintenance payments to more than one former husband or wife under the old rules. Maintenance payments for two agreements under the old rules must be looked at separately. You can get tax relief on the sum of the lower of the two amounts for each agreement. If the sum of the two amounts is less than or equal to £1,830, enter it in box 15.5. If it is more than £1,830, put £1,830 in box 15.5 and the excess in box 15.6.

> **EXAMPLE**
> Jane Spires was divorced from her husband in 1987. Ever since, she has paid him the same amount of maintenance, £2,500 a year under a written agreement. In the year ending 5 April 1998, she paid him the amount he was entitled to. She can get tax relief on the full £2,500 a year because it is paid under the old rules. She enters £1,830 in box 15.5 and the difference (£2,500 minus £1,830 equals £670) goes in box 15.6.

If you make two lots of maintenance payments, one under the old rules and one under the new rules, you may be able to get tax relief under both sets of rules. Work out the amount on which you can get tax relief under the old rules and put the figures in boxes 15.5 and 15.6 (as instructed above). If the figure in box 15.5 is less than £1,830 for the tax year ending 5 April 1998, you can claim under the new rules for maintenance payments which come within those rules. Deduct the figure in box 15.5 from £1,830 and put in box 15.4 the lower of that figure and the amount of maintenance payments you made in the year ending 5 April 1998 under the new rules.

Investing in growing businesses
There are some schemes which encourage investment into growing businesses which require risk capital. These types of investments can carry a high

degree of risk and to compensate investors for carrying this extra risk element, there is a broad range of tax incentives. For more details, see Chapter 8.

Venture capital trusts

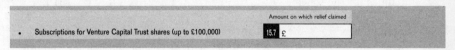

If you invest in a venture capital trust, you are not investing directly in these companies but in a fund like an investment trust which is quoted on the Stock Exchange.

When you buy new ordinary shares in a venture capital trust, you can get income tax relief at 20 per cent on your investment up to £100,000 for the year ending 5 April 1998, as long as you hold your shares for five years. If you are reinvesting the gain made from selling some other asset, you can also claim capital gains tax reinvestment relief on that gain (that is, you can put off paying the capital gains tax until you dispose of your new asset, in this case the shares you hold in the venture capital trust).

Any dividends paid out by the venture capital trust and gains you make on the shares in the trust are all free of tax.

In box 15.7, put the amount you have invested in venture capital trusts, up to a maximum of £100,000.

Enterprise Investment Scheme

You can get tax relief of 20 per cent on investments (not more than £100,000 in the tax year ending 5 April 1998) made in the shares of unquoted trading companies. Any gain you make on the shares will be free of capital gains tax. There are a lot of detailed rules about which companies are eligible and whether you yourself are eligible.

If you have invested in shares eligible for the Enterprise Investment Scheme after 5 April, but before 6 October 1998, you can ask for half the investment up to a maximum of £15,000 (£18,000 proposed in the Budget) to be deducted from your income for the year ending 5 April 1998.

You can claim here in this tax return for an investment only if you have received Form EIS3 from the company in which you invested (Form EIS5 for an investment made through a fund). This form certifies that the company qualifies for the scheme.

Enter in box 15.8 the total investments (up to £100,000) for which you are claiming relief in the tax year ending 5 April 1998. If you have made an investment for which you have not yet received Form EIS3, or form EIS5, don't enter it here. You can either claim before 31 January 1999 by asking your tax office to amend this tax return or you can claim using the form in EIS3 after 31 January 1999.

> **TAX-SAVING IDEA**
> If you are giving to charity, try to arrange to do so either with a covenant or through the Gift Aid scheme. The charity you support can receive more by reclaiming the basic rate tax on what you give.

Enter details of each investment for which you are claiming relief in the section headed Additional information on page 8 of the tax return.

Giving to charity

As well as making donations in the street or in other ways, you can make more formal donations and use the tax system to reduce what it costs you to make the donation. With either a covenant or Gift Aid, you can get tax relief at your highest rate of tax.

Covenants

	Amount of payment
• Charitable covenants or annuities	15.9 £

Enter in box 15.9 the amount you actually paid to the charity (not the gross amount which you agreed to pay). You can get tax relief at your highest rate of tax on payments you make to registered charities if you make them under a deed of covenant. This is a legally binding agreement to make a series of payments and to get the tax relief on payments to charity; they should be capable of continuing for more than three years. You won't get the tax relief if you get significant

> **TAX-SAVING IDEA**
> If you are married and wanting to donate to charity using a covenant make sure that the covenant is made by whichever of you has the highest rate of tax.

benefits from the payments, but you will get tax relief if you are allowed access to the charity's property as a benefit of membership. This includes subscriptions to charities such as the National Trust and those which conserve wildlife for the public benefit, even though you get free or reduced-price entry to the property.

When you make the payment to the charity, you will agree to pay a gross amount, for example, £100 a year. But when you make the payment, you pay only the net amount, because you deduct tax at the basic rate. For the tax year ending 5 April 1998, the basic rate tax is 23 per cent, so you would have handed over to the charity £77, not the £100 you agreed to pay. The charity reclaims the £23 of basic rate tax which you deducted from the Inland Revenue. So the charity receives £100, but it costs you £77. And you can get high-

EXAMPLE

Julia West is a higher rate taxpayer. She has agreed to donate to her favourite charity, the Cricketers Benevolent Foundation, £200 a year. This is the gross amount entered in the covenant. But before she pays over the donation each year she deducts basic rate tax. In the year ending 5 April 1998, she deducted £46 and sent £154 by standing order. The charity reclaimed the £46 from the Inland Revenue. Because she is a higher rate taxpayer, she is entitled to more tax relief and claims it through her tax return. In box 15.9, she enters the amount she actually paid, £154 (not the gross amount of £200 which she agreed to pay). She gets her higher rate tax relief when she works out her tax bill and the amount she has to pay or can claim as a refund on 31 January 1999.

EXAMPLE

Julia West (see above) had to alter her standing order for her covenant for the year ending 5 April 1998 because the basic rate of tax had changed. She cancelled the standing order for £152 and amended it to £154.

er rate tax relief if you pay tax at 40 per cent.

If you don't pay tax at the basic rate, but the lower rate of 20 per cent, or if you are a non taxpayer, you may have to hand money back to the Inland Revenue. If you pay tax at the lower rate for the year ending 5 April 1998, and you had agreed to make a gross payment of £100, handing over £77 to the charity, you will have to repay £3 to the Inland Revenue (this is taken into account when working out your overall tax bill).

It depends on the exact wording of the covenant, but unless you agreed to hand over a fixed net amount, if the basic rate of tax changes you will need to alter how much you pay to the charity. Suppose, for example, the basic rate falls to 22 per cent. For a gross amount of £100, you will need to pay £78.

You can get more information about charitable covenants from the Charities Aid Foundation, King's Hill, West Malling, Kent ME19 4TA.

Annuities and covenants entered into for full value, for genuine commercial reasons in connection with the payer's trade or profession are also eligible for tax relief at the highest rate, but covenants paid to individuals don't get any tax relief.

Gift Aid

		Amount of payment
• Gift Aid		15.10 £

Enter in box 15.10 the amount you actually paid to the charity.

You can get tax relief at your highest rate of tax on single one-off gifts to a charity of £250 or more made during your lifetime (but see p. 26). There is no upper limit. You make the payment by agreeing to pay a gross amount, for example, £1,000. You actually hand over to the charity £1,000 less the amount of basic rate tax. For the tax year ending 5 April 1998, this would be £1,000 less £230 giving a payment of £770 (for the tax year ending 5 April 1999, this would be a payment of £770 after deducting basic rate tax at 23 per cent).

> ### TAX-SAVING IDEA
> If you are married and want to make a donation to charity under Gift Aid, make sure that whichever of you pays the highest rate of tax makes the donation.

If you pay tax at less than the basic rate, you are a lower rate taxpayer or a non-taxpayer, you will have to pay back to the Inland Revenue some of the tax you have deducted. For example, a lower rate taxpayer who had deducted £230 from a gross amount of £1,000 in the tax year ending 5 April 1998 will have to pay £30 to the Inland Revenue.

Closing a business
Even after you have closed a business, you may find that there are certain obligations and expenses which you have to meet. For example, you may need to put right some defect in work which you carried out.

		Amount of payment
• Post-cessation expenses and losses on relevant discounted securities etc	15.11	£

You can deduct some expenses from any other income and gains you have in the year in which the business expense arises, if you have no income from your closed business. The relief is available for expenses incurred within seven years after the business closure. You must claim for the relief by 31 January in the second year after the tax year in which you incurred the expense. So for an expense which you met in the tax year ending 5 April 1998, you must claim by 31 January 2000.

The expenses which qualify for this special relief are:

- costs of putting right defective work you did or faulty goods or services which you supplied and the cost of paying any damages as a result
- premiums for insurance against claims due to defective work or faulty goods and services
- legal and other professional expenses you incur in defending yourself against accusations of defective work or providing faulty goods or services
- debts owed to the business which you included in your accounts but which have subsequently turned out to be bad debts
- cost of collecting debts owed to the business and included in its accounts.

Expenses which don't qualify for post-cessation relief can only be set against future income which comes from the closed business. There are some special rules about unpaid expenses. Ask your tax adviser or your tax office for help.

Enter in box 15.11 the amount of expenses which you want to deduct from your income in the tax year ending 5 April 1998 (and in box 8.5 of the Capital Gains pages the amount you want to deduct from your capital gains). If you are later reimbursed for any expenses or bad debts entered in this section, remember to enter the amount recovered under Any other income (box 13.3 of the tax return – see p. 171).

You also claim in box 15.11 for losses on relevant discounted securities (formerly deep discount bonds and deep gain securities) including a new investment called gilt strips. A loss incurred in the tax year ending 5 April 1998 can be deducted only from the income in the same tax year.

Payments to a trade union or friendly society
Friendly societies supported their members before the arrival of the welfare state by paying sickness benefit, unemployment benefit and widow's pen-

		Half amount of payment
• Payments to a trade union or friendly society for death benefits	15.12	£

sions. Some continue in existence and you can get tax relief on premiums you pay on certain combined sickness and life insurance policies they offer. The tax relief is at half your top rate of tax on the life part of the premium; you can also get the same tax relief on part of your trade union subscription if it includes pension, funeral or life insurance benefits. With the friendly society policy, to be eligible for tax relief the premiums must be £25 or less a month and 40 per cent or less of the premium should be for the death benefit.

Ask your friendly society or trade union to tell you how much of the premium was for pension, life insurance, funeral or death benefit. Enter in box 15.12 half that amount.

ALLOWANCES

Another way of reducing the amount of income tax you have to pay is to claim any allowances to which you are entitled. These are deducted from your income, along with reliefs (deductions), to make your taxable income smaller – and so also your tax bill.

ALLOWANCES *for the year ended 5 April 1998*

Q 16 You get your personal allowance of £4,045 automatically. **If you were born before 6 April 1933, enter your date of birth in box 21.4** – you may get higher age-related allowances

Do you want to claim any of the following allowances? NO ☐ YES ☐

If yes, please read pages 23 to 26 of your Tax Return Guide and then fill in boxes 16.1 to 16.28 as appropriate.

Personal allowances
Everyone gets a personal allowance. It comes automatically; you don't have to claim it in the tax return.

Age-related personal allowances
However, people aged 65 or over during the tax year beginning 6 April 1997, can claim a higher allowance (see p. 00). There is one level of age-related allowance if you were 65 or over during the tax year beginning 6 April 1997 and a still higher rate if you were 75 or over. On the tax return it says if you were born before 6 April 1933, enter your date of birth in box 21.4 to claim the age-related allowance. Box 21.4 is at the bottom of page 7 of the return.

> ### TAX-SAVING IDEA
> You can go back six years to claim an allowance which you forgot at the time or didn't know you were entitled to. You get tax relief at the rate of tax which would have applied if you claimed the deduction at the right time.

Blind person's allowance
Anyone registered as blind with a local authority can claim blind person's allowance. The amount of the allowance for the tax year ending 5 April 1998 is £1,280 and for the tax year ending 5 April 1999 it is £1,330. A registered blind person must be unable to perform any work for which eyesight

	Date of registration (if first year of claim)	Local authority (or other register)
■ *Blind person's allowance*	16.1 / /	16.2

is essential. The partially sighted cannot claim the allowance.

In box 16.1, enter the date you were registered blind if this is the first year you are claiming, and enter the name of the local authority in box 16.2.

If you are not registered until after 5 April 1998 but before 6 April 1999, you can still get the allowance for the tax year ending 5 April 1998 if you can show that you were blind at that date, for example, with an ophthalmologist's certificate.

The requirement for Scotland and Northern Ireland is different from England. You don't need to be registered. You can claim blind person's allowance if you are not able to perform any work for which eyesight was essential. To claim, write Scotland claim or Northern Ireland claim in box 16.2.

If your income is less than your allowances, including blind person's, and you are married and living with your husband or wife, you can transfer the unused part of this allowance to your partner (see p. 43). If both of you are blind, you can claim two allowances.

Transitional allowance

■ *Transitional allowance* (for some wives with husbands on low income if received in earlier years)
• Tick to claim and give details in the 'Additional information' box on page 8 *(please see page 23 of your Tax Return Guide for what is needed)* 16.3
• If you want to calculate your tax, enter the amount of transitional allowance you can have in box 16.4 16.4 £

Transitional allowance is for some wives with husbands on low income which was introduced to ease the changes to the allowances available for married men when independent taxation was introduced. To get this allowance for the year tax ending 5 April 1998 you must be:

- a married woman, and
- getting transitional allowance in the tax year ending 5 April 1997, and
- living with the same husband in the tax year ending 5 April 1998 as you were for the whole of the year ending 5 April 1997.

Your husband must have been resident in the UK for the year ending 5 April

1998, and have written to his tax office asking for the allowance to be given to you.

To claim the allowance tick box 16.3. You will need to enter details about your husband in the Additional information box on page 8 of the return – his name, address, tax reference, National Insurance number and tax office.

If you are working out your own tax bill, you will need to know the amount of the allowance and put it in box 16.4. You can ask either your husband or your tax office for the figure. It should be the amount of transitional allowance you received in the year ending 5 April 1997, less any increase in your allowances in the year to 5 April 1998, or, if lower, the amount of your husband's unused allowances (excluding blind person's and married couple's allowance).

Married couple's allowance
This is an allowance which can be claimed when you marry. There are more details of it in Chapter 6.

The amount of the married couple's allowance for those aged under 65 for the tax year ending 5 April 1998 is £1,830 and higher levels can be claimed by the 65 or over and 75 or over age groups (see p. 41).

Married couple's allowance is automatically given to the husband but it can be split between the two of you or used 100 per cent by the wife. Note, though, that if one of you is 65 or over at the start of a tax year, and entitled to a higher level of married couple's allowance, only the basic amount (£1,830 for the tax year ending 5 April 1998) can be allocated between the two of you. The extra bit always goes to the husband.

Splitting or transferring the married couple's allowance
If you want to do this, you have to plan ahead. You are too late to make these choices for the tax year ended 5 April 1998 and from 6 April 1998, too late to make the choice for the tax year ending 5 April 1999. Write to your tax inspector before 6 April 1999 if you want to share or transfer the allowance for the tax year ending on 5 April 2000.

The same time deadlines apply to altering the allocation.

Married men
A married man can claim married couple's allowance if he was married and living with his wife for at least part of the tax year. He can also claim it if he was separated from his wife before 6 April 1990 but maintaining her volun-

tarily (and not able to claim tax relief on the payments) from separation to 6 April 1997.

Fill in boxes 16.5 to 16.10. Claim married couple's allowance by entering:

- your wife's full name in box 16.5
- her date of birth in box 16.7, if before 6 April 1933
- her tax reference (if known) in box 16.9.

Tick box 16.8 if you and your wife have decided to split the allowance equally between the two of you. Tick box 16.10 if you and your wife have decided to transfer the whole of the married couple's allowance to your wife.

If you married during the tax year ending 5 April 1998 and want to claim all or part of the married couple's allowance (see p. 40), put the date of your marriage in box 16.6. You get one-twelfth of the full married couple's allowance for each month (or part-month) of your marriage (see Chapter 6).

However, there may be two other options open to you:

- if this is a second or later marriage, you may already be claiming married couple's allowance for a previous marriage. If you want to carry on doing this (because you would be able to claim more of the allowance), don't enter anything in box 16.6. And in boxes 16.5, 16.7 and 16.9 fill in the information about your former wife
- or if you have a child living with you, you can claim additional personal allowance instead of married couple's allowance. If you can claim only part of married couple's allowance, you would be better off doing this as you could be entitled to the whole of additional personal allowance (unless you are sharing it or qualify for a higher, age-related married couple's allowance). This would reduce your tax bill. If you make this choice don't enter anything in boxes 16.5 to 16.10, but fill in the additional personal allowance section instead.

Married women

You should fill in boxes 16.11 to 16.15. You can claim married couple's allowance only if you and your husband have agreed to transfer it, but you can demand for it to be split equally between the two of you without his agreement. You must have lived with your husband for all or part of the tax year ending 5 April 1997.

If you have agreed to split the allowance tick box 16.13. If you have agreed to transfer the whole allowance to you, tick box 16.15. Fill in your husband's full name (box 16.12) and his tax reference if you know it (box 16.14).

If you have married since 5 April 1997, enter the date of the marriage in box 16.11 if you want to claim married couple's allowance. If you are still receiving all or your share of the allowance for a previous marriage, don't enter anything in box 16.11 and give details of your former husband in boxes 16.12 and 16.14.

If your husband died in the tax year ending 5 April 1998, you can use only the part of the married couple's allowance which is not used up against your husband's income. This applies even if you had agreed to allocate it differently. If this is the case, do not tick boxes 16.13 or 16.15. Tick instead box 16.26. And if you are filling in a tax return for your husband who has died, do not tick boxes 16.8 or 16.10 because the allowance has first to be deducted from your husband's income.

Additional personal allowance
If you are a single parent, there is an allowance you may be able to claim if the child lives with you. This allowance is known as additional personal allowance. The amount of the allowance is the same as the married couple's allowance (£1,830 for the tax year ending 5 April 1998 and £1,900 for the

tax year ending 5 April 1999). The amount of the relief is restricted to 15 per cent.

You may be able to claim this allowance if at some time in the tax year you are:

- single
- a widow or widower
- divorced
- married but separated (and so not entitled to the married couple's allowance if a man)
- a married man, but your wife is totally unable to look after herself throughout the tax year (but see p. 25 for a change proposed in the Budget).

To get the allowance you must have a child (either your own or someone else's) living with you for the whole or part of the tax year. You can only claim for a child aged 16 or over at the start of the tax year, who is in full-time education at university, school or college or training full-time for at least two years for a trade or profession. If the child is not yours, you cannot claim if the child is 18 or over at the start of the tax year. Your child includes a step-child, adopted child or legitimated child.

It is possible that two people could claim the allowance for the same child because the child lives with each of them for part of the year (who has custody is not the deciding factor). If this applies to you, you can agree with the other what proportion each claims. If you cannot agree, the allowance will be divided up according to the amount of time the child lives with each of you during the tax year. If there are two or more children, you may be able to claim a full allowance each.

If you are living with someone as husband and wife, but are unmarried, you and your partner can claim only one additional personal allowance between the two of you and only for the youngest child. The allowance can be divided up as you wish. If you are not entitled to the allowance for the youngest child, you can't claim it at all.

To claim the allowance, you need to give the name of the child claimed for in box 16.16 and the child's date of birth in box 16.17. Tick box 16.18 if the child lives with you. Fill in box 16.19 if you are claiming for a child over 16 years old.

EXAMPLE

Nicky White is a single parent with two children living with her. Her income is £15,000. She can't claim the married couple's allowance, but she can claim the additional personal allowance (which is the same amount). The allowance is restricted to relief of 15 per cent of £1,830, that is £274.50 for the tax year ending 5 April 1998. Her tax bill is as follows:

Income		£15,000
less personal allowance		£ 4,045
Taxable income		£10,955
Tax bill:		
£4,100 at 20 per cent	£820	
£6,855 at 23 per cent	£1,577	
	£2,397	
less tax relief on additional personal allowance		£274.50
Tax for the year ended 5 April 1998	£2,122.50	

If you and someone else want to share the allowance you will need to fill in boxes 16.20 to 16.23. Enter the name and address of the other person claiming the allowance in box 16.20 and the percentage of the allowance you are claiming in box 16.21. If you cannot agree the percentage for each of you, you will have to give the further information in boxes 16.22 and 16.23 and the Inland Revenue will decide your share.

Widow's bereavement allowance

■ *Widow's bereavement allowance*	• Date of your husband's death	16.24	/ /

You can claim widow's bereavement allowance in the tax year you are widowed and the following tax year (see p. 00). The allowance is £1,830 for the tax year ending 5 April 1998. This is restricted to 15 per cent, as it is with the married couple's and additional personal allowances. For the tax year ending 5 April 1999, the amount is £1,900.

To claim the allowance, enter the date your husband died in box 16.24.

Transfer of surplus allowances

■ *Transfer of surplus allowances* - see page 25 of your Tax Return Guide before you fill in boxes 16.25 to 16.28

• Tick if you want your spouse to have your unused allowances 16.25

• Tick if you want to have your spouse's unused allowances 16.26

Please give details in the 'Additional information' box on page 8 - see page 25 of your Tax Return Guide for what is needed.
If you want to calculate your tax, enter the amount of the surplus allowance you can have.

• Blind person's surplus allowance 16.27 £

• Married couple's surplus allowance 16.28 £

You can transfer any unused amount of married couple's or blind person's allowance to your wife or your husband if you did not have enough income in the year to use up the allowance and you lived with your wife or husband for at least part of that year.

In certain limited circumstances, if a husband cannot use up all his personal allowance, his wife can receive a transitional allowance.

If you want your wife or husband to have the surplus of married couple's and blind person's allowances or transitional allowance, tick box 16.25. In the Additional information box on page 8 of your tax return, give your spouse's name, address, tax reference, National Insurance number and tax office.

If you want to claim and use your spouse's unused allowances, tick box 16.26. Give your spouse's name, address, tax reference, National Insurance number and tax office in the Additional information box on page 8.

If you are working out your own tax bill, enter in boxes 16.27 and 16.28 the amount of the surplus allowances. You can ask your tax office for help if you are not sure of the amount.

OTHER INFORMATION

The last two pages of the basic tax return are where you give additional bits of information about your tax bill, repayments and refunds.

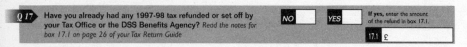

Q17 Have you already had any 1997-98 tax refunded or set off by your Tax Office or the DSS Benefits Agency? *Read the notes for box 17.1 on page 26 of your Tax Return Guide*   NO   YES   If yes, enter the amount of the refund in box 17.1.   17.1 £

If NO, go direct to Q18.

If YES enter the amount you were refunded, either directly from your tax office (including repayments of tax deducted from dividends or other investments) or from your DSS Benefits Agency (such as refunds of tax deducted from jobseeker's allowance). You should also include similar amounts which, rather than being repaid directly to you, have been set against payments of tax you owe.

Enter the amount refunded for the tax year ending 5 April 1998 in box 17.1.

Q18 Do you want to calculate your tax?   NO   YES   If yes, do it now and then fill in boxes 18.1 to 18.9. Your Tax Calculation Guide will help.

Tick YES if you intend to work out your own tax bill. Although daunting, it really should not be a problem for most readers to work out your own tax bill. Chapter 27 will show you how to do it and what to enter in boxes 18.1 to 18.9 and boxes 19.1 to 19.11.

If you are not going to work out your own tax bill, tick NO and go to Q19.

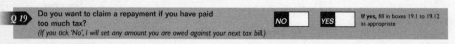

Q19 Do you want to claim a repayment if you have paid too much tax? *(If you tick 'No', I will set any amount you are owed against your next tax bill.)*   NO   YES   If yes, fill in boxes 19.1 to 19.12 as appropriate

Tick YES.

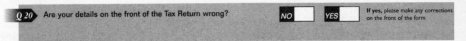

Q 20   Are your details on the front of the Tax Return wrong?   NO ☐   YES ☐   **If yes,** please make any corrections on the front of the form

If they are correct tick NO and go to Q21. If not correct, tick YES and make corrections on the front of the form.

Q 21   Please give other personal details in boxes 21.1 to 21.6

Please give a daytime telephone number if convenient. It is often simpler to phone if we need to ask you about your Tax Return.

Your telephone number   21.1 ☐   Say if you are single, married, widowed, divorced or separated   21.3 ☐

or, if you prefer, your agent's telephone number   21.2 ☐   Date of birth   21.4 ☐ / /

(also give your agent's name and reference in the 'Additional information' box on page 8)   Enter your date of birth if you are self-employed, or you were born before 6 April 1933, or you have ticked the 'Yes' box in Question 14, or you are claiming relief for Venture Capital Trust subscriptions

Enter your first two forenames   21.5 ☐   Enter your National Insurance number (if known)   21.6 ☐☐☐☐

Fill in the details.

In box 21.4, you need to give your date of birth if you are self-employed, or if you are claiming higher age-related personal and married couple's allowances, tax relief on investments in a venture capital trust or relief for pension contributions.

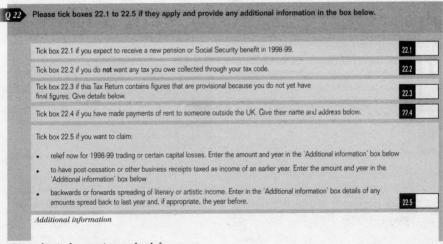

Q 22   Please tick boxes 22.1 to 22.5 if they apply and provide any additional information in the box below.

Tick box 22.1 if you expect to receive a new pension or Social Security benefit in 1998-99.   22.1 ☐

Tick box 22.2 if you do **not** want any tax you owe collected through your tax code.   22.2 ☐

Tick box 22.3 if this Tax Return contains figures that are provisional because you do not yet have final figures. Give details below.   22.3 ☐

Tick box 22.4 if you have made payments of rent to someone outside the UK. Give their name and address below.   22.4 ☐

Tick box 22.5 if you want to claim:

- relief now for 1998-99 trading or certain capital losses. Enter the amount and year in the 'Additional information' box below

- to have post-cessation or other business receipts taxed as income of an earlier year. Enter the amount and year in the 'Additional information' box below

- backwards or forwards spreading of literary or artistic income. Enter in the 'Additional information' box details of any amounts spread back to last year and, if appropriate, the year before.   22.5 ☐

Additional information

Give the information asked for.

If you are on PAYE and owe tax of less than £1,000, it will normally be collected through the PAYE system. You are asked to tick box 22.2 if you do not want this to happen, but do not do so without some thought. PAYE spreads out and delays the payment of your tax.

In box 22.3, you have to say whether any of the figures are provisional. If they are, don't delay sending in your tax return. In the Additional information box, explain which figures are provisional (including the box numbers), why they are provisional and when they will be finalised. If you know you are not going to be able to give reliable figures, because you have lost information or have had to estimate a valuation, for example, explain what they are and how you have arrived at the estimates.

Be warned that if you negligently submit a provisional figure which is inaccurate or unnecessary, you may be liable to a penalty.

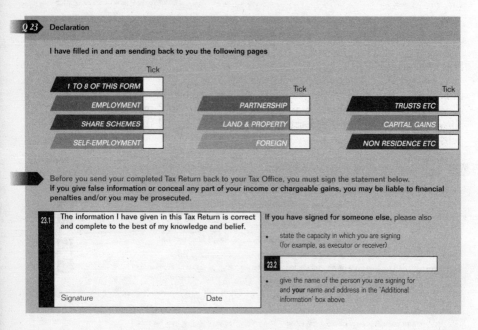

Tick any additional pages you are sending with the basic tax return and sign the declaration. If you are signing for someone else state in what capacity you are doing this.

EMPLOYMENT

Q 1 Were you an employee, or office holder, or director, or agency worker in the year ended 5 April 1998? NO YES EMPLOYMENT YES

It is usually easy to tell whether or not you are an employee. There are some grey areas, however, where the Inland Revenue will seek to tax you as an employee even if you think of yourself as self-employed:

- if you are a company director (even if you own the company)
- if you work on a freelance or consultancy basis, but have to work closely under the control of your boss, working a set number of hours at an hourly rate, say, and at a particular location
- if you work on a casual, part-time basis
- if you work as a temp through an agency. This includes, for example, locum doctors; but it does not apply to entertainers or models working through an agency, or to people who work solely from home
- you have more than one job: you may be classed as an employee for one job, even if you are clearly self-employed in another.

The key significance of being an employee is that in most cases your employer will have to operate PAYE (see Chapter 3) on your earnings from that job and deduct tax and National Insurance before paying you.

For many employees, the advantage of being paid under PAYE is that the right amount of tax on all their income should be deducted from their earnings and so they do not have to worry about paying a separate tax bill. If their income from their job is their only income many also do not need to fill in a tax return. But you may still have to fill one in if:

- you are a higher rate taxpayer and get taxable perks such as a company car or receive investment income
- you have other income which is paid out before tax is deducted, such as some types of investment income
- your tax affairs are complex for any other reason.

If you are an employee and are sent a tax return, you need to tick the YES box at Q1 of the basic tax return and fill in a separate Employment page for each job you have. If you are not sure of your status, check with your tax office.

Your employer

Details of employer

Employer's PAYE reference
1.1

Employer's name
1.2

Date employment started
(only if between 6 April 1997 and 5 April 1998)
1.3   /   /

Employer's address
1.5

Date finished (only if between 6 April 1997 and 5 April 1998)
1.4   /   /

Tick box 1.6 if you were
a director of the company
1.6

and, if so, tick box 1.7
if it was a close company
1.7

Postcode

TAX-SAVING IDEA

A disadvantage of being an employee is that you cannot deduct as many expenses from your taxable income as you could if you were self-employed. So if you are setting up on your own, check that you will meet the Inland Revenue's conditions for self-employment.

So that your tax office can tie up the information on your tax return with that provided by your employer, give your employer's name, address and PAYE reference (shown on the P60 or P45). If the employment started or ended during the tax year ending 5 April 1998, you also need to give the start or end dates of the job, the length of time you worked there, whether or not you are a director (box 1.6) and if it is a close company (box 1.7). This may affect how much tax-free profit-related pay you are entitled to, and how your perks and benefits are taxed.

What is taxed

Broadly speaking, the Inland Revenue seeks to tax any benefit you get from being employed, even if you get it from someone other than your employer. The tax return organises your remuneration into the following categories:

• money (including earnings from working abroad)

- benefits (taxable perks given by your employer) and expenses payments (either flat-rate allowances or reimbursement for expenses you have incurred)
- lump sums received on retirement, redundancy or death.

Not all of these will actually be taxable. But in general, you have to put it all down first, and the tax return then guides you to enter the various tax reliefs which you can deduct, for example, tax relief for expenses incurred in doing your job.

One thing you do not have to enter anywhere on your tax return is details of your National Insurance contributions as an employee. These should all be sorted out for you by your employer.

The date income is taxable

As a general rule, you are counted as receiving income from employment from the earlier of:

- the date you get it
- the date you are entitled to it, even if you do not actually get it till later on.

So if, for example, you are entitled to payment on 15 March 1998, but do not actually receive it until 15 April, you must still include it in your tax return for the tax year ending 5 April 1998. If you receive payment early – on 15 March 1998, for work not completed until 15 April, for example – it is taxable from the date you received it, that is 15 March.

If you are a director, your earnings for a particular period may be decided on one date, credited to you in the company accounts on another date, but not paid out till much later. It is the earliest date that counts, unless the earnings for a particular period were decided before that period ended. In this case, you are treated as receiving them on the last day of the period to which the earnings relate.

The documents you need

Most of the information you need will be on Forms P60, P11D or P9D.

Your P60 is a form your employer must give you by 31 May after the end of the tax year (that is, by 31 May 1998 for the tax year ending 5 April 1998). The P60 is a summary of how much you have been paid, and how much tax has been deducted. If you haven't got a P60, you should be able to find the information from your pay slips. If you left a job during a tax year, the information will be on your P45.

Your employer has to declare to the Revenue any taxable benefits or expenses you receive and the cash equivalent on form P11D or form P9D. Which form you get depends on how much you earn. You should get a copy from your employer by 6 July after the end of the tax year, that is by 6 July 1998 for the tax year ending 5 April 1998.

Note that if you leave a job, you will not automatically be given a form, but your ex-employer must give you one if you ask for it within three years after the end of the tax year in which you left. Your employer has 30 days from receiving your request in which to supply the form (if this is after the normal 6 July deadline).

Your P11D or P9D should be the starting point of all the expenses payments you have received. But you also need to keep receipts or documentation to back up your claim to deduct allowable expenses, particularly if they were not reimbursed by your employer and so did not appear on your P11D or P9D.

If you receive a lump sum from your employer, for example, when you left your job, it may be included on your P60, your P11D, or your P45, or you may just have a letter from your employer. Remember to include only payments that were made because of the change or job loss in the relevant tax year, even if they were actually paid in a different tax year. Your employer should be able to help you decide which category a payment falls within. If there is any doubt, employers can get advance decisions from their tax office, so it is worth talking about the tax consequences with your employer before any payment is made.

MONEY FROM EMPLOYMENT

Income from employment

■ *Money* - see Notes, page EN3

Before tax

• Payments from P60 (or P45 or pay slips) | 1.8 | £

You should enter as money:

- salaries, wages, fees, overtime, bonuses, commission and honoraria (after deducting money you have donated to a payroll giving scheme, or contributed to your employer's pension scheme, see right)
- amounts voted to you as a director and credited to an account with the company, even if you cannot draw the money straight away
- voluntary payments and gifts, whether from your employer or anyone

else, such as tips and Christmas boxes (excluding some small gifts and personal gifts such as long-service awards, see Tax-free fringe benefits on p. 86)
- incentive awards (but see p. 208)
- profit-related pay (excluding any tax-free amount – see p. 208)
- the taxable value of shares withdrawn early from an approved profit-sharing scheme
- sick pay, including statutory sick pay and statutory maternity pay (see p. 208)
- holiday pay
- various payments to do with your employment which are not strictly pay. Examples are golden hellos paid to entice you to join the company; a loan written off because you satisfied or completed an employment condition; payments made to recognise changes in your conditions of service or employment; payments made if you leave a job and agree, in return for a lump sum, not to compete with your employer.

P60 forms vary slightly in design. The figure to look for is your pay 'for tax purposes' or 'this employment pay'. Enter the figure from Form P60 in box 1.8, but check that it does not include employer's contributions to a pension scheme or what you give under a payroll giving scheme (see below). If you were unemployed during the year, your P60 may give details of any jobseeker's allowance you received. Do not enter this in your Employment page – enter it instead in box 11.5 in the basic tax return.

Contributions to an employer's pension scheme
You can get tax relief on contributions you make to your employer's pension scheme, up to a maximum of 15 per cent of your taxable income from the job. This tax relief is given by deducting your contributions from your pay before tax is worked out on it, so giving you relief at your top rate of tax. The figure you enter as taxable pay in box 1.8 should be the figure after deducting pension contributions.

Payroll giving schemes
You can get tax relief on charitable donations of up to £1,200 a year through the payroll giving scheme (sometimes called Give As You Earn, or GAYE) run by your employer. The money is deducted from your pay each week or month and passed straight to the charity by your employer. The donations are deducted from your pay before your tax is worked out on it, in the same way as contributions to an employer's pension scheme, so remember to check that what you enter in box 1.8. is your pay after payroll giving donations.

Incentive awards

Broadly speaking, these are taxable whether you receive them from your employer or from someone else in connection with your job; for example, a car sales representative may receive prizes from the car manufacturer. However, the person paying the award may pay the tax for you, through a taxed award scheme. In this case, the award still counts as part of your income, but the tax paid on your behalf will reduce your tax bill. Whoever makes the award should give you a Form P443 stating the value of the award and how much tax has been paid on it, unless the figures have been included on your P60. You should include the amount of the award in box 1.10 and the tax already paid in box 1.11.

Suggestion scheme awards are tax-free and need not be entered, provided that there is a formal scheme open to all employees, and the suggestion concerned is outside your normal job. If the suggestion is not taken up, the maximum award is £25; if is implemented, the maximum award is 50 per cent of the first year's expected net benefit, or 10 per cent of the benefit over five years, with an overall maximum of £5,000.

Profit-related pay

If you are in a registered scheme, your profit-related pay is tax-free, up to a ceiling of £4,000, or (if lower) 20 per cent of your total pay in the profit period to which the profit-related pay relates. Any profit-related pay above the limit is taxable in the normal way. Your employer should take into account any tax relief when working out the taxable pay shown in your P60. You do not need to enter details of the scheme or tax relief itself in the tax return or the Employment page.

However, the tax relief on profit-related pay is being phased out. The 20 per cent of total pay limit will remain, but the ceiling is being reduced to:

- £2,000 between 1 January 1998 and 31 December 1998
- £1,000 between 1 January 1999 and 31 December 1999
- nil on or after 1 January 2000.

Sick pay and maternity pay

If you are off work through illness or on maternity leave, any payment made to you by your employer, including statutory sick pay (SSP) or statutory maternity pay (SMP), is taxable. It will be taxed before you get it and shown on your P60 or P45 in the same way as other income, and you enter it with your other taxable pay in box 1.8. There are two exceptions to this rule:

- occasionally, SMP or SSP may be paid directly to you by the Department of Social Security. In this case, the benefit is still taxable, but tax is not deducted before it is paid to you and rather than enter it under Employment you should enter it in box 11.7 on page 4 of the basic tax return

- if you pay part or all of the premiums for an insurance policy taken out by your employer to meet the cost of employees' sick pay. In this case, the proportion of the sick pay which arises from your contributions is tax-free and need not be entered on the tax return. Any sick pay arising from your employer's contributions is taxable. Put it in box 1.8.

Tips and other payments

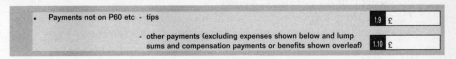

Boxes 1.9 and 1.10 are there to catch any income which does not appear on your P60 (for example, because it is paid by people other than your employer) and for which there is no other place on the Employment page. For example, you should enter in box 1.10 pay from working overseas which you have actually sent to the UK – this may not all be taxable but any tax-free amounts are deducted later on (see p. 219).

Tax deducted

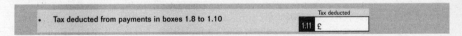

The tax your employer has deducted under PAYE is set against your tax bill. Enter it in box 1.11, together with any other tax deducted (for example, under a taxed incentive scheme). Occasionally, your employer may have given you more tax back as a refund than was actually deducted. If so, remember to enter the amount in brackets.

FRINGE BENEFITS AND EXPENSES

■ *Benefits and expenses - see Notes, pages EN3 to EN6*

Many employers give their employees non-cash fringe benefits, such as a company car or free medical insurance. Generally, you are taxed on the cash equivalent of these benefits (and the same applies, as for pay, if the benefit or expense is paid to you by someone other than your employer). Benefits for your family or household are regarded as a payment to you. However, some types of benefits are tax-free, and others are taxable only for higher-paid employees.

Expense payments you receive are yoked together with benefits in this section and sometimes the dividing line between them can be a fine one; for example, a company car may be a way of covering your travelling costs for work, as well as a perk of the job.

Payments you do not need to enter
There are three sorts of payments which you can ignore when filling out the benefits and expenses section of the Employment supplementary page.

Dispensations
You do not need to enter in your tax return expenses payments which are covered by a dispensation. A dispensation is a special permission from the Revenue which means that your employer does not have to include on your P11D or P9D expenses which would be tax-free anyway. Dispensations are usually given for things like travelling and subsistence expenses on an approved scale: they do not generally cover fringe benefits.

> **T AX - SAVING IDEA**
> Remember – you do not need to enter items covered by a dispensation or PAYE Settlement Agreement.

PAYE Settlement Agreements
The tax on some of your expenses and benefits may already have been paid by your employer under a PAYE Settlement Agreement (PSA). This is a voluntary agreement between an employer and the Inland Revenue under which the employer undertakes to pay the tax due on some types of benefits and expenses. The advantage for your employer is the saving of paperwork; the advantage for you is that you do not need to enter the payments on your return and they are effectively tax-free in your hands. Only some types of benefits and expenses can be covered by this sort of agreement, for example, minor expenses such as taxi fares and one-off payments such as parties for employees.

Tax-free fringe benefits

You do not need to enter the details of any fringe benefits which are tax-free (see p. 86 for a list). Note that there are conditions to be met before most of these benefits can be tax-free. Fuller information is given in Help Sheet *IR207 Non-taxable payments or benefits for employees.*

Payments you need to enter in your tax return

There are some benefits which are always taxable and need to be entered on the tax return. They are assets which are transferred to you (including payments in kind), vouchers and goods paid for by credit cards, living accommodation (with a few exceptions) and mileage allowance.

You may receive other benefits. But if you earn at a rate of less than £8,500 a year and are not a director they will be tax-free and you do not need to enter them on the tax return. Chapter 9 *Fringe Benefits* gives much more detail. It helps you work out whether you are paid at the rate of £8,500 a year or not and helps you work out the taxable value of benefits which you need to enter here.

Assets transferred to you and payments made for you

Payments in kind may be taxed in a number of ways, depending on how much you earn and whether you have the alternative of cash instead (see p. 89 to find out the taxable value). You should be able to get the amount to enter in box 1.12 from your P11D. If you earn less than £8,500, the taxable value is the second-hand value. But if you earn £8,500 or more, the taxable value is the larger of the second-hand value or the cost to the employer of providing the asset.

Payments your employer makes for you, like your phone bill, should also be entered in box 1.12. But don't put assets which remain the property of your employer and which you merely have the use of, or to services supplied by your employer – these go in box 1.22, unless there is a more specific box.

Vouchers and credit cards

		Amount
•	Vouchers/credit cards	1.13 £

You may be given a voucher for a particular service (for example, a season ticket), a credit token or a company credit or charge card. If so, you are taxed on their cash equivalent unless they appear in the list of tax-free fringe benefits on p. 86 (for example, luncheon vouchers, gift vouchers which count as a small gift). Cash vouchers worth a specified amount of cash should already have been taxed under PAYE, so you will not usually have to enter them here as a benefit. If you used vouchers or your company credit card to settle expenses of your job (such as train fares), include the full value of the vouchers or card bill here, but claim a deduction for 'Expenses you incurred in doing your job' on the back of the Employment page.

For vouchers and cards which do count as a taxable fringe benefit, broadly speaking you pay tax on the expense incurred by the person who provided them, less any amount that you have paid yourself. You will not have to pay tax on any annual card fee or interest paid by your employer.

Company credit cards and charge cards are often provided as a convenient way of paying business expenses. If so, you still have to enter the value of any vouchers or goods or services obtained with a credit card or credit token in box 1.13. You can claim any allowable business expenses back in boxes 1.32 to 1.35. For more information see Help Sheet *IR201 Vouchers, credit cards and tokens.*

Living accommodation

The basic taxable charge for any living accommodation (unless it counts as a tax-free fringe benefit, see p. 87), and the extra charge if applicable, should be entered in box 1.14. However, if you have the alternative of getting cash instead of accommodation, and the cash alternative comes to more than the taxable value of the accommodation, you should enter the extra cash in box 1.12 as well as the taxable value in box 1.14. This applies even if you have decided to live in.

There is Help Sheet *IR 202 Living Accommodation* if you want to work out the taxable value in all these situations.

Mileage allowances

If you use your own car for work, most employers pay you a mileage allowance of so many pence per mile. Quite often this is generous enough to allow you to make a profit on it. Any such profit needs to be entered as a benefit in box 1.15. Any loss should be entered in box 1.32.

Which method?

There are three different methods for working out your profit, see p. 91. There are an exact method, a quick method and the Fixed Profit Car Scheme. You do not have to stick with the Fixed Profit Car Scheme, even if your employer operates it, but using the scheme's scales is much simpler than keeping full records. Keep records for a few months to see how similar your actual cost per mile is to the Fixed Profit Car Scheme scale. Then:

- if your car happens to be more expensive to run than average, choose the exact method (but you must keep records of all your expenses)
- if its running costs are average, or cheaper than average, choose the Fixed Profit Car Scheme if your employer runs one, or the Quick method
- if you find that your mileage allowances come to less than the amount of your actual business expenses, do not enter anything in box 1.15 but remember to enter your loss in box 1.32.

Company cars

A company car is taxable only if you earn at the rate of £8,500 a year or more (see p. 93). Put in box 1.16 the cash equivalent of cars made available to you (or to members of your family or household) for private use. Check the figure with your employer or on your form P11D. Help Sheet *IR203 Car benefits and car fuel benefits* gives a calculator.

Fuel for company cars

If you have a company car, you may get free fuel for private use as well. This is taxed according to a fixed scale of charges added to your taxable income (see p. 97) and only taxable if you earn at the rate of £8,500 a year or more.

Enter the amount in box 1.17.

Vans

A van is only taxable if you earn at the rate of £8,500 a year or more (see p. 93). The basic taxable value of a van is £500, but there may be reductions (see p. 98). Enter the adjusted taxable amount in box 1.18.

Interest-free and low-interest loans

Free or cheap loans are only taxable if you earn at the rate of £8,500 a year or more.

The basic rule is that you have to pay tax on the difference between the interest you pay and the interest worked out at an official rate set by the Inland Revenue. But there can be exceptions (see p. 98).

In box 1.19, you should put the cash equivalent (your employer should tell you what this is).

If the loan is for a qualifying purpose (for example, a mortgage to buy a home) you should claim tax relief in box 15.2 or box 15.3.

If the loan is eventually written off, you pay tax on the amount written off. Include the amount with the taxable value of any other loans in box 1.19.

Mobile telephones

A mobile telephone is taxable only if you earn at the rate of £8,500 a year or more.

Enter £200, unless it can be reduced (see p. 99).

Private medical or dental insurance

	Amount
• Private medical or dental insurance	1.21 £

This is taxable only if you earn at the rate of £8,500 a year or more. Enter the taxable amount, which you should find on Form P11D, in box 1.21. For more explanation, see p. 100.

Other benefits

	Amount
• Other benefits	1.22 £

This is a box to sweep up any other taxable perks which you have not already entered elsewhere. Remember, though, that it applies only if you earn at a rate of £8,500 or more. The figures should be shown on your P11D. The main types of benefits you may have to enter here are listed on p. 100.

Expenses payments and balancing charges

	Amount
• Expenses payments received and balancing charges	1.23 £

You should enter here all expenses payments and expense allowances you received, whether or not they are tax-free. You can deduct tax-free expense payments later on in boxes 1.32 to 1.35. The only expenses which you should not enter either here or later on are those for which your employer has a dispensation.

Your expenses payments should be shown in your P11D or P9D. In your P11D they will be broken down into the gross amount received, any contributions you made or amounts on which tax has already been deducted, and the taxable amount. Enter the taxable amount in box 1.23.

Balancing charges are not something you will see on your P11D or P9D. They apply only if you claimed capital allowances on something that you bought for your work and that you have now disposed of (see p. 224).

LUMP SUMS AND COMPENSATION

Income from employment continued

■ *Lump sums and compensation payments or benefits*

You must read page EN6 of the Notes and fill in Help Sheet IR204 **before** *filling in boxes 1.24 to 1.30*

You may have something to enter here if:

- you receive a lump sum when you leave a job, such as redundancy pay
- you retire and received a lump sum from a non-approved retirement scheme (that is, anything other than an Inland-Revenue approved, foreign government or other statutory pension scheme)
- your employer (or ex-employer) paid you a lump sum which you have not already entered as pay (for example, in box 1.8 or box 1.10).

You will need Help Sheet *IR204 Lump sums and compensation payments* in order to work out what to enter in each of the boxes. It is important to enter the right bit in the right category because each is taxed under different parts of tax legislation. You can get various types of tax relief on some categories, but not on others. One payment might be made up of several different types. They may also affect your overall tax calculation, and there is a special lump sums tax calculation guide if you are planning to work out your own tax.

	Tax deducted
. Tax deducted from payments in boxes 1.27 to 1.29	1.30 £

Your employer may deduct tax from any taxable sums you get before paying you. If so, make sure you enter it in box 1.30, so that it is taken into account when working out your tax bill.

Payment expected under the terms of your employment

Taxable lump sums

. From box H of *Help Sheet IR204*   1.27 £

Lump sums that you should enter here include:

- any payment that you receive under the terms and conditions of your contract, or where the expectation that you would get it is firm enough for it to be regarded as part of your contract – for example, a payment based on length of service which it is your employer's established policy to make when a job ends

- payments received in return for you undertaking not to carry out certain actions, sometimes called a restrictive covenant (if not already entered with other pay in box 1.8 or 1.10)
- bonuses on leaving a job (for example, for doing extra work in the period leading up to redundancy). Do not enter redundancy payments themselves in this category – they go in box 1.29, after deducting various reliefs.

All these payments are taxable in full. For tax purposes, they are treated just like the rest of your pay.

Payments from non-approved retirement schemes

| • Retirement and death lump sums | 1.26 £ |
| • From box Q of Help Sheet IR204 | 1.28 £ |

Most pension schemes are approved by the Inland Revenue or statutory schemes, and the lump sums you receive from them are tax-free (within limits). Payments from a non-approved scheme are also tax-free if:
- they arose because of an accident you suffered at work, or
- they were funded by a contribution from your employer on which you have already paid tax, or
- they arose from your own contributions.

If you have any tax-free payments, the total should go in box 1.26. Any taxable payments you receive should be entered in box 1.28.

Other payments

• £30,000 exemption	1.24 £
• Foreign service and disability	1.25 £
• From box R of Help Sheet IR204	1.29 £

Some payments are tax-free altogether if:
- you get them as a result of accident or chronic illness which meant that you couldn't do your job (or they are payments to your family because of your death)
- 75 per cent of your service in the job was foreign service, or if you

worked abroad for least ten out of the last 20 years (and 50 per cent of your time in the job, if longer than 20 years). If you can't meet these conditions, you may still get some relief – see Help Sheet *IR204 Lump sums and compensation payments*.

Enter these payments under reliefs in box 1.25.
The first £30,000 of the following payments are also tax-free:

- redundancy pay (either statutory or at the employer's discretion)
- pay in lieu of notice which is not included in your terms and conditions of employment
- any other payments on leaving a job which were not part of your terms and conditions, and not 'expected' or received as payment for work done.

Enter the first £30,000 (or total received) under reliefs in box 1.24. Anything over £30,000 is taxable and should be entered in box 1.29.

FOREIGN EARNINGS

The broad principle of the UK tax system is that you are taxed on foreign earnings if you are resident or ordinarily resident in this country, even if your permanent home (your domicile) is elsewhere. A full explanation of all these terms is included in Chapter 25. If you think you may be able to claim non-residence you should read that chapter first.

You should include foreign earnings in boxes 1.8 to 1.10 (your employer may already have included foreign earnings in your P60). But if you are a UK resident, or a British citizen, a Crown employee or a citizen of some other countries you can claim personal allowances to set against your income. You may also be able to claim deductions in boxes 1.31, 1.37 and 1.38 which make the possibility of tax on foreign earnings a less fearsome prospect.

Foreign earnings not taxable in the UK

Foreign earnings not taxable in the UK in year ended 5 April 1998 - see Notes, page EN6   1.31 £

In some cases, foreign earnings can be free of UK tax if:

- you were prevented from bringing the earnings into the UK by law, government action, or shortage of foreign currency in the country where they were earned, or
- you are resident but not ordinarily resident in the UK, or
- you are resident and ordinarily resident, but not domiciled in the UK, and the job is carried out wholly outside the country (except for incidental

duties such as attending a directors' meeting in the UK).

This is called the remittance basis. You may be able to claim a deduction on these grounds even if you were non-resident for only part of the year, or if you have included in your tax return income for a different year (for example, if you have only just been able to bring into this country income earned in an earlier year). Help Sheet *IR211 Employment – Residence and Domicile issues* helps you through the calculations to see how much you should enter in box 1.31.

Foreign earnings deduction

■ *Foreign Earnings Deduction*		1.37 £

EXAMPLE

Chris Batty goes to work in Bahrain on a short-term contract, coming home every few months. His diary looks like this:

			running total in each period
3 July 1996	to Bahrain	40 days	40 days
12 August 1996	to UK	20 days	60 days
		(break in qualifying period)	
1 September 1996	to Bahrain	40 days	40 days
11 October 1996	to UK	10 days	50 days
21 October 1996	to Bahrain	120 days	170 days
16 February 1997	to UK	50 days	220 days
5 April 1997	to Bahrain	160 days	380 days
12 September 1997	to UK permanently		

His first visit home is within the 62-day limit, but it is more than one-sixth of the 100 days from when he first went to Bahrain on 3 July to when his second visit to Bahrain ended on 11 October (40 + 20 + 40 = 100). So the first 40 days do not count towards his qualifying period. That only starts at the beginning of his second period in Bahrain (1 September 1996).

His second Bahrain + UK + Bahrain stretch (1 September to 16 February) is 170 days, and the UK visit is comfortably within that. The third Bahrain + UK + Bahrain stretch (21 October 1996 to 12 September 1997) is 120 + 50 + 160 = 330 days; one-sixth of 330 days is 55 days, so his third UK visit does not break his qualifying period either. By now, Chris has reached a qualifying period of 365 days, so all his Bahraini earnings between 1 September 1996 and 12 September 1997 are free of UK tax. He claims his tax-free earnings for the tax year ending 5 April 1998 (received between 6 April 1997 and 12 September 1997) as a foreign earnings deduction in box 1.37.

Even if you are resident (and ordinarily resident) in the UK you can still receive all your foreign earnings up to 17 March 1998 free of UK tax if you spend at least 365 days abroad in a qualifying period. This is called the foreign earnings deduction and you claim it in box 1.37. Note, however, that you cannot claim the foreign earnings deduction if you are taxed on the remittance basis.

You do not need to work for the whole of your absence abroad, and you can make return visits to the UK during the qualifying period, as long as:

- no single visit back to the UK lasts for more than 62 consecutive days, and
- the total number of days you spend in the UK is not more than one-sixth of the total number of days in the visit itself, plus the stretches abroad on either side of the visit.

Whenever you break one of these conditions, a new qualifying period must begin. If you are in the UK at the end of a day (midnight) that day counts as a day spent in the UK. There are more generous special rules for seafarers working on ships abroad (anyone who performs all or most of their duties on a ship, any other duties being merely incidental).

Help Sheet *IR205 Foreign earnings deduction* (or the separate version for seafarers) will tell you if you can claim the deduction. Note, though, that unless you are a seafarer, you can no longer claim the deduction for earnings on or after 17 March 1998.

If you can claim the deduction, enter in box 1.37 the amount of earnings for the tax year ending 5 April 1998 arising from your work abroad during the qualifying period. Remember, though, that you should already have included this amount in your earnings in boxes 1.8 to 1.10. Also note that you should deduct from your qualifying foreign earnings any pension contributions or allowable expenses.

For the tax year ending 5 April 1998, you must claim the deduction by 31 January 1999. However, if your tax position for earlier tax years has not yet been finalised, you may still be able to claim the deduction for those years.

Foreign tax

■ *Foreign tax for which tax credit relief not claimed*   `1.38` £ [   ]

If you work abroad, you may be liable to two lots of tax: tax charged by the country in which you earn the money and UK tax. You have two options for avoiding this double taxation:

- claiming tax credit relief (if you are a UK resident)
- deducting the foreign tax from your foreign earnings.

Because tax credit relief can wipe out all or part of the foreign tax, it is usually the best option, but it is not always available. There are various Inland Revenue working sheets which may help you decide which is the best option for you (see Chapter 19 for more details). If you decide to claim tax credit relief, leave box 1.38 blank. Otherwise, enter the amount of foreign tax.

EXPENSES INCURRED IN DOING YOUR JOB

Income from employment continued

■ **Expenses you incurred in doing your job** - see Notes, page EN7

You should already have entered all the expenses payments and allowances you received in box 1.23. However, not all these expenses will be taxable, and there may be expenses for which you were not reimbursed and on which you can claim tax relief. So you should enter all your tax-allowable expenses, whether or not you were reimbursed, in boxes 1.32 to 1.36.

The only exception is expenses for which your employer has a dispensation (see p. 210). These should not be entered anywhere on your tax return, unless your allowable expenses came to more than the amount covered by the dispensation (in which case you should enter the extra). Your employer should be able to tell you what dispensations exist.

The overall rule is that only those expenses which are expended wholly, exclusively and necessarily in doing your job are allowable, except for travel and related meal and accommodation expenses, which must be necessarily incurred. In both cases, necessarily means that it would be necessary for anybody doing the job, not just necessary for you.

There is no neat list of definitions in tax law, and much depends on previous court judgements. In practice, a

> **T AX - SAVING IDEA**
>
> If your journey counts as business travel, don't forget to include the cost of any meals and accommodation which are attributable to the journey (other than the usual expenses you incur when at your normal place of work).

lot comes down to agreement with your tax inspector and you should keep all the evidence you have (receipts, mileage details and so on) to back up your claims. However, the main tax-allowable expenses are listed below.

Travel and subsistence costs

• Travel and subsistence costs	1.32 £

These include:

- business travel costs, for example fares. If you use your own car for work, the taxable amount of any mileage allowance should already have been entered in box 1.15. However, if you do not get a mileage allowance, or your mileage allowance does not cover the full cost of your business travel, you can enter the costs you bear here. You can claim either the exact amount of your expenses in line with your business mileage (method 1 on p. 92) or a fixed number of pence per mile (method 2 on p. 92). You may also be able to claim capital allowances on the cost of the car, but enter these in box 1.35, not here
- meals and accommodation costs (subsistence) incurred in making the journey
- other business expenses arising because of the journey, for example telephone costs. You cannot deduct personal expenses, such as phone calls home, daily newspapers and personal laundry – but in practice, you may not have had to include these in box 1.23 in any case, since small amounts of personal expenses are tax-free (see p. 88).

A difficult area has long been deciding what is business travel. The cost of travel between your home and your normal place of work is not an allowable expense, but there are special rules for:

- directors who are directors of more than one company in the same group – they can claim the cost of travel between the companies
- a journey for work purposes between your home and somewhere other than your normal workplace. For the year ending 5 April 1998, you can claim the costs of either the actual journey between your home and the temporary workplace, or a journey between the normal place of work and the temporary workplace, whichever is less. This would also apply if you are temporarily absent – that is required to work somewhere other than your normal workplace for not more than 12 months, and you return to your normal workplace afterwards
- people who are required by their employer to work at home (that is, not if it just a matter of personal choice). They may be able to claim the cost of travel from home to other places of work, but in practice few employ-

ees can do this

- travelling workers who are considered to be working the moment they leave home (for example, a commercial traveller). They can claim for journeys which start or finish at home. However, a commercial traveller who operated from a particular office each day, or a computer consultant who worked at a succession of places as part of the same employment (a site-based employee) would not qualify
- some workers in the building and related trades who are covered by working rule agreements between employers' federations and trade unions. The Inland Revenue has agreed that certain travel and lodging allowances paid under such agreements are tax-free
- employees who work outside the UK. The treatment differs depending on whether you work wholly or partly abroad.

If you are claiming home to work travel for one of these reasons, you should include the amount here, and also tick box 1.36. Be prepared to justify your claim.

There are many grey areas, and the record-keeping can be difficult for both employees and employees. A clearer and more generous system started for business journeys made after 5 April 1998. You can now claim the full cost of travelling you are required to incur in the performance of your duties (travel 'on the job'), or travelling to or from a place that you have to attend for your job – so long as attendance is a requirement of your duties, rather than just a matter of personal convenience. You cannot claim the costs of ordinary commuting or private travel.

Ordinary commuting is defined as travel between your home and your permanent workplace. A workplace counts as 'temporary' if you go there for a limited duration or for a temporary purpose, but it loses its temporary status if you spend at least 40 per cent of your working time there over a period which lasts (or is likely to last) for more than 24 months. You do not need to have, or return to, a permanent workplace.

The rules, although clearer, can still be interpreted in different ways depending on the facts of the case. If you are unsure what you can claim, the Inland Revenue guide *Employee Travel – a Tax and NICs Guide for Employers* (to which your employer should have access) gives the full rules and many useful examples.

Fixed deductions for expenses

The Inland Revenue has agreed flat-rate expenses with various trade unions and other bodies to cover the costs of providing equipment and special clothing which is not provided by employers. For example, carpenters and joiners in the building trade can claim a flat-rate £105, uniformed bank employees can claim £40. Ask your union or other staff body if you are covered. You do not have to claim the flat-rate deduction – if you spend more, you can claim more, but if so, you should enter the amount in box 1.35, under other expenses, not here.

Professional fees and subscriptions

• Professional fees and subscriptions

You may pay for membership of a particular body or society which is relevant to your work. You can claim it in box 1.34 as an allowable expense provided that:

- membership of the organisation, or registration with it, is a condition of your job, for example, as a dentist, optician or solicitor
- the organisation is approved by the Revenue as being a non-profit body which exists for a worthy purpose such as to maintain professional standards, and membership is relevant to your work.

Any such organisation should be able to tell you whether it is on the Revenue's list of approved bodies.

Other expenses and capital allowances

• Other expenses and capital allowances

These must be wholly, necessarily and exclusively incurred for work. This means that you cannot claim expenses which merely put you in a position to do your job – for example, a journalist's expenditure on newspapers, employment agency fees, childcare. There are special rules for business entertaining – check with your employer whether these affect you. The expenses you should be allowed are:

- the costs of providing and maintaining tools and special clothing which you have not already claimed a fixed deduction for in box 1.33. Special clothing does not cover clothes which you could wear outside work, even if you would never choose to do so
- the cost of special security needed because of your job – you can claim this only if your employer paid for the security or reimbursed you, and

you have already entered the appropriate amount as a benefit
- costs and expenses if you are held liable for some wrongful act as an employee, or insurance premiums to cover you against such costs
- training expenses for which you are not reimbursed, providing that your employer requires or encourages you to attend the course and gives you paid time off to do so, it is full-time (or virtually so) and lasts for at least four weeks. The expenses allowed are fees (unless you have already had tax relief on these) and the cost of essential books. You may also be able to claim some accommodation or travel costs if you count as being temporarily absent from your normal workplace (see p. 222)
- if you are required to work at home (and do not do so merely from choice) a proportion of the heating and lighting costs, and, for a room used exclusively for work, council tax.

As well as expenses, you may be able to claim capital allowances in this section if:
- you buy equipment such as a computer which is necessary (as defined on p. 221) for your job. You cannot claim an allowance if your employer would have provided the equipment had you not chosen to do so
- you buy a car or other vehicle for use in your job. This does not have to be necessary (as defined on p. 221) and what's more, if you can claim allowances, you can also claim the interest on any loan to buy the car. However, you can claim only the proportion of your capital allowance and loan interest that arises from your use of the car for work.

When you finally dispose of an asset on which you claimed capital allowances there may be a balancing charge to add to your taxable income. (See Chapter 19 for how to work out capital allowances and balancing charges.)

SHARE SCHEMES

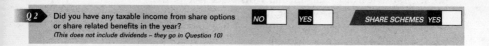

Q2 Did you have any taxable income from share options or share related benefits in the year? *(This does not include dividends – they go in Question 10)*   NO ☐   YES ☐   SHARE SCHEMES YES ☐

Part of your payment from a job may come in the form of shares (or share options – the right to buy shares at a set price at some point in the future) in your employer's company. However, there are special approved schemes under which you can get your shares or options tax-free. You only have to tick the YES box and complete this supplementary page if your shares or share options are not received through an approved scheme, or if you are in a scheme but breach its rules in some respect. You have to complete the back of the supplementary page before the front and you need to fill in a separate page 2 (or a photocopy) for each taxable event arising from a share scheme.

The benefit you get from share schemes may come in the following forms:

- a gift of the shares themselves, or a discount on the purchase price
- an option to buy a set number of shares, at a set price, at a particular time in the future
- dividends from the shares once they become your property
- a capital gain (or loss) arising from movements in the share price once the shares become your property.

The share dividends are taxed like the dividends from any share you own and you enter them at Q10 of the basic tax return (see Chapter 13). The same is broadly true for the capital gains, except that some special rules may apply, for example when deciding what allowable expenditure can be deducted (see below). You give details of capital gains on the Capital gains supplementary pages. The Share scheme supplementary pages apply only on the gift (or discounted purchase) of the shares themselves, or an option to buy them, and to any associated advantages. Occasionally, with some unapproved schemes, they may also apply when you sell the shares themselves.

DIFFERENT TYPES OF SHARE SCHEMES

For tax purposes, share schemes fall within three broad categories:

- approved profit-sharing schemes
- share option schemes – either approved savings-related schemes or discretionary share option schemes (that is, company share option plans and executive share option schemes), or unapproved schemes
- cheap or free gifts of shares through an unapproved scheme (sometimes called share incentive schemes).

You may have come across Employee Share Ownership Trusts (ESOTs) – these are a special type of trust set up to acquire shares in the company and distribute them to employees. For the employee, the shares are taxable in the same way as shares received through an unapproved scheme.

If you received shares or share options which are taxable in the tax year ending 5 April 1998, you will need to declare them on the Share schemes supplementary page, unless they have already been taxed under PAYE or have been included on Form P11D. If under PAYE, you should put the taxable value of the benefit in box 1.8 of the Employment page, and the tax in box 1.11. If on Form P11D, the taxable value goes in box 1.22.

> **TAX-SAVING IDEA**
> As an employee, you do not often have a choice of scheme, since employers are likely either to have just one scheme, or to have one scheme that is open to all employees and another which is open to a select few. But if you know that your employer is considering a scheme, try to make your voice heard so that the scheme which is chosen is one which suits you.

The documents you need

You should have some correspondence from your employer concerning your scheme, including (where relevant) a share option certificate and a copy of the exercise note. You will also need to know the market price of the shares at various dates – if your employer cannot help, ask your local reference library. If the company is not quoted on the Stock Exchange, the market value has to be agreed with the Inland Revenue.

Approved profit-sharing schemes

These are a way of transferring free shares in a company to its employees via a special trust. As long as you stick to the rules, shares you receive under an approved profit-sharing scheme will be tax-free and you will not need to enter them on the Share scheme pages.

The shares will be taxable only if you sell them within three years of being allocated them. However, there is an exception if the shares are sold before the three years (or five years) are up and the job ended because of an injury, disability, redundancy or death or reaching a specified age (between 60 and 75). In this case, tax is due on only 50 per cent of the market value of the shares when allocated.

Working out the tax
If tax is due, the taxable value is the lesser of:

- the initial market value of the shares at the date when they were allocated to you (occasionally, an earlier date may be used) or
- the actual proceeds of selling them, minus your expenses of selling, for example, stockbrokers' commission. If you give them away, the market value at the time of the gift will be used.

Your employer should work out the taxable value for you and deduct the right amount of tax before passing on the proceeds. If you have left the company, the trustees will work out the taxable value and deduct basic-rate tax: enter the taxable amount at box 1.8 and the amount deducted at box 1.11 in the Employment supplementary page. For more information, see Inland Revenue leaflet IR95.

Share option schemes
There are three key events in the life of an option:

- when you are first granted the option
- when you exercise your right to buy (you may decide not to)
- if you cancel the option in return for some benefit.

If you receive your options through an approved scheme, you will never have to pay tax on the grant of the option. You have tax to pay on the exercise of the option only if you fail to meet various conditions. But you will always be taxed if you agree not to use your option in return for some benefit.

To work out the taxable amount (if any), you need to keep records of:

- the date on which each key event takes place
- the number of shares involved
- the share price – both the price you actually have to pay, and the

> **TAX-SAVING IDEA**
> When you take your shares out of an approved profit-sharing scheme or savings-related share option scheme, you can transfer them into a single company personal equity plan (see p. 80), providing you do so within 90 days.

market value at the time of each event
- any cash you contributed for the option, or any cash (or other benefit) you received for cancelling it.

You have to give this information on page 2 of the Share Schemes supplementary pages for each occasion on which your options are taxable.

Approved savings-related share options

Share options					
Read the Notes, pages SN1 to SN5 **before** filling in the boxes					
■ *Approved savings-related share options*					
		Name of company		Tick if shares unlisted	Taxable amount
• Exercise	2.1			2.2	2.3 £
• Cancellation or release	2.4			2.5	2.6 £

These schemes give you the right (or 'option') to buy a set number of ordinary shares in your employer's company at some point in the future, at a price fixed now, but you must do so using savings in a Save-As-You-Earn (SAYE) plan. If you meet the various conditions laid down by the Revenue, you will get your shares tax-free (see Inland Revenue leaflet IR97).

Among other conditions you must agree to:
- save a set amount each month, with a minimum of £5 a month and a maximum of £250
- save for a set period – three years, five years or seven years (the three-year option applies only if you join the scheme on or after 30 April 1996).

The price of the shares (the subscription price) is fixed when you are granted the option, but cannot normally be less than 80 per cent of their market value at that time (or up to 30 days before). So if, for example, shares in Horridges' plc stand at 400 pence, the lowest subscription price is 320 pence. You have no tax to pay when the option is granted to you. You will not have tax to pay when the option is used unless:
- you exercise your option when your company is taken over or sold, and you have not yet had them for three years. In this case, fill in the Exercise column on page 2 of the Share schemes supplementary page (boxes 2.32 to 2.40) and carry the taxable amount to boxes 2.1 to 2.3 on page 1 (see p. 233 for the calculation)
- you benefit from the option in any way other than using it to buy shares

– for example, if you receive compensation for not using or agreeing not to use your option. Fill in the Cancellation/release column on page 2 (boxes 2.34, 2.38 and 2.41) and then carry the taxable amount to boxes 2.4 to 2.6 on page 1.

Approved discretionary share options

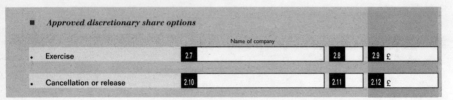

Discretionary schemes may be restricted to groups of employees. Their original name was executive share option schemes, replaced in 1995 by company share option schemes. Broadly, options received under both these schemes are tax-free as long as you exercise them within strict time limits (see opposite).

Unlike savings-related share option schemes, the price at which you can buy the shares under your option must not be less than the market value of the shares when the option is granted (or up to 30 days before). However, you may have been granted a discount of up to 15 per cent of the market value if you:

- were granted options in an Executive Share Option Scheme after 1 January 1992 and before 17 July 1995, and
- your company already had an approved savings-related share option scheme or approved profit-sharing scheme.

If you did receive a discounted option after those dates, this becomes an unapproved share option and you will be taxed on the grant of the option, as well as when it is exercised.

You only have to pay tax on other options if:

> **TAX-SAVING IDEA**
>
> Whether or not you will benefit from a savings-related share option scheme depends on the option price and the share price when you exercise your option.
>
> You do not have to exercise your option if you would make a loss and the return on SAYE schemes is tax-free. So if you are a higher rate taxpayer, or are optimistic that you will make some profit on the shares, joining the scheme is worthwhile.

- you give up the right to exercise the option in return for some benefit, or
- the scheme had ceased to be approved by the time you exercised your options, or
- you exercise the option within three years of being granted it, or
- you exercise the option more than 10 years after being granted it, or
- it is less than three years since you last exercised an option under *any* Executive Share Option Scheme or Company Share Option Scheme.

If the first point applies, fill in the Cancellation/release column on page 2 of the Share schemes supplementary page (boxes 2.34, 2.38 and 2.41) and then fill in boxes 2.10 to 2.12 on page 1. If any of the other conditions apply, fill in the Exercise column on page 2 (boxes 2.34 to 2.40) and then fill in boxes 2.7 to 2.9 on page 1.

Unapproved share options

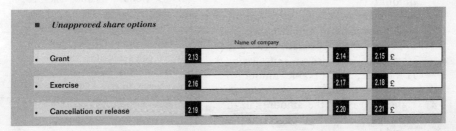

With unapproved schemes, income tax may be payable on both the grant and exercise of an option, or if it is given up in return for some benefit. However, there is no income tax to pay if the option is exercised by your legal representatives after your death, or if the option is not a long option.

A long option is one which can be exercised more than seven years after the date on which it was granted. You pay tax at the time it is granted on the market value of the shares at that time, less the price at which you can exercise the option, less anything you pay for the option. So, there will be no tax to pay if the option is to buy shares at the market value at the time the option was granted. You may have further tax to pay when you finally exercise the option, but you can set against the tax due any income tax you paid when the option was granted.

An option which must be exercised within seven years is not taxable at the time it is granted (except for some non-residents).

How to work out the taxable amount

Whatever type of share option scheme you have, and whether it is approved or unapproved, if the event (the grant, exercise or cancellation) is taxable, the taxable amount is worked out as in the box on the right. You enter the amounts in the right-hand column of page 1 headed Taxable.

EXAMPLE

In 1990 Edward Brough is granted an option which can be exercised at any time between 1 January 1995 and 1 January 2000. This counts as a long option, so he had to pay tax when it was granted. The market value of the shares in 1990 was £3. Edward has the option to buy 1,000 shares at £2. The market value of the shares over which he has the option is £3 × 1,000 = £3,000: he has the option to buy them at £2 × 1,000 = £2,000. The taxable amount is £3,000 – £2,000 = £1,000. As a higher-rate taxpayer, Edward paid £1,000 × 40 per cent = £400 tax on this.

In October 1997 Edward exercised his option. This cost him £2 × 1,000 = £2,000. Since the market price had risen to £3.50, the market value of the shares was £3.50 × 1,000 = £3,500. The taxable amount is £3,500 – £2,000 = £1,500, incurring tax at £1,500 × 40 per cent = £600. However, Edward can set against this the tax he has already paid, so he only actually has to pay £600 – £400 = £200.

Free or cheap shares through an unapproved scheme

Employers have many reasons for offering cheap or free shares. These count as part of your payment from the job. The exact tax treatment depends on whether the shares are counted as your earnings (and entered under Shares received from your employment in boxes 2.22 to 2.24), or treated as a fringe benefit (and entered under Shares as benefits in boxes 2.25 to 2.27), unless these have already been shown under Earnings from employment.

TAX ON THE EXERCISE OF AN OPTION

Step 1: take the market value of the share at the date the option was exercised (which you should have entered in box 2.40) and multiply by the number of shares you actually bought (entered at box 2.36). This gives you the market value of all the shares you have bought.

Step 2: take the price at which you exercised the option (in box 2.37) and multiply by the number of shares you bought (at box 2.36). This is the actual price.

Step 3: deduct the actual price (at Step 2) from the market value (at Step 1). If you paid anything for the option, you can deduct that too. The result is the taxable amount to enter on page 1 of the Share schemes supplementary page in box 2.3, 2.9, or 2.18 as appropriate.

The grant of an option

This is taxable only for an unapproved share option which can be exercised more than seven years after it was granted. The method is the same as if you were exercising the option, except that you start with the market value at the time the option is granted. Fill in the Grant column on page 2 of the Share schemes supplementary page and carry the taxable amount to box 2.15 on page 1.

The cancellation of an option

If you get anything in return for not exercising your option, the taxable amount is what you received, less anything you paid for your option. Fill in the Cancellation column on page 2, and boxes 2.19 to 2.21.

The distinction is fine, but significant: whereas with shares which count as earnings you are taxed on the difference between the market value of the shares and the price at which you acquired them, with shares which count as benefits you are taxed as if you received an interest-free loan from your employer (see p. 98). In some circumstances, this may mean no tax to pay.

You should enter under Shares as benefits (see p. 234):

- shares you are allowed to pay for in instalments (partly-paid shares)
- shares which you buy but where part of the purchase price is deferred, for example, when a particular profit target is met
- any other exceptional cases in which cheap or free shares do not count as earnings.

All other free or cheap shares should go under Shares received from your employment (see p. 234). Even after you have acquired the shares, you may be considered to receive further taxable benefits from them, for example, an increase in their value when a restriction is lifted. You should enter these under Post acquisition charges in boxes 2.28 to 2.30.

Shares received from your employment

You may get some benefit tax-free if the company for which you work decides to sell shares to the public and offers shares on special terms to its employees. You have to distinguish between:

- a discounted price offered to employees
- a priority allocation of the shares.

The discounted price is taxable: you pay tax on the difference between the price you pay and that paid by the general public. Enter the taxable amount under Shares received from your employment. However, the benefit of the priority allocation itself is tax-free and need not be entered unless:

- it is reserved for directors or higher-paid employees, or those who are entitled to it do not all get it on similar terms, and
- the shares reserved for employees in their priority allocation are more than a certain percentage of the overall shares on offer – normally, more than 10 per cent of the total shares on offer.

The calculation is very straightforward. Take the market value of the shares at the time you acquired them. Deduct anything you paid for them. The result is the taxable amount.

E XAMPLE

Linden works for Good Holdings, which has just been offered for sale to the public. Using the priority allocation for employees, Linden bought 500 £1 shares, at the discounted staff price of 80p. Linden is not taxed on the benefit of the priority allocation. However, the discounted price is taxable. The market value of the 500 shares was £1 x 500 = £500, but Linden only paid 80p x 500 = £400. She is taxed on £500 – £400 = £100.

Shares as benefits

Anything entered under this category is treated as an interest-free loan. The

loan is the difference between what you paid and the market value. The loan is taxable only if:

- you count as earning at a rate of £8,500 or more or are a director (see p. 93 for how this is worked out)
- the total amount of all the cheap or interest-free loans from your employer outstanding in the tax year comes to more than £5,000 (see p. 98).

If tax is payable, it will be spread out over the whole life of the loan.

The taxable value of the loan is the theoretical interest you would have paid had you been charged interest at an official rate set down by the government.

Post-acquisition charges

You are charged tax on any further benefit from cheap or free shares. This applies even if you have since left the company. There is no charge if the shares were on offer to the public generally (and you did not buy them through a special offer for employees). Otherwise, you may have further tax to pay on:

- an increase in value when rights or restrictions attached to the shares are changed – for example, if you gain the right to dividends
- an increase in value if the shares are in a subsidiary company. Tax is chargeable on the seventh anniversary of acquiring the shares, or when they are sold, if earlier
- other benefits reserved only for insiders (that is, which are not available to at least 90 per cent of all the shareholders), such as bonus or rights issues of shares, cash, vouchers or tokens.

You need to enter these in boxes 2.28 to 2.30 on page 1 of the Share schemes supplementary page, giving the details on page 2.

SELF-EMPLOYMENT

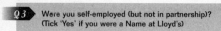

CHAPTER 19

Q3 Were you self-employed (but not in partnership)?
(Tick 'Yes' if you were a Name at Lloyd's)   NO [ ]   YES [ ]   SELF-EMPLOYMENT YES [ ]

If any of your income for the tax year ending 5 April 1998 came from running your own business as a self-employed person, answer YES to Q3 on the basic tax return. You'll need to fill in a separate set of Self-employment supplementary pages for each business you have.

Self-employed people are able to claim more income tax reliefs than employed people and they usually pay less in National Insurance, so you might need to prove to your tax office that you really are self-employed. In general, you'll count as self-employed provided you can answer yes to all of the following questions:

- do you control how your business is run? For example, do you decide what work you take on, where you do the work, what hours you keep?
- is your own money at risk in the business? For example, have you had to pay for your own premises, do you have to finance the lag between incurring costs and receiving payments?
- do you have to meet any losses as well as keeping any profits?
- do you provide the major equipment necessary for your work – for example computer and photocopier for office-based work or machinery for an engineering business? It's not enough that you provide your own small tools – many employees do this too
- are you free to employ other people to help you fulfil the contracts you take on? Do you pay your employees yourself?
- if a job doesn't come up to scratch, do you have to redo it or correct it in your own time and at your expense?

Usually, it will be obvious whether you are an employee or self-employed. But sometimes it's not so clear – for example, if you are newly in business doing work for just one client, perhaps working at a former employer's premises on a freelance basis. Beware if you work through an agency – for example as an agency carer or temporary secretary. Even if you choose whether or not to take on a particular job, you will almost certainly count as an employee rather than self-employed.

If you pay tax and National Insurance as if you are self-employed, but later either your tax office or the Contributions Agency decides you are really an employee, you could face a large bill for back taxes, so it is important to get your status straight right from the start. If you're in any doubt, you can ask your tax office or the Contributions Agency for a written decision about your employment status. If you don't agree with the decision, you can appeal.

BUSINESS DETAILS

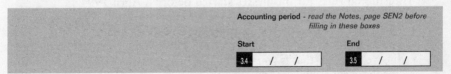

The first part of the supplement simply deals with basic details – the name and nature of your business and the address from which you trade.

Your accounting year

You also need to give the start and finish dates of the accounting period for which you are giving details. Normally, an accounting period is a year long, with the new accounting year starting immediately the previous year ends.

But in the first and last year or two of your business, your accounting year might be longer or shorter (see p. 241).

You may already have given information about your latest set of accounts in last year's return (for example, if your accounting periods overlap). If so, you do not need to give all the information again: you can leave boxes 3.11 to 3.60 and 3.93 to 3.109 blank, but tick box 3.5A (see below). Similarly, if your accounts do not run from the last accounting date, explain why in the Additional information box and tick box 3.7 (see below).

- Tick box 3.5A if you entered details for all relevant accounting periods on last year's Tax Return and boxes 3.11 to 3.70 will be blank | 3.5A |

- Tick box 3.6 if details in boxes 3.1 or 3.3 have changed since your last Tax Return | 3.6 |

- Tick box 3.7 if your accounts do not cover the period from the last accounting date (explain why in the 'Additional information' box below) | 3.7 |

- Tick box 3.8A if you wish to voluntarily disclose that you have applied the anti-avoidance rules in Schedule 22 FA 1995 when calculating your transitional overlap profit for 1997-98 | 3.8A |

- Tick box 3.8B if your accounting date has changed (only if this is a permanent change and you want it to count for tax) | 3.8B |

- Tick box 3.8C if this is the second or further change (explain why you have not used the same date as last year in the 'Additional information' box) | 3.8C |

- Date of commencement if after 5 April 1994 | 3.9 / / |

- Date of cessation if before 6 April 1998 | 3.10 / / |

What profits are taxed
This section of the self-employment pages establishes which profits form the basis of your tax bill for the year ending 5 April 1998, and what information you need to give the Revenue about them. In most cases, your tax bill for the year ending 5 April 1998 will be based on the profits you make during the accounting period which ended during that tax year (the current year basis of taxation).

However, there are special rules if you are in the opening or closing years of the business, have changed your accounting date, or are affected by transitional rules for businesses started before 6 April 1994.

Transitional rules for businesses started before 6 April 1994
If you had already been in business for a while on 6 April 1994, you switch to the current year basis only from the tax year ending 5 April 1998 onwards. Until the tax year ending 5 April 1996, you were taxed on the preceding year basis – that is your tax bill for that year was based on your profits for the accounting year ending in the previous tax year. To make the shift from one basis to another, the tax year ending 5 April 1997 was a transitional year when you were taxed on the average of your profits for the two accounting years ending in the tax years ending 5 April 1996 and 5 April

1997. In most cases, this means that you were taxed on only half the profits you made during those two accounting years.

Although all businesses are now taxed on a current year basis, the transitional rules live on in the form of transitional overlap relief. The transitional rules, in effect, meant that a whole accounting year's profits drop out of the tax assessment process. However, something of this sort would have happened anyway when you eventually closed your business. This is because, under the old tax system, when you opened for business, some profits were taxed twice or even three times. The record would have been set straight under the old closing year rules. Under the new closing year rules, you won't get full relief for this double or triple taxation. So that you don't lose out, the transitional rules identify part of your profits for the tax year ending 5 April 1998 as transitional overlap profits (see example below). These are the profits earned in the period from the start of your accounting year up to 5 April 1997. You will eventually get tax relief on these profits in the same way as for other overlap profits (see p. 242).

For more information see Help Sheet *IR222 How to calculate your taxable profits.*

EXAMPLE

Frank Mills has been in business for ten years, running a take-away food shop. His accounting year runs from 1 August to the following 31 July. His profits for the last few years are as follows:

Accounting year	Profits	Tax year in which taxed
1.8.93-31.7.94	£15,400	Year ending 5 April 1996
1.8.94-31.7.95	£17,800	Year ending 5 April 1997
1.8.95-31.7.96	£17,000	Year ending 5 April 1997
1.8.96-31.7.97	£17,200	Year ending 5 April 1998

For the tax year ending 5 April 1997, Frank's taxable profits were worked out, taking the average of the two accounting years 1994-95 and 1995-96, as follows:

$$(£17,800 + £17,000) \times 365 \div (366 + 365) = £17,376$$

In the tax year ending 5 April 1998, his tax bill is based on profits for his accounting year to 31 July 1997. Out of that year, 248 days fell before 6 April 1997, so he has transitional overlap profits of:

$$248 \div 365 \times £17,200 = £11,687$$

Rules to stop you saving tax

Anyone who has been in business for some years has had an exceptional opportunity to save tax by making as much profit as possible during the two accounting years ending in 1995-96 and 1996-97, because of the transitional rules. There is an advantage in boosting profits for 1997-98 in order to maximise the transitional overlap profits. However, the government anticipated this and passed some stiff anti-avoidance laws designed to stop you saving tax by artificial means. The sorts of activities which might be regarded with suspicion include, for example:

- changing the intervals at which you normally buy in supplies
- altering the accounting treatment of long-term contracts
- bringing forward or deferring routine maintenance
- switching to a different way of calculating your business expenses
- changing the timing or way in which you invoice your customers
- altering your procedure for collecting and paying debts
- changing the date to which you make up your company accounts
- making a financial arrangement with a family member or trust fund, say, which results in profits or expenses being temporarily altered
- agreements to buy back supplies at some future date.

A change to your business or accounting practices or a transaction which, on the face of it, could be regarded as a tax-saving dodge will trigger a tax penalty, unless it passes one of the following tests:

- the motive test – it was made purely for commercial reasons
- the benefit test – the main benefit is not the tax advantage
- the too small to count test. If the profits shifted from one year to another are less than £10,000 or if your average annual turnover is less than £50,000, the change or transaction will be ignored.

Tick box 3.8A if you have adjusted your transitional overlap profits to exclude amounts which would otherwise have been shifted to produce a tax saving. If you fail to adjust your profits for any dubious changes or

> ### TAX-SAVING IDEA
> Are you worried that some change which affects your profits might be interpreted as a measure to save tax during the transitional period? If so, tick box 3.8A on the tax return and reduce the amount of transitional overlap relief claimed in box 3.77.
>
> If applicable, attach a note explaining why you think the anti-avoidance rules should not apply. If the Inland Revenue agrees with you, your transitional overlap profits will be readjusted, saving you tax in the long run. If it disagrees, you won't be able to get the full transitional overlap relief you might have hoped for, but there will be no penalty to pay.

transactions, you will have to pay a penalty. Your transitional overlap profits, on which you can claim relief, will be reduced by $1^1/_4$ times the amount you have incorrectly included.

STARTING OR CLOSING A BUSINESS

If you start a business, special rules say how you will be taxed in the first two or three years.

First tax year during which you're in business

You are taxed on your profits from the date your business started to the end of the tax year (that is the following 5 April). This is worked out by waiting until your first set of accounts is drawn up and then allocating a proportion of those profits to the period up to the end of the tax year. This is usually done on the basis of days. For example, suppose you started in business on 1 January 1998 and your first accounting period runs to 31 January 1999. Out of that first 396-day accounting period, 95 days fall between 1 January to 5 April, so your profits for the tax year ending 5 April 1998 are deemed to be $^{95}/_{396}$ths of the profit for the whole accounting period.

Second tax year during which you're in business

In most cases, the end of an accounting period (not necessarily your first) will fall sometime during this second tax year. Provided you have been trading for at least 12 months, your tax bill will be based on profits for the 12 months up to that date. In the example above, there is an end accounting date falling within the tax year ending 5 April 1999. This is 31 January and, at that date, the business has been running for more than a year. Therefore, tax will be based on profits for the 12 months up to 31 January 1999 – that is $^{365}/_{396}$ths of the profits for the whole accounting period.

If there is an accounting date within the tax year, but you have been trading for less than 12 months, your tax is based on the first 12 months of trading, with a proportion of the profits from your next accounting period being used to make up the full 12 months. For example, suppose you started in business on 1 March 1997 and draw up your accounts to 30 June 1997 and then to each subsequent 30 June. Tax in your second year, the year ending 5 April 1998, would be based on the whole of the profits for the period 1 March to 30 June 1997 (122 days) and and $^{243}/_{365}$ths of the profits for the accounting year from 1 July 1997 to 30 June 1998.

If there is no accounting date at all during your second tax year, tax is based on the profits for the tax year itself – that is from 6 April to 5 April. For example, if you started in business on 1 March 1997 but did not draw up your first accounts until 30 June 1998, an accounting period of 482 days, you would be taxed on $^{365}/_{482}$nds of the profits for that whole period.

Third tax year during which you're in business

If an accounting period at least 12 months after you started up finished during your second tax year, from the third year onwards, you are simply taxed on the profits for the accounting year ending during the tax year – that is normal current year basis.

Where the first accounting period to end at least 12 months after start-up comes to a close in your third tax year of trading, you are taxed on profits for the 12 months to the end of that period. From the fourth year onwards, you are taxed on the normal current year basis.

Overlap profits

As you can see, the opening year rules described above mean that some profits may be taxed twice. For example, for the business which started on 1 January 1998, the profits for the first two years were as follows:

Tax year	Profits on which your tax bill is based
Year ending 5 April 1998	$^{95}/_{396}$ths x profit for accounting period from 1 January 1998 to 31 January 1999
Year ending 5 April 1999	$^{365}/_{396}$ths x profit for the period from 1 January 1998 to 31 January 1999

This means that $(95 + 365) - 396 = 64$ days' worth of profit have been taxed twice. This is called 'overlap profit' and the period over which it arose is called the 'overlap period'. One of the principles of the current year basis tax system is that, over the lifetime of your business, all your profits should be taxed, but only taxed once. Therefore, you are given overlap relief to compensate you for having paid tax on some profits twice in your opening year. But there is a snag: overlap relief is usually given only when you finally close the business down (see p. 244) and inflation in the meantime will reduce its value.

Fiscal accounting

You can avoid all the problems of opening year rules and overlap relief, if you opt for fiscal accounting. This means using the tax year as your accounting year. By Inland Revenue concession, this includes having an accounting date of 31 March, rather than exactly on the tax year end of 5 April. For example, you might have started in business on 1 September 1997, drawing

Jim Newall started working as a freelance computer consultant on 1 July 1995 and drew up his first accounts on 30 April 1996. 30 April is his normal accounting year end. His profit and tax position for the first few years of business was as follows:

Accounting period	Profit for the period
1 July 1995 – 30 April 1996	£ 4,000
1 May 1996 – 30 April 1997	£ 8,500
1 May 1997 – 30 April 1998	£18,500

Tax year	Tax basis	Profits on which tax based
1995-96	Profits for tax year	$280 \div 305 \times £4{,}000 = £3{,}672$
1996-97	First 12 months of trading	$£4{,}000 + (60 \div 365 \times £8{,}500) = £5{,}397$
1997-98	Profits for 12 months to 30 April 1997	£8,500
1998-99	Profits for accounting year ending on 30 April 1998	£18,500

The profit for the period 1 July 1995 to 5 April 1996 is taxed twice, as is profit for the 61 days from 1 May to 30 June 1996. This gives Jim an overlap profit of $£3{,}672 + (61 \div 365 \times £8{,}500) = £3{,}672 + £1{,}420 = £5{,}092$.

up your first accounts on 31 March 1998 and on each 31 March thereafter. Your tax for the tax year ending 5 April 1998 will be based on your profits from 1 September 1997 to 31 March 1998. Your tax for the next year will be based on profits for 1 April 1998 to 31 March 1999 and so on.

For further information see Help Sheet *IR222 How to calculate your taxable profits.*

TAX-SAVING IDEAS

Fiscal accounting makes accounting for tax very simple, especially in your opening years, but it has drawbacks too: you don't have long to make up your accounts and there's only a short delay between making your profits and paying tax on them (see opposite).

If you don't choose fiscal accounting, try to keep your profits as low as possible during the first year or two, so that your overlap profit is small.

Changing your accounting date

Changing your accounting date can bring tax benefits: special rules to determine the profits on which you are taxed can work to your advantage. If you change to a date later in the tax year, you can also use some of the overlap relief you may have acquired so far. But in order to count as a change of accounting date in the Inland Revenue's eyes, all of the following conditions must be satisfied: the first accounting period running up to the new date must not be more than 18 months; you must notify the Revenue in your tax return; and either you must not have made a change of accounting date (effective for tax purposes) in the previous five tax years or, if you have, the Revenue must be satisfied that the latest change is for bona fide commercial reasons.

If you have changed accounting date, you can satisfy the requirement to notify the Revenue by ticking box 3.8B. If you have changed accounting date in previous years, also tick 3.8C and explain your reasons for doing so in the Additional information box.

Closing your business

In the tax years up to the one before closure, you are taxed on the normal current year basis. For the tax year in which you close down, you're taxed on profits from your last accounting date up to the date on which you close down less any overlap profits which you have been carrying forward (see p. 242). The position for a business closing down in the tax year ending 5 April 1999 is summarised below.

> **TAX-SAVING IDEA**
>
> If you were already in business on 6 April 1994 and you have transitional overlap profits, closing down after 5 April 1998 can work to your advantage because you will then get tax relief on the overlap profits.
>
> If you close down in 1997-98 your tax inspector can decide to tax you under rules applying in the old preceding year system if this means you pay higher tax.

Tax year ending	Profits on which your tax bill is based
5 April 1997	Profits for accounting year ending in 1996-97
5 April 1998	Profits for accounting year ending in 1997-98
5 April 1999	Profits from day after end of accounting year ending 1997-98 up to date of closure less overlap profits

There is an exception to the rules described above if you were already in business on 6 April 1994, and closed down in the tax year ending 5 April 1998. In this case, your tax office can decide to tax you under rules applying under the old, preceding year system of taxing profits. This means that for the last two full years of business your tax office can choose to tax your profits on either a preceding year basis or on the basis of your actual profits for those tax years. You cannot get tax relief on your transitional overlap profits. The tax inspector will choose the basis which produces the largest tax bill.

INCOME

If your turnover is less than £15,000 a year

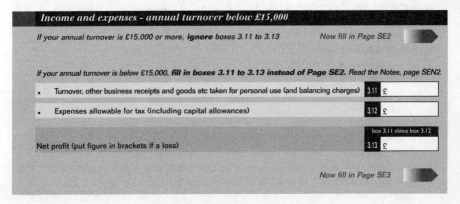

Income and expenses - annual turnover below £15,000

If your annual turnover is £15,000 or more, **ignore** boxes 3.11 to 3.13   Now fill in Page SE2

If your annual turnover is below £15,000, **fill in boxes 3.11 to 3.13 instead of Page SE2**. Read the Notes, page SEN2.

- Turnover, other business receipts and goods etc taken for personal use (and balancing charges)   3.11 £
- Expenses allowable for tax (including capital allowances)   3.12 £

box 3.11 minus box 3.12

Net profit (put figure in brackets if a loss)   3.13 £

Now fill in Page SE3

Complete boxes 3.11 to 3.13. You can get guidance on what expenses are allowable by reading pp. 248 to 254.

You do not need to give full details of your accounts. This does not mean that you can get away without preparing proper accounts – you must have these ready, in case your tax inspector asks to see them, together with all the background paperwork (see p. 12). Note that £15,000 is the annual limit – if your accounts cover a period of under a year, it will be reduced proportionately, and increased if you have a longer accounting period.

Do not complete page 2 of the Self-employed supplement, but go straight to page 3. Turn to p. 255 for guidance on filling in boxes 3.61 and beyond.

If your turnover is £15,000 a year or more

You should complete the details asked for on page 2 of the Self-employed supplementary pages. You don't need to attach a copy of your accounts. If the headings do not tally with the headings you use in your own accounts, don't be tempted to leave any out. Instead, use your judgement to allocate them to boxes on page 2, but make sure that whatever method you adopt this year is followed consistently in future years.

If the period over which you are being taxed is covered by two sets of accounts, you need to complete two Self-employment supplements (unless you have already given all the information in last year's tax return).

If you produce a balance sheet, there is space for the entries on page 4 of the supplement. Enter the amounts in boxes 3.93 to 3.109. If you don't have a balance sheet, leave these boxes blank.

Value added tax (VAT)

You must fill in this Page if your annual turnover is £15,000 or more - read the Notes, page SEN2

If you were registered for VAT, do the
figures in boxes 3.16 to 3.51, include VAT? 3.14   or exclude VAT? 3.15

If your turnover is £49,000 a year or more from 1 December 1997 (£48,000 from 26 November 1996 until then), you must register for VAT. Below that threshold, you can choose whether or not to register. Registration means that you must normally charge your customers VAT on the goods and services that you sell, but you can usually reclaim VAT on the things that you buy to sell, or use, in your business. You must regularly hand over to the Customs & Excise department of the government the net amount of VAT you have collected (or claim a refund if what you are claiming comes to more than the VAT paid by your customers). This VAT does not form part of your profits and needs to be stripped out before your tax bill is calculated. For this reason, the tax office needs to know whether the figures you report in your tax return include VAT or have already had the VAT element stripped out.

If you are registered for VAT, and have entered VAT-inclusive figures, you will need to enter the net amount of VAT paid over to Customs & Excise as other expenses in box 3.50 or the net refund you received over the year as other income/profits in box 3.37. You may have bought capital equipment on which you claim capital allowances (see p. 255) instead of deducting them as expenses. If you are entering VAT-inclusive figures, there won't be an obvious place to enter the VAT on these capital items. You deal with this by adding the VAT to the amount entered in box 3.50 or (if you received a net refund from Customs & Excise) deducting it from the figure entered in box 3.37. Also write in the amount of VAT on capital items in the Additional information box on page 4.

If you are not registered for VAT, you do not charge your customers VAT and the VAT you pay to your suppliers counts as a legitimate business expense. Your figures should include the VAT you have been charged. If you were registered for VAT for part of the year, but not for all, explain why, when the change occurred, and whether your figures are VAT-inclusive or not, in the Additional information box on page 4.

Gross profits

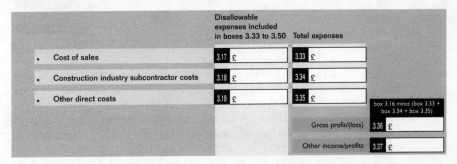

	Disallowable expenses included in boxes 3.33 to 3.50	Total expenses	
• Cost of sales	3.17 £	3.33 £	
• Construction industry subcontractor costs	3.18 £	3.34 £	
• Other direct costs	3.19 £	3.35 £	box 3.16 minus (box 3.33 + box 3.34 + box 3.35)
		Gross profit/(loss)	3.36 £
		Other income/profits	3.37 £

Your taxable profits are the income of your business less all the allowable expenses – that is the expenses you are allowed to deduct under the tax rules.

The starting point for working out your taxable profits is your gross profits. If you are in the business of selling something, this will be the income you get from sales less the cost of buying in the items you sell. If you sell your services, this will be the income you receive. For more information on how to take stock and work in progress into account, see Help Sheet *IR222 How to calculate your taxable profits*.

In your accounts, direct costs (for example, marketing, sales discounts) might include a figure for depreciation of equipment or machinery used in producing your goods. This is not an allowable expense (see Capital allowances on p. 255) and should be entered in box 3.19.

Other income or profits (box 3.37) includes things like income from renting out premises, interest on bank and building society accounts, discounts you get, and so on. If you receive any Business Start-up or Enterprise Allowance, put this in box 3.87, not here.

EXPENSES

• Employee costs	3.20 £		3.38 £	
• Premises costs	3.21 £		3.39 £	
• R~~~irs	3.22 £		3.40	
• Depreciation and loss/ (profit) on sale	3.31 £		3.49 £	
• Other expenses	3.32 £		3.50 £	

Put the total of boxes 3.17
to 3.32 in box 3.53 below

total boxes 3.38 3.50

Total expenses 3.51 £

You don't need to complete page 2 of the Self-employment supplement if your annual turnover is less than £15,000. If it is £15,000 or more you need to allocate your costs and expenses to boxes 3.17 to 3.50. In the boxes in the right-hand column you should enter total expenses under each heading. In the left-hand column you should enter the amount of any expenses not allowed but which have been included in the right-hand column.

You total the amounts in boxes 3.17 to 3.32 and enter the total in box 3.53.

Deducting an expense from your business income has the effect of giving you tax relief at your top rate(s) of tax, so it is important to claim all the expenses you can. According to tax law, you get tax relief on an expense only if it is incurred wholly and exclusively for business. Strictly speaking, this means you can't get relief at all on expenditure which is partly for your private benefit. In practice, the Inland Revenue does allow you to claim a proportion of some costs where something – for example, your car or home – is used partly for business. However, your tax office may baulk at some expenses which arise because of a joint business and private purpose – for example, combining a trip abroad to see a client with a holiday.

TAX-SAVING IDEAS

Claim all the allowable expenses you can. If you're not sure whether an expense is allowable, deduct it from your taxable profits but ask your tax office to confirm whether this is correct.

If you work from home, beware of allowing any part of it to be used exclusively for business. Although you might be able to claim more relief against income tax, you could become liable for business rates and, when you eventually come to sell the home, there could be capital gains tax to pay on part of the home (see p. 62).

It is hard to lay down hard and fast rules which apply to all businesses. Different types of businesses can claim different expenses and to a different extent. It is up to you to show that any claim is justified within the context of your own line of work.

You can claim expenses you incur before you open for business if they would have been allowable anyway. If your business started on or after 6 April 1995, treat them as expenditure incurred on the first day of business.

Expenses which you incur after you close down can be set against any late income which comes into the closed business. However, if there is no income, tax relief on the expenditure is usually lost. With a few particular types of expense, you can get tax relief by setting the expenses against any other income or gains you have for up to seven years (in box 15.11 of the basic tax return, see p. 188).

Employee costs

. Employee costs	3.20 £	3.38 £

Normally allowed
Salaries, bonuses, overtime, commissions etc paid to your employee, together with the add-on costs, such as National Insurance contributions, pension and insurance benefits. The costs of hiring locums to stand in for you or fees paid to people to whom you subcontract work. Training. Council tax paid on behalf of employees if a genuine part of the pay package, taxed as normal through PAYE. Include the cost of employing your wife, husband or other family member in the business, provided their pay is reasonable for the work done. Costs of entertaining staff – for example, a Christmas party.

Not allowed
Your own wages, National Insurance, income tax, pension costs (though you can get personal tax relief for these), your drawings from the business. Wages to employees which remain unpaid nine months after the accounting date (although they can be deducted in the accounting period in which they are eventually paid). Payments to family members if excessive for the work done – be especially careful employing young children which might, in any case, be illegal.

Premises costs
Normally allowed
If you work from dedicated business premises, include any rent, business

rates, water rates, cost of lighting, heating, power, insurance, cleaning, security, and so on. If you work from home, you can claim a proportion of your home related expenses – for example, heating, lighting, power, cleaning, maintenance. If part of the home is used exclusively for business, part of your mortgage interest. Also part of your council tax, though the tax rules are not clear on whether it's enough just to work from home or whether part of it must be dedicated exclusively to business use. The proportion you claim must relate to your business use of the home – for example, based on the number of rooms used or floor area. You should explain the basis used in the Additional information box on page 4 of the supplement.

Not allowed

Cost of buying premises (see Capital allowances on p. 255), costs relating to any part of the premises not used for business.

EXAMPLE

Hannah Brown has converted the garage at her home into an office which is used exclusively for her computer software business. She can claim part of her household expenses as allowable expenses for business purposes and, because she uses part of the home exclusively for business, she can also claim part of her mortgage interest. She makes the following calculation:

add up total household expenses	£1,800
add up the number of rooms in the house, ignoring separate toilets, halls and landings (unless large enough to be used as rooms)	8 rooms
divide the expenses by the number of rooms to give a cost per room figure	£1,800 ÷ 8 = £225 per room
multiply the cost per room by the number of rooms used for business (or by the relevant fraction of a room, if a room is used only partly for business)	1 x £225 = £225

She also claims one-eighth of her mortgage interest as a business expense. This comes to $1/_8$ x £3,600 = £450. However, Hannah may become liable for business rates and capital gains tax on the garage when she sells her home.

Repairs

	3.22 £	3.40 £
• Repairs		

Normally allowed
General maintenance and repairs to your business premises and machinery, cost of replacing small tools.

Not allowed
Costs of alterations and improvements (see Capital allowances on p. 255), costs relating to any part of the premises not used for business, general reserve for repairs.

General administrative expenses

	3.23 £	3.41 £
• General administrative expenses		

Normally allowed
Office expenses, such as postage, telephone, stationery, printing, subscriptions to trade journals, professional fees, cost of computer software (unless bought at the same time as hardware, on which capital allowances can be claimed, see p. 255), accountancy and audit fees and regular expenses not included elsewhere.

Not allowed
Personal expenses, payments to political parties, most donations and fees to clubs, charities and churches. Any non-business part of a cost.

Motor expenses

	3.24 £	3.42 £
• Motor expenses		

Normally allowed
Costs of running a vehicle used in your business – for example, insurance, servicing, repairs, road tax, breakdown insurance, parking charges, fuel, hiring or leasing charges. A proportion of those costs if you also use the vehicle privately.

Not allowed
Travel between your home and business premises. Cost of buying a vehicle

(see Capital allowances on p. 255). Parking fines, other fines.

Travel and subsistence

• Travel and subsistence	3.25 £	3.43 £

Normally allowed
Rail, air and taxi fares, hotel accommodation.

Not allowed
Cost of lunches.

Advertising, promotion and entertainment

• Advertising, promotion and entertainment	3.26 £	3.44 £

Normally allowed
Advertising, mail-shots, free samples, gifts up to £10 a year to clients provided they promote your firm or its products or services and are not food or drink.

Not allowed
Entertaining clients, business associates etc (only entertaining staff is allowed), gifts except those specifically allowed (see above).

Legal and professional costs

• Legal and professional costs	3.27 £	3.45 £

Normally allowed
Fees charged by accountants, auditors, solicitors, surveyors, stocktakers and so on, professional indemnity premiums.

Not allowed
Legal costs of buying premises, equipment etc (treated as part of their cost – see Capital allowances on p. 255), legal expenses on forming a company, cost of settling tax disputes, fines etc as a result of acting illegally.

Bad debts

| | Bad debts | 3.28 £ | 3.46 £ |

Normally allowed
Items you have sold or amounts you have invoiced but for which you no longer expect to be paid. A proportion of a bad debt given up under a voluntary arrangement. If in a later tax year you are paid, include the amount recovered in box 3.37 (other income/profits).

Not allowed
General pool for bad debts.

Interest

| | Interest | 3.29 £ | 3.47 £ |

Normally allowed
Interest and arrangement fees for a business loan or overdraft.

Not allowed
The part of loan payments which represents capital repayments.

Other finance charges

| | Other finance charges | 3.30 £ | 3.48 £ |

Normally allowed
Charges on your business current account, credit card interest and fees, the interest element of hire purchase charges, leasing payments.

Not allowed
The part of any payment which represents capital repayment.

Depreciation and loss/(profit) on sale

| | Depreciation and loss/ (profit) on sale | 3.31 £ | 3.49 £ |

Not allowed
None of these costs are allowable – instead you claim capital allowances (see p. 255). The figure you enter at 3.49 should exactly match the amount you

put in box 3.31 – unless some of the costs relate to finance leases, in which case ask your tax office what you can deduct.

Other expenses

Normally allowed

Any expenses which you haven't found a place for in boxes 3.33 to 3.49. For example, any insurance premiums not included elsewhere, contributions (up to 30 March 2000) to Business Links, trade and part or all of professional subscriptions which secure some benefit for your business or to societies which have an arrangement with the Inland Revenue.

Not allowed

The non-business element of any expenses included in box 3.50. This includes, for example, ordinary clothing even if you bought it specially for business and would not normally wear it otherwise, buying a patent (see Capital allowances right), cost of computer hardware and any software bought at the same time (see Capital allowances right).

Tax adjustments to net profit or loss

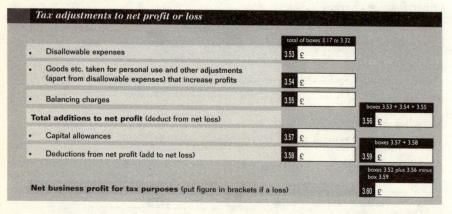

All the expenses which are not allowable are added together and the total entered in box 3.53. In the next box, you must enter the profit attributable to any goods which you took for personal use. These are added to your profits.

CAPITAL ALLOWANCES

When you buy capital items for your business – that is things which will be in use for many years – you are not allowed to set the full cost against your business income in the year you buy the item. In your ordinary business accounts, you'll deduct depreciation each year which varies from business to business and is not allowed as an expense. Instead you deduct capital allowances calculated according to standard rules.

To be eligible for capital allowances, the item you have bought must generally be wholly and exclusively for business use. But, as with allowable expenses (see p. 248), in some cases, you can claim a proportion of the allowance if the item is used partly for business and, in part, privately.

How much you can claim
The basic capital allowance is called a writing-down allowance and it is available for plant and machinery (which covers most of your ordinary business equipment), cars and vans, patents and know-how. In general, capital allowances are not given for what you spend on buying business premises (for example a shop or office), but industrial and agricultural buildings and some hotels with ten or more bedrooms are exceptions. Expenditure which qualifies for allowances is lumped together in one or more pools and you can claim a certain proportion of the pool at the end of each tax year as a writing down allowance.

The maximum you can claim is:
- 25 per cent a year for machinery, plant, vans, patents, know-how (and see box on p. 256)
- 25 per cent a year for cars but, for any car costing over £12,000, there is also a cash limit of £3,000 a year
- 4 per cent a year for industrial and agricultural buildings and qualifying

hotels, and an initial allowance in the first year of 100 per cent for industrial buildings in an enterprise zone. If part of this is not claimed, you can claim 25 per cent a year of the remaining cost.

You can claim less than the maximum. It would be worth restricting your claim if your taxable profits or income were so low that some of the maximum allowance would be wasted. The allowance is not lost. The effect is to carry forward a higher value of assets in your pool of expenditure. This increases the value of the maximum writing-down allowances you can claim in future years. For example, suppose your pool of expenditure is valued at £10,000. If you claimed the full writing-down allowance of 25 per cent, the allowance would be £2,500 and the value of the pool carried forward would be £7,500, so next year you could claim up to 25 per cent x £7,500 = £1,875. If instead, you claimed only a 10 per cent allowance in the first year, the pool carried forward would be £9,000 and the maximum allowance in the second year would be 25 per cent x £9,000 = £2,250.

Various categories of capital expenditure have to be allocated to their own separate pools. These are:

- any car costing more than £12,000 must be hived off to its own pool and the writing-down allowance is limited to the smaller of 25 per cent or £3,000 in each year. Cars costing £12,000 or less are in another pool. Vans, lorries and so on do not count as cars
- industrial and agricultural buildings
- an asset used partly for private use must have its own pool and you can claim only a proportion of the allowance reflecting the proportion of business use
- short-life assets. Capital equipment (other than cars) which you expect to have a useful life of no more than five years can be put in a separate pool. The advantage of doing this is that you get tax relief on the full cost of the item more rapidly than if it were in the general pool of expenditure (see Buying and selling capital items right).

You do not get capital allowances on items you lease rather than buy. Instead the leasing charge counts as an allowable expense (see p. 253). If you buy something on hire purchase, the capital element of the charges can qualify for capital allowances but the interest element is treated as an allowable expense (see p. 253).

Buying and selling capital items

When you buy an item of capital, its cost is added to the appropriate pool of expenditure. This increases the year-end value of the pool on which the writing-down allowance is worked out.

When you first start in business, you might take into the business capital equipment you already own – for example a desk, shelving, a computer. Although no money changes hands, you are treated as having sold the item to your business and you can claim capital allowances in the normal way. Value each item at its second-hand market value given its age, state of repair and so on.

When you sell a capital item, the amount you get for it (up to its original cost) is deducted from the expend-iture pool. Occasionally, this may be more than the total value of the pool, in which case, the excess (called a balancing charge) is added to your profits or (taxable income) for the year, increasing your tax bill. These are entered in boxes 3.62, 3.64, 3.66 and 3.68 and the total is added to your profits at box 3.55.

If you sell the item for less than its written-down value – at the extreme, you might scrap it for nothing – the shortfall remains in your pool of expenditure and continues to be written down. So you could be claiming allowances on an item for many years after you have sold it. Only when you finally close down the business can you claim a balancing allowance for any remaining value of the pool. This is where short-life assets come into their own.

> ## TAX-SAVING IDEAS
>
> Do not claim more capital allowances than needed to reduce your taxable profits to the level of your personal allowances.
>
> Earmarking a capital item as a short-life asset means you can get full tax relief on the cost of the item in just five years.
>
> If you buy software at the same time as you buy a computer, it will count as a capital item for which you claim capital allowances. Buy the software separately and it does not count as capital, so you can get immediate tax relief by claiming its cost as an allowable expense.

If you scrap a short-life asset within five years, you can claim tax relief on the difference between what you get (if anything) for the asset and its written-down value. The relief is given in the tax year in which you scrap it – you don't have to wait until the business closes down. If, having declared an asset as short life, you actually go on using it beyond five years, it is transferred into your general pool of expenditure and treated like any other capital item.

If you are registered for VAT, the amount you put in your expenditure pools should not include VAT. If you are not registered for VAT, you claim capital allowances on the cost including VAT.

Claiming capital allowances

Capital allowances are given as a deduction in working out your taxable profits for the year. Enter the capital allowances you are claiming in boxes 3.61, 3.63, 3.65 and 3.67 and the total is deducted from your profits at box 3.57.

EXAMPLE

Joe Morris has been running a dairy since 1978. He makes up his accounts to 31 December each year. For the year to 31 December 1997, he made the following purchases and sales of capital items:

Date	Capital item	Purchase/sale price
10 March 1997	New van bought	£17,000
5 May 1997	Old van sold (cost £12,000 when new)	£ 5,000
2 November 1997	Second-hand cream separator bought	£38,000

On 31 December 1996, after claiming writing-down allowances, Joe's general pool of capital expenditure stood at £158,000. Because the cream separator was bought between 1 July 1997 and 2 July 1998, Joe can claim an initial allowance of 50 per cent x £38,000 = £19,000. The van was bought before the initial allowance was available (unfortunately, as a goods-carrying van rather than a car it would have qualified). Joe adds this to his existing pool of expenditure and deducts the £5,000 from selling the old van. This gives a general pool at 31 December 1997 of £158,000 + £17,000 − £5,000 = £170,000. Joe can claim a maximum writing-down allowance of 25 per cent x £170,000 = £42,500. This gives allowances of £19,000 + £42,500 = £61,500 to set against his taxable income for the year. In fact, he has only enough profits and other income to use up £37,000 of the allowances. His capital pool at 1 January 1998 (including the balance of the expenditure on the cream separator) becomes £170,000 + £19,000 − £37,000 = £152,000.

Adjustments

So far, in completing the Self-employment supplement, you have entered figures for one particular accounting period. As explained on p. 238 this may not be the same as the period over which you are actually taxed. This peri-

Adjustments to arrive at taxable profit or loss

Basis period begins `3.71 / /` and ends `3.72 / /`

- Tick box 3.72A if the figure in box 3.88 is provisional `3.72A`
- Tick box 3.72B if the special arrangements for certain trades detailed in the guidance notes apply `3.72B`

Profit or loss of this account for tax purposes (box 3.13 or 3.60) `3.73 £`

Adjustment to arrive at profit or loss for this basis period `3.74 £`

- Overlap profit brought forward `3.75 £`
- Deduct overlap relief used this year `3.76 £`

- Overlap profit carried forward `3.77 £`

Adjustment for farmers' averaging `3.78 £`

od is known to the Inland Revenue as your basis period. After the first two or three years in business, your basis period (and the dates you enter in 3.71 and 3.72) will normally be the same as your accounting period. But in the early years of the business, or if you change your accounting date, you may have to enter different dates.

EXAMPLE

Sam started his business as a self-employed landscape gardener on 6 July 1997. His basis period for the tax year ending 5 April 1998 is the period between 6 July 1997 and 5 April 1998. He draws up his first set of accounts on 5 June 1998. In all the boxes up to 3.73 he enters the figures for his first accounting period, running to 5 June 1998. His profit in this accounting period was £8,000. Because he was only in business for 274 of the 365 days in the year to 5 April 1998, his profits for the tax year were 274/365 x £8,000 = £6,005. At box 3.74 he enters an adjustment (in brackets) of £8,000 – £6,005 = £1,995.

If your basis period does differ from your accounting period, you have to make an adjustment in box 3.74 by allocating a proportion of the profits made in your first accounting period to the tax year. This is explained on p. 238 and in Help Sheet *IR222 How to calculate your taxable profits*. Remember to enter the adjustment in brackets if it is a deduction.

If you are a foster carer or adult carer, or you run a business overseas, you may not need to complete the whole of the Self-employment pages. Tick box 3.72B if this applies.

Overlap relief

You may pay tax on the same lot of profits twice. These profits are called 'overlap profits' and they arise if your basis period for one year has overlapped with that for another year. This can happen if your accounting date is not 5 April, either because of the special rules for new businesses (see p. 241) or because of the transition to the current year basis of taxing profits (see p. 238). You can use your overlap profits to reduce your profits if you closed your business in the year to 5 April 1998, or if you changed your accounting date.

Enter your total overlap profits in box 3.75, and the amount you want to set against your profits in box 3.76. If you ticked box 3.8A on page 1 of the Self-employment supplement, remember to make the adjustment to meet the anti-avoidance rules (see p. 240).

You can carry forward any unused overlap profits to set against the profits from the same business in future years, but you cannot set them against other types of income. If you are continuing your business, enter any unused amount in box 3.77. If you are closing down or selling your business, deduct all the overlap profits and you will end up with a loss on which you may qualify for tax relief.

LOSSES

If you make a loss, you can get tax relief on it. There are several ways in which tax relief can be given.

Other income or gains for this year

Net profit for 1997-98 (if loss, enter '0')	3.79 £
Allowable loss for 1997-98	3.80 £
• Loss offset against other income for 1997-98	3.81 £

Complete box 3.81 to set the loss against other income you have during 1997-98 – for example from working for an employer or from your savings. If this does not use up all the loss, you can ask for the rest to be set against any taxable capital gains for tax year ending 5 April 1998. If any loss still remains, you can ask for relief on it to be given in some other way. The time limit for making this choice with respect to losses made in the accounting period being declared for the tax year ending 5 April 1998 is 31 January 2000.

Other income and gains for the previous year

• Loss to carry back	3.82 £

Complete box 3.82 to carry back the loss to the tax year ending 5 April 1997 to set against your income from any source for that year. If this does not use up the full loss, you can ask for the rest to be set against any capital gains for the tax year ending 5 April 1997. If some loss still remains, you can ask for relief on it to be given in some other way. The time limit for making this choice is 31 January 2000.

Other income for earlier years

You can ask for a loss made in the first four years of the business to be carried back and set against income (but not gains) for the previous three tax years – that is, those ending 5 April 1995, 1996 and 1997. The loss is set against the earliest year first. The time limit for this choice is also 31 January 2000.

> ### TAX-SAVING IDEAS
>
> If you are a basic rate taxpayer, carrying back losses to the tax year ending 5 April 1997 when the basic rate of income tax was 24 per cent will give you higher relief than setting losses against income or gains for the tax year ending 5 April 1998 when the basic tax rate is 23 per cent.
>
> You do not have to make up your mind about how to get tax relief for your losses straightaway. You have a while to wait and see how your business affairs turn out. But the time limits for each option are strict, so don't delay so long that you miss them.

Future profits

• Loss to carry forward (that is allowable loss not claimed in any other way)	3.83 £

Complete box 3.83 to carry the loss forward to set against your future profits from the same business. It will be set against the next profits you make with any remaining loss being rolled forward to set against the next profits and so on until the loss is completely used up. You have until 31 January 2004 to make this choice.

Closing down

If your business closed down during the tax year ending 5 April 1998, you have a further option. A loss you made during your last 12 months of trading can be set against your profits for the three previous tax years – that is

> # EXAMPLE
>
> Sonja Frisk has been an antiques dealer for the last ten years. Normally, she makes a reasonable living but, in 1997, the sale of some expensive artifacts fell through and Sonja made a £7,000 loss for the tax year.
>
> Sonja could set the remaining loss against other income which she had in the tax year ending 5 April 1998 from a part-time job lecturing in art history at the local university. Alternatively, she can carry back her loss to the tax year ending 5 April 1997, or carry it forward to set against future profits from her antiques business. She doesn't want to use her loss this year, because she will pay only 20 per cent tax on her lecturing income, compared with the 24 per cent top rate of tax she paid last year; nor is she keen to carry forward her loss because she does not expect to pay a higher rate of tax in future. She claims to carry back her loss to the year ending 5 April 1997, qualifying for tax relief of 24 per cent x £7,000 = £1,680.

you can go back to the tax year ending 5 April 1995. The time limit for this choice is also 31 January 2004.

For more information see Help Sheet *IR227 Losses*.

NATIONAL INSURANCE

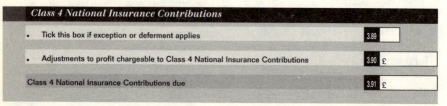

Running your own business, you will usually have to pay National Insurance contributions (NICs) both for yourself and for any people you employ. You will have to pay: Class 2 contributions at a flat-rate of £6.15 a week in the tax year ending 5 April 1998 and £6.35 a week in the tax year ending 5 April 1999. If your profits are less than £3,480 in the tax year ending 5 April 1998 or £3,480 in the tax year ending 5 April 1999, you can opt not to pay. However, Class 2 NICs help you to qualify for certain state benefits, such as jobseeker's allowance and incapacity benefit, so it might be better to carry on paying even if your profits are low. Class 2 contributions are paid direct to the Contributions Agency, usually by direct debit.

You may also have to pay Class 4 contributions. Unlike other types of National Insurance, Class 4 contributions do not entitle you to any state benefits – they are simply a tax on profits which is collected along with your income tax. In the tax year ending 5 April 1998, Class 4 NICs were payable at a rate of 6 per cent on profits over £7,010 up to £24,180. For the tax year ending 5 April 1999, the rate is unchanged, but the lower and upper profit limits are increased to £7,310 and £25,220, respectively. There are no Class 4 NICs to pay on profits below the lower limit and above the upper limit. If your profits are less than the lower limit, you do not pay any Class 4 NICs at all.

A few groups of people are excluded from having to pay Class 4 NICs. They include people over state pension age (currently 60 for women and 65 for men), people under age 16 if they have been granted an exemption by the Contributions Agency (ask for leaflet CA03 at your local Contributions Agency) and people who are not resident in the UK.

In some circumstances, you might have earnings which count as profits of your business and on which Class 4 NICs might be payable, but which have already had Class 1 NICs deducted – for example, where part of your income derives from fees for teaching in a school. There is a cap on the overall amount you have to pay in National Insurance, so it may be that Class 4 NICs won't be payable after all. However, you usually don't know whether this is the case until after part of the Class 4 NICs would have become payable, so you can ask to have payment deferred until the position is known.

If you are either excluded from paying Class 4 NICs or your Contributions Agency has agreed that you can defer paying them, you should tick the box at 3.89 and put 0 in boxes 3.90 and 3.91. In all other cases, leave box 3.89 blank. If you have any losses which have been carried forward to set against your profits for the tax year ending 5 April 1998, enter them in box 3.90 because they can also reduce your profits used for working out Class 4 NICs. If you have paid interest for business purposes but it has not been deducted

---

Example

Jim Newall has profits for income tax purposes of £8,500 for the tax year ending 5 April 1998. These are also the profits on which his Class 4 NICs are based. They are calculated as follows:

Profit for Class 4 NICs purposes	= £8,500
Less lower profit limit	= £7,010
Amount chargeable (£8,500 – £7,010)	= £1,490
Class 4 NICs at 6 per cent x £1,490	= £89.40

in working out your profits for income tax purposes, you might be able to deduct it for Class 4 NICs purposes. If this applies enter the amount of interest also in box 3.90.

Box 3.91 invites you to write down the amount you owe in Class 4 NICs. You don't have to do this sum yourself. Provided you send in your tax return by the 30 September deadline, you can leave the box blank and let your tax office do the sums. If you prefer to work out your Class 4 NICs yourself, there is a calculator included in the notes accompanying your Self-employment supplement. (The calculator is not suitable if you run more than one business, see Help Sheet *IR220 More than one business.*)

Class 2 and Class 4 contributions are not allowable expenses and can't be deducted when working out your profits for income tax purposes. If you have employees, you have to pay employer's Class 1 NICs for them if they earn more than the lower earnings limit (£62 a week for the tax year ending 5 April 1998 and £64 a week for the tax year ending 5 April 1999). In this case, the amount you pay counts as an allowable expense (see p. 249).

> # TAX-SAVING IDEAS
>
> Losses can be used to reduce your Class 4 National Insurance contributions as well as your income tax bill.
>
> If you're paying both Class 1 and Class 4 National Insurance on some of your income, ask to have the Class 4 liability deferred until you know precisely how much is due. Otherwise, you could end up paying too much in contributions.

PARTNERSHIP

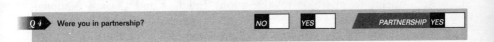

CHAPTER 20

Q4 Were you in partnership? NO ☐ YES ☐   *PARTNERSHIP* YES ☐

If you are in business with one or more partners, you should answer YES to Q4 in the basic tax return and fill in the Partnership supplement. There are two versions:

- short version. Use this if the partnership income is from trading profits or interest from bank or building society accounts which has already been taxed at the savings rate. This version will be adequate for most partners

- full version. If your partnership earnings are more complex because you have untaxed investment income, foreign income or income from land and property, for example, you'll need to complete this longer supplement.

The partnership should already have provided you with a Partnership Statement summarising your share of the profits, losses and other income. If you received the full statement, you need the full version of the supplementary pages; if you received a short statement, you need only the short supplement. If you haven't received a Partnership supplement or you need the full version, phone the Inland Revenue Orderline (see p. 143).

You and your fellow partners are jointly responsible for the partnership tax return, although one partner may be nominated to deal with it. This is a separate document from the partnership supplement. Profits are calculated on the return as if the partnership were a single person using largely the same rules as for a self-employed person (see Chapter 19). How profits are shared between partners depends on your partnership agreement.

Once the partner dealing with the tax return has worked out the taxable profits for the partnership as a whole, he or she must show each partner's share of the profits, losses and tax paid on the Partnership statement at the end of the Partnership return. The Partnership statement gives each individual partner the information needed to complete their own Partnership supplement. Each partner is then responsible for the tax on their own share of the profits.

Each partner is treated as if they were carrying on a business on their own, and the short version of the Partnership supplement is very similar to the Adjustments to arrive at taxable profit and loss and Class 4 National Insurance sections of the Self-employment supplement (see pp. 262-4). The other sections of the supplement simply summarise your share of any tax that the partnership has already paid. For this reason, we have not gone through the Partnership supplement in detail.

Becoming a partner

Partnership details	
Partnership reference number	Partnership trade or profession
4.1	4.2
• Date you started being a partner (if during 1997-98) 4.3 / /	• Date you stopped being a partner (if during 1997-98) 4.4 / /

When you join a partnership, the normal opening rules described on pp. 241-3 apply. The period on which your tax is based is likely to be different from the accounting year for the partnership. The dates you put in boxes 4.5 and 4.6 should reflect how the opening year rules apply to you. The opening year rules may result in overlap profits (see p. 242) on which you can eventually claim tax relief either when you leave the partnership or, possibly, if the partnership accounting date is changed. Once the special opening year rules have worked through, you are taxed on the normal current year basis. The period on which your tax is based will then be the same as the accounting year of the partnership, so you put the start date of the partnership year in box 4.5 and the end date in box 4.6.

Ceasing to be a partner
If you leave a partnership you are treated as if you are closing down your own business. The normal closing rules apply (see p. 244), including the claiming of tax relief on any overlap profits carried forward from the opening years.

LAND AND PROPERTY

 Q5 Did you receive any rent or other income from land and property in the UK?   NO   YES   LAND & PROPERTY YES

If you ticked the YES box against Q5 on page 2 of the tax return, you will need the Land and property supplementary pages. Many people renting out the odd room in their home may have to do little more than tick one box on the first page. But there is also space for details of more substantial lettings businesses and for income from holiday homes.

If you take in lodgers in your home, providing meals and other services, this may amount to a form of business and details should be entered on the Self-employment supplementary pages (see Chapter 19). Income from property abroad is entered on the Foreign pages (see Chapter 22).

The documents you need
You will need details of the rents you have received and any receipts or invoices for expenses. With furnished holiday lettings, you will also need records of the periods the properties were available for letting out.

If any of these properties is jointly owned, remember to enter only your share from these documents when filling in the tax return.

THE RENT A ROOM SCHEME

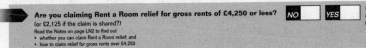 **Are you claiming Rent a Room relief for gross rents of £4,250 or less?** (or £2,125 if the claim is shared?)
Read the Notes on page LN2 to find out
• whether you can claim Rent a Room relief; and
• how to claim relief for gross rents over £4,250   NO   YES   If 'Yes', and this is your only income from UK property, you have finished these Pages

The rent a room scheme means that a modest rent from letting out furnished accommodation in your home is tax-free. The scheme applies whether you own your home or are yourself a tenant. But it must be your only or main home (see p. 53) and in the UK. And you cannot claim rent a room relief if you have gone abroad or moved into job-related accommodation (see p. 59).

For the tax year ending 5 April 1998, you could have rent before deduction of any expenses of up to £4,250 tax-free. If you are married or share your home, the income is treated as belonging to the person who actually rents out the room. If you were jointly letting the rooms with your husband, wife or partner you can each have rent before deduction of any expenses of up to £2,125 tax-free.

If your gross rent is below these levels, tick the YES box. If this is your only letting income, there is nothing more to enter – you don't even need to bother claiming expenses.

For the tax year beginning 6 April 1998, the amount of rent before deduction of any expenses you can have tax-free remains at £4,250 – or £2,125 if you are jointly letting the rooms.

Rent just above the rent a room scheme level?

If your gross letting income – that is rent before deduction of expenses – is higher than the maximum for the rent a room scheme, you have two options:

- you can choose to pay tax on the amount by which the gross rent exceeds the maximum (that is, £4,250 for the tax year ending 5 April 1998)
- you pay tax on the letting income in the same way as any other property income – you pay tax on the net income (the rent after deduction of various expenses and allowances).

Tax-saving idea

If your income from renting out rooms in your home is expected to be somewhat over £4,250 in the tax year which began on 6 April 1998, think about claiming rent a room relief. It will pay you to claim if the amount by which the gross rent exceeds £4,250 is less than your net income after deductions.

Example

Natalie Lean lets out three rooms in her house, bringing in a total of £150 a week in rent. This means her gross rental income for the tax year beginning 6 April 1998 will be £7,800, on which she could claim expenses and allowances of £2,350.

If the rental income is taxed as normal property income, she will pay tax on £7,800 – £2,350 = £5,450. But if she claims the rent a room relief, she will pay tax on the excess of the gross rental income of £7,800 over £4,250 – that is, on £3,550.

Rent a room relief means Natalie will pay tax on £1,900 less income.

If your gross letting income is just over the rent a room maximum, you will almost certainly be better off with the first option. For example, if your gross letting income was £4,500 in the tax year ending 5 April 1998, you could choose to pay tax on £4,500 – £4,250 = £250.

If you want to choose the first option, tick the NO Box and put the rent before deduction of expenses in box 5.20 on the second page. Don't enter any expenses in boxes 5.24 to 5.30, or claim any capital allowances in box 5.36 (or wear and tear allowance in box 5.37). Enter the tax-free amount you are claiming under the rent a room scheme in box 5.35 (either £4,250 or £2,125) and don't enter any claim for losses.

If you want to choose the second option (that is the income taxed as other property income), tick the NO box and follow the instructions for Other property income (see p. 274).

FURNISHED HOLIDAY LETTINGS

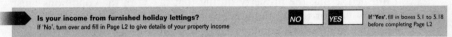

Is your income from furnished holiday lettings?
If 'No', turn over and fill in Page L2 to give details of your property income

NO □ YES □ If 'Yes', fill in boxes 5.1 to 5.18 before completing Page L2

If you have no income from short-term furnished lettings, tick the NO box and turn over to page L2 and to p. 274.

Tax benefits of furnished holiday lettings
Income from furnished holiday lettings is treated differently from other forms of property income, to reflect the fact that it is a form of business for many owners. This offers several tax benefits:

- you can claim capital allowances on plant and equipment (see p. 255)
- losses can be set off against other income for the same or next tax year and losses in the first four years of the business can be deducted from other income from the previous three years (see p. 260)
- it counts as relevant earnings for tax relief on pension contributions (p. 75)
- you can claim the special business reliefs for capital gains tax (p. 128).

To count as furnished holiday lettings, the property must meet all the following conditions for the year ending 5 April 1998:

- be available for letting to the general public on a commercial basis (that is, with a view to a profit) for at least 140 days
- actually let for at least 70 of those days
- not let for more than 31 days in a row to the same person in a period of at least seven months.

If you first started letting the property during the tax year ending 5 April 1998, these conditions must be satisfied for the first 12 months of letting. If you finished letting the property during that tax year, the conditions must have been met for the 12 months ending with the last letting. If you own more than one furnished holiday letting, you can average out the letting and occupancy periods between all of them.

Income

Furnished holiday lettings

. Income from furnished holiday lettings   5.1 £

Enter the total income from all your furnished holiday lettings in the UK for the tax year ending 5 April 1998 – before any deductions such as agents' commission. Include any income for services provided to tenants, such as cleaning, linen hire and use of additional facilities. Also include any money received from insurance policies for loss of rent.

Expenses

■ *Expenses* (furnished holiday lettings only)

If your total property income is less than £15,000, enter your total expenses in box 5.7, as Other expenses – you don't need to give details of individual expenses. If your total property income is over this limit, you need to list expenses separately:

Rent, rates, insurance, ground rents etc

• Rent, rates, insurance, ground rents etc	5.2 £

Enter the amount of rent, business rates, council tax, water rates, ground rent and insurance premiums on the furnished holiday lettings (including for insurance against loss of rents) in box 5.2.

Repairs, maintenance and renewals

• Repairs, maintenance and renewals	5.3 £

Claim in box 5.3. Any work that prevents the property deteriorating is a repair – such as painting and damp treatment. You can't claim here the cost of improvements, additions or extensive alterations, but if the work makes repairs unnecessary you can claim part of the outlay equal to what the repairs would have cost.

If you aren't claiming capital allowances for the furniture, fixtures and fittings, you can claim a renewals deduction for the cost of replacing them. If the new items are better, you cannot claim the full cost. And if any of the old items are sold, the proceeds should be deducted from the amount you claim.

Finance charges

• Finance charges, including interest	5.4 £

Enter in box 5.4 the cost of any loan you took out to buy the property – including interest paid and charges for setting up the loan.

Legal and professional costs

• Legal and professional costs	5.5 £

You can claim legal and professional expenses for a letting of less than a year, including fees for agents, surveyors and accountants and commission. You can also claim such costs when renewing the lease for a longer letting provided it is for less than 50 years. But you cannot claim expenses incurred in the first letting of a property for more than a year. Nor can you claim costs of registering title to land, getting planning permission or in connection with the payment of a premium on renewal of a lease. Enter the total in box 5.5.

Cost of services provided

Cost of services provided, including wages   **5.6** £

You can claim as an expense the cost of services such as gardening, cleaning and porterage. You can't claim the cost of your own time, but you can claim the cost of paying other people such as a member of your family.

Enter the total in box 5.6. If you are paid for any services you provide, this should be included as part of the income in box 5.1.

Other expenses

	total of boxes 5.2 to 5.7
Other expenses **5.7** £	**5.8** £

Other expenses include advertising costs, stationery, telephone calls, rent collection and travel to the property when solely for the letting.

Add together the figures in boxes 5.2 to 5.7 and enter the total in box 5.8.

Net profit

Net profit (put figures in brackets if a loss)   box 5.1 *minus* box 5.8   **5.9** £

Net profit is income minus expenses. Deduct the figure in box 5.8 from that in box 5.1 and put the amount in box 5.9, in brackets if it is a loss.

Tax adjustments

■ *Tax adjustments*

• Private use   **5.10** £

Private use
If a furnished holiday letting is partly used for your own enjoyment or that of friends staying rent-free, this counts as private use. Part of the costs must be apportioned to this private use, and cannot be claimed as an expense. If it was available for letting for nine months of the year and used by you for the rest of the time, you can claim only three-quarters of the costs of owning it. (You can still claim the full costs of letting it out as expenses.)

There are two ways to make an adjustment to reflect private use. You can enter the appropriate share of the costs in boxes 5.2 to 5.7, but let your tax inspector know what you've done. Or, better, you enter the costs in full in these boxes and enter in box 5.10 a figure for private use which is deducted from the total.

Capital allowances and balancing charges

You can claim capital allowances for the cost of buying furniture, machinery such as a lawnmower or equipment such as a water pump. If you get rid of an item you have claimed capital allowances on, a balancing charge may be added to your profits to reflect its second-hand value. There's more on p. 255 about capital allowances and balancing charges. You might also find it useful to get Help Sheet *IR250 Capital allowances and balancing charges in a rental business* from the Orderline.

Enter the amount of any capital allowances you are claiming for the tax year ending 5 April 1998 in box 5.13 and the amount of any balancing charge in box 5.11. Add the figures in boxes 5.10 and 5.11 together and enter the total in box 5.12. Total boxes 5.9 and 5.12 and subtract the amount in box 5.13.

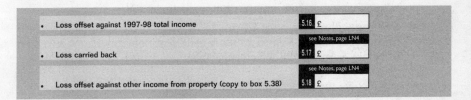

If the answer is a negative number, you have made a tax loss on your furnished holiday lettings. Enter 0 in box 5.14 and put the amount of the loss in box 5.15. If you have made a profit, enter it in box 5.14.

Losses

• Loss offset against 1997-98 total income	5.16 £	
• Loss carried back	5.17 £	see Notes, page LN4
• Loss offset against other income from property (copy to box 5.38)	5.18 £	see Notes, page LN4

Any loss in box 5.15 can be used to reduce the amount of tax you pay on other income or capital gains in the tax year ending 5 April 1998 or earlier tax years:

- other income for the tax year ending 5 April 1998 (enter the amount you wish to claim in box 5.16)
- capital gains for the same tax year – include the amount you wish to claim in the total you enter in box 8.5 of the Capital gains supplementary pages (see p. 298)
- income and gains for earlier tax years – enter the amount you wish to claim in box 5.17.

If you haven't used all the loss in box 5.15, you can set off what remains against other property income for the tax year ending 5 April 1998. Enter what is left in box 5.18 and copy it into box 5.38 on page L2 of the Land and property supplementary pages.

OTHER PROPERTY INCOME

Income

Copy the figure for profits on furnished holiday lettings from box 5.14 to box 5.19.

Rents and other income from land and property

Enter in box 5.20 the total income from all your lettings in the UK except furnished holiday lettings for the tax year ending 5 April 1998 – before any deductions such as agents' commission. Include the following:

- rent you will receive after 5 April 1998 which is payment in arrears for the tax year ending 5 April 1998 (equally, leave out any rent received on or before 5 April 1998 which is payment in advance for rent for periods after 5 April 1998)
- any income for services provided to tenants, such as cleaning, gardening

or porterage
- any money received from insurance policies for loss of rent
- ground rent and feu duties
- grants from local authorities for repairs (you can claim the cost of repairs as an expense)
- payments for using your land – for example, to shoot or graze.

If any tax has been deducted from the income before you get it, enter the total in box 5.21. The figure you enter in box 5.20 should be the before-tax amounts – so should include the amount in box 5.21.

If you own and let the property jointly with someone else, enter only your share of the income in box 5.20, and your share of the expenses lower down. If you only know your share of the profit after expenses, enter this in box 5.20 or any loss in box 5.29.

Chargeable premiums

If you receive a premium from a tenant in return for granting a lease, you will have to pay income tax on part of it if the lease lasts less than 50 years (and capital gains tax on the rest). Any work the tenant agrees to do for you on being granted a lease counts as a premium.

If you are paid the premium in instalments, the total premium is still taxable in the year the lease is granted. But if paying in one go would cause you hardship, you can ask your tax inspector to allow you to pay by yearly instalments. The maximum number of instalments is eight (or the number of years you are getting the premium over, if less).

The proportion on which you will have to pay income tax is calculated as follows:
$$\frac{51 - \text{number of years of the lease}}{50}$$
So if the lease is a 20-year one, the proportion of the premium which is taxable is:
$$\frac{51 - 20}{50} = \frac{31}{50}$$
Enter the amount of the premium which is taxable in box 5.22. Add the figures in boxes 5.19, 5.20 and 5.22 together and enter the total in box 5.23.

Expenses

Expenses (do not include figures you have already put in boxes 5.2 to 5.7 on page L1)

• Rent, rates, insurance, ground rents etc	5.24 £	
• Repairs, maintenance and renewals	5.25 £	
• Finance charges, including interest	5.26 £	
• Legal and professional costs	5.27 £	
• Costs of services provided, including wages	5.28 £	total of boxes 5.24 to 5.29
• Other expenses	5.29 £	5.30 £

If your total property income for the tax year ending 5 April 1998 is less than £15,000, go straight to box 5.29 and enter your total expenses in it. If your total property income is over this limit, you need to list the expenses incurred in the tax year ending 5 April 1998 separately.

The details of what expenses you can claim in boxes 5.24 to 5.29 are given under Furnished holiday lettings on pp. 271-2. Note that with furnished property, you can claim a renewals deduction in box 5.25 for the cost of replacing furniture, fixtures and fittings, but not if you are already claiming a wear and tear allowance on the property (see opposite).

Don't include any expenses you have already claimed in boxes 5.2 to 5.7.

Add together the figures in boxes 5.24 to 5.29 and enter the total in box 5.30.

Net profit (put figures in brackets if a loss)

	box 5.23 minus box 5.30
	5.31 £

Subtract the figure in box 5.30 from that in box 5.23 to find the net profit or loss on the letting. Enter the figure in box 5.31, in brackets if it is a loss.

Tax adjustments

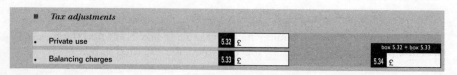

Tax adjustments

• Private use	5.32 £	
• Balancing charges	5.33 £	box 5.32 + box 5.33
		5.34 £

Example

Miriam Patel has divided most of her house into furnished rooms which she lets out, providing cleaning. The total yearly income is £9,640 but she can deduct these expenses:

- a proportion of the outgoings on the house (council tax, water rates, gas, electricity and insurance) which add up to £2,400 a year. Miriam is letting out three-quarters of the house and claims this proportion
- the cost of cleaning (cleaner's wages plus materials) – £1,300 a year
- an allowance for wear and tear of the furniture and furnishings – Miriam claims the actual cost of replacement (£300 for this year).

Thus Miriam's tax bill would be calculated as follows:

Total rent received	£9,640
Less expenses	
Three-quarters of the outgoings of £2,400 a year	£1,800
Cost of cleaning	£1,300
Cost of replacing furniture and furnishings	£300
Total allowable expenses	£3,400
Taxable rental income	£6,240

If Miriam does the cleaning, no allowance can be made for her time. But if she pays someone else to do the work (her mum, say), she can claim this cost as an allowable expense.

Box 5.32 is where you enter a figure for any private use of the property, in the same way as for furnished holiday lettings (see p. 272).

Any balancing charges (see p. 273) should be put in box 5.33. Add together the amounts in boxes 5.32 and 5.33 and put the total in box 5.34.

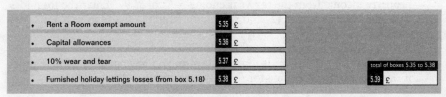

Enter in box 5.35 any tax-free amount you are claiming under the rent a room scheme (see p. 267). Otherwise leave it empty.

If you want to claim capital allowances (see p. 255), enter the amount in box 5.36. You can't claim capital allowances if you let a furnished home (other than as furnished holiday lettings). You can instead claim a renewals deduction for the cost of replacing such items (in box 5.25 above). Or you can claim a wear and tear allowance in box 5.37 of 10 per cent of the rent less service charges and local taxes. Once you have chosen a method, you can't switch. And if you have been using a different method of allowing for wear and tear agreed with your tax inspector before 6 April 1976, you can carry on using it.

You should already have filled in box 5.38 if you wish to set off a loss on furnished holiday lettings against other property income (see box 5.18).

In box 5.39 enter the total of boxes 5.35, 5.36, 5.37 and 5.38.

Adjusted profit (if loss enter '0' in box 5.40 and put the loss in box 5.41)	boxes 5.31 + 5.34 minus box 5.39	5.40 £
Adjusted loss (if you have entered '0' in box 5.40)	boxes 5.31 + 5.34 minus box 5.39 5.41 £	
• Loss brought forward from previous year		5.42 £
Profit for the year	box 5.40 minus box 5.42	5.43 £

Add the figures in boxes 5.31 and 5.34 together and subtract the figure in box 5.39. If the answer is a negative number, you have made a tax loss on your property interests. Enter 0 in box 5.40 and put the amount of the loss in box 5.41. There are several ways that a tax loss on property income can be used to reduce your tax bill (see boxes 5.44 to 5.46, below).

If you have made a profit, enter it in box 5.40. You can reduce this – and the amount of tax you pay on your property income – if you made a loss on property income from the tax year ending 5 April 1997. Enter the total loss from that year in box 5.42, and subtract it from the figure in box 5.40.

If the answer is a negative number, enter 0 in box 5.43 and put the balance in box 5.45. If the answer is more than zero, you have made a taxable profit on your property income for the tax year ending 5 April 1998.

Losses

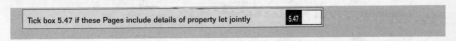

• Loss offset against total income	5.44	£
• Loss to carry forward to following year	5.45	£
• Pooled expenses from 'one estate election' carried forward	5.46	£

You can deduct a property income loss from other forms of income for the tax year ending 5 April 1998. However, you can set off some of the loss in box 5.41 against other income only if you have claimed capital allowances in box 5.36. Even then, the maximum loss you can set off in this way is the amount of capital allowances minus any balancing charge – box 5.36 minus box 5.33.

If this is what you want to do, enter the amount you wish to deduct in this way in box 5.44. Alternatively, a loss which reflects an excess of capital allowances over balancing charges can be carried over to next year and set against your income for the tax year ending 5 April 1999. If this is what you would like to do, make a note of the figure to enter in the 1999 tax return.

Finally, any other unused losses can be carried over to deduct from future profits from property – enter these in box 5.45. If the figure in box 5.43 is 0 you will have already entered the right figure in box 5.45. If the figure in box 5.40 is 0, you find the figure to enter in box 5.45 by adding together the figures in boxes 5.41 and 5.42 and subtracting the figure in box 5.44.

Ignore box 5.46 unless you own agricultural land. If you think it might apply to you, ask for Help Sheet *IR251 Agricultural land and land managed as one estate* to see what you should enter.

Tick box 5.47 if these Pages include details of property let jointly	5.47

Tick box 5.47 if you own and let property jointly with someone else – and give the name and address of the person who keeps the records in the Additional information box on page 8 of the basic tax return (see Chapter 16).

FOREIGN

Q6 Did you have any taxable income from overseas pensions or benefits, or foreign companies or savings institutions, offshore funds or trusts abroad, or from land and property abroad or gains on foreign insurance policies?

NO ☐   YES ☐

Have you at any time made, or been associated with, a transfer of assets which has resulted in income becoming payable to a foreign entity or have you benefited in any way from such a transfer made by someone else?

NO ☐   YES ☐

Do you want to claim tax credit relief for foreign tax paid on foreign income or gains?

NO ☐   YES ☐   FOREIGN YES ☐

If you ticked any of the three YES boxes at Q6 on page 2 of the basic tax return, you will need the supplementary pages called Foreign. These have space to give details about your foreign savings, pensions and benefits, property income and other investment income from abroad. Earnings from work abroad should be entered in the Employment, Self-Employment or Partnership pages of the tax return as appropriate. Similarly, details of capital gains on overseas transactions should be entered in that supplement.

This chapter tells you how to fill in the Foreign pages, and about the expenses and allowances you can claim. But the tax treatment of people who live abroad is beyond the scope of this guide. If this applies to you, seek professional advice from your bank or accountant.

How foreign income is taxed
Income from abroad is taxable in the UK, even if you have already paid foreign tax on it. You can deduct any foreign tax paid from the income before working out your UK tax bill – so you pay UK tax only on what you get after paying foreign tax.

But in most cases, you can instead claim a deduction from your UK tax bill to reflect the foreign tax paid, known as tax credit relief. This is likely to mean paying less in UK tax than if you simply deduct the foreign tax from the gross income before working out the tax bill.

However, working out the amount of tax credit relief can be complicated and this guide assumes you are leaving the calculations to your tax inspector. If you feel up to the calculations, you can use the guidance notes sent out by the Inland Revenue to calculate your tax credit relief and thus your UK tax bill on such income.

Note that if the amount of foreign tax is adjusted on or after 17 March 1998, you must notify your tax inspector if it means any deduction for that tax was bigger than it should have been.

> ### EXAMPLE
>
> Bill Livingstone made £2,500 after expenses last year letting out his villa in Freedonia. He paid the equivalent of £400 tax on this to the Freedonian tax authorities.
>
> In calculating his UK tax, he could have simply deducted the £400 of Freedonian tax from the £2,500 and paid tax on £2,100. Since he paid tax on the income at the basic rate of 23 per cent, the tax bill would have been £483.
>
> But he claimed tax credit relief, so the full £2,500 was taxable at 23 per cent – £575 in tax. He could then deduct the £400 of Freedonian tax, making his UK tax bill just £175.

What income is taxed

The instructions below are for people who are domiciled in the UK and ordinarily resident here. Their foreign income is taxed on an arising basis – when they get it or it is credited to them, not when it is brought back to the UK. You should enter the amounts you got in sterling, using the exchange rate at the time the income arose.

There are different rules for people who are not domiciled or ordinarily resident in the UK. The latter is likely to apply to you only if you don't visit the UK regularly and either have no home here or spend less than 91 days on average here in a tax year. If it does apply, you will need to fill in the Non-residence supplementary pages (see p. 303). And your foreign income will be taxed on a remittance basis – enter the amounts of income received in the UK and the equivalent share of any foreign tax deducted from it.

Tax-free foreign income

The following types of foreign income are tax-free in the UK:

- pensions paid by Germany or Austria to the victims of Nazi persecution and to pensioners who have fled from persecution
- the extra foreign pension paid to you if you have been retired because you were disabled by injury on duty or by a work-related illness
- any part of a pension from overseas that reduces the amount of tax-free

UK war widows' and dependants' pensions
- social security benefits which are similar to UK benefits that are tax-free – child benefit, maternity allowance, guardian's allowance, child's special allowance, widow's payments, incapacity benefit (only for the first six months if it began on or after 13 April 1995), attendance allowance, disability living allowance and severe disablement allowance.

A tenth of overseas pensions funded by an overseas employer or pension fund is tax-free in the UK unless it is taxed on a remittance basis (see p. 281).

Income stuck in a foreign country

In some cases, you will be unable to remit foreign income to the UK because it arises in a country which has exchange controls or is short of foreign exchange. If income is unremittable, give details of the amount of income and foreign tax in the currency of the country concerned – you will be unable to give other information asked for.

The documents you need

You will need to gather together dividend vouchers for overseas shares, bank statements for overseas bank accounts, pension advice notes, foreign property bills – as well as details of any foreign tax paid.

FOREIGN SAVINGS

Foreign savings

Fill in columns A to E, and tick the box in column E if you want to claim tax credit relief.

Country A ▼ tick box if income is unremittable	Amount before tax B	UK tax C	Foreign tax D	Amount chargeable E ▼ tick box to claim tax credit relief
■ *Dividends, interest, and other savings income* - see Notes, page FN4	£	£	£	£
	£	£	£	£
	£	£	£	£

On page F1 give details of foreign interest, dividends and other savings income for the tax year ending 5 April 1998 unless you are taxed on a remittance basis (see p. 281).

The following types of such income should not be included:
- foreign income dividends received from a UK company – you should enter details of these on page 3 of the basic tax return
- distributions by a foreign company in the form of its shares (but enter details of any cash alternative you took instead)

- stock dividends from foreign companies
- bonus shares from a scrip issue by a foreign company
- capital distributions – for example, the return of your capital or distributions in the course of a liquidation.

Enter each source of income on a separate line. If any of these types of income is from joint holdings, enter your share only. In column A give the name of the country where the income arose and tick the box if the income cannot be remitted to the UK. In columns B, C, D give the amount of income before tax, the amount of any UK income tax deducted and the amount of foreign tax paid.

Under double taxation agreements signed between the UK and more than 100 countries, tax should be deducted from investment income by the foreign country at a reduced rate which is then taken into account in calculating your UK tax bill. If the figure in column D is more than you should have paid under such an agreement, ask the foreign tax authority for a refund.

The amount you enter in column E depends on whether you wish to claim tax credit relief:

- if you intend to claim it, enter the amount in column B and tick the box
- if you are not claiming tax credit relief, enter the figure in column B less any foreign tax in column D.

Add up the figures in column C and enter the total in box 6.1. Put the total for column E in box 6.2.

Foreign savings income taxable on the remittance basis and foreign income from overseas pensions or social security benefits or from land and property abroad

On page F2, give the same information for foreign pensions, social security benefits and property income. And if you are taxed on your foreign income on a remittance basis (see p. 281), this is where you give details of foreign interest, dividends and other savings income.

Pensions and social security benefits

Exclude pensions and benefits which are free of UK tax – see p. 281. If only part of a payment is free of UK tax, give the amount which is not exempt in column E.

INCOME FROM FOREIGN LAND AND PROPERTY

Income from overseas property is taxed in much the same way as that from UK property (see p. 274). You can deduct expenses including the cost of managing the property and collecting the income (for example, paying an agent). If you buy equipment, you may be able to claim a capital allowance or some other form of deduction (see p. 277). And you can deduct loan interest on the property.

As for UK property, there are certain expenses you cannot claim. These include personal expenses – such as the costs incurred while the property is not let. Nor can you claim any loss you make when you sell the property.

There is space on page F2 of the Foreign supplement for details of the income and tax paid on overseas property and land. But before you fill this in, you must turn to page F4 and complete a copy of it for each property, giving details of the income, expenses and other deductions for the tax year ending 5 April 1998. If your foreign income is taxed on a remittance basis (see p. 281), you do not need to complete page F4.

OTHER OVERSEAS INCOME

Disposals of offshore funds, income from non-resident trusts and income received by trusts or companies abroad	6.5 £

This is where you give details of miscellaneous other types of overseas income. If you have these complex investments, you should take specialised tax advice.

Disposals of holdings in offshore funds

The income from an offshore fund should be entered as savings income on page F1 of the foreign pages. Here you must give details of any gain made on cashing in part or all of your investment unless the fund qualifies as a distributor fund – one which distributes most of its income as dividends. This is to stop investors rolling up income in offshore funds to create capital gains and reduce their income tax bills.

If the fund does not count as a distributor fund, enter the gain in box 6.5. If you have received an equalisation payment from a distributor fund, you should enter the part of the gain taxable as income in box 6.5. The taxable amount will be shown on the voucher given to you by the fund manager.

Income from non-resident trusts

If you are entitled to the income from a trust that is not resident in the UK, enter the amount from foreign sources in box 6.5. Any of the trust's income from UK sources should have been entered in the appropriate boxes of the Income part of the tax return as if it had been paid direct to you.

Any income paid to you from a non-resident trust at the discretion of the trustees should be entered in box 6.5.

Income received by trusts or companies abroad

If you have transferred assets so the income is paid to anybody abroad – such as a company or trust – and you get a benefit from it, enter the income or capital sum received in box 6.5.

Also enter the value of any payment or benefit such as a loan received from other sorts of offshore funds such as offshore bonds. You must include the amount of any unexpended income from such sources – income held in trust or by a company on your behalf. Give the full name of the trust in the Additional information box at the foot of the page, or the name and address of the company receiving the income. If you have these complex types of investments, you should take specialised tax advice.

Foreign life insurance policies

	Number of years	Notional Income Tax	Gains
• Gains on foreign life insurance policies etc	6.6	6.7 £	6.8 £

Give details here of any gains you have made on foreign life insurance policies – whether because the policy has come to an end or because you have drawn some benefit from it. Enter the number of years you have held the policy in box 6.6 and the gain in box 6.8.

Most such gains are simply added to your taxable income because no foreign tax has been paid on them. If foreign tax has been deducted, you may be able to get a 'credit for notional basic rate tax' which means the gain will be taxed only at the difference between the basic and higher rate in the same way as a UK life insurance policy gain (see p. 168). Enter the amount of any notional income tax credit in box 6.7.

TAX CREDIT RELIEF

With all types of foreign income, you can simply deduct any foreign tax already paid from the income before working out the UK tax bill. But you

See Notes, page FN11

Enter in this column the Page number in your Tax Return from which information is taken. Do this for each item for which you are claiming tax credit relief ▼	Country A		Foreign tax D	Amount chargeable E	tick box to claim tax credit relief ▼
			£	£	
			£	£	
			£	£	

are likely to pay less UK tax if you claim tax credit relief which reduces the UK tax bill to reflect the foreign tax already paid.

This section is for calculating tax credit relief on all your foreign income, including that from investments, pensions, benefits and property already entered above. But you can also claim the relief on foreign income from employment, self-employment and partnerships which you will have entered elsewhere on the tax return.

First you must enter details of these other forms of foreign income. Give the country the income arose in, the amount of foreign tax paid on it and the gross amount of the income before deduction of foreign tax. In the first column, give the page number of the tax return where the income is fully reported.

Next, there is room to enter the amount of tax credit relief you wish to claim on all of your foreign income. This is only for people who want to do the sums themselves – if you don't want to get involved in the calculations, go on to the next section.

If you want to work out your tax credit relief, you need to use the Tax Credit Relief Working Sheet on page FN14 of the Tax Return Guide. There are full instructions beginning on page FN12, and all the data you need to complete it on the following pages. You won't be able to complete the working sheet until you have completed most of the rest of the tax return. Some of the figures you have to enter on it are drawn from the Tax Calculation Guide which you use to work out your overall tax bill.

• If you are calculating your tax, enter the total tax credit relief on your income in box 6.9   6.9 £

Fill in a separate working sheet for each item of foreign income you wish to claim relief for. Enter the total amount you wish to claim in box 6.9.

See Notes, page FN12

Amount of gain under UK rules	Period over which UK gain accrued	Amount of gain under foreign tax rules	Period over which foreign gain accrued	Foreign tax paid D	tick box to claim tax credit relief ▼
£	days	£	days	£	
£	days	£	days	£	
£	days	£	days	£	

The bottom half of the page is for details of capital gains you wish to claim tax credit relief on. Help Sheet *IR261 Tax Credit Relief: Capital Gains* tells you what to enter and how to do the sums if you wish to calculate the tax credit relief on your foreign gains.

. If you are calculating your tax, enter the total tax credit relief on your gains in box 6.10   6.10 £

If you have calculated the tax credit relief on your capital gains, enter the total in box 6.10.

TRUSTS

Q7 — Did you receive any income from any trust, settlement or estate of a deceased person? NO ☐ YES ☐ TRUSTS ETC YES ☐

If you ticked the YES box at Q7 on page 2 of the basic tax return, you will need the supplementary page called Trusts etc. You should give details about taxable income from trusts and other forms of settlement such as a transfer of assets, and from the estates of people who have died. In some cases, you may have to give details of income from trusts you have set up. Even though the money has been paid to someone else, it may be treated as yours.

The documents you need
You require details of any income received. With a payment from a discretionary trust, the trustees should have given you a certificate R185 setting out the details; personal representatives handling the estates of people who have died should give similar statements when handing over income.

If you have directly or indirectly provided funds for a settlement and are not sure whether the income will be treated as yours, Help Sheet *IR270 Trusts and settlements – income treated as the settlor's* should help. Ask the Orderline (p. 143).

INCOME FROM TRUSTS AND SETTLEMENTS

Income from trusts and other forms of settlement comes with a tax credit which reflects the amount of tax already deducted from it or deemed to have been paid on it. What you receive is the net (after-tax) amount of income. To find the gross (before-tax) amount, you need to add back the tax credit. You can find out the amount of the tax credit from certificate R185 or similar statement the trustees should give you.

How trust income is taxed

The amount of the tax credit depends on the type of trust:

- trust with an interest in possession where you have the 'absolute right' to the income from the trust. The tax credit will be at the rate of 20 per cent of the grossed-up amount of savings income, such as interest and share dividends; for other sorts of income, such as rents or royalties, it will be at the basic rate of tax – 23 per cent for the tax year ending 5 April 1998
- a discretionary trust where the trustees have discretion about paying out the income. The tax credit will be 34 per cent of the grossed-up income.

If the tax credit is more than the amount of tax you would have paid if the grossed-up income had come direct to you, you can claim a rebate. For example, if you get interest or share dividends from a trust and your income – including the grossed-up trust income – is too low to pay tax, you could reclaim all the tax credit which comes with it.

With a discretionary trust, anyone not liable to higher rate tax can reclaim part of the tax credit. Any payment you receive from the trust will come with a tax credit of 34 per cent of the grossed-up amount. But if you pay tax at no more than the basic rate – even after the grossed-up trust payment is added to your income – you should have paid tax on the payment at 23 per cent in the year ending 5 April 1998. You can thus reclaim the difference of 34 – 23 = 11 per cent of the grossed-up amount.

Higher rate taxpayers will have to pay extra tax on income from either sort of trust. With a discretionary trust, this would be an extra 6 per cent of the grossed-up amount (the difference between the 40 per cent higher rate and the 34 per cent tax credit that comes from the trust).

Trust income that might be treated as yours

If you have directly or indirectly provided funds for a settlement, the income from those funds may be treated as yours – even though you haven't received it.

The sorts of trust which might produce an income that would be treated as yours include:

- a trust you set up for your husband or wife or children
- a trust that has lent money to you or your spouse
- a trust where the capital would come back to you if the beneficiaries died before becoming entitled to it.

This treatment might also apply if you make some investments on behalf of your children unless they are over 18 or married – for example, opening a savings account in their names. Any income from such investments is treated as yours unless it is £100 a year or less before tax. This exception applies to gifts from each parent, so a child can have up to £200 a year before tax in income from gifts from both parents without a problem.

You can't get round this by giving the funds to someone else who passes them on to your child. You would still have indirectly provided the funds and the income would be yours. The same would be true if you settled some money on a friend's child in return for him doing the same for you.

This income should be included as your own in Q10 in the basic tax return and not entered on the Trusts etc pages unless you create a proper trust.

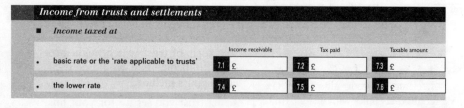

Income from trusts and settlements			
■ Income taxed at	Income receivable	Tax paid	Taxable amount
• basic rate or the 'rate applicable to trusts'	7.1 £	7.2 £	7.3 £
• the lower rate	7.4 £	7.5 £	7.6 £

Enter the income from trusts in the tax year ending 5 April 1998 in these boxes. For discretionary trusts, put the actual amount received in box 7.1, the tax credit in box 7.2 and the gross income in box 7.3 (this should be the sum of boxes 7.1 and 7.2). Also include here any income from trusts or settlements which is treated as yours even though you haven't received it.

For income from a trust with an interest in possession on which the tax credit is at the 23 per cent basic rate, give the same details in boxes 7.1, 7.2 and 7.3. For savings income on which the tax credit is at the 20 per cent lower rate, enter the details in boxes 7.4, 7.5 and 7.6.

You don't need to enter the following here:

- scrip dividends or foreign income dividends received from a trust with an interest in possession and paid by UK companies, authorised unit trusts or open-ended investment companies – give details of these on page 3 of the basic tax return (see p. 159)
- income from foreign sources paid to you by a trust with an interest in possession – give details on the Foreign supplementary pages (see p. 284)
- income from a discretionary trust where the trustees are not resident in the UK for income tax purposes – this should also go on the Foreign pages (see p. 284).

INCOME FROM ESTATES

You do not pay income tax on anything you inherit from a dead person. And if you inherit something that produces an income, such as money in a bank savings account, you should enter the interest in the appropriate part of the main tax return.

However, you should give details in this section of the tax return of income you receive from the estate while it is being wound up by the personal representatives – the executors or administrators. You would be entitled to this income if you were a residuary beneficiary – the person or one of the people who gets what is left after all the specific bequests and legacies have been made.

Such income will come with a tax credit in the same way as a trust with an interest in possession. Some of this income will have been taxed at the basic rate (23 per cent for the tax year ending 5 April 1998) and some at the lower rate for savings income of 20 per cent. For most types of income, this tax will be repayable if it is more than you would have paid; but the tax is not repayable for some types of income such as gains on life insurance policies and UK stock dividends.

The statement supplied by the personal representatives – tax certificate R185E – will show you the rate the income has been taxed at and whether it is repayable or not. Enter the details given on the statement for the tax year ending 5 April 1998 in boxes 7.7 to 7.18. Give the name of the estate and the total amount paid to you in the Additional information box at the bottom of the page.

■ *Income bearing*

	Income receivable	Tax paid	Taxable amount
• basic rate tax	7.7 £	7.8 £	7.9 £
• lower rate tax	7.10 £	7.11 £	7.12 £
• non-repayable lower rate tax	7.13 £	7.14 £	7.15 £
• non-repayable basic rate tax	7.16 £	7.17 £	7.18 £

In some cases, income accrued during the life of the dead person and paid into the estate after their death will come to you after being taken into account in calculating the inheritance tax bill on the estate. There is a special tax relief that stops you having to pay higher rate tax on such income – ask your tax inspector for details.

Income from foreign estates
If you get income from a foreign estate, it will not have borne full UK tax – either because the personal representatives are outside the UK tax net or because the estate is that of someone who died while domiciled outside the UK and has income from non-UK sources. In this case, enter the full amount of such income in boxes 7.7 and 7.9. Don't enter anything in box 7.8, even if some foreign tax has been deducted.

If the foreign estate has some income from UK sources, it will have paid some UK tax. In this case, you can reduce the amount entered in boxes 7.7 and 7.9 by the following amount:

$$\frac{\text{net amount of income subject to UK tax}}{\text{total estate income less UK tax}} \times \text{total estate income before UK tax}$$

Foreign tax paid

• Total foreign tax for which tax credit relief not claimed	7.19 £

If you have been paid income from an estate which has already been taxed in a foreign country, you may end up paying two lots of tax on it: tax in the foreign country and tax in the UK. You may be able to reduce the amount of UK tax you pay on the income to reflect the foreign tax paid – this is known as tax credit relief. You claim this on the Foreign supplementary pages (see p. 285).

If you don't want to claim tax credit relief – which can be quite complicated – you can instead deduct the foreign tax you have paid from the income. Enter the amount in box 7.19.

Leave box 7.19 blank if you are claiming tax credit relief.

CAPITAL GAINS

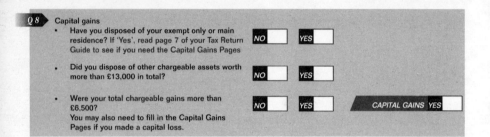

CHAPTER 24

Q 8 Capital gains
- Have you disposed of your exempt only or main residence? If 'Yes', read page 7 of your Tax Return Guide to see if you need the Capital Gains Pages   NO ☐ YES ☐
- Did you dispose of other chargeable assets worth more than £13,000 in total?   NO ☐ YES ☐
- Were your total chargeable gains more than £6,500? You may also need to fill in the Capital Gains Pages if you made a capital loss.   NO ☐ YES ☐   CAPITAL GAINS YES ☐

If you have ticked any of the three YES boxes at Q8 on page 2 of the basic tax return, you will need the supplementary pages called Capital gains. These ask for details of taxable gains you have made on buying and selling assets such as shares, unit trusts and property. You may also have to report a taxable gain even though you haven't sold something – if you give it away, for example. And if you have made a loss on such assets, you should give details here also, since it might reduce your overall tax bill now or in the future.

This chapter tells you how to fill in the Capital gains supplementary pages. Chapter 10 explains how the tax works in detail with examples of the sometimes complicated calculations needed to fill in these pages. It also explains how to claim all the reliefs and allowances to minimise your capital gains tax bill.

The documents you need
You will need details of anything you have spent on buying or selling or maintaining the value of assets. With shares and unit trusts, you need any paperwork relating to share issues while you owned them or company reorganisations.

For assets owned on 31 March 1982, you may also need details of their value on that date (see p. 111). Use catalogues, press advertisements or stock market share price records to value them.

With assets that are jointly owned, you need enter only your share of any gains. With a husband and wife, the gain or loss is split 50:50 between them unless they have told their tax inspectors that the asset is not owned equally (see p. 105).

CHARGEABLE GAINS AND ALLOWABLE LOSSES

The first page of the Capital gains pages has space at the top for you to write your name and the tax reference you will find on the front of your basic tax return. Once you have filled in these two boxes, turn over to page CG2 which has to be completed before you can fill in the rest of page CG1.

1 Description of asset	2 tick box if shares are unquoted ▼	3 Disposal proceeds	4 Net gain (loss)	5 tick box if estimate or valuation used ▼	6 tick box if assets held at 31 March 1982 ▼	7 tick box if relief claimed ▼	8 Further information
.		£	£				
		£	£				

This page is for giving details of each taxable disposal made during the tax year ending 5 April 1998. If you are likely to run out of space on page CG2, make photocopies before filling it in. Put your name and tax reference on each sheet.

Include anything you have been given as a result of the reconstruction or takeover of a company, building society or mutual insurance company (see p. 121). But you don't need to enter any details of disposals of assets on which gains are tax-free. Thus you should leave out possessions which are worth £6,000 or less when you disposed of them – these are known as chattels (see p. 113). However, if you made a loss on the disposal of a chattel, you should give details since it can be used to reduce your tax bill.

In some circumstances, you may need to give details of capital gains or losses on this page even though you haven't disposed of the assets they relate in the tax year ending 5 April 1998. For example, if you have been given something and agreed to take over the gain from its previous owner (hold-over relief), you have to pay tax on that gain if you become non-resident within six years of the end of the tax year in which the gift was made (see p. 126).

Column 1: Give details to identify the asset – the address of property, for example. With shares or unit trusts, give the name of the company or unit trust fund manager, types of shares or units and the number disposed of.

Column 2: Tick if the shares were unquoted – that is, not listed on the Stock Exchange or the Alternative Investment Market (AIM).

Column 3: Enter the total disposal proceeds, including any cash or other asset to be received in the future. But if the disposal was a gift or a sale to a connected person you should enter the market value of the asset (see p. 106). For capital gains tax, a connected person includes your husband or wife, your business partner and their spouse, a relative of yours or these others (brother, sister, parents, child, grandchild) and the spouse of one of these relatives.

If you have been given the right to something in the future in return for the disposal, this should also be included unless it would be taxed as income (for example, dividends or royalties). If it is not clear what you will get in the future – as with a share of any profits – include an estimate in the disposal proceeds. When that uncertain part is finally paid, this will count as another disposal – the right to the share of the profits will have been exchanged for real cash. There will then be another capital gain or loss to report at that time.

Column 4: Enter the chargeable gain or allowable loss, putting losses in brackets. See p. 105 for how to work out the gain or loss.

If claiming reliefs such as reinvestment relief, enter the amount after deduction of the relief and give details of the relief claimed in column 8. You don't have to submit the calculations done to reach these figures, but you can if you want to.

Column 5: Tick this box if your figures include any estimates – of market value, for example, or future payments in return for the disposal.

Column 6: If you owned the asset on 31 March 1982, tick this box – there are special rules for calculating the gains and losses on such assets (see p. 111).

You should also tick the box if you will be treated as if you owned the asset on that date. This would apply, for example, if the asset had been given to you by someone who owned it on that date and you had agreed to take over that person's gain on it (hold-over relief – see p. 126).

Column 7: Tick this box if you have claimed any one of the many reliefs which reduces the chargeable gain on disposing of an asset in the tax year ending 5 April 1998. These include private residence relief for your only or main home (p. 60), retirement relief when you retire from your business (p. 128), roll-over relief when you replace business assets (p. 129) and reinvestment relief when you invest in certain types of small companies (p. 127).

Column 8: Give any other relevant details on the disposal, including which reliefs have been claimed and why you have used estimates.

When you have completed page CG2, add together the chargeable gains in column 4 and put the total at the bottom. Do the same for the allowable losses. Then turn back to page CG1.

Enter the total chargeable gains for the tax year ending 5 April 1998 from the bottom of page CG2 in box 8.1.

Enter the total allowable losses for the tax year ending 5 April 1998 in box 8.2. This is the total from the bottom of page CG2, minus any losses from unquoted shares in trading companies you are claiming to deduct from your income (see p. 83).

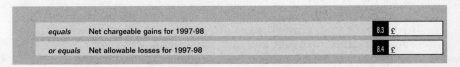

If box 8.2 is less than box 8.1, you have made a net chargeable gain for the tax year ending 5 April 1998. Subtract box 8.2 from box 8.1 and enter the result in box 8.3. If the amount in box 8.3 is £6,500 or less, put 0 in box 8.8 and go to the capital losses section (p. 299). If the amount in box 8.3 is more than £6,500, continue with box 8.5.

If box 8.2 is more than box 8.1, you have made a net allowable loss for the tax year ending 5 April 1998. Subtract box 8.1 from box 8.2 and enter the result in box 8.4. Put 0 in box 8.8 and go on to the Capital losses section (opposite).

minus	Trading losses, losses from furnished holiday lettings, post-cessation expenditure, or post-employment deductions which can reduce chargeable gains	8.5	£

There are losses on several types of income you can deduct from a net chargeable gain if you haven't enough income to set them off against:

- any trading losses from self-employment (p. 261) or a partnership
- losses from furnished holiday lettings (p. 269)
- certain expenses incurred in the seven years after you have closed a business which would have been allowable against business income (post-cessation expenditure) – for example, bad debts, costs of rectifying faulty work (p. 189)
- certain expenses incurred by employees up to six years after they have left their jobs (post-employment deductions) – for example, insurance premiums for policies that pay out against claims of faulty work.

If you have such losses, you can enter them here up to the amount in box 8.3.

minus	Allowable losses brought forward (see Notes, page CGN6 for the amount to include)	8.6	£

You can deduct any allowable losses left over from previous tax years from your net chargeable gains (see p. 114). If you have enough losses held over, you can reduce your net chargeable gains to £6,500, the amount that is tax-free for the tax year ending 5 April 1998.

If your losses from previous years are not big enough to reduce your net chargeable gains to £6,500, enter the full amount carried over in box 8.6. Then put 0 in box 8.17 and box 8.18, and go to box 8.7, below.

If your losses from previous years are more than enough to reduce your net chargeable gains to £6,500, enter in box 8.6 the amount that, combined with any figure in box 8.5, will bring net chargeable gains down to £6,500 exactly. Then go to box 8.7.

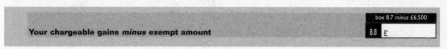

		box 8.3 *minus* (box 8.5 + box 8.6)
equals	Chargeable gains for 1997-98	8.7 £

Add the figures in boxes 8.5 and 8.6, and subtract the total from the figure in box 8.3. Enter the result in box 8.7.

	box 8.7 *minus* £6,500
Your chargeable gains *minus* exempt amount	8.8 £

You can have up to £6,500 of chargeable gains free of capital gains tax in the tax year ending 5 April 1998 (see p. 114). So subtract £6,500 from the figure in box 8.7 to find your taxable chargeable gain for the tax year. Enter the result in Box 8.8. If your net chargeable gain was £6,500 or less or you have made a net allowable loss for the tax year, you should already have entered 0 in this box.

• Additional liability in respect of offshore trusts	8.9 £

If you are the beneficiary of a trust which is not resident in the UK or is also resident in another country (a dual resident trust), you may be liable to capital gains tax on anything you receive from the trust – whether it be cash, a loan or an asset. You need to give details in box 8.9 of the amount of tax due on what you have received in the tax year ending 5 April 1998. To work this out, use the calculator on Help Sheet *IR301 Capital gains on benefits from non-resident and dual resident trusts.*

CAPITAL LOSSES

This part of the Capital gains pages helps you keep track of your allowable losses from previous years and this year – it will be useful when you come to fill in next year's tax return.

This year's losses

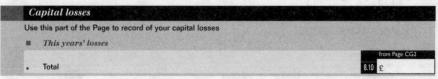

Capital losses	
Use this part of the Page to record of your capital losses	
■ *This years' losses*	
	from Page CG2
• Total	8.10 £

The first few boxes are for losses for the tax year ending 5 April 1998. Put in box 8.10 the total allowable losses for the year – the figure from the bottom of page CG2.

| • Used against gains | 8.11 | £ |
| • Used against earlier years' gains (see Notes, page CGN7) | 8.12 | £ |

Enter in box 8.11 the amount of the allowable losses for the tax year ending 5 April 1998 used to reduce your chargeable gains in that year. This is the figure in box 8.2 if this is less than box 8.1; if box 8.2 is bigger than box 8.1, enter the figure in box 8.1.

Personal representatives clearing up the estate of someone who has died can carry unused losses back to earlier tax years and effectively claim a tax rebate for the estate (see p. 115). Enter any amount this applies to in box 8.12.

			amount claimed against income of 1997-98	box 8.13A + box 8.13B
	8.13A	£		
• Used against income (see Notes, page CGN6)	8.13B	£	amount claimed against income of 1996-97	8.13 £

If you have made losses on shares in unquoted trading companies, you can set them off against income from the same tax year or the previous tax year. For more information, see Help Sheets *IR286 Income tax losses for new shares you have subscribed for in unlisted trading companies* and *IR297 Enterprise Investment Scheme and Capital Gains Tax.*

If you make such a claim, enter the amount claimed against income for the tax year ending 5 April 1998 in box 8.13A, and the amount against the previous tax year in box 8.13B. Add the two and enter the total in box 8.13.

| | box 8.10 minus (boxes 8.11 + 8.12 + 8.13) |
| • This year's unused losses | 8.14 £ |

Add the amounts in boxes 8.11, 8.12 and 8.13 and subtract the total from the amount in box 8.10. Enter the result in box 8.14 – this is the total unused losses for the tax year ending 5 April 1998 which can be carried forward to future tax years.

Earlier years' losses

| ■ *Earlier years' losses* | | |
| • Unused losses of 1996-97 (see Notes, page CGN3) | 8.15 | £ |

The next few boxes record what has happened to losses carried forward from previous tax years. Enter in box 8.15 the amount carried over from the tax year ending 5 April 1997. You can find the figures you need on your tax return for the year ending 5 April 1997. Add the figures in boxes 8.16 and 8.17 of that tax return to fill in box 8.15 on this year's tax return.

* Used this year (losses from box 8.15 are used in priority to losses from box 8.18)   8.16 £

Enter in box 8.16 the amount of the losses from the tax year ending 5 April 1997 used this year and included in the total in box 8.6. If box 8.6 is blank, put 0 in this box. If there is any figure in box 8.6, you should enter it here up to the amount in box 8.15, so you use up losses from the tax year ending 5 April 1997 before losses from earlier years.

box 8.15 minus box 8.16

* Remaining unused losses of 1996-97   8.17 £

Subtract the amount in box 8.16 from the amount in box 8.15 and enter the result in box 8.17. This is the remaining unused losses from the tax year ending 5 April 1997.

* Unused losses of 1995-96 and earlier years   8.18 £

Enter in box 8.18 the total of any unused losses from the tax year ending 5 April 1996 and earlier tax years. You can find this figure in box 8.12 of your tax return for the year ending 5 April 1997.

box 8.6 minus box 8.16

* Used this year (losses from box 8.15 are used in priority to losses from box 8.18)   8.19 £

Box 8.19 records the amount of losses from the tax year ending 5 April 1996 and earlier tax years used in the tax year ending 5 April 1998. It can be found by subtracting the amount in box 8.16 from the amount in box 8.6. If box 8.6 is blank, put 0 in this box.

Total of unused losses to carry forward
Finally, the tax return has space to note down the totals of losses you can carry forward to future tax years.

box 8.14 + box 8.17

* Carried forward losses of 1996-97 and later years   8.20 £

Add the amounts in boxes 8.14 and 8.17 and enter the total in box 8.20.

This is the amount of losses for the tax years ending 5 April 1997 and 5 April 1998 you can carry forward.

- Carried forward losses of 1995-96 and earlier years

box 8.18 minus box 8.19

8.21 £

Subtract the amount in box 8.19 from the amount in box 8.18 and enter the result in box 8.21. This is the amount of losses for the tax year ending 5 April 1996 and earlier tax years which you can carry forward.

NON-RESIDENCE

 Q 9 Are you claiming that you were not resident, or not ordinarily resident, or not domiciled, in the UK, or dual resident in the UK and another country, for all or part of the year?

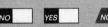 NO ☐ YES ☐ NON-RESIDENCE ETC YES ☐

If you are a resident of the UK, you are liable for UK tax on all your income whether it comes from within the UK or abroad. But, if you count as a non-resident, there is no UK tax on your income from abroad, only on any income which originates in the UK.

If you want to claim non-residence (or non-domicile) for the tax year ending 5 April 1998, you need to fill in the green Non-residence Supplement which you can get through the Orderline (see p. 143). You are likely to need this if:

- you are normally a UK resident but you are working abroad for an extended period
- you have been a UK resident but you are going to live abroad permanently or indefinitely – for example because you are retiring abroad
- you have been resident elsewhere but you are based in the UK for now or you have returned for permanent residence.

This guide cannot give you all the detail you may need so you should consult a professional adviser.

Residency is not defined in the tax laws, but broadly it means the place where you usually live. Because different countries use different criteria to decide who is resident, it is possible to count as a resident of more than one country at the same time, in which case you could pay two lots of tax on the same income. However, the UK has double taxation agreements with many countries to avoid this situation.

In general, payment of UK taxes depends on whether or not you were resident during the particular tax year in question. Occasionally, it may hinge on where you are ordinarily resident. Again, there is no hard and fast definition, but basically your ordinary residence is the country you are resident in year after year, which you use as your base, returning to it for extended periods, and probably where you have an established home.

Your domicile can be the key to whether or not there is tax on foreign income and gains you receive and any inheritance tax to pay on your estate when you die. Your country of domicile is the place which you consider to be your permanent home and where you would intend to end your days. You can have only one country of domicile and it is not necessarily the country in which you are resident or ordinarily resident. Claims for foreign domicile should be made as soon as possible on form DOM1.

Note that even if you are non-resident for tax purposes, you might still be able to claim the UK personal tax allowances to set against your income from UK sources, for example, if you are a citizen of a Commonwealth country or a European country within the European Economic Area (this includes the UK), a Crown employee (or a widow or widower of someone who was a Crown employee) or employed by a UK missionary service.

If your intention is to be out of the country for less than four years, you can continue to pay any mortgage on your UK home through MIRAS and so claim the tax relief on it (see p. 53).

A word of warning: there are Inland Revenue concessions which might apply to you. You can claim the concessions, providing you don't use them simply as a means of avoiding tax. If the Inland Revenue suspects that tax avoidance is your main motive, it will refuse you the concession.

How do you count as being non-resident?
If you have generally been considered as a UK resident, to count as non-resident for tax purposes, you need to pass all four of the following tests:

- the motive test
- the absent for a whole tax year test
- the 183 days test
- the 91 days test.

The notes which accompany the Non-residence Supplement include a calculator which will help you to work out whether you pass all these tests.

The motive test
You will pass this test if you go abroad to work full-time, providing the other tests are also met. Whether or not your job is full-time is judged, first, by comparing your hours with the norm in the UK, but if your job is less struc-

tured it will be assessed on its own merits and in the light of what is normal for your type of work and the country you are going to. You could also count as working full-time if you have two or more part-time jobs.

By concession, if you count as non-resident because of your work abroad, your wife or husband, if they go with you, will also count as non-resident, providing they pass the other tests.

Another way to pass the test is if you go abroad to live permanently or at least indefinitely. The Inland Revenue will want evidence that this is your intention – for example, that you have bought a home abroad or you are going to marry someone in another country. If you still have a UK home, it wants to know how that fits with your plans to live overseas. Once you've lived abroad for three years, it will be accepted that you are non-resident.

If you can't pass this test at the time you go away, the situation can be reviewed later on, if new evidence of your motive becomes available or once you have been abroad for three years.

The absent for a whole tax year test
To count as non-resident for a tax year, if you work abroad, your job must last for at least a whole tax year and you must be out of the country for the whole tax year or longer, except for visits within the other rules (see below). Similarly, if you go to live abroad permanently or indefinitely, you must be out of the country for at least a whole tax year.

By concession, in the year you leave and the year you return, you can count as non-resident for just part of the year, provided that year is part of a longer period of non-residency. If you want to claim this split year treatment, you must give details of your date of arrival in or departure from the UK in box 9.25 or box 9.26 of the supplementary pages.

The 183 days test
You will always count as resident for the tax year if you spend 183 days or more in the UK. There are no exceptions to this rule. For example, if you make visits back home during a period working abroad, the total of your visits during any tax year must come to less than 183 days if you are not to lose your status as a non-resident. For the purposes of this rule and the next, the days on which you travel do not count as days spent in the UK.

The 91 days test
In addition to the 183 days test, the average time you spend in the UK must come to less than 91 days in a tax year. This is worked out over the period

since you left until you have been away for four tax years. After that it is worked out over the most recent four tax years. You are allowed to ignore periods you had to spend in the UK for reasons beyond your control – for example, because someone in your family was ill.

How do you count as being non-domiciled in the UK?

Your domicile is relevant only if it will affect the tax you must pay, so unless you fall into one of the following categories, you do not need to fill in boxes 9.27 to 9.31, and you should also leave box 9.5 blank. The tax areas which might be affected are where:

- you have income or gains from foreign investments which you will not be bringing in full into the UK
- you are claiming UK tax relief on contributions to a foreign pension scheme made out of earnings from a non-UK resident employer
- the costs of travelling between the UK and your normal home have been paid by your employer
- you worked abroad for a non-UK employer and have not brought all the earnings into the UK.

You can have only one domicile at a time and there are three ways in which it can be established: by birth, by dependency or by choice. From birth, you normally have the domicile of your father – that is not necessarily the same as the country in which you were born. If the domicile of the person on whom you are dependant changes, so will yours. Similarly, if you become dependant on someone else of a different domicile, your own domicile will fall into line with that. Women no longer acquire their husbands' domicile on marriage. Once you reach age 16, you have the right to choose a new domicile but the change is not easily made. You would need to show that you had settled in the new country of domicile with a view to staying there permanently. Your home, business interests, social and family ties, and the form of any will would all be relevant, but other factors could also be just as important.

> **TAX-SAVING IDEAS**
>
> If you go to work or live abroad, make sure your trips back home average less than 91 days a year and come to less than 183 days in any single tax year to avoid paying UK taxes on your overseas income.
>
> Taking a long lease of three years on a home abroad would help to show that you intended to live abroad permanently.
>
> If you are returning permanently to the UK after a period of non-residence abroad and you have been saving through an offshore roll-up fund (see p. 284), make sure you sell your investment before you become a UK resident again. If you don't, you will become liable for tax on the rolled-up income.

ILLING IN THE TAX CALCULATOR

Q18 Do you want to calculate your tax? NO ☐ YES ☐ If yes, do it now and then fill in boxes 18.1 to 18.9. Your Tax Calculation Guide will help.

The objective of the new self-assessment system of tax collection is that you, the taxpayer, should be able to calculate your own tax bill. If you prefer to leave it to your tax inspector, you can do so – provided you send the tax return back in time for this to be done (see p. 14). But if you have left it too late for the Inland Revenue to do the calculations – or you want to seize control of your tax affairs – tick the YES box at Q18 on page 7 of the tax return and open the green Tax Calculation Guide on page 5. There you will find the tax calculation working sheet you need to fill in which this chapter takes you through step by step. The next chapter has examples of how two typical taxpayers might do the sums.

Have you made a chargeable capital gain?

If you have made a chargeable capital gain in the tax year ending 5 April 1998 there is a special Tax Calculation Guide. If you entered a figure in box 8.8 on page CG1 of the Capital gains supplementary pages, ask the Orderline for the Tax Calculation Guide (Capital gains).

This version of the tax calculator is largely the same as the standard one. If you need help filling it in, send for our extra guide (see p. ix).

When you might not want to work out your own tax

Anyone with enough determination can calculate their own tax. But some people's tax affairs are quite complicated and it will need a great deal of determination:

- foreign income from savings, pensions, benefits or property – you may be able to claim tax credit relief against any foreign tax you have paid on the income. If you want to claim tax credit relief, you can calculate your tax bill only if you have worked out the amount (see p. 285)

- non-resident – the tax treatment of people who live abroad is beyond the scope of this guide
- Lloyd's underwriters – you have your own tax return to fill in to reflect the special rules for taxing your income
- ministers of religion – you also have your own tax return
- farmers – special rules in various parts of the tax system.

See also the box below on special tax circumstances.

If you want the Inland Revenue to calculate your tax, remember to send your tax return back on time – normally by 30 September (see p. 14).

FILLING IN THE TAX CALCULATION WORKING SHEET

The working sheet begins on page 5 of the Tax Calculation Guide by asking you to bring together all your income for the tax year ending 5 April 1998

SPECIAL TAX CIRCUMSTANCES

There is a special Tax Calculation Guide if in the tax year ending 5 April 1998 you received certain lump sums or income that comes with a notional tax credit for basic rate tax. Ask the Orderline for the Tax Calculation Guide (Lump sums etc) if you entered figures (other than zeros) in any of the following boxes elsewhere in the tax return:

- box 6.8 on page F2 of the Foreign section of the tax return, or boxes 12.5 or 12.8 on page 4 of the Income section – a chargeable gain on a life insurance policy
- box 1.29 on page E2 of the Employment section – a lump sum or compensation payment on leaving a job
- box 7.18 on page T1 of the Trusts etc section – income from the estate of someone who died which came with a notional tax credit at the basic rate
- box 12.12 on page 4 in the Income section – a refund of surplus additional voluntary contributions from a pension scheme.

This special Tax Calculation Guide spreads a chargeable life insurance gain over several years to reduce the tax bill on it (see p. 169). It also steers you through the complicated rules for deducting your various tax allowances and reliefs from other sorts of income.

If you have these types of lump sum and income with a notional tax credit, **and** you have a chargeable capital gain for the tax year, ask the Orderline for the Tax Calculation Guide (Capital gains and lump sums).

---

to find your total taxable income. You will need to draw figures from your tax return, so have it handy.

> **Total income from:** *(copy figures from your Tax Return)*

The first 11 boxes ask you to enter details of your income by drawing on figures you have entered in various parts of the tax return. Most people will not have to enter an amount in every box – only in the boxes that relate to the sort of income they receive.

- **Employment** *including* benefits and *minus* expenses for **each** employment

	First employment	Other employments	*If any of the sums on this page result in a negative amount, enter a zero in the appropriate box*
Add income in boxes 1.8 to 1.10, 1.12 to 1.23, 1.27 and 1.28	£	£	
Deduct any figures in boxes 1.31 to 1.38	£	£	
Total taxable income	£	+ £	= **W1** £

Start with your employment income from working for someone else or a company in the tax year ending 5 April 1998 – you will need amounts from the Employment section of the tax return.

First enter the total of earnings, expenses and the value of fringe benefits from your main job in the top box in the first column. Your earnings are in boxes 1.8, 1.9, 1.10 on page E1 of the Employment section; expenses and fringe benefits are in boxes 1.12 to 1.23 inclusive. You must also include in this total any amounts for taxable lump sums in boxes 1.27 and 1.28 on page E2.

Then enter the amount of the above income which is not taxable in the second box down in the first column – boxes 1.31 to 1.38 in the Employment section inclusive. Subtract the total in the second box from that in the first box to get the total taxable income from your main job and enter this in the third box in the first column.

If you have employment income from more than one job, put the same totals for all the other jobs added together in the three boxes in the second column. The third box in the second column will then have your total taxable income from all jobs other than your main one.

Add the totals in the two boxes in the third row to get your total taxable income from employment, and enter this in box W1.

- **Share schemes** (from box 2.31) W2 £

If you received any taxable income from share options or share-related fringe benefits in the tax year ending 5 April 1998, enter the total in box W2. This is the amount in box 2.31 on page S1 of the Share schemes supplementary pages.

- **Self-employment** (from box 3.88) W3 £

If you received income from being self-employed in the tax year ending 5 April 1998, enter the total taxable profits in box W3. This is the amount in box 3.88 on page SE3 of the Self-employment supplementary pages.

If you have more than one lot of income from self-employment, add together the total taxable profits from each and enter the grand total in box W3.

- **Partnerships** (from boxes 4.35, 4.70 and 4.73) W4 £

If you received income from partnerships in the tax year ending 5 April 1998, enter your share of the partnership's taxable income in box W4. This is found by adding the amounts in boxes 4.35, 4.70 and 4.73 on the Partnership supplement. (If you have had to complete only the short version, there is no box 4.35 to worry about.)

If you have more than one lot of income from partnerships, add together the amounts for each and enter the grand total in box W4.

- **UK land and property** (from box 5.43) W5 £

If you received income from letting out rooms, homes, land or other property in the UK during the tax year ending 5 April 1998, enter your total profit in box W5. This is the amount in box 5.43 on page L2 of the Land and property supplementary pages.

- **Foreign income** (from boxes 6.2, 6.4 and 6.5) W6 £

If you received income from abroad from investments, pensions, benefits or property, enter the amount chargeable to tax for the tax year ending 5 April 1998 in box W6. This is found by adding the amounts in boxes 6.2, 6.4 and 6.5 on pages F1 and F2 of the Foreign income supplementary pages.

> **• Trusts, settlements or estates of deceased persons**
> (add together any figures in the 'right hand' column of the Trusts etc pages and deduct any figure in box 7.19) **W7** £

If you received taxable income from trusts, other forms of settlement such as a transfer of assets or the estates of people who have died, enter the amount for the tax year ending 5 April 1998 in box W7. This is found by adding the amounts in boxes 7.3, 7.6, 7.9, 7.12, 7.15 and 7.18 on page T1 of the Trusts etc supplement and subtracting any amount in box 7.19.

> **• UK savings and investments** (total any figures in the 'right hand' column on page 3 of your Tax Return) **W8** £

If you received any income from UK savings and investments in the tax year ending 5 April 1998, enter the total taxable amount in box W8. This is found by adding the taxable amounts entered in the Income section on page 3 of the tax return: boxes 10.1, 10.4, 10.7, 10.8, 10.11, 10.14, 10.17, 10.20, 10.23, 10.26, 10.29 and 10.32.

> **• UK pensions, retirement annuities and benefits** (add together any figures in the 'right hand'
> column of Question 11 on page 4 of your Tax Return *minus* any deduction in box 11.13) **W9** £

If you received any UK pension, social security benefit or income from a retirement annuity in the tax year ending 5 April 1998, enter the total taxable amount in box W9.

This is found by adding the following amounts in the third Taxable amount column in the Income section on page 4 of the tax return: boxes 11.1, 11.2, 11.3, 11.4, 11.5, 11.6, 11.7, 11.9 and 11.12. Then subtract any amount in box 11.13.

> **• Maintenance and alimony received** (from box 12.3) **W10** £

If you received taxable maintenance or alimony in the tax year ending 5 April 1998, enter the amount in box W10. This is the amount in box 12.3 in the Income section on page 4 of the tax return.

> **• Other income** (copy the figure in box 13.3 *minus* any figure in box 13.5) **W11** £

Box W11 is for any other income you received in the tax year ending 5 April 1998 that was not entered somewhere else on the tax return. The figure to enter is the amount in box 13.3 in the Income section on page 4 of the tax return, minus the amount in box 13.5.

Total W12 £ Total column above

Add the amounts in boxes W1 to W11 and enter the total in box W12. This is your total taxable income for the tax year ending 5 April 1998.

> ## Deductions for

This is where you enter the various deductions you are allowed to set against your total taxable income in the tax year ending 5 April 1998. You won't be asked here to give details of deductions which lead to a fixed reduction in the amount of tax you pay since these are entered later in boxes W40 to W46.

• **Personal pension** (add together any figures in boxes 14.5, 14.10, 14.15, 14.16 and 14.17) W13 £

If you are claiming tax relief for contributions to a personal pension or retirement annuity for the tax year ending 5 April 1998, enter the total contributions claimed in box W13. You can find this amount by adding the amounts in boxes 14.5, 14.10, 14.15, 14.16 and 14.17 in the Reliefs section on page 5 of the tax return.

• **Vocational training** (multiply any figure in box 15.1 by $^{100}/_{77}$) W14 £

If you are paying for certain types of vocational training, you can get tax relief on the cost (see p. 180). You get tax relief at the basic rate automatically by paying reduced fees. But you need to enter here the before-tax-relief amount you paid in the tax year ending 5 April 1998 in case you are due some tax relief at the higher rate.

To find the before-tax-relief amount, take the amount you entered in box 15.1 in the Reliefs section on page 5 of the tax return and multiply it by $^{100}/_{77}$. Enter the answer in box W14.

• **Interest on qualifying loans** (from box 15.3) W15 £

Enter the amount of interest you paid in the tax year ending 5 April 1998 on which you can get tax relief in box W15. The amount to enter is in box 15.3 in the Reliefs section on page 5 of the tax return. Note that this amount excludes interest on loans to buy your only or main home where the tax relief on has been given through MIRAS (see p. 53).

> • **Maintenance or alimony paid** (see the notes on page 2 of this Guide) **W16** £ _____

The amount of tax relief you get on maintenance or alimony paid depends on whether they are dealt with under the new rules for payments since 1988 or the old rules that previously applied (see p. 182). You will already have had to decide whether the new or the old rules applied in filling in boxes 15.4, 15.5 and 15.6 in the Reliefs section on page 5 of the tax return.

This is what you fill in here for the tax year ending 5 April 1998:

- if the payments are made under the new rules, leave box W16 blank. Then enter the amount from box 15.4 in box W42.6 on page 6 of the Tax Calculation Guide
- if the payments are made under the old rules, enter the amount from box 15.6 in box W16 and the amount from box 15.5 in box W42.6
- if the payments are made under both sets of rules, leave box W16 blank. Then add together any amounts in boxes 15.4 and 15.5 (one of them may be blank), and enter the total in box W42.6.

> • **Charitable covenants, annuities and Gift Aid payments**
> (multiply any figures in boxes 15.9 and 15.10 by $^{100}/_{77}$) **W17** £ _____

You can get tax relief on regular gifts made to charity by covenant and on larger one-off gifts under the Gift Aid scheme (see p. 188). You get tax relief at the basic rate automatically by handing over the gifts after deducting tax at the basic rate. But you need to enter here the before-tax-relief amount of such gifts in the tax year ending 5 April 1998 in case you are due some tax relief at the higher rate (or have had too much tax relief and must pay some back). Do not include any gifts made under payroll-giving schemes.

To find the before-tax-relief amount, add the amounts you entered in boxes 15.9 and 15.10 in the Reliefs section on page 5 of the tax return and multiply the total by $^{100}/_{77}$. Enter the answer in box W17.

> • **Losses and post-cessation expenses** (from boxes 3.81, 4.15, 4.61, 5.16, 5.44, 8.13A and 15.11) **W18** £ _____

If you have made losses from being self-employed, working in a partnership or letting property, you can set them off against other income. The same is true of capital losses on disposing of assets and – in certain circumstances –

expenses incurred after you wind up a business or leave a job. This is where you enter such amounts in the tax calculation working sheet.

To claim such losses, add the following amounts:

- box 3.81 on page SE3 of the Self-employment supplement
- box 4.15 on page P1 of the Partnership supplement – plus, if you get the full four-page version of this section, box 4.61 on page P3
- box 5.16 on page L1 and box 5.44 on page L2 of the Land and property supplement
- box 8.13A on page CG1 of the Capital gains supplement
- box 15.11 on page 5 in the Reliefs section of the basic tax return.

Enter the total in box W18.

Enter the amount from box 15.12 in the Reliefs section on page 5 of the tax return in box W19.

Add the amounts in boxes W13 to W19 and enter the total in box W20. This is your total deductions that can be set against total taxable income for the tax year ending 5 April 1998.

Subtract the amount in box W20 from the amount in box W12 and enter the answer in box W21. This is your total income less deductions for the tax year ending 5 April 1998.

Now copy the amount in box W21 into box W22 at the top of page 7 of the Tax Calculation Guide where the calculations start on the amount of tax you must pay.

CALCULATING THE TAX DUE

Pages 6 and 7 of the Tax Calculation Guide work out the amount of income tax due on your total income less deductions. The working sheet will now calculate the income tax due on your total income after taking account of all the allowances and reliefs you can claim for the tax year ending 5 April 1998 – including personal allowances.

This involves some complications because there are different tax rates for different types of income. For example, up to £26,100 of savings income is taxed at 20 per cent for the tax year ending 5 April 1998. But only £4,100 of other sorts of income is taxed at 20 per cent, and the next £22,000 is taxed at the basic rate of 23 per cent.

The tax calculation working sheets therefore go through a four-step process to work out your tax bill. You don't need to understand it to do the sums – so if you want to get on with it, just jump on down to Reliefs, below. But for those who want to understand the calculation, the four steps are:

1. Work out how much tax you would pay if your total income after all allowances and reliefs was taxed at the lower rate of 20 per cent.
2. If your total income after all allowances and reliefs is more than £4,100, 3 per cent of the excess apart from any savings income is added to your tax bill. This 3 per cent means non-savings income over £4,100 is taxed at 23 per cent.
3. If your total income after all allowances and reliefs is more than £26,100, higher rate tax is due on the excess at 40 per cent. So 17 per cent of the excess is added to your tax bill. This means that non-savings income over the £26,100 limit has been taxed at 40 per cent (20 + 3 +17 per cent). But savings income has been taxed at only 37 per cent (20 + 17 per cent).
4. This step adds 3 per cent of savings income over £26,100 to your tax bill, bringing it up to the 40 per cent higher rate (37 + 3 per cent).

Reliefs
- you get basic rate relief automatically - further relief will be due if you are liable to higher rate tax.

Fill in any boxes on this page that apply to you and copy to page 7. Then work through remaining boxes on pages 7 and 8

- **Pension payments**
  (from boxes 14.15 and 14.17)   W23.1 £

- **Vocational training**
  (from box W14)   W23.2 £

Copy to W23

Total W23.3 £

If you have made payments on which you have already had tax relief at the basic rate of 23 per cent, these payments must be added back here if you are not to get a second lot of tax relief:

- if you made contributions to a personal pension or free-standing additional voluntary contribution plan, add the amounts in boxes 14.15 and 14.17 in the Reliefs section on page 5 of the tax return and enter the total in box W23.1
- if you made payments for vocational training, enter the amount in box W14 on the previous page of the Tax Calculation Guide in box W23.2.

Add the amounts in boxes W23.1 and W23.2 and enter the total in box W23.3. Now follow the dashed line to box W23.

You should have already filled in box W22 with the amount in box W21 on page 5 of the Tax Calculation Guide. Fill in box W23 with the amount in box W23.3, along the dashed line on the opposite page. Then add the amounts in boxes W22 and W23 and enter the total in box W24.

Now go to Allowances given as a deduction from your income on the opposite page of the tax calculation working sheet.

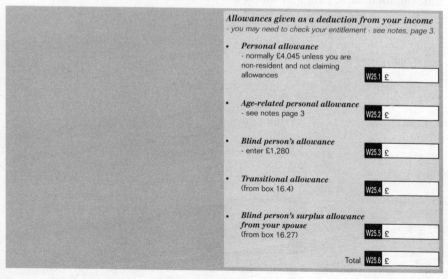

This section is to enter allowances that can be deducted from your income before tax is calculated. Enter the following allowances only if you have claimed them in the Allowances section on page 6 of the tax return:

NEGATIVE ANSWERS?

If any of the sums you are asked to do in filling in pages 6 and 7 of the Tax Calculation Guide produce a negative number, enter 0 as the answer.

- box W25.1 – your personal allowance. Enter £4,045
- box W25.2 – any extra personal allowance you are entitled to if born on or before 5 April 1933. Enter 0 if born on or after 6 April 1933; otherwise see box on p. 319 for what to enter
- box W25.3 – blind person's allowance. Enter £1,280
- box W25.4 – transitional allowance for some wives whose husbands have a low income (see p. 192). Enter the amount in box 16.4 in the Allowances section on page 6 of the tax return
- box W25.5 – blind person's surplus allowance your spouse cannot use up. Enter the amount in box 16.27 in the Allowances section on page 6 of the tax return.

Add boxes W25.1 to W25.5 and enter the total in box W25.6. Now follow the dashed line to box W25.

Enter the amount in box W25.6 in box W25. Subtract the amount in box W25 from the amount in box W24 and enter the result in box W26.

Multiply the amount in box W26 by 20 per cent ($^{20}/_{100}$), and enter the answer in box W27. If the answer is not an exact amount of pounds, include the pence in the figure you enter in box W27.

If the amount in box W26 is £4,100 or less, leave boxes W28 to W38 blank and go to box W39, on p. 308. Otherwise go to Savings income taxable at the lower (20%) rate on the opposite page of the tax calculation working sheet (see over).

Savings income taxable at the lower (20%) rate

- *Partnership savings*
  (from boxes 4.35 and 4.70)

  W28.1 £

- *UK savings*
  (from box W8)

  W28.2 £

- *Foreign savings*
  (from box 6.2)

  W28.3 £

- *Trusts, settlements and estate income*
  (from boxes 7.6, 7.12 and 7.15)

  W28.4 £

  Total W28.5 £ → *Copy to W28*

This part of the tax calculator works out how much of your income should have been taxed at the 20 per cent rate for savings:

- box W28.1 – your share of partnership savings income. Add the amounts in boxes 4.35 and 4.70 in the Partnership supplementary pages (if you have filled in the short version, there is no box 4.35)
- box W28.2 – UK savings income. Enter the amount in box W8 on the first page of the tax calculation working sheet
- box W28.3 – foreign savings income. Enter the amount in box 6.2 on page F1 of the Foreign supplementary pages
- box W28.4 – income from trusts, settlements and the estates of deceased persons. Enter the total of boxes 7.6, 7.12 and 7.15 on page T1 of the Trusts etc supplementary pages.

Add the amounts in boxes W28.1 to W28.4 and enter the total in box W28.5. Now follow the dashed line to box W28.

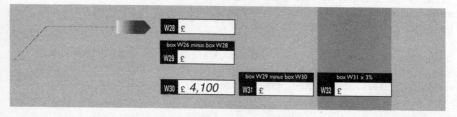

Enter the amount in box W28.5 in box W28. Subtract the amount in box W28 from the amount in box W26 and enter the result in box W29.

BORN ON OR BEFORE 5 APRIL 1933?

If you were born on or before 5 April 1933, you qualify for extra personal allowance for the tax year ending 5 April 1998 – provided your total income is below £15,600 (see p. 10). This box helps you work out how much you are entitled to.

First add the amount in box W21 to the amount in box W19. Enter the amount here – this is your total income:

_____ **Amount A**

Then enter the following maximum amount of extra personal allowance for people of 65 and over as Amount B:

- if you were born on or after 6 April 1923 and on or before 5 April 1933 – £1,175
- if you were born on or before 5 April 1923 – £1,355.

_____ **Amount B**

If Amount A is £15,600 or less, enter Amount B in box W25.2.

If Amount A is more than £15,600, subtract £15,600 from Amount A and enter the answer as Amount C:

_____ **Amount C**

Multiply Amount C by $^1/_2$ _____ **Amount D**

If Amount D is more than Amount B, enter 0 in box W25.2.

If Amount D is less than Amount B, subtract Amount D from Amount B and enter the answer in box W25.2.

Subtract the amount in box W30 (£4,100) from box W29 and enter the result in box W31.

Multiply the amount in box W31 by 3 per cent ($^3/_{100}$) and enter the exact answer (including pence) in box W32.

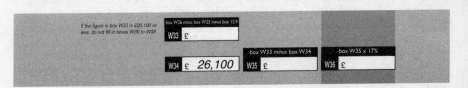

If the figure in box W33 is £26,100 or less, do not fill in boxes W35 to W38

box W26 minus box W23 minus box 12.9
W33 £

W34 £ *26,100*   box W33 minus box W34 **W35** £   box W35 x 17% **W36** £

Add the amount in box W23 to the amount in box 12.9 in the Income section on page 4 of the tax return. Subtract the total from the amount in box W26 and enter the answer in box W33.

If the amount in box W33 is £26,100 or less, leave boxes W35 to W38 blank and go straight to box W39, below.

If the amount in box W33 is more than £26,100, subtract the amount in box W34 – £26,100 – from it and enter the answer in box W35. Multiply the amount in box W35 by 17 per cent ($^{17}/_{100}$), and enter the exact answer (including pence) in box W36.

Look at boxes W28 and W35 to see which is the lower. Enter the lower of the two in box W37. Multiply the amount in box W37 by 3 per cent ($^{3}/_{100}$), and enter the exact answer (including pence) in box W38.

Add boxes W27, W32, W36 and W38 and enter the total in box W39 to find the income tax due for the tax year ending 5 April 1998. There are still some further adjustments to be made, however.

Add the amounts in boxes 15.7 and 15.8 in the Reliefs section on page 5 of the tax return, and enter the total venture capital trust and enterprise investment scheme subscriptions in box W40.

Multiply the amount in box W40 by 20 per cent ($^{20}/_{100}$), and enter the exact answer (including pence) in box W41.

Now go to Allowances and reliefs given in terms of tax on the opposite page of the tax calculation working sheet. This section is to enter allowances that have to be used to reduce your tax bill rather than the amount of your taxable income – because the tax relief is restricted to 15 per cent.

Allowances and reliefs given in terms of tax
- these reduce your tax bill - you may need to use the Question 16 notes on pages 23 to 26 of the Tax Return Guide and starting on page 3 of this Guide.

• *Married couple's allowance*
- see notes, pages 4 and 9

 £

The first such allowance is the married couple's allowance. If both of you were born on or after 6 April 1933, the allowance for the tax year ending 5 April 1998 was £1,830 – though this is reduced if you were married for only part of the tax year (see p. 44). The married couple's allowance goes to the husband unless the wife has asked for half of it to be set off against her income (£915 each) or both have agreed the whole £1,830 goes to the wife. Enter the amount you are entitled to in box W42.1.

If either husband or wife was born on or before 5 April 1933, the husband may be entitled to a higher married couple's allowance – see box below for how to calculate the amounts both husband and wife should enter in box W42.1.

WERE EITHER OF YOU BORN ON OR BEFORE 5 APRIL 1933?

If you or your spouse were born on or before 5 April 1933, you may be entitled to a higher rate of married couple's allowance for the tax year ending 5 April 1998. There are two parts of your married couple's allowance:

• the basic £1,830 married couple's allowance which goes to under-65s – you can allocate this between you in the same way as they can

• an extra amount which goes only to the husband – but this may be reduced if the husband's total income for the tax year ending 5 April 1998 was more than £15,600.

The calculator on the next pages will help you both work out how much you are entitled to. There is a worked example on p. 346.

MARRIED COUPLE'S ALLOWANCE - CALCULATOR FOR THE 65S AND OVER

	Husband	Wife
Basic married couple's allowance	£_____ J	£_____ K

Extra married couple's allowance:

Husband's total income:	£	L
Subtract from Amount L:	£15,600	
Total income over £15,600:	£_____	M
Maximum extra allowances:	£	N
Multiply M by 1/2	£_____	P
Subtract P from N	£	Q
Maximum extra married couple's allowance:	£	R

Enter the smaller of
Amount Q or Amount R: £_____ S

Total married couple's allowance: £_____ T (J + S) £_____ K

The basic married couple's allowance

The basic married couple's allowance of £1,830 goes to the husband unless arrangements have been made to split it between you or allocate it to the wife:

- if the basic married couple's allowance is all to go to the husband, enter £1,830 as Amount J and enter a 0 as Amount K
- if the basic married couple's allowance is to be divided between you, enter £915 as both Amounts J and K
- if the basic married couple's allowance is all to go to the wife, enter 0 as Amount J and £1,830 as Amount K.

Amount K is the figure to enter in box W42.1 of the wife's tax calculation working sheet for the tax year ending 5 April 1998.

The extra married couple's allowance

The next step is to calculate how much extra married couple's allowance the couple is entitled to – all of this goes to the husband.

First find the husband's total income by adding the amount in Box W21 of his tax calculation working sheet to the amount in Box W19. Enter the answer in the calculator above as Amount L.

Then subtract £15,600 from Amount L and enter the answer as Amount M – the amount of husband's total income over £15,600. If Amount L is less than £15,600, enter 0 as Amount M.

Now enter the maximum extra allowances – personal and married couple's – the husband is entitled to for a couple of your ages as Amount N in the calculator above. You can find the figure to enter in the third column of the table below.

Maximum extra allowances for the tax year ending 5 April 1998

Husband born	Wife born	Amount N	Amount R
On or after 6 April 1933	Before 6 April 1933 but after 5 April 1923	£1,355	£1,355
	On or before 5 April 1923	£1,395	£1,395
Before 6 April 1933 but after 5 April 1923	Before 6 April 1933 but after 5 April 1923	£2,530	£1,355
	On or before 5 April 1923	£2,570	£1,395
On or before 5 April 1923	Any time	£2,750	£1,395

If Amount M is 0, copy Amount N into Amount Q – you are entitled to the maximum extra allowances.

If Amount M is more than zero, halve it and enter the answer as Amount P. Subtract Amount P from Amount N and enter the answer as Amount Q. Then enter as Amount R the maximum extra married couple's allowance you are entitled to – you can find the figure in the fourth column of the Table.

Finally, compare Amount Q with Amount R and enter the lower of the two as Amount S. This is the extra amount of married couple's allowance the husband is entitled to.

Total husband's married couple's allowance
Add Amount S to Amount J and enter the total as Amount T – the amount of married couple's allowance the husband gets for the tax year ending 5 April 1998. Amount T is the figure to enter in box W42.1 of the husband's tax calculation working sheet.

- *Married couple's surplus allowance*
  (from box 16.28)

  W42.2 £

- *Additional personal allowance*
  - usually £1,830, may be split with
  another person - see the notes

  W42.3 £

- *Widow's bereavement allowance - £1,830*
  (if your husband died in 1996-97 or
  1997-98 and you have not remarried)

  W42.4 £

- *Interest on home loans (other
  than MIRAS)* (from box 15.2)

  W42.5 £

- *Maintenance and alimony*
  (boxes 15.4 and 15.5 - see the
  notes for box W16)

  W42.6 £

Total W42.7 £

Enter the following amounts:

- box W42.2 – married couple's surplus allowance unused by your spouse (see p. 198). Enter the amount in box 16.28 in the Allowances section of page 6 of the tax return
- box W42.3 – additional personal allowance. Enter your share of the £1,830 (see p. 195)
- box W42.4 – widow's bereavement allowance. If you are a widow whose husband died during the tax year ending 5 April 1998 or the previous tax year, enter £1,830 unless you have remarried
- box W42.5 – interest on loans to buy your only or main home. Enter the amount in box 15.2 in the Reliefs section on page 5 of the tax return
- box W42.6 – maintenance and alimony payments you make. You should have completed this box when filling in box W16 on the previous page of the tax calculation working sheet.

Add the amounts in boxes W42.1 to W42.6 and enter the total in box W42.7. Now follow the dashed line to box W42.

box W42 x 15%

W42 £   W43 £

Enter the amount in box W42.7 in box W42. Multiply this amount by 15 per cent ($^{15}/_{100}$), and enter the exact answer (including any pence) in box W43. Then go to Notional tax on the opposite page of the tax calculation working sheet.

- **Partnership notional tax**
  (from box 4.78) `W44.1 £`

- **Notional tax on UK scrip dividends
  and FIDs** (from boxes 10.22,
  10.25, 10.28 and 10.31) `W44.2 £`

- **Notional tax on estate
  income** (from box 7.14) `W44.3 £`

Copy to W44

Total `W44.4 £`

Some types of income come with a notional tax credit – which reduces the amount of tax you have to pay on it but cannot be repaid if it is more than you should have paid. This section stops any such notional tax being repaid if it is more than your tax bill for the year:

- box W44.1 – your share of a partnership's notional tax. Enter the amount in box 4.78 on the Partnership supplementary pages
- box W44.2 – notional tax on UK scrip dividends and foreign income dividends. Enter the total of boxes 10.22, 10.25, 10.28 and 10.31 from the Income section on page 3 of the tax return
- box W44.3 – notional tax on income from the estates of dead persons. Enter the amount in box 7.14 on page T1 of the Trusts etc supplementary pages.

Add the amounts in these three boxes and enter the total in box W44.4. Now follow the dashed line to box W44.

`W44 £`

Enter the amount in box W44.4 in box W44.

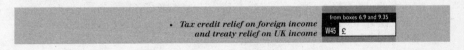

- **Tax credit relief on foreign income
  and treaty relief on UK income** *from boxes 6.9 and 9.35* `W45 £`

If you have foreign income from savings, investments, pensions, benefits or property and have paid tax on it in another country, you can claim tax credit relief to reduce your UK tax bill. If you are claiming tax credit relief – and you have been able to work out the amount – you will have written the amount in box 6.9 on page F3 of the Foreign supplement. And if you are allowed relief from some UK tax under a treaty because you are resident in another country, you may have entered a figure in box 9.35 of the Non-residence pages. Add the amounts in boxes 6.9 and 9.35 (if any) together and enter the total in box W45.

boxes W41 + W43 + W44 + W45

W46 £

Add the amounts in boxes W41, W43, W44 and W45 and enter the total in box W46.

Income Tax due, after allowances and reliefs   If the figure in box W46 is more than the figure in box W39, enter a zero   box W39 minus box W46   W47 £

Subtract the amount in box W46 from the amount in box W39 and enter the result in box W47.

Remember that if the answer is a negative number, enter 0 in box W47.

• *Recoverable tax on charitable covenants, annuities and Gift Aid payments* (box W17 x 23%)   W48 £

Take the amount you entered in box W17 on page 5 of the Tax Calculation Guide and multiply it by 23 per cent ($^{23}/_{100}$). Enter the exact answer in box W48. This stops you getting two lots of basic rate tax relief on gifts to charity made by covenant or through the Gift Aid scheme.

• *Class 4 National Insurance Contributions* (from box 3.91 or box 4.25)   W49 £

If you have income from being self-employed, enter the amount of Class 4 National Insurance contributions you must pay in box W49. The figure to enter is in box 3.91 on page SE4 of the orange Self-employment supplement. If you have income from a partnership, the figure to enter in box W49 can be found from the Partnership pages in box 4.25.

If you have more than one source of income on which Class 4 National Insurance contributions are due, you need Help Sheet *IR220 More than one business* to calculate the amount.

Income Tax and Class 4 National Insurance Contributions	boxes W47 + W48 + W49
	W50 £

Add the amounts in boxes W47, W48 and W49 and enter the exact total (including pence) in box W50. This is the total amount of income tax and Class 4 National Insurance contributions due on your income for the tax year ending 5 April 1998. Copy the amount in box W50 into box W50 at the top of page 8 of the Tax Calculation Guide.

TAX ALREADY PAID OR ACCOUNTED FOR

The next page of the tax calculation working sheet covers the last leg of the calculation: working out how much tax you need still to pay – or the rebate you are entitled to.

First you must add up the tax you have paid already on your income for the tax year ending 5 April 1998.

You should have already filled in box W50 with the amount in box W50 at the foot of the previous page.

Next look for your PAYE Coding Notice for the 1997-98 tax year and see if there is an adjustment to collect unpaid tax from previous tax years. If there is, copy the figure for the amount of tax being collected into box W51. Then enter the same amount in box 18.1 on the Other information section on page 7 of the tax return.

If you can't find your PAYE Coding Notice for 1997-98, ask your tax inspector whether there was any such tax collected, and the amount.

Add the amounts in boxes W50 and W51 and enter the total in box W52.

Tax paid at source	
Employment (from boxes 1.11 and 1.30)	W53.1 £

Enter in box W53.1 the amount of tax deducted from your earnings from jobs in the tax year ending 5 April 1998. You can find this by adding the amount in box 1.11 on page E1 of the Employment supplementary pages and the amount in box 1.30 on page E2. If you have more than one job, add together the amounts from each of them.

- *Self-employment* (from box 3.92) W53.2 £ [   ]

Most self-employed people have no tax deducted from their earnings before they receive them. But self-employed subcontractors in the construction industry receive payment after tax has been deducted. Enter in box W53.2 the amount of tax deducted in the tax year ending 5 April 1998. You can find the amount in box 3.92 on page SE4 of the Self-employment supplement.

- *Partnerships* (from box 4.77) W53.3 £ [   ]

If you have income from a partnership, enter in box W53.3 your share of any income tax paid at source on its income in the tax year ending 5 April 1998. The amount is in box 4.77 on the back page of the Partnership supplementary pages.

- *UK land and property* (from box 5.21) W53.4 £ [   ]

Enter in box W53.4 any income tax deducted from income from letting out property in the tax year ending 5 April 1998. The amount is in box 5.21 on page L2 of the Land and property supplementary pages.

- *Foreign income* (from boxes 6.1 and 6.3) W53.5 £ [   ]

If any UK tax has been deducted from foreign income, enter in box W53.5 the amount deducted in the tax year ending 5 April 1998. The amount can be found by adding any amount in box 6.1 on page F1 of the Foreign supplementary pages to any amount in box 6.3 on page F2.

- *Trusts, settlements or estate income* (from boxes 7.2, 7.5, 7.8 and 7.11) W53.6 £ [   ]

Tax deducted from trusts, other forms of settlement such as a transfer of assets or the estates of people who have died should have been entered in the following boxes on page T1 of the Trusts etc supplementary pages: 7.2, 7.5, 7.8 and 7.11. Enter the total in box W53.6.

- **UK savings** (from boxes 10.3, 10.6, 10.10, 10.13, 10.16 and 10.19) W53.7 £

If you received any income from UK savings and investments in the tax year ending 5 April 1998, enter the total tax deducted from it in box W53.7 . This is found by adding the tax deducted from the following boxes in the Income section on page 3 of the tax return: 10.3, 10.6, 10.10, 10.13, 10.16 and 10.19.

- **UK pensions, retirement annuities and benefits** (from boxes 11.8 and 11.11) W53.8 £

If tax was deducted from a UK pension, social security benefit or income from a retirement annuity in the tax year ending 5 April 1998, enter the total in box W53.8. The amount should be the total of boxes 11.8 and 11.11 in the Income section on page 4 of the tax return.

- **Other income** (from box 13.2) W53.9 £

Box W53.9 is for the tax deducted from any other income you received in the tax year ending 5 April 1998 that was not entered somewhere else on the tax return. Enter the amount in box 13.2 in the Income section on page 4 of the tax return.

Total W53.10 £   W53 £

Add boxes W53.1 to W53.9 and enter the total in box W53.10. Then copy this total to box W53.

- **Tax due for 1997-98 included in the 1998-99 PAYE tax code** W54 £   box W53 + box W54 W55 £

Copy to box 18.2 in your Tax Return

If your PAYE tax code failed to collect all the tax due during the tax year ending 5 April 1998, your tax inspector will normally adjust your PAYE code for the tax year ending 5 April 1999 to collect this underpayment. Since the inspector has made these arrangements, there is no need for you to make good the underpayment in calculating the amount you need to pay. So you add the amount that is to be collected in the tax year beginning 6 April 1998 back in here as tax that is accounted for.

To see if you need to enter anything here, find the last PAYE Coding Notice sent to you for 1997-98 – the tax year ending 5 April 1998. If your PAYE code was reduced, there will be a figure described as 'estimated underpayment' at the bottom of the notice. Enter the amount of the underpayment in box W54.

If you can't find a PAYE Coding Notice for the year or are unsure what to enter, ask your tax inspector.

Then copy the amount in box W54 into box 18.2 on page 7 of the tax return.

Finally, add box W53 and box W54 and enter the total in box W55.

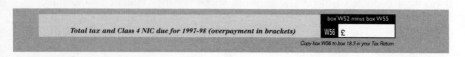

Total tax and Class 4 NIC due for 1997-98 (overpayment in brackets)   box W52 minus box W55   W56 £

Copy box W56 to box 18.3 in your Tax Return

Subtract box W55 from box W52 and enter the answer in box W56. This is the amount of income tax and Class 4 National Insurance contributions due for the tax year ending 5 April 1998.

If the answer is a negative amount, you have paid too much – enter the figure for the overpayment in brackets.

Now copy the amount in box W56 into box 18.3 on page 7 of the tax return.

Do you owe tax or are you due a rebate?

Tax owed or overpaid in 1997-98

• *1997-98 tax already refunded*
(from box 17.1)   W57A £

This part of the tax calculation working sheet works out whether you owe tax for the tax year ending 5 April 1998, or whether you are due a rebate.

If you ticked the YES box to Q17 on page 7 of the tax return, you have already received a tax rebate for the tax year ending 5 April 1998. This would happen, for example, if you had claimed back tax deducted from savings income because you expected it to be more than your overall tax bill (see p. 68).

Enter in box W57A the amount of any such repayment – the amount you have already entered in box 17.1 on page 7 of the tax return. But do not include any repayment which was made against income from on or before

5 April 1997 – for example, if you have had trading losses carried back to set against income from earlier tax years.

Have you paid too little tax for the tax year ending 5 April 1997 – or earlier tax years? It is unlikely, but it could happen if you have closed down a business and have since received some income from it – post-cessation receipts – which you want added to the year the business ceased (see p. 188). You need to recalculate your tax bill for the tax year you backdate the receipts to and enter any extra tax and Class 4 National Insurance contributions here.

You could also find yourself owing tax from earlier years if you are in one of the narrow range of professions that allows you to spread your income over several tax years – a farmer, writer or artist, for example. If this raises your income for earlier years, you need to recalculate your tax bill for those earlier years and enter the extra amount here.

If there is unpaid tax for earlier years, enter the amount in box W57 and copy it into box 18.4 on page 7 of the tax return. If you are unsure about this, ask your tax inspector for help.

Then add boxes W56, W57A and W57 and enter the total in box W58.

Have you paid too much tax for the tax year ending 5 April 1997 – or earlier tax years? This could happen if you want to set losses against income from such earlier years, or to carry back personal pension or retirement annuity payments (see p. 78). Farmers can also reduce their tax on earlier years if they are averaging their income.

Again you need to recalculate your tax bill for the tax year you have carried the losses or payments back to. Do not include losses or payments you have already claimed relief on.

Enter the tax and Class 4 National Insurance contributions you now think were overpaid in box W59. Tick box 18.5 on page 7 of the tax return and copy the figure in box W59 to the Additional information box on page 8 of the tax return. If you are unsure about this, ask your tax inspector for help.

You may already have made payments on account of tax and Class 4 National Insurance contributions for the tax year ending 5 April 1998. The two payments on account were due on 31 January 1998 and 31 July 1998.

Add the payments made and enter the total in box W60. Don't include interest charged for late payment, penalties for making late returns or other surcharges. If in doubt about what to enter, ask your tax inspector.

Then add the amount in box W60 to the amount in box W59 and enter the total in box W61.

If the amount in box W61 is smaller than the amount in box W58, you owe tax for the tax year ending 5 April 1998. If the amount in box W61 is larger than the amount in box W58, you have paid too much tax for that tax year.

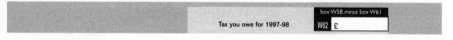

If you owe tax for the tax year ending 5 April 1998, subtract the amount in box W61 from the amount in box W58 and enter the answer in box W62. If the amount you owe is less than £1,000, you can choose to have it collected from your income through PAYE in the tax year beginning 6 April 1999. If it is more than £1,000 – or you want to pay it off sooner – you must pay it by 31 January 1999 with your first payment on account for the tax year beginning 6 April 1998. See opposite for how to calculate the amount of the payment on account.

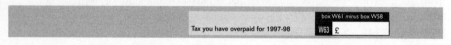

If you have overpaid tax for the tax year ending 5 April 1998, subtract the amount in box W58 from the amount in box W61 and enter the answer in box W63. You may be able to get a rebate now, depending on the amount of the payment on account you have to make for the tax year which began on 6 April 1998 – see below.

WORKING OUT YOUR PAYMENTS ON ACCOUNT

The next stage in calculating your tax is to work out what payments on account you need to make for the tax year beginning 6 April 1998. How any underpayment for the previous tax year is collected – and whether you can claim a rebate of overpaid tax – depends on the amount of these payments.

Payments on account for 1998-99

Your payments on account for the tax year beginning 6 April 1998 are based on your income tax and Class 4 National Insurance contributions due for the tax year ending 5 April 1998 – the figure you entered in box W56. Normally you will be asked for two payments, each of half this total, one due on 31 January 1999, the other on 31 July 1999.

However, you will not have to make payments on account for the tax year which began on 6 April 1998 if the total is less than £500 or less than 20 per cent of your total tax including what is deducted at source. This next part of the tax calculation working sheet checks whether you have to make payments on account – and if so, how much.

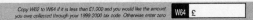

Copy W62 to W64 if it is less than £1,000 and you would like the amount you owe collected through your 1999-2000 tax code. Otherwise enter zero | W64 £

If the tax you owe for the tax year ending 5 April 1998 – the amount in box W62 – is less than £1,000, you can choose to have it collected from your income through PAYE in the tax year beginning 6 April 1999. If this is what you want to do, enter the amount in box W62 in box W64.

If the amount in box W62 is £1,000 or more – or you do not want your underpayment collected through PAYE – enter 0 in box W64.

If W65 is *less than £500* you do not need to make payments on account. Leave box 18.6 blank and tick box 18.8 on your Tax Return. If W65 is *equal to or more than £500, carry on* | box W56 minus box W64 | W65 £

Subtract the amount in box W64 from the amount in box W56 and enter the answer in box W65.

If the amount in box W65 is less than £500, you do not need to make payments on account for the tax year beginning 6 April 1998. Tick box 18.8 on page 7 of the tax return and leave box 18.6 blank. If the amount in box W65 is £500 or more, move on to the next line.

Add the amounts in boxes W47, W44 and W48 and enter the total in box W66. This is the amount of income tax due after allowances and reliefs.

Then enter in box W67 the amount of Class 4 National Insurance contributions due from box W49.

Add boxes W66 and W67, and enter the total in box W68. Multiply box W68 by 20 per cent ($^{20}/_{100}$) and enter the answer in box W69.

If the amount in box W65 is less than the amount in box W69, you do not need to make payments on account for the tax year beginning 6 April 1998. Tick box 18.8 on page 7 of the tax return and leave box 18.6 blank.

If the amount in box W65 is equal to or larger than the amount in box W69, you will have to make payments on account for the tax year beginning 6 April 1998. Move on to the next line.

Halve the amount in box W65 and enter the answer in box W70. This is the amount of each of your payments on account for the tax year beginning 6 April 1998.

The amount in box W70 is normally the amount you should now enter in box 18.6 on page 7 of the tax return as your first payment on account for the tax year (include any pence). However, you are entitled to pay less than this amount if you think smaller payments will cover your tax bill for the tax year beginning 6 April 1998. There are two reasons why you might feel it appropriate to make lower payments on account:

- your income for the tax year beginning 6 April 1998 will be lower than the previous year's
- you expect to be able to claim higher allowances and reliefs for this year than for last year.

No payments on account are needed if you expect your tax bill for the tax year beginning 6 April 1998 to be less than £500 or 80 per cent or more of the tax will be collected at source. For example, if more of your income is to be taxed under PAYE or comes from savings where tax is deducted at source, you might need to make no payments on account.

If you think that lower payments on account are needed, work out carefully how much you think should be paid. Put this estimate in box 18.6 on page 7 of the tax return and tick box 18.7. Then explain your reasons in the Additional information box on page 8 of the tax return.

It is probably better to pay slightly more rather than too little in your payments on account. If you pay too much, you will get interest on it; if you pay too little, you will pay interest. There are penalties in the form of fines if you are caught trying to hoodwink your tax inspector in setting payments on account. And remember, if you make the payments on account calculated in the Tax Calculation Guide on time, there is normally no interest to pay even if your tax bill turns out to have been much higher.

• 1998-99 tax you are reclaiming now	18.9 £

Enter here details of tax you wish to claim back from the tax year ending 5 April 1998 for either of the following:

- trading losses in the tax year beginning 6 April 1998 – give details in the Additional information box on page 8 of the tax return
- pension payments you want to bring back from the tax year beginning 6 April 1998 – you entered these in boxes 14.4, 14.9 or 14.14 in the Reliefs section on page 5 of the tax return.

You will need to recalculate your tax bill for the tax year ending 5 April 1998 to take account of these backdated reliefs using the tax calculation working sheet. The amount to enter in box 18.9 is the difference between the figure you entered in box W56 on page 8 of the Tax Calculation Guide without backdating the reliefs and then after backdating the reliefs.

Working out your payment due on 31 January 1999

You have now worked out what your payments on account should be for the tax year beginning 6 April 1998. But if you owe tax for the tax year ending 5 April 1998, this must also be paid with the first payment of account by 31 January 1999. And if you are entitled to a rebate, this can reduce your first payment on account. This last part of the Tax Calculation Guide on page 11 tells you how much you have to pay by 31 January 1999.

If you owe tax for the tax year ending 5 April 1998 – that is, if you have entered a figure in box W62 – complete the top half of this working sheet. If you have overpaid tax for the tax year – you have entered a figure in box W63 – complete the bottom half.

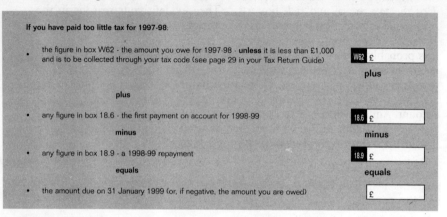

If you have paid too little tax for 1997-98:

• the figure in box W62 - the amount you owe for 1997-98 - **unless** it is less than £1,000 and is to be collected through your tax code (see page 29 in your Tax Return Guide)   **W62** £

plus

• any figure in box 18.6 - the first payment on account for 1998-99   **18.6** £

minus

• any figure in box 18.9 - a 1998-99 repayment   **18.9** £

equals

• the amount due on 31 January 1999 (or, if negative, the amount you are owed)   £

If you paid too little tax in the tax year ending 5 April 1998, enter in the top line the amount you owe from box W62 on page 8 of the Tax Calculation Guide. But if it is less than £1,000 and you want it collected through PAYE, enter 0.

Then enter the amount of your payment on account for the tax year beginning 6 April 1998 – from box 18.6 on page 7 of the tax return. If you are claiming any repayment of tax for losses or pension payments made in the tax year beginning 6 April 1998, enter the amount from box 18.9.

Add the amount in box W62 to the amount in box 18.6 and subtract the amount in box 18.9. The answer is the amount you must pay by 31 January 1999 – enter it in the box on the bottom line.

If you paid too much tax in the tax year ending 5 April 1998, enter in the top line the amount overpaid from box W63 on page 8 of the Tax Calculation Guide.

If you are claiming any repayment of tax for losses or pension payments made in the tax year beginning 6 April 1998, enter the amount from box 18.9 on page 7 of the tax return.

Then enter the amount of your payment on account for the tax year beginning 6 April 1998 – from box 18.6.

Add the amount in box W63 to the amount in box 18.9 and subtract the amount in box 18.6. The answer is the amount the Inland Revenue owes you – enter it in the box on the bottom line.

You can claim your rebate by ticking the YES box by Q19 on page 7 of the tax return.

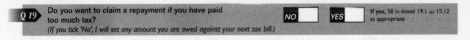

Q 19 **Do you want to claim a repayment if you have paid too much tax?** `NO` [   ] `YES` [   ] If yes, fill in boxes 19.1 to 19.12 as appropriate
(If you tick 'No', I will set any amount you are owed against your next tax bill.)

If you owe the Inland Revenue any amounts from previous years, your tax inspector will deduct these from any rebate. If you tick the NO box the rebate will be used to reduce your next tax bill.

If you want the rebate to be sent to you, tick box 19.1. If you would prefer it to be paid into your bank or building society account or to someone else you nominate, tick box 19.2.

Give the details of the bank or building society account in boxes 19.3 to 19.7.

If you want the rebate to go to someone else, give details of your nominee in boxes 19.8 to 19.12.

CASE STUDIES IN FILLING IN THE TAX CALCULATOR

In this chapter, we follow a simple case study to show how easy it is for most people to calculate their own tax bills. We run through the tax calculation working sheet for Mary Emmanuel – a company executive with a range of fringe benefits and income from a portfolio of savings and investments.

On p. 345, we also follow through the calculations for Gerard Mallory – a pensioner with income from pensions and investments.

MARY EMMANUEL WORKS OUT HER TAX

Mary Emmanuel earned £34,500 from her job in the tax year ending 5 April 1998. She has a company car, which has a taxable value of £4,714. And she gets free private medical insurance at work for herself and her family. This is worth £560 in the tax year ending 5 April 1998.

She also has freelance earnings from writing, which earned her £6,750 in the tax year ending 5 April 1998.

She has the following types of investment income – all in the UK:

- interest on her bank and building society accounts – a total of £107 after deduction of tax at 20 per cent (a gross amount of £134)
- interest from a National Savings Investment Account – £525 paid gross, without deduction of tax
- dividends from various shares she owns – a total of £288, with tax credits of £72 (a gross amount of £360)
- distributions from unit trusts – £150 with £37 of tax credits (£187 gross).

She can claim as an expense of her main job the £120 a year subscription she pays to her professional association. In the tax year ending 5 April 1998, she paid £180 after tax relief under a covenant to charity. She paid £2,772 into her personal pension scheme in the tax year ending 5 April 1998: this is after deduction of tax at the basic rate of 23 per cent – a gross amount of £3,600 for the year. And she and her husband jointly pay £4,800 a year in mortgage interest, paid net of tax relief under MIRAS (see p. 53).

Mary has been married for several years, and the married couple's allowance is split between her and her husband. Both are in their 30s.

Mary has no chargeable capital gains, so she completes the standard tax calculation working sheet.

Total income from
Mary starts on the first page of the tax calculation working sheet, adding together her total income.

Her income from her first employment is her salary of £34,500 (from box 1.8 in the Employment supplementary pages), plus the value of her fringe benefits: £4,714 for her company car (box 1.16) and £560 for free medical insurance (box 1.21). That makes total income from her first job of £34,500 + £4,714 + £560 = £39,774. Mary enters £39,774 in the top line under First employment.

In the second line, she enters the £120 subscription to her professional association she can claim as an expense – from box 1.34 in the Employment supplementary pages.

She deducts the £120 in the second line from the £39,774 in the first line and enters £39,654 as her total taxable income from her first job in the third line.

She has no other employment, so she leaves the second column blank. She therefore copies the £39,654 in the third line of the first column into box W1.

The freelance earnings from writing count as income from self-employment. So Mary enters £6,750 in box W3 – she gets this figure from box 3.88 on page SE3 of the Self-employment supplement.

The only other income Mary has is from her UK savings and investments: £134 in interest from her bank and building society accounts (in box 10.4 on page 3 of the tax return); £525 in interest from her National Savings Investment Account (box 10.8); £360 from share dividends (box 10.17); £187 from unit trust distributions (box 10.20). This gives a total taxable amount of £134 + £525 + £360 + £187 = £1,206 – which she enters in box W8.

She adds the £39,654 in box W1, the £6,750 in box W3 and the £1,206 in box W8 to get a total of £47,610. She enters £47,610 in box W12.

Deductions for
Mary now enters details of her deductions in the tax calculation working sheet.

She starts with her gross personal pension payments of £3,600 from box 14.15 on page 5 of the tax return. She enters £3,600 in box W13.

Then she turns to the £180 a year of payments she makes net under covenant to charity (box 15.9 on page 5 of the tax return). She multiplies this by $^{100}/_{77}$ to get £233.77 – the gross amount which she enters in box W17.

Although she gets tax relief on her mortgage interest payments, she does not claim any deduction in calculating her tax. She gets the tax relief through MIRAS by making payments net of tax relief.

She adds the £3,600 in box W13 to the £233.77 in box W17 to get total deductions of £3,833.77. She enters this amount in box W20. Then she deducts the amount in box W20 from the amount in box W12: £47,610 – £3,833.77 = £43,776.23. She enters £43,776.23 in box W21 as her total income less deductions.

Reliefs
Mary turns to the next page of the tax calculation working sheet. She copies the figure of £43,776.23 into box W22 at the top of the page.

She now has to add back the personal pension payments, since she will already have had the tax relief on them by paying them net of basic rate tax relief. So she enters £3,600 (box 14.15 on page 5 of the tax return) in box W23.1. There is no figure to enter in box W23.2, so she enters £3,600 in box W23.3, and copies this into box W23.

She adds the amounts in boxes W22 and W23: £43,776.23 + £3,600 = £47,376.23. She enters £47,376.23 in box W24.

Allowances given as a deduction from your income
Mary's only allowance given as a deduction against her income is her personal allowance of £4,045. She enters £4,045 in box W25.1 and as the total in box W25.6. She then copies it into box W25.

She deducts the amount in box W25 from the amount in box W24; £47,376.23 – £4,045 = £43,331.23. She enters £43,331.23 in box W26.

Mary then multiplies £43,331.23 by 20 per cent: £43,331.23 x $^{20}/_{100}$ = £8,666.25. She enters £8,666.25 in box W27.

Savings income taxed at the lower (20%) rate
Mary's only income which is taxed at the lower rate of 20 per cent is her £1,206 from UK savings and investments (already entered in box W8). She enters £1,206 in box W28.2 and as the total for this section in box W28.5.

She then copies £1,206 into box W28. She subtracts this from the amount in box W26: £43,331.23 – £1,206 = £42,125.23. She enters £42,125.23 in box W29.

Mary subtracts box W30 from box W29: £42,125.23 – £4,100 = £38,025.23. She enters £38,025.23 in box W31.

She multiplies the amount in box W31 by 3 per cent: £38,025.23 x $^{3}/_{100}$ = £1,140.76. She enters £1,140.76 in box W32.

Next she calculates the figure to enter in box W33. There is no amount in box 12.9 of the Income section of the tax return, so she subtracts the amount in box W23 – £3,600 – from the amount in box W26 – £43,331.23. She enters the answer in box W33: £43,331.23 – £3,600 = £39,731.23.

The amount in box W33 is more than £26,100, so Mary subtracts the £26,100 in box W34 from the £39,731.23 in box W33: £39,731.23 – £26,100 = £13,631.23. She enters this in box W35 and then multiplies it by 17 per cent: £13,631.23 x $^{17}/_{100}$ = £2,317.31. She enters £2,317.31 in box W36.

Then Mary compares the amounts in boxes W28 (£1,206) and W35 (£13,631.23) to see which is the lower. She enters £1,206 in box W37 and then multiplies it by 3 per cent: £1,206 x $^{3}/_{100}$ = £36.18. She enters £36.18 in box W38.

Box W39 is the total of boxes W27, W32, W36 and W38: £8,666.25 + £1,140.76 + £2,317.31 + £36.18 = £12,160.50.

Mary has not invested in a venture capital trust or the Enterprise Investment Scheme, so she leaves boxes W40 and W41 blank.

Allowances and reliefs given in terms of tax
Mary enters her half of the married couple's allowance in box W42.1 – £915. Although she gets tax relief on mortgage interest, this is not entered here –

she gets it direct from the lender by making payments net of tax relief through MIRAS.

So the total for allowances and reliefs given in terms of tax is £915 – she enters this in box W42.7, and copies it across to box W42. She multiplies £915 by 15 per cent: £915 x $^{15}/_{100}$ = £137.25. She enters £137.25 in box W43.

Mary has received no income with notional tax credits, so she leaves W44 blank. And she has no tax credit relief to claim from foreign investments – she leaves box W45 blank also.

Box W46 is found by adding boxes W41, W43, W44 and W45: in Mary's case, this is 0 + £137.25 + 0 + 0 = £137.25. She deducts this from the amount in box W39: £12,160.50 – £137.25 = £12,023.25 and enters £12,023.25 in box W47.

Mary has given herself tax relief on her covenant payments which must now be allowed for. She takes the £233.77 she entered in box W17 and multiplies it by 23 per cent: £233.77 x $^{23}/_{100}$ = £53.77. She enters £53.77 in box W48.

She does not have to pay any Class 4 National Insurance contributions, so she leaves box W49 blank. Her total tax bill for the year is therefore the total of boxes W47, W48 and W49: £12,023.25 + £53.77 + 0 = £12,077.02. She enters £12,077.02 in box W50, and copies it over to box W50 at the top of the next page of the tax calculation working sheet.

Income tax and Class 4 NIC due
Mary has had no adjustment to her PAYE code for the tax year ending 5 April 1998 to collect unpaid tax from earlier tax years. So she leaves box W51 blank and copies £12,077.02 in to box W52.

She now finds out how much tax has been paid at source on her income. For her earnings from her main job, she finds she has paid £8,529 through PAYE (from box 1.11 on page E1 of the Employment supplementary pages for her main job). She enters £8,529 in box W53.1.

No tax has been paid on her earnings from her freelance writing, so she enters 0 in box W53.2.

On her savings income, she finds the amounts of tax deducted or credited from the following boxes on page 3 of the tax return:

• bank and building society interest – box 10.3 shows £27

- share dividends – box 10.16 shows £72
- unit trust distributions – box 10.19 shows £37.

Interest on National Savings Investment Accounts is paid gross, so no tax has been deducted.

Mary adds these amounts of tax together: £27 + £72 + £37 = £136. She enters £136 in box W53.7.

She then adds the amounts in boxes W53.1, W53.2 and W53.7: £8,529 + £0 + £136 = £8,665. She enters £8,665 in box W53.10, and copies it into box W53.

No tax for the tax year ending 5 April 1998 has been included in the next year's PAYE code, so Mary enters 0 in box W54 and enters £8,665 in box W55.

She subtracts this amount from box W52: £12,077.02 – £8,665 = £3,412.02. She enters £3,412.02 in box W56 – her income tax and Class 4 National Insurance contributions due for the tax year ending 5 April 1998. She copies this total to box 18.3 on her tax return.

Tax owed or overpaid in 1997-98
No tax for the tax year ending 5 April 1998 has already been refunded, nor is there any unpaid tax for earlier years, so she enters 0 in boxes W57A and W57. Box W58 is thus the same as box W56 – £3,412.02.

Mary did not overpay tax in earlier years, so she enters 0 in box W59. She has, however, made two payments on account of £830 each for the tax year ending 5 April 1998: one due on 31 January 1998; the other due on 31 July 1998. So she enters twice £830 = £1,660 in box W60. This is also the amount to enter in box W61.

Box W62 tells Mary the tax she still owes: box W58 – box W61: £3,412.02 – £1,660 = £1,752.02. This will be collected with Mary's first payment on account for the tax year beginning 6 April 1998. She now goes on to calculate how much the payment will be.

Payments on account for 1998-99
The amount in box W62 is more than £1,000, so Mary enters 0 in box W64. Box W65 is therefore the same as box W56 – £3,412.02.

Box W56 is the amount of tax and Class 4 National Insurance due for the tax year ending 5 April 1998. But no payments on account will be needed if it is less than £500 (which it isn't) or less than 20 per cent of Mary's overall tax bill including tax collected at source. The next bit of the working sheet checks this second condition.

First, it asks for Mary's total tax from box W47: she enters £12,023.25 in box W66. No Class 4 National Insurance contributions are due, so Mary enters 0 in box W67 and £12,023.25 in box W68. She enters 20 per cent of £12,023.25 = £2,404.65 in box W69. Since the amount in box W56 is more than this, payments on account will be needed for the tax year beginning 6 April 1998.

Each payment on account is half the figure in box W65: half of £3,412.02 = £1,706.01. Mary enters £1,706.01 in box W70, and copies it into box 18.6 on page 7 of the tax return.

Payment due on 31 January 1999

Lastly Mary turns to page 11 of the Tax Calculation Guide to work out how much is due on 31 January 1999. This will be:

- the amount of tax owed from the tax year ending 5 April 1998 from box W62 – £1,752.02
- plus the amount in box 18.6 – £1,706.01
- minus any figure in box 18.9 – £0 for Mary.

This gives an answer of £1,752.02 + £1,706.01 + £0 = £3,458.03, which is the amount due on 31 January 1999.

The second payment on account for the tax year beginning 6 April 1998 will be due by 31 July 1999 – this is £1,706.01.

GERARD MALLORY WORKS OUT HIS TAX

Gerard Mallory, 67, has retired and lives with his wife Eva, 66. His main income is from pensions:

- the state retirement pension – he received £3,247 in the tax year ending 5 April 1998
- his pension from his former job – £11,583 in that tax year.

In addition, Gerard has income from savings and investments, most of which is paid after deduction of tax at 20 per cent. He has received a gross amount of £4,429, with tax of £713 having been paid on £3,566 of this.

All their married couple's allowance is deducted from Gerard's income. Since he has no chargeable capital gains, he completes the standard tax calculation working sheet.

Total income from
Gerard starts by entering his income totals on the first page of the tax calculation working sheet. He enters 0 in each of boxes W1 to W7, since he has none of those sorts of income.

Box W8 is for the total taxable amount of income from savings and investments shown on page 3 of his tax return. This comes to £4,429.

Box W9 is for his total taxable amount of pension income, from page 4 of the tax return. He adds the £3,247 state retirement pension in box 11.1 to the £11,583 occupational pension in box 11.12: £3,247 + £11,583 = £14,830. He enters £14,830 in box W9.

He enters 0 in boxes W10 and W11. He adds the amounts in boxes W1 to W11: £4,429 + £14,830 = £19,259. He enters £19,259 as the total in box W12.

Deductions for
Gerard has no deductions to enter in boxes W13 to W19. So he enters 0 for total deductions in box W20, and enters £19,259 in box W21 as his total income less deductions.

Reliefs
Gerard copies the £19,259 to box W22 at the top of the next page of the tax calculation working sheet. He makes no payments for personal pensions or vocational training, so there is nothing to enter in the Reliefs boxes at the top of page 6. He enters 0 in box W23, and enters £19,259 in box W24.

Allowances given as a deduction from your income
Gerard enters the £4,045 personal allowance in box W25.1.

Since he was born on or before 5 April 1933, he may be entitled to an extra amount of personal allowance on account of his age. Gerard was born on or after 6 April 1923, so the maximum extra he is entitled to is £1,175.

However, Gerard's total income is more than £15,600, so the amount of extra allowance is reduced by £1 for each £2 over this limit. Gerard uses the calculator on p. 319 of this guide to work out whether he is entitled to any extra allowance.

First, he works out his total income – the amount in box W21 plus the amount in box W19: £19,259 + £0 = £19,259. This is Amount A.

Then he enters the maximum amount of extra personal allowance for someone of his age as Amount B: £1,175.

Since Amount A is more than £15,600, he subtracts £15,600 from Amount A: £19,259 – £15,600 = £3,659. This is Amount C.

Gerard multiplies Amount C by $1/_2$: £3,659 x $1/_2$ = £1,829.50. This is Amount D. Since Amount D is more than Amount B, Gerard is not entitled to any extra personal allowance on account of his age, so he enters 0 in box W25.2.

Gerard is not entitled to any of the other allowances in this section, so the total is box W25.1 + box W25.2: £4,045 + £0 = £4,045. He enters £4,045 in box W25.6 and copies it across to box W25.

He then deducts the amount in box W25 from the amount in box W24: £19,259 – £4,045 = £15,214. He enters £15,214 in box W26.

Gerard then multiplies £15,214 by 20 per cent: £15,214 x $20/_{100}$ = £3,042.80. He enters £3,042.80 in box W27.

Savings income taxed at the lower (20%) rate
Gerard's only income which is taxed at the lower rate of 20 per cent is his £4,429 from UK savings and investments (already entered in box W8). He enters £4,429 in box W28.2 and as the total for this section in box W28.5.

He copies £4,429 into box W28 and subtracts this from the amount in box W26: £15,214 – £4,429 = £10,785. He enters £10,785 in box W29.

Gerard subtracts box W30 from box W29: £10,785 – £4,100 = £6,685. He enters £6,685 in box W31.

He multiplies the amount in box W31 by 3 per cent: £6,685 x $3/_{100}$ = £200.55. He enters £200.55 in box W32.

There is no amount in box 12.9 of the Income section of the tax return or in box W23. So he enters the £15,214 in box W26 in box W33.

Since the amount in box W33 is less than £26,100, Gerard leaves boxes W35 to W38 blank and moves on to box W39. He adds the amounts in boxes

W27, W32, W36 and W38: £3,042.80 + £200.55 + £0 + £0 = £3,243.35.

Since he has not invested in a venture capital trust or the Enterprise Investment Scheme, Gerard leaves boxes W40 and W41 blank.

Allowances and reliefs given in terms of tax
Gerard and his wife were born on or before 5 April 1933, so he may be entitled to a higher married couple's allowance on account of his age. Gerard was born on or after 6 April 1923, so the maximum extra he is entitled to is £1,355. Gerard uses the calculator on p. 322 to work out whether he is entitled to a higher married couple's allowance – and if so, how much.

First, he enters the basic married couple's allowance of £1,830 as Amount J, since it is all to be set against his income. He enters 0 as Amount K – Eva gets none of the married couple's allowance.

The next step is to calculate how much extra married couple's allowance the couple is entitled to – all of this goes to the husband. This depends on his total income, which he had already calculated above when working out his personal allowance. It is the amount in box W21 plus the amount in box W19: £19,259 + £0 = £19,259. He enters this as Amount L.

Then he subtracts £15,600 from Amount L: £19,259 – £15,600 = £3,659. He enters £3,659 as Amount M – the amount of his total income over £15,600.

Gerard looks at the table on p. 323 to find the maximum extra allowances – personal and married couple's – for a couple aged 67 and 66. This is £2,530 so he enters this as Amount N.

He halves Amount M: $^1/_2$ x £3,659 = £1,829.50. He enters £1,829.50 as Amount P. He subtracts Amount P from Amount N: £2,530 – £1,829.50 = £700.50. He enters £700.50 as Amount Q.

Then Gerard enters as Amount R the maximum extra married couple's allowance he is entitled to, which is £1,355, according to the table on p. 000. The lower of Amount Q (£700.50) and Amount R (£1,355) is Amount Q. So he enters £700.50 as Amount S – the extra married couple's allowance he is entitled to.

Gerard adds Amount S to Amount J: £700.50 + £1,830 = £2,530.50. He enters £2,530.50 as Amount T – the amount of married couple's allowance he gets for the tax year ending 5 April 1998. It is also the amount to enter in box W42.1 on Gerard's tax calculation working sheet.

Gerard is entitled to none of the other allowances and reliefs given in terms of tax, so he enters £2,530.50 in box W42.7 and copies it across to box W42. He then multiplies box W42 by 15 per cent: £2,530.50 x $^{15}/_{100}$ = £379.58. He enters £379.58 in box W43.

Gerard has received no income with notional tax credits, so he leaves W44 blank. And he has no tax credit relief to claim from foreign investments, so he leaves box W45 blank also.

Box W46 is found by adding boxes W41, W43, W44 and W45: £0 + £379.58 + £0 + £0 = £379.58. Gerard deducts this from the amount in box W39: £3,243.35 – £379.58 = £2,863.77 and enters £2,863.77 in box W47.

There is nothing for Gerard to enter in boxes W48 and W49. So he enters £2,863.77 in box W50, and copies it over to box W50 at the top of the next page of the tax calculation working sheet.

Income tax and Class 4 NIC due

Gerard has had no adjustment to his PAYE code for the tax year ending 5 April 1998 to collect unpaid tax from earlier tax years. So he leaves box W51 blank and copies £2,863.77 to box W52.

He now finds out how much tax has been paid at source on his income. For his savings income, he finds the amounts of tax deducted or credited from the boxes in the second column of page 3 of the tax return – £713. He enters £713 in box W53.7.

Box W53.8 is for the tax deducted from his pension income. Although the state retirement pension is taxable, it is paid without deduction of tax; instead his pension from his job comes with tax on both pensions having been deducted under PAYE. He entered the figure for tax deducted from his occupational pension in box 11.11 on page 4 of the tax return. He enters this figure, £1,978, in box W53.8.

Gerard adds the amounts in boxes W53.7 and W53.8: £713 + £1,978 = £2,691. He enters £2,691 in box W53.10, and copies it into box W53.

No tax for the tax year ending 5 April 1998 has been included in the next year's PAYE code, so Gerard enters 0 in box W54 and enters £2,691 in box W55.

He subtracts this amount from box W52: £2,863.77 – £2,691 = £172.77. He enters £172.77 in box W56 – his income tax and Class 4 National Insurance contributions due for the tax year ending 5 April 1998.

The £172.77 is, in fact, the tax due on the £863 of investment income that was paid without deduction of tax. His tax inspector will probably try to collect this from his occupational pension in future years by making an adjustment to his PAYE code for Untaxed interest (see p. 365).

Tax owed or overpaid in 1997-98
No tax for the tax year ending 5 April 1998 has already been refunded, nor is there any unpaid tax for earlier years – so Gerard enters 0 in boxes W57A and W57. Box W58 is thus the same as box W56 – £172.77.

Gerard did not overpay tax in earlier years, nor was he asked to make any payments on account for the tax year ending 5 April 1998, so he enters 0 in boxes W59, W60 and W61.

Box W62 is the tax Gerard still owes: box W58 – box W61: £172.77 – £0 = £172.77. This is will be collected through PAYE in the tax year beginning 6 April 1999. And since Gerard's tax bill for the tax year ending 5 April 1998 was less than £500, he will not have to make payments on account for the tax year beginning 6 April 1998.

KEEPING AN EYE ON YOUR TAX AFFAIRS

The introduction of self-assessment means you can take control of your tax affairs, and make sure you don't pay a penny more than you should. But even if you do all the sums, there are several forms the Inland Revenue will send you that you need to check to make sure you aren't paying too much.

This chapter tells you how to check three of the most important forms:

- the Tax Calculation which your tax inspector issues after you send in your tax return – correcting any mistakes and setting out his or her calculations of your tax bill
- the PAYE Coding Notice sent to people who work for someone else – this tells your employer how much tax to deduct from your pay
- the Statement of Account sent to taxpayers who have income from being self-employed, rent from letting out property or income from investments paid without deduction of tax.

TAX CALCULATION

Once you have sent in your tax return, the Inland Revenue checks through it for any obvious errors – such as arithmetical mistakes or failing to copy figures correctly from one part to another. If you have decided not to work out your own tax bill, it is calculated for you. And even if you have done the sums yourself, the Inland Revenue checks your answers by running the figures through its computers. The Tax Calculation form tells you the result of this process, the total tax the inspector thinks you owe and the amount of any payments on account you have to make. Check this carefully as soon as it arrives and challenge your tax inspector if you don't agree with the figures.

The first page of the Tax Calculation form summarises the figures:

- first it says if there are any corrections to your tax return – if there are, they will be listed on the back of the first page
- then it tells you the total amount of income tax plus capital gains tax owed for the tax year – the calculation will be set out on the second sheet

- lastly it says what the tax inspector calculates as the two payments on account you have to make towards the next year's tax bill (see p. 15).

Below is a guide to checking the Tax Calculation form for the tax year ending 5 April 1998. If you're checking it for a different tax year, you will need to adjust some of the instructions for the different tax rates and thresholds. If you need help checking a Tax Calculation form for the tax year ending 5 April 1997, send for our guide (see p. ix).

If there is anything you don't understand on the Tax Calculation form, write or phone your tax office for clarification. And if you disagree with the tax inspector's figures, do the same – otherwise you will be expected to pay up.

Checking a Tax Calculation form

If you have calculated your own tax bill, checking the Tax Calculation form is straightforward. It is simply a matter of comparing the figures you worked out on the green Tax Calculation Working Sheet with the inspector's calculation. Below, we give the numbers of the relevant boxes on the working sheet – the W numbers for the standard version, the G numbers for the version in the Tax Calculation Guide (Capital Gains).

If you have left it to the tax inspector to do the sums, you will need a copy of your tax return and a calculator to check the figures.

Either way, you are unlikely to find all the headings below – only the ones which apply to your tax circumstances.

Total income

This adds together all the income declared on your tax return – from working for an employer, self-employment, freelance work, pensions and taxable benefits, rents, interest on savings, share dividends and unit trust distributions. If you did your own tax calculation, it should be the same as box W12 (G12). If you didn't do the calculation yourself, go through your tax return for all the before-tax income figures (pp. 309-311) and add them together.

Total deductions

This is the total deductions you have claimed on your tax return, such as personal pension contributions, maintenance or alimony payments where you get tax relief and some loan interest. The total should be the same as the figure in box W20 (G20) on the working sheet.

If you didn't do your own calculations before, you will need to find all the right figures on your tax return (see pp. 312-4). With vocational training payments and payments to charity by covenant or Gift Aid, you need to gross up the figures on the tax return to find the before-tax relief amounts. For the tax year ending 5 April 1998, multiply by $^{100}/_{77}$.

Total income less deductions
This is a simple subtraction sum which should produce the same result as box W21 (G21) on the working sheet.

If you have made any payments for personal pensions or vocational training, they now have to be added back. You have already had tax relief on these at the basic rate of tax (23 per cent for the tax year ending 5 April 1998). Adding back the grossed-up amounts makes sure you don't get two lots of tax relief and gives any higher rate tax relief you are due. The figure should be the same as box W23 (G23) on the working sheet.

Allowances that reduce taxable income
Next deduct the allowances that are taken off your total income to reduce the amount you pay tax on. These are the personal allowance, blind person's allowance, transitional allowance, the extra allowance you are entitled to if you are 65 or over and blind person's surplus allowance.

The total is the amount in box W25 (G25) of the working sheet. If you haven't done your own tax calculations, check you've got the right amount of allowances – see p. 10 for the amounts, together with p. 192 for transitional allowance and p. 191 for blind person's surplus allowance. If you are entitled to the extra age-related allowance, see p. 322 for how to calculate the amount.

Taxable income
Subtracting your total allowances from your total income less total deductions gives your taxable income. The tax bill on this is calculated in up to four stages:

- income tax @ 20% on all your taxable income, as if it was all taxed at the lower rate – the answer should be the amount in box W27 (G27) of the working sheet
- income tax @ 3% on everything over £4,100 to collect basic rate tax at 20 + 3 = 23 per cent – the answer should be the amount in box W32 (G35) of the working sheet
- income tax @ 17% on everything over £26,100 to collect higher rate tax at 23 + 17 = 40 per cent – the answer should be the amount in box W36 (G45) of the working sheet
- additional tax due on savings income for higher rate taxpayers, where tax has been deducted at source at 20 per cent – income tax at an extra 3 per

cent of this income means it is taxed at 20 + 17 + 3 = 40 per cent. The answer should be the amount in box W38 (G48) of the working sheet.

Adding these figures together gives income tax due, which should be the amount in box W39 (G49) of the working sheet.

Allowances which reduce tax

There are some allowances that reduce the amount of the tax bill by a fixed amount, rather than reducing the amount of income the tax bill is calculated on. They include investments in venture capital trusts and the Enterprise Investment Scheme, where the tax relief is 20 per cent of the amount invested within limits. Any tax relief for such investments is deducted now – the amount is in box W41 (G58) of the working sheet.

Much more common is the tax relief for married couple's allowance and other allowances restricted to 15 per cent of the amount. These are married couple's surplus allowance (p. 198), additional personal allowance (p. 195), widow's bereavement allowance (p. 198), mortgage interest tax relief (if not given through MIRAS – see p. 181) and part of some maintenance and alimony payments (see p. 182). To find the amount of married couple's allowance you are entitled to, see p. 322.

These allowances must be added together here (box W42 on the working sheet, or G59), and multiplied by 15 per cent to get the amount of tax relief (W43 or G60). Also deducted here is any tax credit relief (p. 285 – box W45 or G62) and notional tax deducted from income such as scrip dividends (p. 157 – box W44 or G61).

Income tax due after allowances and reliefs

The result of deducting these allowances from income tax due is income tax due after allowances and reliefs – the amount in box W47 (G64) of the working sheet. There is still some tax to be added, however, before getting to the total for the year:

- tax on charges – the basic-rate tax relief on payments to charities by covenant or Gift Aid in box W48 (G65) of the working sheet, which can be found by multiplying the amount you hand over by $^{23}/_{77}$
- Class 4 National Insurance contributions paid by the self-employed in box W49 (G66) of the working sheet – you should have entered the amount in box 3.91 on page SE4 of the Self-employment supplement or box 4.25 of the Partnership pages
- unpaid tax for earlier years coded out in this year – this should be in box W51 (G68) of the working sheet or on your PAYE Coding Notice for the

tax year ending 5 April 1998.

Once all of these figures have been added, you should have the total amount of Income tax and National Insurance contributions for the tax year – the figure in box W52 (G69) of the working sheet.

Tax deducted at source
The next figure will be the amount of tax you have already paid through deductions from some types of income before you get it. If you worked out your own tax bill, the amount is in box W53 (G70) of the working sheet. If you didn't work out your own bill, you need to comb through your tax return to find the various amounts and total them (see pp. 327-9 for guidance on where to find the figures).

Unpaid tax in code for later year
Your tax inspector may already have decided to collect some tax for the tax year ending 5 April 1998 through higher PAYE deductions in the following tax year. If so, the amount – in box W54 (G71) of the working sheet will be subtracted from the amount you owe overall. The figure can be found on the last PAYE Coding Notice you were sent for 1997-98 (see p. 327).

Income tax and National Insurance contributions due
You now have the total amount of income tax and National Insurance contributions due – this should be the same as the amount in box W56 (G73) of the working sheet. If more tax has been deducted at source than you should have paid, there could be a minus figure – this is the refund you are owed. If it is notional tax that cannot be refunded (for example, from scrip dividends or foreign income dividends), this will be noted.

Most people are more likely to owe some tax, and in most cases this will be the end of the tax calculation. But if you have capital gains, there may be a few more steps to work through.

Capital gains tax
This tells you the assessable capital gain, the amount which is entered in box G28 on the working sheet (Capital gains). If you didn't work out your tax bill, the figure can be found in box 8.8 on page CG1 of the Capital gains supplement.

The capital gains tax due is calculated in three stages:
- lower rate @ 20% on all your assessable gains – the answer is the amount in box G29 of the working sheet
- basic rate @ 3% on all your assessable gains (the amount in box G36) –

but if less than £4,100 of your lower rate band is taken up by non-savings income, the unused part is deducted from your assessable gains before multiplying by 3 per cent (the amount in box G40)
- higher rate @ 17% on all your assessable gains less any amount taxed only at the lower or basic rate (the amount in box G52).

Any liability from offshore trusts must be added. The amount is in box G54 of the working sheet and can be found in box 8.9 on page CG1 of the Capital gains supplement.

And any tax credit relief on gains can be deducted. The amount is in box G55 of the working sheet and can be found in box 6.10 on page F3 of the Foreign supplement.

The result is capital gains tax due, which should be the same as the amount in box G56 of the working sheet.

Add capital gains tax due to income tax and National Insurance contributions due to get total tax and National Insurance contributions due. This should be the same as the amount in box G74 of the working sheet.

Checking the payments on account
The tax inspector will say whether you need to make payments on account during the next tax year, beginning 6 April 1998. You will not have to make payments on account if income tax and Class 4 National Insurance contributions owed for the tax year ending 5 April 1998 is less than £500 or less than 20 per cent of your total tax including what is deducted at source.

If you worked out your own tax bill, you did the calculations to see if payments on account were due in boxes W64 to W70 of the working sheet (G82 to G90). The amount of each payment on account should be half the figure in box W65 (G85).

If you did not work out your own tax bill, the amount of any payments on account is half the figure for income tax and National Insurance contributions due in the inspector's calculation. To see if you need to make the payments:
- add the following amounts from the inspector's calculation: income tax due after allowances and reliefs, notional tax, tax on charges and Class 4 National Insurance contributions
- find 20 per cent of the total
- if the result is the same as or less than income tax and National Insurance contributions due, you have to make payments on account.

PAYE CODING NOTICE

This form sets out the calculations your tax inspector has made in setting your PAYE code for the tax year. Your employer will use the code to work out how much tax should be deducted from your pay. People with two jobs should have two PAYE codes – and two Coding Notices.

If you have retired, any pensions you get from an employer's pension scheme or personal pension will also have tax deducted from them before you receive the money. Again, you should have a PAYE code for each one if you have more than one substantial pension.

Your PAYE code reflects the amount of allowances your tax inspector estimates you can set against your earnings in the current tax year. It may also be adjusted to collect tax on fringe benefits and income such as freelance earnings, odd pensions and savings interest. The amounts are based on information given in your tax return, by your employer and by other organisations that send details of payments to the Inland Revenue.

E X A M P L E

Harold Svensen checks his Coding Notice for the 1999-2000 tax year – the one beginning 6 April 1999. This is the code for his main job with Viking Shipbuilders.

He first sees that he has been given the right tax allowances for the year (the figures are those for the previous tax year, when the Coding Notice was sent out):

- £60 a year for his subscription to his professional body
- £4,195 personal allowance
- £1,900 married couple's allowance.

That makes total allowances of £6,155. The following amounts are deducted from this:

- £150 for Harold's membership of a local sports club paid by the company
- £2,146 for the benefit of his company car
- £1,074 allowance restriction, to keep the tax relief a basic rate taxpayer such as Harold gets on the married couple's allowance to 10 per cent (see p. 25).

Thus Harold has total deductions of £3,370. Harold's tax-free amount for the year is £6,155 – £3,370 = £2,785. His tax code is found by dropping the last digit to get 278; the letter to be added is T, because he has a company car. So Harold's code is 278T.

If you have been given the correct code or codes, you will have paid the right amount of tax on your income by the end of the tax year. But if there has been a mistake, you may pay too much – and have to wait for a rebate. And although paying too little tax may seem attractive, you will have to make up any underpayment in the following tax year – often in one go if it is more than £1,000. So it makes sense to check your PAYE code carefully whenever you receive a Coding Notice.

Checking a Coding Notice

The main figures on a PAYE Coding Notice are in two columns. The first lists the allowances that are to be set off against this income to reduce the tax bill on it. If this is your main source of income, the Coding Notice should normally list all your allowances unless they are specifically to be set off against other types of income (for example, against rents or freelance income). See p. 357 for the details of what might appear in this column.

The second column lists amounts that will be deducted from your allowances in order to collect extra tax. For example, if you have taxable fringe benefits, their taxable value will normally be in this column. So will other sources of untaxed income, such as freelance earnings, taxable state pensions and benefits and income from savings that have not been taxed. See p. 359 for how to check this column.

Total deductions are subtracted from total allowances to find the amount of income covered by this PAYE code which can be tax-free during the tax year. This is then converted into a PAYE code – normally by knocking off the last figure and adding one of the following letters:

- L – you have been given the personal allowance for those aged under 65
- H – you have also been given the married couple's allowance for those aged under 65 or the additional personal allowance
- P – you have been given the personal allowance for those aged 65 to 74
- V – you have also been given the married couple's allowance for those aged 65 to 74.

So if your only tax allowance is the single person's allowance of £4,195 and you have £160 deductions for fringe benefits, your total tax-free amount for the year will be £4,195 – £160 = £4,035. Your code is found by knocking off the last figure to give you 403, and adding L because you get only the single person's allowance. Your PAYE code will be 403L.

When it comes to deducting tax from your pay, the employer's tax tables will say that an employee with a code of 403 was entitled to tax-free pay during the tax year of £4,039 – divided equally over the year.

The letters after the number mean that if the main allowances change, your PAYE code can be adjusted by your employer or pension provider. So if the single person's allowance is increased from £4,195 to £4,395 in the budget, everyone with an L code will automatically get an extra £200 of tax-free pay.

If the code ends in the letter T, your tax position is more complicated – you may be getting other allowances, for example, blind person's allowance or allowances for people aged 75 and over. You could also get it if you have fringe benefits such as a company car, or have asked for it because you don't want your employer to know what allowances you are entitled to. Changes cannot be made automatically if you have this sort of code and you will have to wait longer for the tax office to make the adjustments.

K codes
If the amount of deductions is more than your allowances, you will have a PAYE code that begins with a K. This is calculated as follows:

- subtract the deductions from the allowances – the answer will be a negative number
- take the last figure off the number
- reduce that number by one
- put a K in front of the answer to give a PAYE code.

E X A M P L E

Sanjay Patel is a single man, and his only tax allowance is the personal allowance of £4,195. However, he has a company car with a taxable value of £4,650, so his tax-free amount for the year is £4,195 – £4,650 = – £455.

His PAYE code is therefore found by dropping the last digit to get 45. Then he subtracts 1 to get 44 – giving a code of K44. With a PAYE code of K44, Sanjay would have £449 added to his pay for the year before the tax was worked out (instead of having some allowances deducted).

K codes have to be recalculated every time the tax allowances change or there is some alteration in your circumstances.

PAYE codes with more than one source of income
There are special PAYE codes which don't have numbers or which have numbers which don't stand for tax allowances. These are mainly used for deducting tax from second or third sources of income:

- BR – this income is all to be taxed at the basic rate. This is where other sources of income have had all your allowances set against them and used

PAYE Coding Notice

This form shows your
tax code for the tax year

| 1999-2000 |

Please keep all your coding notices. You may need to refer to them if you have to fill in a Tax Return.

846

MR H SVENSEN
143 WENDOVER ROAD
LONDON

SW14 5NJ

HM INSPECTOR OF TAXES
LONDON PROVINCIAL 24
GRAYFIELD HOUSE
5 BANKHEAD AVENUE
SIGHTHILL
EDINBURGH   EH11 4AE

Tax Office telephone ☎	Date of issue
0131 453 7200	12 JAN 1999

Please quote your Tax reference and National Insurance number if you contact us

Tax reference	National Insurance number
976/52425	YR 61 53 51 C

Your tax code for the year shown above is

| 319T |

This tax code is used to deduct tax payable on your income from

VIKING SHIPBUILDERS

If you move to another job, your new employer will normally continue to use this tax code.
The tax code is made up as follows:

The *'See note'* columns below refer to the numbered notes in the guidance leaflet P3 *Understanding Your Tax Code*. Leaflet P3 also tells you about the **letter part** of your tax code.

Check that the details are correct. If you think they are wrong, or you have any queries, contact your Tax Office (details above).

This coding notice replaces any previous notice for the year. You should pass it to your agent if you have one.

See note	Your tax allowances	£	See note	Amounts taken away from your total allowances	£
10	PROFESSIONAL SUBSCRIPTIONS	60	30	BENEFITS IN KIND	150
01	PERSONAL ALLOWANCE	4195	30	CAR BENEFIT	2146
02	MARRIED ALLOWANCE	1900	25	ALLOWANCE RESTRICTION	661
	Total allowances	**6155**		**Total deductions**	**2957**

Your tax free amount for the year is £ 3198 , making your Tax Code 319T

See example overleaf

The **Tax free amount** is the difference between your **Total allowances** and **Total deductions**.

If necessary we will use this box to give you further information about your tax code

up the amount of income which is taxed at the lower rate
- D – this income is all to be taxed at the higher rate. This is where other sources of income have had all your allowances set against them and used up the amount of income which is taxed at the lower and basic rates
- DT – you are not entitled to any tax-free pay, but this source of income is to be taxed first at the lower rate, then the basic rate and perhaps eventually the higher rate
- NT – this income should be paid without any tax being deducted, perhaps because it is less than your tax-free allowances.

Your tax allowances
In checking your PAYE Coding Notice, make sure you have all the allowances and deductions you're entitled to.

Personal allowance
This will give the amount you are entitled to for your age (see p. 191).

If you are 65 or over, you are entitled to a higher rate, but this is reduced if your total income is over a set limit – £16,200 for the tax year beginning 6 April 1998. If your tax inspector thinks you are over this limit, you will find an estimate of your total income against estimated income. If you think this is wrong – because you have stopped getting some income, for example, tell your tax inspector.

Married allowance
This will give the amount of married couple's allowance you are getting (see p. 40). Again, there is a higher amount if you are 65 or over, which is reduced if your total income is over a set limit (see p. 42 for the exact rules).

Other allowances
Any other allowances you are entitled to should be listed, including widow's bereavement allowance (p. 198), additional personal allowance (p. 195) and blind person's allowance (p. 191).

Expenses
Deductions for job expenses (either the amount paid or the flat-rate amount for your job – see p. 221) and subscriptions to professional bodies (p. 224).

Pensions, retirement annuities and superannuation
There should also be entries for deductions which you are allowed to claim on death and superannuation payments (p. 189) and retirement annuity payments (p. 175).

> ### Example
> Gerry Walker makes £500 gross (before tax relief) in personal pension payments in the tax year beginning 6 April 1998. Since the basic rate of tax for the tax year is 23 per cent, he gets basic rate tax relief of 23 per cent of £500 = £115. So he actually hands over £500 – £115 = £385.
>
> But Gerry pays tax at the higher rate, so he is entitled to tax relief of 40 per cent of £500 = £200. The extra £85 (£200 – £115) is given by increasing his tax allowances by £212.50, since 40 per cent of £212.40 is £85.

If you make contributions to a personal pension scheme, you get tax relief at the basic rate automatically, by paying lower premiums (see p. 78). But if you pay tax at the higher rates, there will be a entry on your Coding Notice to give you the extra relief.

Charity gifts relief and taxed annual payment

You can get tax relief on single gifts to charity of £250 or more – Gift Aid (see p. 188). You get tax relief at the basic rate by deducting the amount before handing over the gift; if there is higher rate tax relief due, this is given here as charity gifts relief which operates in the same way as for personal pension payments.

Likewise, higher rate tax relief on gifts made by covenant to charity (see p. 186) is given under taxed annual payment.

Maintenance payments

If you are entitled to tax relief on maintenance payments you are required to make to a former spouse or child, this is where you get it. (See p. 45 for the complicated rules about the amount.)

Building society interest and loan interest

If you are entitled to tax relief for interest paid on mortgages or other loans which are not in the MIRAS system (see p. 53), this is where the amount you can claim is entered.

There may also be an entry for beneficial loan interest if you get a cheap or interest-free loan from your employer for a purpose that would entitle you to tax relief on interest paid – for example, a mortgage on your only or main home. There will be tax on the benefit which will be collected elsewhere on the Coding Notice – this entry gives you the tax relief.

Lower rate tax allowance

If this is a PAYE code for a second source of income, it will normally be a BR code which means all this income is taxed at the basic rate (see p. 361). But if your first source of income isn't big enough to use up all the amount of income taxable at the lower rate (£4,300 in the tax year beginning 6 April 1998), you will get an allowance here to reduce the amount of tax paid on the second source of income.

Balance of allowances

There may be an allowance here in the code for a second source of income where the first source isn't big enough to use up all your allowances.

Other items

Lots of other less common tax allowances and deductions can be included in this column – including losses from self-employment (p. 260) or letting property (p. 273), vocational training tuition fees (p. 180), tax relief on Enterprise Investment Scheme investments (p. 185) and wife's transitional relief (p. 192).

Amounts to be taken away from your tax allowances

These amounts reduce the amount of your tax-free pay and thus increase the amount of tax deducted from your earnings or pension.

Allowance restriction

Several tax allowances are restricted to tax relief at 15 per cent only – for example, married couple's allowance and additional personal allowance. You will have been given these allowances in the first column, but the PAYE system would then give you tax relief at your top rate of tax. Allowance restriction will recover the extra tax relief you would get if this happened.

For basic rate taxpayers, the amount of the restriction in the tax year beginning 6 April 1998 should be £661 for the married couple's allowance (or any other allowance worth £1,900 for the tax year). For lower rate taxpayers, the allowance restriction should be £475.

For the tax year beginning 6 April 1999, the tax relief on these allowances will fall to 10 per cent. This means the restriction on an allowance of £1,900 will rise to £1,074 for a basic rate taxpayer and £950 for a lower rate taxpayer.

If you expect your top rate of tax to have changed in this tax year, this restriction might be too large or too small. If so, tell your tax inspector so the right amount of tax is deducted through PAYE.

> ## EXAMPLE
>
> Betty Pinder gets additional personal allowance – £1,900 at 15 per cent only for the tax year beginning 6 April 1998. This means she should get tax relief of 15 per cent of £1,900 = £285.00. But Betty pays tax at the higher rate of 40 per cent – so if the allowance of £1,900 is set against her income, the PAYE system would give her tax relief of 40 per cent of £1,900 = £760. This is £760 – £285 = £475 more tax relief than she should receive.
>
> Betty's tax inspector corrects this with an Allowance restriction of £1,187. By deducting this amount from her allowances, the Inland Revenue recoups 40 per cent of £1,187 = £475.

Married allowance to wife

This is for married men where the wife is to receive half or all the married couple's allowance given in the allowances column.

State pension and state benefits

If you receive taxable state pension or other benefits, these are paid without deduction of tax. The amount you will receive during the tax year will be entered here, reducing your tax-free allowances to be set against any other earnings or pensions.

If you are a married man, the amount will not include any state pension based on your National Insurance contributions paid to your wife if 60 or over. This will be treated as your wife's and she can set her own personal allowance against it (see p. 162).

Small amounts of other pensions may be included here to collect tax on them. For example, armed forces pensions, other occupational pensions or income from personal pension schemes. If these are larger sources of income, they may be taxed under PAYE by the organisation making the payments with their own PAYE code.

Jobseeker's allowance and incapacity benefit

This is the taxable amount of jobseeker's allowance or incapacity benefit you are due to get in the tax year.

Car benefit, van benefit and car fuel benefit

If you have a company car or van available for private motoring, the taxable benefit will be included here (see p. 98 for how it is worked out). Likewise, if your employer pays for fuel for private use, there will be an entry here (see p. 97).

Check the amount of car benefit has been reduced if you do more than 2,500 miles a year on business trips or the car is four years old or more during the tax year. Any contributions for private mileage should be deducted from the benefit. And there are special rules to reduce the tax paid on vans that are not available to you all the time (see p. 98).

Employer's loan benefit

This amount is the taxable benefit of any interest-free or low-interest loans from your employer (see p. 98). If you are entitled to tax relief on some of the interest paid (for example, on the first £30,000 of a loan to buy your home), this will have been entered in the first column under Beneficial loan interest.

Other fringe benefits

There will be special entries if your employer pays for private medical insurance (p. 100), provides you with a mobile phone (p. 99), pays your home telephone expenses or provides any other benefits in kind (see p. 100).

If you get a taxable allowance for work expenses – for using your home or car, for example – this will be entered as Taxable expenses payments. Some of these costs may be claimed as expenses against tax and should then be entered in the first column against Job expenses.

Part-time earnings, tips and commission

Tax on small amounts of earnings can be collected here – for example, on small amounts of part-time earnings, tips (p. 209), commission (p. 207) and other types of income from employment.

Maintenance payments received

If you receive maintenance payments which are taxable, the taxable amount will be here (see p. 166).

Property income

If you receive small amounts from letting out rooms or other property, the tax can be collected here from your earnings under PAYE.

Untaxed interest

This amount collects tax on interest you are expected to get during the tax year which will not have tax deducted from it first – for example, from National Savings Investment Account (see p. 154).

This income is taxed at 20 per cent only (see p. 66). So if you pay tax at no more than the lower rate of 20 per cent the actual amount you are expected

Gerry Walker gets £200 of interest from his National Savings Investment Account in the tax year beginning 6 April 1998. He should pay tax of 20 per cent of £200 = £40. But he is a basic rate taxpayer, so adding £200 to his taxable income would collect too much – 23 per cent of £200 = £46.

Gerry's tax inspector adds £174 to Gerry's income with an Untaxed interest deduction from his PAYE code. This will collect the right amount, since 23 per cent of £174 = £40.

to receive will be entered here. But if you pay tax at the basic rate on your income – 23 per cent for the tax year beginning 6 April 1998 – the amount entered here will be less than you actually get. This is to avoid too much tax being collected on it.

Taxed annual payment
If you have deducted tax relief at the basic rate from covenant payments, but are entitled to tax relief at the lower rate only, this amount will take back the extra tax relief you have given yourself.

Loan interest restriction
You are entitled to tax relief on mortgage interest on loans of up to £30,000 at 10 per cent only for the tax year beginning 6 April 1998 (see p. 53). The MIRAS system automatically gives you the right amount of tax relief, but if the loan is not in the MIRAS scheme, you will have claimed the tax relief direct from the Inland Revenue. The deduction for this interest should have been in the first column; this amount is what is needed to restrict your tax relief to 10 per cent.

Lower rate tax adjustment
This adjustment is made if you are paying tax at the lower rate on more than one source of income and too much of your income is being taxed at this rate (that is, more than £4,300 in the tax year beginning 6 April 1998).

Basic rate tax restriction
This is a similar adjustment if you have income from more than one source and too much has been taxed at the basic rate (more than £27,100 in the tax year beginning 6 April 1998).

Higher rate tax adjustment
Higher rate taxpayers receive interest, dividends and some other sorts of income after deduction of tax which covers any basic rate tax due. This adjustment collects any extra higher rate tax due on such income.

> **E XAMPLE**
>
> Betty Pinder pays tax at the higher rate and receives £1,000 of interest and dividends. This is paid after deduction of tax at 20 per cent: 20 per cent of £1,000 is £200, so she receives £1,000 – £200 = £800 of savings income net.
>
> But Betty should have paid tax at 40 per cent on the gross amount – 40 per cent of £1,000 = £400. So she owes another £400 – £200 = £200. To collect this £200, a higher rate tax adjustment of £500 is made. By adding £500 to Betty's taxable income, she will pay 40 per cent of £500 = £200 on her income taxed under PAYE.

Tax underpaid

If you have underpaid up to £1,000 of tax in a previous tax year, the Inland Revenue will normally try to collect this by an adjustment to your PAYE code.

> **E XAMPLE**
>
> Gerry Walker owes £450 in tax unpaid from the tax year ending 5 April 1998 and pays tax in the tax year beginning 6 April 1998 at the basic rate of 23 per cent only. His tax inspector adds the following amount to his taxable income for the tax year to collect the £450:
>
> $$£450 \times \frac{100}{23} = £1,957$$

Allowances allocated elsewhere

If your allowances listed in the first column are more than the amount of income covered by this Coding Notice, the surplus may be allocated to other sources of income (and thus other Coding Notices). This entry in the second column is for any allowances thus allocated to other sources of income.

Other items

Lots of other less common types of income and adjustments can be included in this column. For example, if you have a balancing charge to add to your income because you claimed capital allowances in an earlier year (see p. 257).

STATEMENT OF ACCOUNT

If you have income of £500 or more in a tax year from being self-employed,

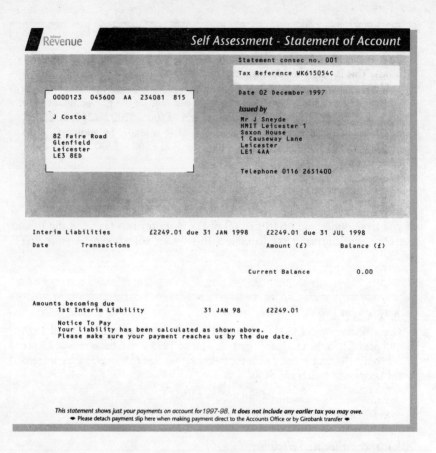

Self Assessment - Statement of Account

Statement consec no. 001

Tax Reference WK615054C

0000123 045600 AA 234081 815

Date 02 December 1997

J Costos

82 Faire Road
Glenfield
Leicester
LE3 8ED

Issued by
Mr J Sneyde
HMIT Leicester 1
Saxon House
1 Causeway Lane
Leicester
LE1 4AA

Telephone 0116 2651400

Interim Liabilities   £2249.01 due 31 JAN 1998   £2249.01 due 31 JUL 1998

Date   Transactions   Amount (£)   Balance (£)

Current Balance   0.00

Amounts becoming due
    1st Interim Liability   31 JAN 98   £2249.01

Notice To Pay
Your liability has been calculated as shown above.
Please make sure your payment reaches us by the due date.

This statement shows just your payments on account for 1997-98. It does not include any earlier tax you may owe.
☛ Please detach payment slip here when making payment direct to the Accounts Office or by Girobank transfer ☚

from letting out property or from investments which pay out income without deduction of tax, you will normally have to make two payments of tax on account against your final tax bill for the year. However, there will be no need to make such payments if most of your tax – 80 per cent or more – is deducted from your income at source.

If you do have to make payments on account, the first is due on 31 January during the tax year, the second by 31 July after it has finished. The amounts are based on the income you got in the previous tax year.

If you are calculating your own tax bill (see p. 14), it is up to you to work out the amounts. But if you ask your tax inspector to do the calculations, the amounts will be notified to you in two Statements of Account sent out by the Inland Revenue: one around December during the tax year; the other around the end of the tax year.

Unless you appeal against a Statement of Account, you must pay the tax requested on it by the right date – paying late could mean an interest charge (see p. 16). So it is vital to check the statement. If it demands more than you should pay in the current tax year, you can ask for the payments to be reduced. But you must do this before the date the payment is due. This section of the guide tells you how to check a statement and how to claim a reduction.

How to reduce your payments on account

If you think your tax bills for the types of income covered by a Statement of Account will be lower than in the previous year, you can claim to make a lower payment on account than the Inland Revenue is asking for. This might happen if your income has dropped off – for example, you have received less in rent, profits from your business or on the investment income which is received without deduction of tax. Or your tax bill might be less because you are entitled to claim higher allowances and deductions against your income – if you have married, for example, or made a large investment in the Enterprise Investment Scheme (see p. 81).

If this is the case, work out your expected tax bill for this tax year carefully. Then calculate how this should be divided between the two payments on account. If you should be paying less than the Inland Revenue is asking for, make your claim to pay less on Inland Revenue form SA303. A copy is sent out with every Statement of Account – if you have lost yours, ask your tax office for another copy. You must send this back before the payment on account is due.

If later you realise you could pay still less, you can make a further claim – as long as it is before the payment is due. If you discover after making the first payment that it was too much, you can reduce the second payment on account to compensate.

It is probably better to pay slightly more rather than too little in your payments on account. If you pay too much, you will get interest on it; if you pay too little, you will pay interest. There are penalties in the form of fines if you are caught trying to hoodwink your tax inspector in the amounts you pay. And if you make the payments on account demanded on time, there is normally no interest to pay even if your tax bill turns out to have been much higher.

TAX-FREE INCOME

Income from a job
Check with your employer if you are uncertain about whether any of these forms of income is taxable

- work-related expenses you are reimbursed for by your employer covered by an agreement with the Inland Revenue that they do not need to be declared (see p. 221)
- some fringe benefits, such as canteen meals and Christmas parties provided for all staff, special clothes for the job and subscriptions to approved professional societies (see p. 86)
- foreign service allowances paid to diplomats and other servants of the Crown
- the first 15p a day of luncheon vouchers
- goods and services your employer lets you have cheaply (see p. 86)
- miners' free coal or cash allowances in lieu of coal
- long-service awards so long as they are not in cash and are within set limits (see p. 87)
- awards from approved suggestions schemes (see p. 208)
- payments for moving to higher-cost housing areas, within set limits (see p. 88)
- genuine personal gifts – for example, wedding presents
- pay received under a registered profit-related pay scheme – within limits (see p. 208)
- earnings from working abroad for prolonged periods before 17 March 1998 (see p. 218)

Income on leaving a job
Check with your ex-employer

- statutory redundancy payments
- wages in lieu of notice
- gratuities from the armed forces
- lump-sum compensation for an injury or disability that means you can no longer do the job

- tax-free lump sum instead of part of a pension and certain other ex gratia payments on retirement or death
- up to £30,000 of other compensation on leaving a job, including counselling and outplacement services (see p. 216)

Pensions and benefits
Check with the organisation paying the pension or benefit

- state pension Christmas bonus
- war widows' and orphans' pensions and equivalent overseas pensions
- widow's payment
- certain compensation payments and pensions paid to victims of Nazi persecution
- war disablement pensions
- additional pensions paid to holders of some bravery awards such as the Victoria Cross
- the part of a pension paid to a former employee who retires because of a disability caused by injury at work or a work-related illness which is in excess of the pension paid to an employee who retires on normal ill-health grounds
- income support paid to people aged 60 or over, single parents with a child under 16 and those staying at home to look after a severely disabled person. Part of income support paid to unemployed people may be tax-free – see your statement of taxable benefits (p. 163)
- jobfinder's grant, most youth training scheme allowances, employment rehabilitation and training allowances
- family credit
- housing benefit and council tax benefit
- improvement and renovation grants for your home
- payments from the social fund
- maternity allowance (but statutory maternity pay is taxable)
- child benefit, one-parent benefit, school uniform grants
- additions for dependent children paid with a state pension or social security benefit
- guardian's allowance
- student grants
- incapacity benefit for first 28 weeks (and if paid to replace invalidity benefit)
- industrial disablement benefits
- disability living allowance, disability working allowance
- attendance allowance

Investment income
If in doubt, check with the organisation paying the income

- interest on National Savings Certificates (and Ulster Savings Certificates if you normally live in Northern Ireland), National Savings Children's Bonus Bonds
- interest and terminal bonuses on bank and building society Save-As-You-Earn (SAYE) schemes
- first £70 of interest each year from National Savings Ordinary Account (£140 for married couples with a joint account)
- dividends and other income from a personal equity plan (PEP), so long as no more than £180 is drawn out in interest (see p. 80)
- interest on a tax-exempt special savings account (TESSA) kept open for the full five years – provided some of it is reinvested for the term of the account (see p. 81)
- income from an individual savings account (ISA) – to be introduced from 6 April 1999 (see p. 83)
- dividends on ordinary shares in a venture capital trust (see p. 83)
- part of the income paid by an annuity
- amount paid out by a regular-premium life insurance policy such as an endowment policy or a unit-linked one – including money paid out on the death of the policyholder (see p. 71)
- loan interest paid to members of a credit union

Other tax-free income
If in doubt, check with the organisation paying out the money

- what you receive under maintenance agreements made on or after 15 March 1988 and any increases in maintenance paid on agreements made before that date (see p. 45)
- up to £4,250 a year of income from letting out a furnished room in your only or main home – the rent a room scheme (p. 267)
- gambling winnings (as long as it is not your business)
- lottery winnings
- premium bond prizes
- income from qualifying life insurance policies that pay out on death – for example, mortgage protection policies, family income benefit policies (see p. 168)
- income from insurance policies to cover mortgage payments if you are sick or unemployed
- income from a permanent health insurance policy, creditor insurance and some long-term care policies
- pay-outs under some accident insurance policies (usually group ones)
- interest on a delayed settlement for damages for personal injury or death
- compensation for being wrongly sold a personal pension (paid following the review ordered by the Securities and Investments Board)
- interest on a tax rebate

GROSSING-UP TABLES

Some forms of income are paid net – after some tax has been deducted from them. For example, 20 per cent tax is normally deducted from the interest on savings accounts in banks and building societies before it is paid out to you or added to your account (unless it is a tax-exempt special savings account or individual savings account). In working out your tax bill, you may need to know how much the income was before the tax was deducted – the gross income.

You can find the gross income by grossing-up the net income using the ready reckoners below. With most forms of investment income, tax will have been deducted at 20 per cent, so that is the rate in the first ready reckoner. The second is for grossing-up income where tax has been deducted at the basic rate of 23 per cent which applies for the tax year ending 5 April 1998 and the tax year beginning 6 April 1998.

If the tax rates change, you can use the following formula to work out the grossed-up income:

$$\text{Amount paid to you net } \times \left(\frac{100}{100 - \text{rate of tax}} \right)$$

So if, for argument's sake, the rate of tax was 15 per cent, and you received £85 after tax, the grossed-up amount of the income would be:

$$£85 \times \left(\frac{100}{100 - 15} \right)$$

$$= £85 \times \frac{100}{85}$$

$$= £100$$

Grossing-up when tax is deducted at 20 per cent

Net amount £	Gross amount £	Net amount £	Gross amount £	Net amount £	Gross amount £
1	1.25	10	12.50	100	125.00
2	2.50	20	25.00	200	250.00
3	3.75	30	37.50	300	375.00
4	5.00	40	50.00	400	500.00
5	6.25	50	62.50	500	625.00
6	7.50	60	75.00	600	750.00
7	8.75	70	87.50	700	875.00
8	10.00	80	100.00	800	1,000.00
9	11.25	90	112.50	900	1,125.00
				1,000	1,250.00

EXAMPLE

Gary Loudon receives building society interest of £1,793 in the tax year ending 5 April 1998. He must gross up this net interest at 20 per cent as follows:

Net income	Gross income
£1,000	£1,250.00
£700	£875.00
£90	£112.50
£3	£3.75
TOTAL £1,793	£2,241.25

Grossing-up when tax is deducted at 23 per cent

Net amount £	Gross amount £	Net amount £	Gross amount £	Net amount £	Gross amount £
1	1.30	10	12.99	100	129.87
2	2.60	20	25.97	200	259.74
3	3.90	30	38.96	300	389.61
4	5.19	40	51.95	400	519.48
5	6.49	50	64.94	500	649.35
6	7.79	60	77.92	600	779.22
7	9.09	70	90.91	700	909.09
8	10.39	80	103.90	800	1,038.96
9	11.69	90	116.88	900	1,168.83
				1,000	1,298.70

Example

Peggy Cronin receives net income of £4,375 in the tax year beginning 6 April 1998, from which tax has been deducted at the basic rate of 23 per cent. She finds the gross income as follows:

Net income	Gross income
£4,000	£5,194.80
£300	£389.61
£70	£90.91
£5	£6.49
TOTAL £4,375	£5,681.81

USEFUL LEAFLETS

You can get all these leaflets free from your tax office.

Introductions to self-assessment
SA/BK1 Self-assessment – a general guide
SA/BK2 Self-assessment – a guide for the self-employed
SA/BK3 Self-assessment – a guide to keeping records for the self-employed
SA/BK4 Self-assessment – a general guide to keeping records
SAT 3   Self-assessment – what it will mean for employers

General guides to the Inland Revenue
IR37   Appeals against tax
IR73   Inland Revenue investigations: how settlements are negotiated
IR141   Open government
SVD1   Shares Valuation Division – an introduction
AO1   How to complain about the Inland Revenue
COP1   Mistakes by the Inland Revenue
COP2   Investigations
COP6   Collection of tax
COP10   Information and advice
COP11   Enquiries into tax returns by local tax offices

Income tax for particular groups
IR41   Income tax and job seekers
IR60   Income tax and students
IR80   Income tax and married couples
IR90   Tax allowances and reliefs
IR91   A guide for widows and widowers
IR92   A guide for one-parent families
IR121   Income tax and pensioners

Income tax and international issues

IR20	Residents and non-residents – liability to tax in the UK
IR58	Going to work abroad?
IR138	Living or retiring abroad – a guide to tax on your UK income and pension
IR139	Income from abroad? A guide to UK tax on overseas income
IR140	Non-resident landlords, their agents and tenants

Income tax – general

IR1	Extra-statutory concessions (plus supplement with latest concessions)
IR45	What to do about tax when someone dies
IR46	Income tax and corporation tax – clubs, societies and associations
IR65	Giving to charity – how individuals can get tax relief
IR75	Tax reliefs for charities
IR87	Letting and your home
IR93	Separation, divorce and maintenance payments
IR113	Gift Aid – a guide for donors and charities
IR115	Tax and childcare
IR119	Tax relief for vocational training
IR122	Volunteer drivers
IR123	Mortgage interest relief: buying your home
IR125	Using your own car for work
IR144	Income tax and incapacity benefit

Savings and investments

IR68	Accrued income scheme – taxing securities on transfer
IR78	Personal pensions: a guide for tax
IR89	Personal Equity Plans (PEPs) – a guide for potential investors
IR110	A guide for people with savings
IR114	TESSA – tax-free interest for taxpayers
IR129	Occupational pension schemes – an introduction
IR137	The Enterprise Investment Scheme
IR150	Taxation of rents – a guide to property income
IR152	Trusts – an introduction
IR153	Tax-exemption for sickness or unemployment insurance payments

Employees

480	Expenses and benefits – a guide for tax
IR16	Share acquisitions by directors and employees – explanatory notes
IR34	Pay As You Earn
IR42	Lay-offs and short-time work
IR69	Expenses payments: Forms P11D – how to save yourself work

IR95	Approved profit-sharing schemes – an outline for employees
IR97	Approved save as you earn share option schemes – an outline for employees
IR101	Approved company share option plans – an outline for employers
IR133	Income tax and company cars from 6 April 1994 – a guide for employees
IR134	Income tax and relocation packages
IR136	Income tax and company vans – a guide for employees and employers
IR145	Low-interest loans provided by employers

Self-employed
CWL1	Starting your own business?
IR24	Class 4 National Insurance contributions
IR56	Employed or self-employed? A guide for tax and National Insurance
IR72	Investigations: business accounts
IR105	How your profits are taxed

Income tax – construction industry
IR14/15	Construction industry tax deduction scheme
IR40	Construction industry: conditions for getting a sub-contractor's tax certificate
IR116	Guide for sub-contractors with tax certificates
IR117	A sub-contractor's guide to the deduction scheme
IR148	Are your workers employed or self-employed – a guide to tax and National Insurance for contractors in the construction industry
IR157	Workers in building and construction – help with tax for employers and the self-employed

Employers
480	Expenses and benefits – tax guide
CWG1	Employer's quick guide to Pay As You Earn and National Insurance contributions
CWG2	Employer's further guide to Pay As You Earn and National Insurance contributions
IR64	Giving to charity – how businesses can get tax relief
IR109	Employer compliance reviews and negotiations
IR132	The taxation of company cars from 6 April 1994: employers' guide
IR136	Income tax and company vans – a guide for employees and employers
IR155	PAYE settlement agreements

Capital gains tax
CGT4	Capital gains tax – owner-occupied houses

CGT6   Retirement relief on disposal of a business – capital gains tax
CGT11   Capital gains tax and small businesses
CGT14   Capital gains tax – an introduction
CGT16   Capital gains tax – indexation allowance, disposals after 5 April
         1988

Inheritance tax
IHT2*   Inheritance tax on lifetime gifts
IHT3   Inheritance tax – an introduction
IHT8*   Alterations to an inheritance following a death
IHT14*   Inheritance tax – the personal representative's responsibilities
IHT15*   Inheritance tax – how to calculate the liability
IHT16*   Inheritance tax – settled property
IHT17*   Inheritance tax – businesses, farms and woodlands
IHT18*   Inheritance tax – foreign aspects

*Available from the three Capital Taxes Offices:
England and Wales: Ferrers House, PO Box 38, Castle Meadow Road,
Nottingham, NG2 1BB (0115-974 2400)
Scotland: Mulberry House, 16 Picardy Place, Edinburgh EH1 3NB
(0131-556 8511)
Northern Ireland: Dorchester House, 52-58 Great Victoria Street, Belfast
BT2 7QL (01232-236633)

Business Economic Notes
These give information on how tax inspectors approach particular business-
es such as travel agents, road hauliers, hairdressers and funeral directors.
You can get them from:

Inland Revenue Reference Library
Room G9
South West Wing
Bush House
Strand
London WC2B 4RD

They cost £2 each (cheques payable to INLAND REVENUE).

INDEX